BEAN
by
BEAN

BEAN

by

BEAN

Crescent Dragonwagon

WORKMAN PUBLISHING ⟟ NEW YORK

Library of Congress Cataloging-in-Publication
Data is available.

ISBN 978-0-7611-3241-7

Cover design by Faceoutstudio
Cover photo composite:
© pixelsaway/Veer
© StockFood
© Brian Leatart/FoodPix/Getty Images
Interior design by Sara Edward-Corbett
Illustrations copyright © by Eleanor Davis

Workman books are available at special
discounts when purchased in bulk for
premiums and sales promotions as well
as for fund-raising or educational use.
Special editions or book excerpts also can
be created to specification. For details,
contact the Special Sales Director at the
address below, or send an e-mail to
specialmarkets@workman.com.

Workman Publishing Company, Inc.
225 Varick Street
New York, NY 10014-4381
www.workman.com

Printed in the United States of America
First printing December 2011
10 9 8 7 6 5 4 3 2

ACKNOWLEDGMENTS:

On this, my 50th published book, it's dawned on me that usually, the writer's nearest, dearest friends and family appear last in acknowledgments, by which time they're usually reduced to "words cannot express . . ." I'm reversing this unfair practice while I still have plenty of words. Thank you, David R. Koff: taster of virtually every recipe here, annual putter-upper of poles, around which grateful beans of countless varieties have joyfully twirled for . . . let's see, can it be *nine years*? The beans are not the only grateful ones, David. Life sent us a Black Valentine; how tender and succulent is this surprising, prolific pod we continue opening.

Thank you, Charlotte Zolotow: now a very old bean (96)—you grow dearer and dearer to me and, in altered state, continue to surprise, delight, and inspire me . . . perhaps even more than when you were in your so-called right mind. Thank you, Hawa Diallo, to whom one day Charlotte said, "I'm adopting you!" Hawa, how glad I am that Charlotte made sisters of us, though we'd already done so. Thank you for peanut butter stew, black-eyed pea fritters, late-night conversations, walks, workouts, and mornings of dancing and singing with me, Charlotte, and Youssou N'dour. Peace and love! Long may we both keep cooking for, and feasting at, life's mysterious and abundant table. Amen.

And Chou! Thank you, Chou-Chou Yearsley, you strang of purls you. Maker of pies, finder of paise, old, good friend, co-adventurer, compadre in mischief-making, stalwart during hard times. Life has certainly put us on to soak and simmer, together and separately. Are we tender yet?

I would say so. And part of the reason I can say so is because we have known tough as well as tender. Sweet, *the* Sweetness, as well as bitter.

Thank you, Judith Reichsman, my darling Vermont jumping bean, dancing bean, sweet and sustaining bean . . . We have proved, in summer, that she who laps last laps best, and in winter, that snow-covered capsicums are chilly peppers indeed. Amoro grando por allo seasonales, Judeborita!

Now. A capitalized THANK YOU to you, Edite Kroll. With all the changes in our industry and our lives, where would I be, and how could I bear being there, without your tough-minded, tender-hearted self? Integrity, loyalty, smartness, general kick-ass attitude—you steadily live this amidst the changes, a be-here-now Zen bean in a very, very no-nonsense business pod. Not everyone can stand up to a dragon, but not only do you, fearlessly, but I would never ever dream of exhaling *you* into toast! Thank you, thank you, thank you.

ACKNOWLEDGMENTS

Gaelen and Richard, keepers of the cairns, the most neighborly neighbors I have ever had . . . thank you. May we keep sharing many figurative bouquets of vernal wildflowers, and wintertime pots of beans—for you two only, made without garlic.

Where acknowledgments in this particular book are concerned, the praises of the core cadre of my Facebook pals—30 or 40 of you, you know who you are—must be sung loud and clear. You are actual, not cyber, pals; how I love our close-in-conversation back-and-forths, even though we are scattered all over the globe. Your consistent encouragement, ideas, advice, tweaks, witticisms; your expressed enthusiasm for this project (and previous ones) when it remained, interminably it felt, like a book-to-be—I am *so grateful*. The long, slow period between a book's caterpillar and butterfly phases is dark, cramped, and isolated. But you guys! I could always hear you cheering just outside the cocoon. May I live up to all your kind and generous words, and may every recipe nourish and delight you.

Now, on to the kitchen. Servings (with seconds and thirds) to all those who've generously shared recipes: Dee Mulvahill (and her friend Fern), Gina Meadows, Ellen Levine, Genie Reece (where are you, Genie?), Lisa Esposito (you poet-of-the-bean-and-carnitas-you), neighbor Dorothy Read, Nanci McDermott (the security guy, too . . . thanks again), Jennifer Yaukapolus, David Levington and Ellen Greenlaw, Jill Nusinow, and Julie Reimer. Ruth Eichor, Elsie Freund, and David Yearsley, special posthumous thanks—may you rest all the better for knowing we enjoy, still, the same good foods you once cooked for us. Thanks, too, to those who shared quotes (especially Diane Abu-Jaber; our inadvertent e-conversation has been a pleasure), information, kindness, and enthusiasm.

And now to the world beyond the kitchen: Thanks to Workman Publishing, with whom I have been traveling for a long, long time. Frijole-decorated acknowledgments go to the usual suspects, Suzanne Rafer and Kylie Foxx McDonald. A few new ones: Kathie Ness, thank you for bringing respect and clarity to chaos. Bob Miller, you confidence-instiller you, I am very glad you are part of Workman. Rebecca Carlisle, you are one smart, energized, on-it, alert, innovative, thoughtful, well-organized, enthusiastic cookie. And I am loving working with your on-it self. Dear Workmaniacs, may we continue to work together in ever-new configurations as collaborators and colleagues. And, as always, thank you, Peter Workman, original usual suspect/Workmaniac, for recognizing me back in the way-back, when I hadn't even yet germinated into sprouthood.

May all of us, like beans, continue to nourish each other as we are nourishing the world around us, in every phase. Bit by bit, bite by bite, bean by bean.

ꙩ ꙩ ꙩ *Contents* ꙩ ꙩ ꙩ

Bean Basics
The A, B(ean), Cs

A primer for all things bean. Everything you've ever wondered about selecting, preparing, cooking, and storing dried beans, fresh beans, shell beans, canned beans, and dehydrated beans—including, yes, a revolutionary method for making beans more belly friendly.

Hummus, Where the Heart Is
Leguminous Starters

Small plates and sumptuous bowls beckon nibblers, grazers, and feasters alike. From rich dips like Newly Minted Puree of Fresh Favas (page 43) and the exotic Marrakech Melange (page 36), to surprising party munchies like Gotcha-Hotcha Sweet-Smoky Cocktail Peanuts (page 28), these satisfying starters are the pillars of any appetizer spread.

Soulful Simmer
Soups for Spirit and Substance

Explore the globe with bean soup, the very potage our ancestors—even the biblical Jacob and Esau—made for thousands of years. Ladle up the flavors of the Middle East with Syrian Zucchini-Chickpea Soup (page 61), then journey to Kilimanjaro for Tanzanian Black-Eyed Pea & Coconut Soup (page 72). Nourish and soothe with Noodled Japanese Broth with Tofu & Bean Threads (page 79); turn up the heat with India's Kerala-Style Dahl (page 85); and trace the bean's journey through Europe with belly-filling Pasta e Fagioli (page 96) and garlicky Caldo Verde (page 102). End in the New World on a high note: rich, golden, avocado-and-egg flourished Fanesca.

Cool Beans
Salads for Every Season

Crunchy or tender, hearty or light—here, green beans and dried beans dance together and apart. The cool bean takes many forms, from sprightly starter salads—Sugar Snap Pea, Orange & Spinach Salad with Citrus-Mint Vinaigrette (page 134)—all the way to full-meal salads, like Dragon-Style Dan-Dan Noodles with Baked Tofu, Bean Sprouts & Crisp Vegetables (page 147).

Chili Weather

Chili spans the color spectrum: from Brown Bean Chili with Sweet Potatoes (page 180) to White Chili with White Beans, Poblanos & Hominy (page 182). You'll find chili variations from all cardinal directions, and, of course, their go-to go-withs: cornbreads, fixins, even salsas.

CHAPTER 6 — 185

Superior Stews, Companionable Curries

The plot thickens, or, rather, the soup does, enticing us into the realm of luscious curries and satisfying stews. Whatever you choose to call them, these hearty bowlfuls—like Dorothy Read's Yellow-Eye Beans Redux (page 190) and Mellow Coconut-Tempeh Curry with Spinach, Zucchini & Sweet Potatoes (page 206)—will surprise, tempt, and sustain you.

CHAPTER 7 — 213

Bountiful Bean Bakes, Comforting Casseroles

Bubbling and beckoning, these oven-baked beauties are truly hot items. Old-Fashioned, Down-Home All-Day Baked Beans (page 216) with Steamed Boston Brown Bread (page 219) and Vegetarian Cassoulet (page 234). Baked Beans Brazilian with Olives & Cheese (page 230), several methods for oven-baked tofu, and Summer Garden Potpie with Cheese-Herb Drop Biscuits (page 240). All are served up golden-brown and piping hot.

CHAPTER 8 — 251

Home on the Range
Simpatico Skillets and Stir-Fries

Stovetop beans are one-pot wonders: They can be both contemplative, slow-cooked simmers and quick-fire weeknight dinners. You'll discover falafel, both Traditional (page 260) and Neo-Traditional (page 264); the so easy and so good CD's Beans & Greens Pasta with Lemon, Garlic & Chile (page 273); and nearly infinite variations on the stir-fry. There's even Socca (page 277)—addictive chickpea flatbread—to soak up any leftover skillet sauce.

CHAPTER 9 — 299

Beans and Grains
Earthy Soul Mates

It's a perfect marriage: Beans and grains complete each other in traditional dishes like Mjeddrah (page 301), Dragon-style Dancin' John (page 312), and two styles of Red Beans & Rice (pages 306 and 308). And they delight in imaginative bean-grain two-steps like Maya's Magic Black Beans with Eggplant & Royal Rice (page 314). All are heavenly matches made on earth.

CHAPTER 10 — 319

Sweet Beans
In Which Legumes Dessert You

Let's champion the versatility of the legume! Julie's Peanut Butter Chocolate Chip Oatmeal Cookies (page 322) are sure to satisfy your sweet tooth. So, too, will the tart Lime Tofu Mousse-Custard (page 330) and the luscious spiced navy bean custard that fills "Don't Hurt Yourself" Bean Pie (page 327). And of course, this dessert chapter wouldn't be worth a hill of beans without Red Bean Ice Cream (page 339)—a delicious ending to our leguminous journey.

INTRODUCTION

HOW TO KNOW BEANS

"What shall I learn of beans, or beans of me?"
—Henry David Thoreau, Walden

Thoreau devoted a chapter of *Walden* to "the common small white bush bean"; he'd devoted a growing season of his two years in the woods to their raising. "I cherish them," he wrote of his beans. "I hoe them, early and late I have an eye to them; and this is my day's work."

Let us, too, have an eye to the bean. Hold one in the palm of the hand. Discreet, self-contained as an egg, spotted or speckled, dark or light, it's such a small package holding so much. Inspiration for tonight's dinner, perhaps a soup or stew? Sure, and no more and no less important than all it contains.

Soften, now, to time, as that bean, soaked in water, would soften. You'll see more life than seems possible in something so tiny. Eye the future and there, if you allow that bean to sprout, you have the stuff of tomorrow's salad or stir-fry. Look further: Bury that bean in soil, and it sprouts. Emerging from the earth, roots growing down, shoots and leaves growing up, it becomes a bush or a vine climbing a pole, tendrils curled—tenacious, poetic. This is a miracle beans have in common with any other seed. Yet, unique among plant families, beans and their kin generously give back to the soil; they are—it almost defies belief—*self-fertilizing*.

Look backward, too. The bean resting in your astonished palm is a direct link to the members of our own human family: the bean-growers, -sowers, and -eaters of ten thousand years ago in the Americas and the Middle East, in Africa, India, China, Japan. Had they not labored, no little package of life in its shiny coat would rest there under your scrutiny, ready to tell its secrets to anyone who will listen. Or remain silent, doing its work anyway.

Take your inquiry in another direction and you'll see, in this small, perfect package a nutritional cornucopia: protein, fiber, carbohydrate, vitamins A, C, and B-complex, omega-3 fats, calcium, potassium, phosphorus, selenium, zinc, copper, magnesium; and some pesky sugars known as oligosaccharides. It is these sugars, indigestible to humans, that give beans their nudge-nudge, grade-school-jokey, scatological reputation. Which is not worthy of them, or us, and which is easily dealt with once you understand a few bean basics (see page 1). Perhaps we should not be surprised that something as powerful as the bean has an explosive quality: When beans arrived in the Old World—first from the Middle East, then from the Americas—their protein and their ability to enrich, as opposed to deplete, the soil in which they are grown literally changed the face of Europe. Lynn White Jr., in *Medieval Technology and Social Change*, writes:

It was not merely the new quantity of food produced by improved agricultural methods, but the new type of food supply which goes far towards explaining, for northern Europe at least, the startling expansion of population, the growth and multiplication of cities, the rise in industrial production, the outreach of commerce, and the new exuberance of spirits which enlivened that age. In the full sense of the vernacular, the Middle Ages, from the tenth century onward, were full of beans.

Thoreau and I, as you can see, are far from the first to meet in the bean field. "Field," not only as a cultivated piece of ground, but as an area of inquiry and observation. Humanity and beans have kept company together a long time—for all recorded history.

The contexts of this meeting, both earthy and sublime, include supper (sustenance, succulence, sensual pleasure, nourishment) and soul (poetry, art, spirituality): meals and myth. Look closely at some of humankind's largest directional shifts and achievements, and you will find behind them . . . beans.

Members of the Leguminosae family (which includes beans, peas, lentils, and such idiosyncratic kin as peanuts and jicama) appear in the Bible often, where, among many mentions, they are pivotal in the Old Testament account of what many take to be the classic tale of sibling rivalry, that of Jacob and Esau. (I take the tale quite differently, see page 58; it describes, handily and beanily, another one of those large directional human shifts.) The Sufi poet and mystic Rumi (1207–73) wrote "Chickpea to Cook," a dialogue in which a disgruntled chickpea argues with its cook, who turns out to be its spiritual mentor and fellow traveler. Mark Twain wrote about bean soup in *A Tramp Abroad*; Shakespeare mentions peas in *As You Like It, A Midsummer Night's Dream, Henry IV,* and *Twelfth Night.* And let's not forget two leguminous nursery tales: In one, Jack's trade of a cow for a handful of beans leads him into gigantic trouble, and in the other, a pea gives a princess a particularly restless night. More contemporaneously, in the 2009 film *Cold Souls*, the character played by Paul Giamatti has his angsty soul extracted. What does it look like? A chickpea. Beans have penetrated the human psyche at least as much as they've nourished countless human bodies.

"Back when I was a sprout . . ."

Beans have also been my day's work for the last few years. They were my work as well during a much earlier period of my life, back in 1970–72, when I wrote the ancestor of this book, *The Bean Book: Cooking, Planting, Growing, Harvesting, Drying, Eating, and Just Thinking About Them* (it cost $2.45). I was eighteen then; I'm in my late fifties now. But in a less focused manner, beans and I have been together all those years in between. When I was a young freelance writer of uncertain and unpredictable income, bean soups nourished me, simmering gently and comfortingly as I worked. They cost little and made a tiny bit of meat (which I then ate; I no longer do) go a long, long way. They nourish me, and those I cook for, still.

Beans have certainly come up, up, in the world since I first began writing about them. Once lacking in social standing, associated with poverty, they're now chic side dishes, even entrées, at many of the world's finest restaurants, treated with respect. Once reviled nutritionally as little more than starch, they are now praised, both for what they are (carbohydrate that is low-glycemic, i.e., slower to turn to sugar in the body, judiciously mixed with protein, fiber, and a bountiful collection of vitamins), as well as what they are not (meat, with its saturated fat, cholesterol, excess calories, secondhand antibiotics, and large eco-footprint and expense).

Once limited in canned form to seven or eight varieties, and in dried to about twelve, today about fifteen varieties of canned beans and about twenty dried are to be found in your average supermarket. And if you go online to a specialty store, you'll find hundreds of varieties, including such captivatingly named beans as Tongues of Fire, Flor de Mayo, Indian Woman, nightfall, Mortgage Lifter, Rattlesnake,

Christmas limas, gigandes, and Petite Estoria lentils. One bean in particular, the soybean, has done such an about-face in terms of availability, a trajectory that has taken it from primarily animal feed to nutritional superstar, that I myself find it hard to believe. Yet it's true: In 1969, in New York City, if you wanted tofu, you got on a subway heading downtown and shopped at a Chinatown grocery. I know; I did it. Today, every Walmart in the country carries tofu, and most supermarkets offer countless soyfoods, ranging from frozen edamame to various meat analogs.

To V or not to V: Leguminous Options

The bean's slow-but-steady renaissance parallels, in part, the journey I took in my own eating. When I was sixteen and lived in a commune, if the food was vegetarian more than two nights in a row, I'd jones for meat to such an extent that I'd take the subway to the Middle Eastern section of Brooklyn and order lamb. But as I aged, several skeins of interest—environmentalism, nutrition and health, the range of agricultural and animal husbandry practices possible (some respectful and some brutal to earth, as well as to plants and animals), social justice, history, the astonishing number of human beings on this vast green globe who go to bed hungry each night, and yes, my own

love of good eating and the practice of cooking—coalesced. Gradually, for me, a plant-based diet became the way of eating that felt best on many levels; and once again, beans were there.

Being a "laissez-fare" vegetarian, I am not here to proselytize or advocate a meatless diet; indeed, I've included in this book many of my long-ago with-meat standbys. Though it's been many years since I've eaten these dishes, my meatist friends tell me they're just as tasty as I remember them. Choosing how and what to eat is such an individual and intimate matter: We all have our reasons and experiences for choosing as we do. While many still insist on conflating a vegetable-centric diet with self-denial and deprivation (and many, on the other side, flaunt an ill-founded and alienating sense of moral superiority about not consuming meat), eating, to me, remains a delight both reliable and ever-varying. As a vegetarian I give as much care and attention, from the sensual pleasure point of view, to what I put in my mouth and the mouths of those I love as I did when I ate lamb and pork, beef and chicken, and fish.

So, I've learned to cook beans in countless ways above and beyond the meaty. Whatever your preferences and choices, you'll find ways with beans that fit them here. Green and dried herbs, fresh and toasted spices, garlic, ginger, onions, and other aromatics, vegetables, stocks, oils, butter, coconut fat, condiments, and pickles—all these befriended me and the beans I cooked, and cook still, and will befriend you in your kitchen. Meat, in most cases, is optional.

Multiplicitous Meals

Beans are equally amiable as entrées (Vegetarian Cassoulet, page 234) and side dishes (Three Sisters Salad with Fresh Corn and Zucchini Ribbons, page 133); for lunch (Mr. Puppevich's Ho-made Fishcake-style Tofu Cakes, page 257) and dinner (Mjeddrah, page 301); and even for breakfast (Fastest-Gun-in-the-West Huevos Rancheros con Frijoles, page 270, The Best Vegetable Hash, page 256). Beans can start a meal (Classic Hummus Bi Tahini, page 30, Gotcha-Hotcha Sweet-Smoky Cocktail Peanuts, page 28) or finish it (White Chocolate & Peanut Butter Banana Cream Pie, page 332, Rose of Persia Cake, page 334). Beans can be curry (pages 199–207), chili (pages 157–184), ragout (page 282), soup (pages 51–126), or salad (pages 127–156). They can also be bread (Socca, page 277), pancakes (Neo-Classic Crepes, page 280), cookies (Julie's Peanut Butter-Chocolate Chip Oatmeal, page 322), even ice cream (Red Bean Ice Cream, page 339).

Deep Feast

What have I learned of beans, then? My answer to Thoreau's question is on every page of this book (as well as on my website and blog—www.dragonwagon.com and www.deepfeast.com—plus Facebook and Twitter [@cdragonwagon], into which my bean obsession has naturally also flowed).

It's impossible, of course, to answer the part of Thoreau's query in which he wonders what beans will learn of him. But if I could give voice to beans, I can tell you what I'd hope they'd say of me: "She treated us with respect, imagination, and gratitude. She cooked us with exuberance. She used us as a way to join hands with others all over this spinning green planet on which we ride together, each of us, in turn, eating and being eaten." I think beans must know, as I do, that life's contract requires full participation, whether we are legume or human.

Let us participate, then, and celebrate, sprouting, growing, making tendrils; maturing, harvesting, and being harvested; cooking, eating, being eaten; letting the next generation rediscover the poignant joy of the feast. Let us join hands at a table the size of the world. Let's eat.

There's Room for Everyone at the Table: About the Recipe Tags

Cooking, eating, and feeding others is best done with generosity and a spirit of inquiry. For me, how to provide for what someone does or doesn't eat is fun—a creative challenge, not a hassle. I am, after all, the creator of the first birthday cake my friend Judith (who does not eat flour or any sweetener except apple juice concentrate) was able to have in *twenty years*.

But it's not so fun and creative for those who avoid, say, gluten, because they choose to or must (due to allergies, celiac, and so on). It's a capital-H Hassle to say, over and over, "Does this have any gluten in it?" Or, to look at recipes, get excited about them, then find that wheat flour has made an appearance.

I hope the recipe tags throughout this book will simplify this:

Vn means a recipe is vegan; it has no animal products of any kind in it.

Ve means it is vegetarian; it contains dairy products and/or eggs, but no meat, fish, or chicken.

Gf means it is gluten-free; it contains no gluten flours, such as wheat.

Me means it's meatist; it contains meat, fish, or chicken, or something made with them (such as fish sauce or chicken stock).

Now, you may have a moment when you go "Whoa! How can this be vegan *and* meatist?" Easy, my dear . . . look at the ingredients list and you'll inevitably find "2 cups vegetable *or* chicken stock" or "2 slices of bacon (optional)." Please, don't freak out. You gluten-free folks, same thing: "2 tablespoons flour *or* 1½ teaspoons cornstarch" or "8 ounces noodles (optional)."

I'm holding your hand as much as I can here, but you still have to use discrimination. For instance, I call for "tamari soy sauce," not "tamari soy sauce, or, for you gluten-free eaters, wheat-free tamari soy-sauce." I presume gluten-free eaters know the fine points of tamari and gluten. If a recipe asks for "honey, agave, or sugar," and is marked both vegan and vegetarian, I presume vegans will know to choose agave or sugar, not honey.

It's intimate, the choices we make about what to put in our bodies. Beans want us to be happy. They're amenable: How else could they be both a vegetarian staple in some circles, and, in others, an ingredient that elicits an automatic throw-in-a-ham-hock response?

However you eat, beans and I welcome you, with respect and joy, to the table. Your place is set, and there's more than enough for seconds.

CHAPTER 1

BEAN BASICS

The A, B(ean), Cs

Which came first, the bean . . . or the bean? Plant your first garden, open your first package of bean seeds, and you'll see that a bean seed is a bean! The very same plump little ovoids that you see in bins at your local co-op or in bags at the supermarket—that's what's in your seed packets. Could you plant the beans you get at such stores? Sure (assuming they are untreated whole beans, not, say, split peas). Certainly if you plant a dried pinto bean, you will get a plant covered with pods in which, eventually, you'll find those same pinto beans, each of which is both an edible seed and a potential future pinto bean plant. Each bean or pea, no matter its variety, is the mature seed of itself, freed of the comforting pod in which it grew. Each contains within it the materials needed to re-create itself.

Podded Pleasures

The word *legume* itself means "true pod." If you want to know beans, you have to know pods.

A pod is a kind of purse of vegetal flesh, made of two equal-size flaps seamed on the two long sides, culminating in a short tip on each end. One tip, the stem end, attached the pod to the plant. The other was once the site of the now-fallen-off blossom, which heralded the arrival of this same pod; it's called, naturally, the blossom end, though by the time you buy it, the blossom is no more. And what this sutured pod holds is the seeds for the next generation of bean plant—hence the root word of legume: "to gather."

Now, when we eat a green bean or an edible-pod pea, these seeds are immature, stillborn; were we to split the pod, we would see tiny, barely formed seeds.

A bean's pod is what we eat when we eat a green bean. But stay with me here: What we're actually eating is the seed case of the immature bean, not a bean at all. Hence "green" bean—not only pertaining to color, but meaning youthful, as when Shakespeare's Cleopatra refers to her youth as her "salad days, when [she] was green in judgment." And when they are really fresh and carefully prepared, I believe green bean pods to be among the most succulent of vegetables (I dare you to try the Greek-style green beans on page 284 and see if you don't agree).

PERUSE YOUR PODS

Examine the pods before you pick or buy; they give many useful clues, such as, in the garden, when to pick and, in the market, whether the green bean is old and tough or will be forgivingly tender when cooked. The tiny, not-much-thicker-than-a-pencil-lead beans called fillet beans or haricots verts are adorable and tender, the baby version of regular-size green beans, but no different in flavor from their slightly more grown-up kin, which have stayed on the bush or vine a few days, maybe a week, longer. Fillet beans usually cost quite a bit more, too. The older beans may be less precious, but they have more interior bean flesh to outer skin; they're beanier to my taste, though they may not look as cute.

When choosing green beans—which, remember, may be green or yellow or purple, and rounded or flat, depending on variety— select those with consistently smooth, even pod-sides. Avoid those with bumpy indentations; by the time you can see the pod swelling pregnantly with the beans, the pod itself will be tough and leathery, not tender (though the beans within will be succulent).

Check for freshness at the market thus: Pick up a pod and break it in two. A fresh bean will snap, crisply and audibly, into two distinct pieces—hence another slightly

old-fashioned but still common, so-very-apt name for green beans: snap beans. If the bean merely bends, it's been sitting in the produce section too long and is past its prime, making for disappointing eating. (No need to do this test when picking from your garden; you'll know when your beans are, well, full of beans then.)

Another thing a snap will tell you: whether or not the bean's pod has "strings"—thin threads of relatively tough fiber that edge the pods along one or both side-seams. These threads, when left attached to the pod, are unpleasant to bite into. A snap reveals them. This doesn't mean, however, that you should avoid beans with strings. Many delicious beans and edible-pod peas do have 'em. Now, some people will tell you strings have been bred out of green beans: not true. Some varieties are stringless, others still have them, and some with-string varieties are exceptionally well flavored. So don't let strings dissuade you; just remove them as instructed in Basic Green Bean Cookery, page 10.

Bean Varieties

As for dried beans, there are hundreds of varieties available. (There are eight major categories of edible bean, botanically speaking, which relate to their geographic origins. See the charts on page 344 for more.) At your local supermarket, you'll likely find pintos, kidneys, red beans, navy beans, lima beans, black-eyed peas, lentils, and split peas. And depending on where you live, you might also find a host of other varieties (soldier beans in the Northeast, for example, or pigeon peas in areas with a large Caribbean population). Each bean has a slightly different appearance, flavor, texture, cooking time, and culinary idiosyncrasy.

Before you get overwhelmed by this bean fecundity, however, know that *beans are more alike than they are different*—the same basic cooking methods apply (at least as far as dried beans are concerned)—and a seasoning that tastes good with one bean will almost surely be tasty (though perhaps not traditional) with another. With the exception of the swift-cooking, no-need-to-soak legumes (lentils, split peas, split chickpeas, black-eyes), the two delicate-skinned beans (large limas and black soybeans), and the tough-skinned fava (which must be peeled post-soaking), all dried beans can be used interchangeably. The only thing that varies is the length of time needed to reach tenderness. In other words, you could use lentils instead of black beans in your favorite black bean soup recipe, and it'd still be good (though it would cook much more quickly).

All cooking times listed in the charts on page 346, unless otherwise stated, assume the raw beans have been soaked to full hydration. That means, as you'll learn on page 16, there's no pale dry spot in the center of a split-open bean after soaking.

Beans: What's in Them for You

What is the makeup of a bean nutritionally? First, and uniquely among edible plants, it has protein. The Leguminosae and their kin, and the products made from them (like tofu and tempeh), are protein-dense: the single most concentrated source of plant-based protein in the world. Between 6 and 11 percent of beans' cooked weight is protein; ½ cup of cooked beans, depending on the variety, has about 8 grams (an egg, by contrast, has 6). While it is true that in most cases the protein in legumes is "incomplete" (that is, short on a couple of the essential amino acids), the grains we so often and naturally eat with beans are abundant in the amino acids legumes lack. It's a handy reciprocity. Add a slice of bread, a helping of pasta, a scoop of rice, or a tortilla with your beans, and you have protein perfecto. (The exception to the rule here: the soybean, which *does* contain complete protein.)

Although "protein complementarity" is stated elsewhere in this book and in many other places (having first been popularized in 1971 in Frances Moore Lappé's *Diet for a Small Planet*), its perfection—and the fact that beans and grains together just taste so good and right (black beans and rice! falafel and pita bread! cornbread and chili!)—remains amazing to me. (I am also amazed by the fact that there are still lots of people who don't yet know about protein complementarity, or who believe it to be more complex than it is, or who still consider plant-based protein inferior to animal-derived—so now that you know better, spread the word.)

But it's not only that beans, with their few missing nutritional pieces supplied by grains, are full of protein equal in quality to that derived from animal sources. It's that bean protein is in many ways superior to that derived from animals: It has no cholesterol, it's low in fat, and it's high in fiber. And since a bean, even a non-organically raised one, is lower on the food chain than a cow, it lacks the intrinsic concentration of pesticides that rises when we consume higher-ups. Beans are not fed antibiotics or growth hormones, nor do they carry the common freight of general contemporary animal husbandry practices. Beans are not raised in feedlots or stacked in cages, with the environmental degradation inherent in such practices. Growing beans not only hurts no one and nothing, it quietly enriches the soil in which beans are raised. And healthy soil and food systems are perhaps the ultimate nutritional benefit.

Beans are packed with B vitamins (though some vitamins, being water-soluble, are lost during soaking and cooking). They're high in iron, calcium, and phosphorus, and of course fiber; as a class of foodstuff, beans have more fiber than virtually anything edible except the bran in grains. Beans are rich in complex carbohydrates, too—the starch that gives them their creamy, satisfying heartiness. When you're fed on beans, you're well and truly fed.

Hopefully you already know that high-protein, carbohydrates-are-spawn-of-the-devil diets are just plain wrong; that it's all in the nature and amount of the carbohydrate. And bean carbohydrate is not mere starch. In her *Good Food Book*, Jane Brody calls bean carbs "nutritional wonders" and points out that they've been proven to drastically improve the stability of blood sugar levels in diabetics. She adds that "on diets containing substantial amounts of beans, many adult-onset diabetics have been able to reduce greatly or eliminate entirely their dependence on insulin and other medications to control blood sugar." Why? Probably, at least in part, because legumes are digested very slowly—one of the very qualities that makes them such a stick-to-the-ribs food.

Still not a bean convert? Consider the "Mexican Paradox," examined in a study by Northern Arizona University. Like the "French Paradox," much discussed a few years back, the Mexican Paradox highlights the fact that the Mexican diet is as high as or higher than the American diet in saturated fats, yet the Mexican population has far lower rates of heart disease. In France, the missing piece of this puzzle turned out to be phytochemicals called phenols, which are commonly found in red wine and which help the body break down LDL cholesterol (the "bad" kind) so that it can't clog arteries. The Mexican diet is rich in a foodstuff containing a similar, related phytochemical: polyphenolics. These appear, also, to aid the human body in assimilating the "bad" cholesterol and rendering it harmless. What are polyphenolics found in? Beans, especially black beans and pintos.

But let me return to the larger nutritional profile already mentioned: that it's not only what beans do for us, but what they do for our shared habitat, Earth. Beans are the single cultivated plant family that actually *benefits* the soil, enriching it rather than depleting it during the growing process. How is this possible? Legume family members have beneficial nodules on their roots that verifiably *add* nitrogen to the soil, instead of using it up. Some legumes do so much good that they are planted as a "green manure," to enrich the soil naturally between greedier crops such as corn and wheat.

Could there be a plant more generous than the bean?

Unmaking the Mischief of the Musical Fruit

Raffinose, stachyose, and verbascose— are they hoodlums hanging out at the corner when they should be at school or gainfully employed? No, these "splendidly disreputable-sounding" characters (as the *Laurel's Kitchen* folks put it) are complex sugars, collectively called oligosaccharides. They hang out in beans and cause us trouble. Oligosaccharides cannot be broken down by our digestive enzymes; instead, our intestinal bacteria ferment them during digestion. This fermentation causes most of the gas attributed to beans (though beans are also high-fiber foods, and those unaccustomed to eating such foods also tend to suffer flatulence when they first start fibering up). The quantity of gas produced, how uncomfortable it is physically or socially, and whether or not it is odiferous depend on several factors, largely within your control.

★ *The cooking method.* Oligosaccharides are water-soluble and can, with proper soaking and cooking, be washed out to a great degree (see The De-Gassifying Method, page 16).

★ *What the bean is cooked or eaten with.* Historically, certain herbs and spices were supposed to mitigate the gas-making effects of beans. As with most pieces of folk wisdom, there's something to this; quite a few herbs and spices thus recommended (see page 8) have a carminative effect.

★ *What the bean is* not *cooked or eaten with.* One of the most popular families of bean amendments, particularly in America, is something sweet—as in the "Boston baked bean" lineage. Indeed, this is a tasty way to go. But while delicious, brown sugar, honey, et al., can spell trouble for those sensitive to beans, because these drop still more carbs into the digestive tract for the bacteria to work on. Pay attention: If sweetened beans don't work for you, omit them, eat them in small quantities, or try some Beano (see box, page 9).

★ *The variety of bean used.* The least "flatulating" legumes are said to be (in this order) lentils, split peas, adzuki beans, mung beans, black-eyed peas, and anasazi beans (one of the old heritage beans). All are lower in oligosaccharides. In the low to middle range probably (because they've not been tested, to my knowledge, for oligosaccharides) are the other non-hybridized heritage beans, such as tepary, calypso, nightfall, and so on. Mid-range are chickpeas, black beans, and white beans. Higher still are limas and navy beans, with whole soybeans being the highest.

★ *The form in which you eat beans.* Soybeans may be difficult to digest in whole-bean form, but as tofu, tempeh, or TVP (see box, page 179), virtually no one has a problem with them because most of the oligosaccharides have been removed in the process of their manufacture.

★ *How well-cooked the beans are.* Since the oligosaccharides are water-soluble, it is logical to suppose that an all-the-way-cooked-through-to-softness bean, which has been totally rehydrated, would have less of them, while a bean still somewhat firm would have more. This is the case. Fortunately, "fully done" is the precise degree at which beans taste their best. When is a bean done? It should be soft enough that you can mash it against the roof of your mouth with your tongue, without resistance. On the other hand, it should not be disintegrating.

★ *The age of the beans.* Beans keep indefinitely on your kitchen shelf and can be cooked years after being harvested. But that doesn't mean they *should* be. I once made an elaborate soup that required just a half cup or so of lentils. I discovered, midway through cooking, that the only lentils I had were ancient, sitting in a jar in a dusty, hard-to-reach corner of my pantry. I used them, and, Reader, they like to never soften! Lentils can cook in as little as fifteen or twenty minutes; these cooked in the soup for hours, never got there, and finally disintegrated into tough little shards. They never got creamy. And those shards were "flatulating," as well as unpleasant to eat.

"New-crop" beans—those from the most recent harvest—cook more quickly than old, sometimes even more quickly than a recipe says. Moreover, they cook to smooth creaminess, a major standard by which haute beanery is measured, and the indicator that the oligosaccharides are in decline. I wouldn't go so far as to say to throw out last fall's beans when this fall rolls around—besides, you have no way of knowing for sure when your store-bought beans were harvested—but know that age is a factor in the end results.

★ *How often you eat beans.* If all this is beginning to seem more trouble than it's worth, take heart in a University of California–Berkeley study in which bean-eating subjects "reported greater tolerance and less discomfort by the end of a three-week period of bean eating."

★ *In what quantity you eat beans.* Eat a lot of beans once in a while, and you'll almost certainly have problems (unless you use Beano, see the box on page 9). But eat small amounts of beans on a daily basis, with occasional large portions, and you should be fine. This supports the study above; the body adjusts. Good old body.

★ *Individual bean tolerance.* Individual responses to oligosaccharides vary. You and your spouse/partner/pal might react differently; some beans might be a problem and some not. Experiment, take note, and give your body time to adapt.

Helpful Herbs and Soothing Spices

I mentioned that many traditional cultures use various herbs and spices to deflate the effect of beans. A closer look:

★ In Germany and other parts of Central Europe, summer savory is called "the bean herb." Beans were almost invariably cooked with a few sprigs added (and perhaps a little more, fresh, sprinkled over the top of each bowl). Bay leaf is often cooked with beans for this reason, as well as its very compatible flavor.

★ In India, carminative cumin, ginger, and cilantro are frequently cooked with beans. A strong hot tea of cumin seeds, *jeera vellam*, is commonly poured in home kitchens as a standard digestive after the midday meal—the largest (usually beaniest) meal of the day.

★ Used throughout Mexico and Central America, one of the most famous herbs of bean side-effect alleviation is epazote (*Chenopodium ambrosiodes*), which has a lovely herbal-floral flavor when cooked with beans and/or rice dishes. I've used it both fresh and dried. You can find it at Mexican or South American specialty groceries, where it may be called pazote, worm weed, wormseed, or Mexican tea. In recent years, it's become widely available as a garden herb; you can probably find it at any local nursery with a good herb section. Diana Kennedy, thc doyenne of Mexican cooking, in her book *The Cuisines of Mexico*, says that it's an acquired taste, but that once one has it, cooking black beans without epazote is "unthinkable."

★ Many Asian cultures, as well as those who follow macrobiotics, swear by cooking dried beans with a piece of kombu (a thick seaweed that looks a little like a dark green piece of lasagna noodle) for its de-gassifying effects.

If using dried herbs, try about 2 teaspoons per pound of dried beans, added after the beans have been soaked and drained but before they are cooked. For the Indian-style spices, which are often sautéed before being added, or for fresh herbs, just follow the specific recipes.

BEAN NO? BEAN YES!

If you have real problems despite your attention to these factors, but want the benefits of beans in your life, try Beano. Made by the company AkPharma and available at natural foods markets and some drugstores, it comes in a teeny plastic squeeze bottle. All you do is drip a few drops on your first bite of beans. Made of a benign food-grade mold, Beano contains a digestive enzyme that neutralizes the oligosaccharides before they get inside you. Problem solved. No, you can't cook with it (heat breaks it down), nor can you stir it into a whole pot—it must be on that *first spoonful* of beans in order to work its magic. Oh: How, you ask, does Beano taste? Wholly unobjectionable—like soy sauce. Really, truly. No problem.

And in case the notion of Beano seems too weird to you, know that Rancho la Puerta, one of the most luxurious spa-resorts in North America, keeps bottles of the stuff sitting out on the condiment tray in the dining room.

A BEGINNER'S BEANERY

Here are the absolute ABCs: all you need to know in order to change fresh green beans or dried beans into succulent ingredients. From these basics onward to dinner, in countless ways.

Basic Green Bean Cookery: A Many-Hued Palette

The same rules as to cooking and doneness apply to both the familiar green beans and the *non*-green green beans that are part of the abundant midsummer yields at farmer's markets and in home gardens. Proceed happily toward these figuratively "green" (as in fresh, young, still-tender) beans, which may be:

★ pale yellow (mild green bean flavor, sometimes called "wax" beans; varieties include Eureka, Gold Mine, and Mellow Yellow)

★ deep violet-purple (classic green bean taste, these sadly revert to green when cooked, with the cooking water turning, unbelievably, turquoise! Varieties include Purple Queen and Violetto)

★ mottled (slightly fleshier versions of green beans, often grown for dried beans but glorious as young edible-pod beans too; I love the red and white Italian Rose and the pale green and reddish purple Dragon's Tongue)

GREEN BEAN YIELDS & EQUIVALENTS

1 pound fresh green beans = 3½ to 4 cups sliced beans. Serves 4 to 6 as a side dish or salad.

1 pound fresh green beans, steamed and pureed (see box, page 11) = 2½ cups thick puree (for pâtés), 3 cups slightly thinner puree (for soups).

★ slightly gray-green, with wide, flattened rather than pencil-shaped pods (Italian pole beans, Romanos, and Romas; their robust flavor is hearty, their texture meaty)

And those green beans may not even be beans as such at all, but rather edible-pod peas, also known as sugar snaps, *mange-touts*, or, when slightly flattened in shape, snow peas.

Here's how to prepare green beans—of any variety or color—for cooking:

1. Give them a good rinse. Drain.

2. Snip, pinch, or cut off the tough stem end of the bean pods, as well as any spoiled spots and any brown blossom remnants clinging to the tail end. You need not

remove the tail itself, though some people do, feeling that leaving it on is sloppy and that it could catch in your throat. (If your grandmother "tipped and tailed" her green beans, you'll probably do so, too, or it won't seem right.) I leave them on and have never run into an identifiable or unpleasant tail after the dish is cooked.

3. Break or snap a bean in half. If you see a string, break each pod close to the stem end and pull down firmly; the strings (if there are any, they run down both sides) will curl back from the bean and zip off. Sometimes you can get both strings from the stem end; if you only get one, pinch off the blossom end, too, and pull the other string from the opposite side. That's it!

Beans are one vegetable that, to me, are *not* usually at their best cooked tender-crisp. They should be tender, yes, though never, ever boiled to the gray falling-apart stage too many of us may remember from summer camp or school cafeterias. (The few exceptions to this are noted.) They must retain shape, and some texture, but I have really come to think they are much tastier when not chewy or crisp at all, unless maybe you're using them in a salad or a stir-fry, or if they are exceptionally slender and young. If you eat your green beans tender-crisp and only tender-crisp, you are missing remarkable depth of flavor and silken texture. Trust me, you are. It took me years of living in the South to fully get this. But once I did (and once you do), there was no going back.

BASIC GREEN BEAN PUREE

Want to make an ordinary vegetable soup full of soul, or an almost-instant cream soup that is beyond wonderful? Want to fill your freezer with harvested beans in season from your garden or farmer's market, but find you're running out of space? Want to make a luscious, silky vegetarian pâté, such as Ellen Levine's Vegetarian "Chopped Liver" à la Dragon on page 45? Puree your green beans.

1. Steam or blanch trimmed green beans to tenderness, just past tender-crisp (see pages 12–13). Drain, reserving the cooking water, and rinse with cold water. Let them cool to room temperature.

2. Transfer up to 1 pound cooked green beans at a time to a food processor, allowing ½ to ⅔ cup bean cooking water per batch (if using the puree for pâtés, use a tablespoon or two of water at the most—as little as you can get by with). Buzz smooth.

3. Refrigerate, freeze for up to 6 months, or use in a recipe ASAP. Feel very lucky.

BUZZ

So, unless they are itty-bitty skinny haricots verts (fillet beans), tender-ish even before cooking, it is usually advisable to precook green beans before using them in the recipe. Here's how:

1. Bring a pot—the size depends on the amount you're precooking—of water to a full boil, allowing sufficient water to cover the green beans to a depth of 1 inch. Ideally, you want a pot of water so big, and at such a vigorous boil, that the water won't stop boiling with the addition of the beans. (If you use spring or filtered water rather than ordinary tap water, which usually is chlorinated and fluoridated, your beans will taste incrementally better; see the box, below.)

2. Drop in the washed, trimmed green beans.

3. If you want them barely blanched, keep them in just until the color brightens

The Secret Ingredient

There's a universal, un-exotic secret ingredient in most recipes. It's water.

Just as the same wine-grape varieties, and the wines made from them, taste different when grown in different soils, so do soups, beverages, and beans taste different depending on the water with which they are cooked. Some waters are better than others. If you're extremely lucky (and live in the country), the water that comes out of your tap is good, clean, uncontaminated well water. If you live in a more populated area, you're on city water. What comes out of your tap is almost certainly surface, not well, water: This is the water you see when you drive by a city's reservoir. Unlike well water (and many spring waters), it's relatively low in minerals. It's also subject to easy pollution: runoff from pesticides and herbicides, animal wastes, floods, storms, lawn fertilizers, construction dust, and so on. To make it potable, municipalities process it with filtration systems and additives (like chlorine and fluoride). Because urban sources of water, and water levels in lakes and reservoirs, vary greatly from season to season, cities adjust their processing accordingly. Water tastes noticeably different not only city to city, but season to season and home to home; its character is further affected by the pipes it passes through.

Because of the variability of city-sourced water, I highly recommend spring or well water for drinking and cooking.

Now, I know that many people follow this advice as far as drinking goes, but don't for the water they use in tea, coffee, and soup, or to cook pasta or beans; it would be absurd and prohibitively expensive. For them, a water filtration system is the way to go. These come in all price ranges, from by-the-pitcher types to those that are installed at the faucet. You want a filter that leaves the trace minerals but removes the particulate municipal additives and any other contaminants. Incrementally, everything you eat or cook tastes better when made with good, clean water. Most people notice it immediately in coffee and tea; but consider the beans, their dryness plumped by nothing but water. Better water equals better beans.

a bit, maybe 30 seconds to 1 minute. This might be good for beans that you're going to use in a salad (where you may want residual crispness) or beans that you'll be cooking again. But in most cases, I leave the beans in a little longer, 3 to 4, even 5 minutes. At this point, they lose their slight characteristic fuzz and are a bit more tender.

4. Drain the cooked beans in a colander, saving the cooking water for soup stock, if you like. Immediately run cold water over the beans to stop the cooking process and prevent sogginess.

Note: If preferred, steam the green beans, about the same range of time as above, on a collapsible steamer basket set over boiling water. This keeps more of the water-soluble nutrients in the beans.

Basic Semi-Mature Bean Cookery

The next stage of bean edibility is what's usually called a shell bean or shellie, seldom seen these days unless you live out in the country or shop where there are large metropolitan farmer's markets. A shell bean is a bean that has matured past the edible-pod stage but is itself edible once cooked. The pod, now fully pregnant with beans, is swollen and bumpy and must be shucked off (or hulled, or, yes, shelled—it all results in the same thing: removed) to free the starchy beans themselves. They may be white or buff,

pink, blue-black, mottled, or dotted with an eye of brown or black—depends on the variety. At this stage the beans are fully formed, in pods that are by now large and leathery but still colored and not yet dry. With that pod removed, these shell beans can be cooked and eaten as they are—for somewhat longer than you'd cook fresh in-pod green beans, but much more briefly than you'd cook dried beans.

Many beans, such as black-eyed peas and kidney beans, are edible and prized in all three stages: as young (green) bean, shell bean, and dried bean—more bean generosity. All beans, of any variety, if allowed to reach the semi-mature phase, are shell beans, but a few varieties are grown especially for shellies: in the South, lady peas, crowder peas, and black-eyes. In the North, occasionally you'll see large, beautifully streaky red and white or purple and white pods that contain shell beans that are also streaked; the reds are similarly Tongues of Fire beans, the purple, Dragon's Tongue. But you don't find them in markets that often, because they don't keep well.

Almost anything made with dried beans can be made with shell beans, but much more quickly. A dried black-eyed pea, for instance, takes about an hour to an hour and a half to become tender. A fresh black-eyed shell bean is there, *so* there, in fifteen to twenty minutes. But because shell beans are such a seasonal delicacy, I hardly ever just substitute them for cooked dried beans in an elaborate recipe. Nor do I puree them.

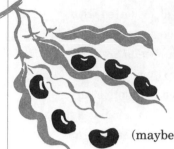

I cook them, by the method I'm about to give, and enjoy them ultra-simply: a pat of butter, some cornbread on the side (maybe a scallion, too, and a sliced garden tomato . . . you try this for supper and see if I'm not right).

For the exception to the rule, fava beans, see page 44.

BASIC SHELL BEANS

1. Snap off the stem ends of the pods to open them. Run your thumb down the inside of each pod to remove the beans. Discard the pods.

2. Place the shelled beans in a pot, and add water to barely cover. Bring to a boil, turn down to a simmer, and let cook for anywhere from 7 to 20 minutes (it depends on the size and variety of the bean; see chart, page 344).

3. Taste for doneness: The bean or pea will be tender and creamy, with no hint of raw starch.

....

SHELL BEAN YIELDS & EQUIVALENTS

....

1 pound shell beans in the pod = 2½ to 3 cups shelled beans without the pods. Serves 4 to 6 as a side dish or salad, 2 to 3 as a main dish (with cornbread).

....

BASIC HALF-AND-HALF SHELL BEANS

Shell beans are often a delicacy known to gardeners only, and the beans mature over a period of time on the plant; so if you grow your own, you're likely to have both green beans and shellies at once. (And you could probably fake it if your local farmer's market has both green and shell beans at the same time.) They can be cooked together. If you feel so inclined, add a slice or two of bacon, cut up, to the beans as they cook. It's been more than forty years since I've eaten them thus, but I remember finding them simple but addictive—and to my West Texan then-husband, they were heaven on earth. Here is how to combine shell and green beans in one glorious pot:

1. Gather, from garden or market, shell beans and green beans in a ratio of 2 to 1.

2. Snap stem ends off the shell bean pods to open them. Remove the beans. Discard the pods.

3. Place the shelled beans in a pot, and add water to barely cover. Bring to a boil, turn down to a simmer, and let cook for 5 minutes.

4. Meanwhile, trim the stems from the green beans, and cut them into about 1-inch lengths. After the shell beans have cooked for 5 minutes, drop in the green beans. Let them cook until the shell beans are tender, anywhere from 7 to 20 minutes more (it depends on the size and variety of the shell bean;

the green beans may be a little more done than you're used to, but they are delicious this way).

Basic Dried Bean Cookery

To convert a dry, hard bean to creaminess requires soaking (usually) and cooking (always). Why don't I use any one method in every single dried-bean recipe in this book? Because there *is* no single method that's best for every recipe and for every moment you want beans. Since your bean-soaking and -cooking options are several, and in many cases interchangeable (in quite a few cases, you can even use canned beans instead of soaked and cooked dried beans), I've laid them all out. Though there are soaking and cooking combinations I use more than others, there aren't any that I haven't used at some time. I've offered the pros and cons of each method (some have speed on their side, for example, or yield a more nutritious result), so you can decide which one works best for you on any given day.

SOAKING IT IN

Before you get cooking you will likely need to get soaking. Almost all slow-to-cook dried beans (that is, everything except lentils, split peas, black-eyed peas, and adzuki and mung beans) do better when they've been soaked. Why? Soaked beans cook in about a third of the time of unsoaked, and their texture is uniformly creamy. Also, soaking beans—if you then discard the soaking water—gets rid of many of the oligosaccharides that cause flatulence (see page 6). Now, you do lose some B-vitamins—though not protein—in the water-discarding process, but if you avoid eating beans because of the discomfort, social or physical, they cause you, well, you're not getting those nutrients anyway.

Unless otherwise specified by your chosen cooking method or recipe, you can soak beans overnight (lengthy but simple), use the quick-soak method (faster, still simple), or use the pressure-cooked quick-soak method (quickest but slightly more complex). The main difference is the amount of haste you're in. (The De-Gassifying Method on page 16 is a special case: It requires an overnight soak, with a huge quantity of water.)

In all cases, your first step is the same: sort and pick through the beans, sifting them with your fingers into a colander to remove any tiny rocks, pebbles, or pieces of straw, as well as the odd moldy bean (unlikely) and (often) little bits of dried mud. Then rinse them well under room-temperature running water.

After the beans are rinsed, soak them using one of the methods that follow. You'll know your beans are soaked adequately when they are much inflated in appearance;

plus when you split one in half, you'll be able to see that it's fully hydrated: It will be the same color all the way through. If it's not fully hydrated, you'll see a paler dry spot at the center of the split-open bean, showing clearly how far the water has penetrated. This tells you that the beans need to soak longer.

Overnight Soaking

This is the way I usually soak beans, but then I am a plan-ahead kind of gal. This

yields a nominally better product texturally, evenly creamy all the way through.

1. In a large bowl or pot, soak picked-over, rinsed beans in enough water to cover them to a depth of at least 1 inch. (The more water you use for soaking and then drain off,

THE DE-GASSIFYING METHOD

If you have major difficulty with bloating post-beans, this method of bean soakery and cookery will solve or greatly diminish the problem. Devised by the USDA's Northern Regional Research Center, it gets rid of most of the flatulence-causing oligosaccharides.

Now, I must point out that although the method is effective, I wonder if it's worth the trouble. Why not just try to get your body used to eating beans? While the technique itself is not exactly difficult, it can be a hassle; it takes a while and requires a few water changes. And you need rather large cooking vessels, because you need to use large amounts of water. Also, you throw

out every scrap of cooking liquid, making this method inappropriate when the recipe calls for cooking in stock, or when you otherwise want a nice, thick, flavorful cooking liquid, as in a soup or stew. It's better for a bean that will be cooked tender but then used dry, without a sauce—in a salad, say, or pureed for a burger or spread. But if you're eager to de-gassify, here's how:

1. In a very large pot or bowl, using 9 cups of water to 1 cup of beans, soak picked-over and rinsed beans, covered or not, for 4 to 5 hours or overnight.

2. Drain and rinse the soaked beans thoroughly under running water, place them in

a large, heavy pot, and cover them again with water in the same 9-to-1 ratio. Bring to a hard boil, turn the heat down to medium-low, and simmer, covered, for 30 minutes. Drain the beans, discarding the cooking water.

3. Assuming the beans are not yet done, return them to the pot, and cover them with water yet again—third time now!—in the same 9-to-1 ratio. Bring to a hard boil, turn down to a simmer, and cook, covered, stirring every half hour or so and adding more liquid as needed, until the beans are tender. Discard the cooking water and use the beans as you like.

the more oligosaccharides you discard. I use a lot of water.) Soak them at room temperature, covered or not, for 6 to 8 hours or overnight. (If it is very warm, however, refrigerate them.)

2. When the beans are hydrated (split one open—it should be the same color all the way through), pour off any remaining soaking water, turn the beans into a colander, and rinse them under cold water (preferably filtered) several times. Proceed to cook.

Quick Soaking

I do this pretty often, too, if I get in a beany mood and forgot to get 'em soaking the night before.

1. Place picked-over, rinsed beans in a medium-large pot. Add enough water to cover them to a depth of at least 1 inch.

2. Quickly bring the water to a hard boil, and cook the beans for 5 minutes. Turn off the heat and let the beans stand, covered, for 1 hour. (You can repeat this if you like, both for oligosaccharide removal and for faster actual cooking.)

3. Pour off any remaining soaking water, turn the beans out into a colander, and rinse them under cold water (preferably filtered) several times. Proceed to cook.

Pressure-cooked Quick Soaking

Even faster, and amazingly good results.

1. Place the picked-over, rinsed beans in the pot of a large pressure cooker. Add 3 cups of water for the first cup of dried beans and 2 cups for each cup thereafter. Lock the lid in place, and bring to high pressure according to the manufacturer's instructions.

2. For smaller beans (such as adzuki, navy, tepary), once the cooker has reached high pressure, count to 10, turn off the heat, and let the pressure release naturally for 10 minutes before unlocking the lid. Let medium beans (black beans, kidneys) cook for 1 to 2 minutes at high pressure; let the pressure release naturally for 15 minutes before unlocking the lid. Allow 3 minutes at high pressure for large beans (like large limas) or hard beans (chickpeas); let the pressure release naturally for 20 minutes before unlocking the lid.

3. After the lid is removed, turn the beans into a colander, drain off any remaining water, and rinse them thoroughly, several times, with running water. Proceed to cook.

SOAKING/COOKING OPTIONS: VARIATIONS ON A THEME

The same basic elements: a big pot, water (or another liquid), soaked beans, stove or slow-cooker. The main difference: which method was used to soak the beans. There are pros and cons to each.

Stovetop Cooking, Overnight Soak

This is my favorite method, but then, I work at home.

Pros: To my mind, best finished product. Very easy, basically unattended cooking time. High soothe factor, especially in cold weather: It's just pleasing to have a pot simmering, good bean-cooking aromas scenting the air and steaming up the windows. Overnight soaking gives you that satisfying I-got-a-jump-on-things feeling.

Cons: You must plan in advance; the cooking time is long and slow. While you don't have to stay in the immediate vicinity, as with a pressure cooker, you do have to kind of be around.

How to: Place the overnight-soaked beans in a large, heavy pot (I usually give it a spritz of oil beforehand). Cover with water (or whatever liquid is called for in the recipe) to a depth of 1 inch (unless your recipe instructs you to do otherwise). Bring to a hard boil, turn down to low, and simmer, covered, stirring every 30 to 45 minutes, until the beans are tender (see chart, page 344, for specific cooking times). Add more liquid as needed.

Stovetop Cooking, Quick Soak

Almost as good as the previous. I often do this if I've failed to plan ahead.

Pros: Good results, and you don't have to plan too far ahead.

Cons: A nominally less perfect texture than from the overnight soak. Nominally more work on cooking day than soaking overnight.

How to: Place the quick-soaked beans (see page 17) in a large, heavy pot; if you're not using a well-seasoned cast-iron or nonstick pot, spray it with oil first. Cover with water or whatever liquid is called for in the recipe to a depth of 1 to 2 inches (if your recipe says otherwise, listen to it). Bring to a hard boil, turn down to low, and simmer, covered, stirring every half hour or so, until the beans are tender. Add more liquid as needed.

Slow Cooking, Soaking Method of Your Choice

This is my second-favorite method of cooking beans—and you don't have to work at home to use it. I also like to cook beans for doneness on the stovetop, then transfer them to the slow-cooker with seasonings for their final transformation.

My friends who work outside the home tell me it makes for a mighty nice welcome when you walk in the door dead tired after a long and interactive day to find a comforting bean-cooking aroma that does all but bring you your pipe and slippers.

Pros: Pretty darn hassle-free. You don't have to be there to watch the bean pot; it can cook all day while you're at work, or all night while you're asleep. It's ready when you are (and how often can you say that about anyone or anything in the world?).

Con: You must own a slow-cooker.

How to: Place the soaked, rinsed beans in a slow-cooker set to high, add water to cover, and cook, covered, for 1 hour. Turn down to low and let cook slowly till the beans are tender, 6 to 8 hours. Check on the beans every so often, adding liquid if needed.

Pressure Cooking, *Without* Presoak

As much as I love my pressure cooker, I prefer cooking presoaked beans in it unless I'm in a flat-out hurry; beans with some kind of presoak have a superior creaminess of texture.

Pros: Speediest bean cooking method there is. Especially good for bean soups. Also good in an emergency—drop-in guests, little in the pantry or fridge, say.

Cons: You have to stick around for it. You have to own a pressure cooker and be comfortable using it. Because beans tend to foam during cooking, it's a good idea to add a little oil, especially with older pressure cookers. The oil partially prevents foaming, but adds a higher fat content. It's tough to check for doneness; you have to open the pot, taste a bean, and then, if it's not done, pressure up again or cook longer conventionally. Minimal oligosaccharide removal occurs because the size of the pressure cooker limits the amount of water you can use.

How to: Place the rinsed, *unsoaked* beans in the pressure cooker, adding 1 teaspoon to 1 tablespoon oil, depending on the size of the cooker, per cup of beans (this is optional in contemporary "second-generation" pressure cookers but is required in old-fashioned jiggle-tops). Add water (or the liquid called for in the recipe) to cover the beans to a depth of about 1½ inches (don't fill the pot more than halfway—these puppies expand). Lock the lid in place and cook under high pressure anywhere from 2 to 3 minutes (for small beans such as adzukis, baby limas) to 10 to 18 minutes (for larger/harder beans like favas and chickpeas). Allow the pressure to release naturally. Check for doneness; simmer them conventionally if

AN IMPORTANT NOTE ON BEAN COOKERY, REGARDLESS OF METHOD

Never—*except in the case of black soybeans and large limas*—should you add salt to beans until they are tender. The same goes for any acidic ingredient (vinegar, lemon juice, even tomatoes). Why?

These ingredients toughen the outer coats, or skins, of beans, which in most cases are already the toughest part of the bean for the water to hydrate.

Large limas and black soybeans are exceptions to this rule; they have unusually tender skins that tend to slip off, leaving you with a mushy-textured puree. Therefore, salt them before cooking, even the soaking water.

they are not quite tender, or, if they are very underdone, bring them back to high pressure for another minute or two.

Speed Beans: Two Alternatives

Okay, you got home late, bean-hungry. Will you go to hell if you use a shortcut? No.

CANNED BEANS

For healthy, quick beans, you can always . . . open a can. Canned beans are one of the few shortcut foods that really are equally wholesome as the from-scratch variety (though perhaps excessively salty) and taste almost as good. In many recipes, they are, in fact, perfect.

A few provisos in using canned beans:

★ They are not environmentally sound; their packaging, and the manufacturing of that packaging, wastes resources. Try to limit use of canned goods when possible, especially when it comes to foodstuffs that have easy, environmentally sound alternatives, as beans do.

★ Herbs, spices, and flavorings cannot be cooked in, as the beans are already cooked. (However, there are plenty of savory recipes in which the seasonings can be added later to great effect.)

★ Read labels, especially if you are a vegetarian. Some canned bean varieties have animal products added to them,

or may be excessively salty or sweet. Canned beans are generally quite salty. If you're limiting your sodium intake, or just find them too salty for your taste, cook beans from scratch whenever possible, and rinse the canned beans before cooking with or eating them.

★ You can't use The De-Gassifying Method (page 16) since the beans are precooked. If you have problems with digestion when eating canned beans, try the dried bean method; you may be happily deflated.

Even with these potential drawbacks, you can't beat canned beans to jump-start any number of quick, satisfying suppers, and you'll find many recipes here that do so. Canned beans are a quick down-and-dirty way to turn leftovers into a full, or at least fuller, meal. That leftover sauté of vegetables from last night? Reheat it with a can of beans and maybe a minced jalapeño, and serve it with rice: voilà. That last bit of potato salad? Toss it with a can of drained chickpeas, scoop the whole thing onto a bed of romaine with some good tomatoes, a scattering of fresh herbs, a shower of crumbled feta or Gorgonzola, maybe a lashing of olive oil and a squeeze of lemon— and you have dinner for a hot summer night. Ad infinitum.

DEHYDRATED BEANS

These are a miracle product that should be on everyone's cupboard shelf. Run, don't walk, to your natural foods store and see if they have them. *You want the kind that lists two ingredients, and only two: flaked dehydrated beans and salt.* Watch out if the ingredient list is any longer! You want plain, not preseasoned, dehydrated beans. (The seasoned, sadly, are much easier to find but are an inferior product. Avoid them. Why, oh, why do they muck 'em up? Don't get me started.)

Plain dehydrated beans are easily reconstituted with boiling water: You pour the water over them, let them sit for 10 minutes, and voilà, a thick, delicious, smooth, satisfying puree, like refried beans, only without the fat. You want a quick way to do burritos, enchiladas, side dishes, or dips like 7-Layer Tex-Mex Mountain (page 41)? This is it. You can also add a few tablespoons of dehydrated bean flakes to any thinnish simmering vegetable soup; they'll thicken it deliciously, adding body, flavor, and protein.

Taste Adventure makes two types of unseasoned bean flakes: black bean and pinto. In some parts of the country they're widely available; in others, not. If you want to order them by mail—and serious bean-eaters or vegans *will* want to—go to www.tasteadventure.com. You do have to order a case, but trust me, once you've experienced how good these beans are, you'll go through it in no time.

P.S. Dehydrated beans are not only almost ready to eat, they're also light and easily transportable— terrific backpacking food if you like to camp out.

P.P.S. Remember, when the flakes are rehydrated they make a *smooth* product. Thinned with water, they make a perfect almost-instant soup; made with less water, they yield a dish the consistency of mashed potatoes. Follow the package directions, then play around.

However, if you want whole-bean texture, not puree, either cook your beans from scratch or open a can.

Chill Out: Bean Freezing

My general cooking practice, for beans and anything else, is this: Cook once for several meals. For beans especially, always cook more than you need. Freeze some for future dishes, and use some now, incorporating them into several different meals in different ways. (They are so versatile they do not feel in the least like leftovers. For example, a black bean soup is nothing like a five-bean salad in which some of those same black beans are a featured player.)

Beans freeze perfectly, both plain and in most iterations; I almost always make a double batch of Dahl (page 81) and freeze the extras; ditto most bean soups (unless they contain potatoes, which do not freeze well). Chili seems to get even better when prepared, frozen, thawed, and reheated.

Freeze any cooked beans in airtight freezer containers, filling the containers no more than three-quarters full. Beans stay happily frozen for up to six months. Thaw them overnight in the fridge before reheating them.

A Final Basic

Let me send you off into the world of leguminous cooking, then, with this: Culinarily speaking, a bean, though nutritionally powerful, is innocent and unassertive. In its life as an ingredient, it is humble, an object of potential, not actuality. Nothing wrong with that.

Not all are born great; some, as Shakespeare said, achieve greatness, and some have greatness thrust upon them. It is up to the cook to thrust greatness upon the bean as generations of our kind around the world have done. The bean is waiting for you to tease from it its goodness, to make a bowl or plate stalwart, satisfying, and succulent.

Beans and humans have partnered for a long time. May this book, a pound of beans, and you renew and celebrate that partnership together.

CHAPTER 2

HUMMUS, WHERE THE HEART IS:

Leguminous Starters

In the beginning was the bean, in terms of human agriculture. But also, in the beginning *is* the bean, or can be; beans can start almost any contemporary meal off brilliantly. That brilliance especially shines in hand-to-mouth eating.

Not hand-to-mouth as in living in straitened circumstances, paycheck to paycheck—though it's true that beans, being so inexpensive, can help make leaner times much more filling and pleasurable. Instead, add to *those* inherent virtues legumes' ability to become dishes that are transported *by* hand *to* mouth: "finger food." But for the down-to-earth, gutsy, lusty bean, isn't such a phrase overly delicate? Bean beginnings deserve more carnal semantics. Popping open an emerald-green edamame pod, a few crystals of coarse salt sparkling on it, with a fingernail; then quickly traveling the interior length of the pod with a thumb, severing the row of sweet, neat oval green soybeans into your mouth in a gesture as automatic and unthinkingly physical as, say,

a monkey peeling a banana—would it not be twee to call this "finger food"? Hand to mouth: slightly primitive, direct, without the intermediary utensil or cocktail napkin.

Tortilla chips invite a dive into an artfully constructed mountainous Tex-Mex pile (see page 41): avocado, sour cream or Greek yogurt, olives built around a base of superb slow-cooked chile-enriched frijoles. Accept that invitation, and . . . hand to mouth. A similar dive, with vastly different flavors, calls from the Middle East: garlicky lemon-spiked hummus (page 32) with a hooked arc of really crisp, really red pepper: hand to mouth. Or visit Ashkenazi Europe with traditional green bean–based "chopped liver," such as Ellen Levine's on page 45, smoothed onto a grainy cracker. And no crudité, cracker, or chip is required at all for the addictive, mess-with-your-head Gotcha-Hotcha Sweet-Smoky Cocktail Peanuts: hand to mouth.

As free of utensils as they are of fuss, such bean beginnings start meals and parties, serve as snacks or lunches, or are offered as cocktail nibbles. Conveniently, many are best enjoyed at room temperature, and most give themselves to advance preparation, wholly or in part.

When beans are part of the hand-to-mouth journey—so basic that it's almost atavistically satisfying—the journey is gratifyingly good.

THE BEAN,
THE WHOLE BEAN,
AND (ALMOST) NOTHING
BUT THE BEAN

A perfect, and perfectly simple, starting point: the bean itself. Two kinds of bean lend themselves to ultra-straight-up treatment: soybeans and peanuts. Both can be served in their pods or already shelled. In-pod, in my view, is best for snacking.

Edamame, particularly, are fun to snack on while sitting around a coffee table in the living room before dinner, just talking and snapping pods. These bright green legumes, pronounced *ed-uh-MAH-may*, are simply fresh (as opposed to dried) soybeans. They go by a lot of names—green soybeans, sweet beans, beer beans, immature soybeans—and are a staple starter at American Japanese restaurants, where they're served hot and freshly boiled, sprinkled with a bit of coarse sea salt, just as they've been in parts of Asia for more than two thousand years.

It'd be hard to find an easier, healthier, more conversation-friendly food than a bowl of edamame. But if there is one, it might be roasted-in-the-shell peanuts, one of edamame's many cousins. The way we eat and shell peanuts is almost identical to what we do with edamame, though the peanut, being an American native (South America; from Peru and Brazil, to be precise), is more "ours" geographically than the Asian soybean. We even, in the American South, boil fresh peanuts: a regional, seasonal roadside delicacy, which at first bite you kind of go "ennhh," but which has you scrabbling for more by the end of your first bag. But we don't stop there. We make a spread out of them (peanut butter) and a candy (peanut brittle). While these are not in the purview of this chapter, something else we do— glaze peanuts with sugar, hot spices, and salt, to make a great cocktail nibble—is. See page 28, and munch on, baby.

EDAMAME IN THE POD

If you have a vegetable garden and can grow beans, you can grow soybeans too, and experience fresh not-ever-in-their-lives frozen, edamame. If you don't garden but do frequent farmer's markets, you may also likely have this experience. But frozen edamame in the pod are pretty darned good, too—a great quick snack while you're making dinner and the ravening hordes are growing restless and cranky.

Gardeners: Purchase seed for edible soybeans at www.wannamakerseeds.com or www.evergreenseeds.com. Edible soybeans reach peak sweetness and are harvest-ready a month after blossoming. At this point, the seeds themselves are full-size, starting to bulge against the bright-green, not-yet-yellowed pods. Buyers: Select fresh soybeans with pods at this same point.

If you've purchased edamame fresh and still on the stem, bundled together, you'll have a bunch of perhaps a dozen bushy branches, rubber-banded at one end. Pick the pods off the branches, discard everything but the pods, and follow the directions below. **Vn** **Gf**

About 1 tablespoon salt

About 1 pound fresh or 1 bag (14 ounces) frozen edamame pods

Coarse sea salt, for serving

1 Place the 1 tablespoon of salt, or more to taste, in a large pot of water and bring to a rolling boil over high heat.

2 Drop in the edamame and cook until the pods begin to rise to the top, 3 to 4 minutes for frozen edamame and 6 to 8 minutes for fresh. Try a bean straight from the pod; you want it to be slightly crunchy, tender-crisp, and bright green (when you open the pod, the beans should not be dull gray-green). If you'd like the beans a bit softer, boil 2 to 3 minutes longer.

3 Drain the edamame pods into a colander, and transfer them to a serving bowl. Sprinkle coarse sea salt over the pods. Serve hot, with an extra bowl in which to toss the rapidly emptied-out pods. To eat them, simply split open the pod with your thumb, and pop the beans from their casing and into your soon-to-be-very-happy mouth.

Serves 2 to 4 as an appetizer or snack

Goober Peas

When you were a kid, did you ever sing the cheerful folk song "Goober Peas," perhaps in elementary school or at summer camp? Or maybe you heard a recorded version, by Burl Ives, or the Kingston Trio, or Tennessee Ernie Ford? Or perhaps a nonrecorded version—because although he frequently covers it in live shows, he's never put it on an album—by Elton John (*of all people,* one is tempted to add)?

Well, "Goober Peas" is not what it seems.

During the last years of the Civil War, Confederate soldiers and civilians were cut off from the rail lines and their own farms. There was often little to eat aside from peanuts, aka "goober peas." Parse the song's lyrics in this context and you'll hear sarcasm, bravado, and a litany of wartime conditions in that particular time and place—horse-thievery, poverty, small miseries (fleas), large miseries (monotony, hunger, knowing you were defeated), humor, and longing:

Sitting by the roadside on a
summer's day,
Chatting with my
messmates, passing time
away,
Lying in the shadows
underneath the trees,
Goodness, how delicious,
eating goober peas.

Peas, peas, peas, peas
Eating goober peas
Goodness, how delicious,
Eating goober peas.

When a horse-man passes, the
soldiers have a rule,
To cry out their loudest,
"Mister, here's your mule!"
But another custom,
enchanting-er than these,
Is wearing out your grinders,
eating goober peas.

Just before the battle, the
General hears a row,
He says "The Yanks are
coming, I hear their rifles
now."
He turns around in wonder,
and what d'ya think he sees?

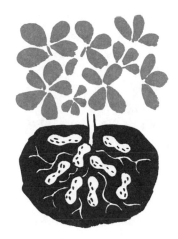

The Georgia Militia . . .
eating goober peas!

I think my song has lasted
almost long enough,
The subject's pretty
int'resting, but rhymes are
mighty rough.
I wish the war was over, so
free from rags and fleas,
We'd kiss our wives and
sweethearts, and gobble
goober peas.

A true folk song, it has no author as such. But the sheet music was first published in New Orleans in 1866, by one A. E. Blackmar.

Gotcha-Hotcha Sweet-Smoky
COCKTAIL PEANUTS

Sweet and heat, smoke and crunch, salt, sesame seeds . . . these peanuts are addictive and easy to make, too. A bowl on the table is an invitation to casual conviviality; a Mason jar of 'em with a ribbon around it is a great bread-and-butter gift or holiday token. Imagine peanut brittle without the brittle (just that glaze of crunchy sweetness) and an aftertaste of "Yowza!" and you'll have the idea. **Vn** **Gf**

Vegetable oil cooking spray (optional)

1 cup white or turbinado (raw) sugar

2 teaspoons red chile powder (see Note)

1 to 2 teaspoons cayenne

½ to 1 teaspoon freshly ground black pepper

2 tablespoons smoked sweet Hungarian paprika (regular paprika is okay in a pinch, but smoked really adds intensity!)

2 tablespoons sesame seeds

1 pound dry-roasted, unsalted peanuts (about 2½ cups)

Fine sea salt, to taste

1 Preheat the oven to 325°F.

2 Spray a large, heavy nonreactive sauté pan with oil. (If you have a heavy nonstick pan, skip the oil.)

3 Add 1 cup water and the sugar to the pan, and bring to a boil over high heat. Continue to boil, giving it a whisk or two, until the sugar has dissolved, making a clear, hot syrup, about 1 minute. Stir in all the remaining ingredients *except* the salt.

4 Reduce the heat to medium-high and cook, stirring nearly constantly, until the syrup is much thickened (there should be very little liquid left), 8 to 10 minutes.

Toward the end, pay extra-close attention: You want to prevent the peanut mixture from sticking or burning (you may need to turn the heat down slightly).

5 Line a rimmed baking sheet with a silicone baking mat (see box, page 29). If you don't have one, you can very generously spray the baking sheet with oil or line it with parchment paper, but the silicone baking mats, bless their hearts, make cleanup a snap.

6 Transfer the peanut mixture to the baking sheet, spreading it out evenly. Bake, stirring every 5 minutes or so, until the peanuts have deepened in color and there's no sign of liquid, 15 to 20 minutes. Test the peanuts by blowing on one: If the syrup turns into a crisp, caramelized coat, they're there. Let the nuts cool slightly on the baking sheet; then break up any clumps, and salt the nuts. Let them cool completely before packing them into an airtight container. They keep at room temperature for a week to 10 days.

Makes about 2½ cups

Note: Be sure to use red chile (with an e) powder—just dried, ground red chiles—as opposed to chili (with an i) powder, which is a spice mixture used to make the stew of the same name.

VARIATIONS

Gotcha-Hotcha Nuts-and-Bolts: Don't salt the peanuts. Rather, combine them with an equal amount of sesame sticks (salty, sesame-spiked mini-crackers, which are available in bulk at most natural foods markets). This is just the perfect munchy combination, to my taste. For me, it has entirely replaced the (frighteningly expensive) bowl of mixed roasted salted nuts I occasionally have cause to set out. **Vn**

Gotcha-Hotcha Indian-Spiced Sweet-Hot Peanuts: These are Gotcha-Hotchas with an intriguing spice-market's worth of flavor notes. Omit the sesame seeds and add the following spices to the unflavored, unseasoned syrup and peanuts in step 3: 2 teaspoons toasted whole cumin seeds or 1 teaspoon ground cumin; 1 tablespoon toasted whole coriander seeds or 1½ teaspoons ground coriander; 1 tablespoon red chile powder; 1 to 2 teaspoons cayenne; 1 teaspoon ground cinnamon; ½ teaspoon freshly grated nutmeg; ½ teaspoon ground ginger; 1 tablespoon smoked paprika; and 2 tablespoons black mustard seeds. **Vn** **Gf**

Bhel of the Ball: Go to the nearest Indian grocery and purchase a 24-ounce bag of Bhel Mix, a time-honored snack in itself: a slightly spicy combination of puffed rice and tiny crisp-fried chickpea noodles. Toss one batch of cooled Gotcha-Hotcha Indian-Spiced Sweet-Hot Peanuts (and, if you like, a handful of raisins) with the Bhel Mix. Serve in bowls for irresistibly intriguing grazing. **Vn** **Gf**

American-style Bhel of the Ball: You say there's no Indian grocery near you? Okay, fine, be like that. While the Gotcha-Hotcha Indian-Spiced Sweet-Hot Peanuts are baking, toast 2 teaspoons of curry powder in a dry skillet over medium heat, stirring frequently, until fragrant and a slightly deeper gold, about 2 minutes. Toss it into a large mixing bowl along with 2 tablespoons nutritional yeast (see page 109), ½ teaspoon cayenne, and ½ to 1 teaspoon salt. Add about 8 cups freshly popped popcorn (from ¼ cup unpopped) and toss well. When the peanuts have cooled, add them, too, and toss well. (If you like, you can also toss in 2 cups sesame sticks.) **Vn**

SILPAT, S'IL VOUS PLAÎT

Rubbery-feeling to the fingers, silicone baking mats—Silpat being the first, but no longer the only, brand—are flexible sheets of food-grade silicone in which a mesh of fiberglass threads is embedded. What's the big deal about 'em? Place your Silpat on a cookie sheet or baking pan, and put anything that needs baking on top of it. Anything—from a meringue to a sweet potato to a batch of glazed peanuts. Pop the whole shebang into the oven at any temp up to 500°F, roast or bake to your heart's content, and know that no messy, soak-forever-scrub-to-get-off, burned-on gunk is in your future.

Silpats can be used thousands of times, almost anywhere you'd need a greased pan or one lined with parchment paper. After use, simply handwash the Silpat in warm soapy water. It's that easy. Even, say, the burned-on, molasses-thick juice that oozes out of a baking sweet potato will peel right off.

The only way to hurt a Silpat is to use a knife on it. So don't. Silicone baking mats are available at houseware stores such as Sur la Table, Williams-Sonoma, and Bed Bath & Beyond.

DIPS, SPREADS & SLATHERS

Dreamily, creamily, unctuously smooth, or hit up with spice and crunch, bean-based spreads, slathers, and dips have found their way onto toasts, chips, and vegetable dippers all over this round-as-a-chickpea world. Legumes, pureed, take beautifully to a universe of flavor combinations. Their bland starchiness softens sharp flavor edges (raw garlic, hot chiles) and is very amenable to surprises (roasted vegetables, fruit zest or juice). Their smooth seductiveness makes any meal heartier and more protein-rich. As appetizers, they have the added benefit of being less pricey and lower in saturated fat than their sour cream- or cheese-based counterparts. Infinitely variable, they smooth themselves into the cultures of many regions: Middle Eastern (hummus), Mexican/Tex-Mex (refried beans, multilayer dips), Mediterranean/French/Italian/ North African (pureed beans plus each region's signature herbs and aromatics, often topping a disc of crisped rustic bread). No need, with such choices, to spread ourselves too thin. Let's begin.

Classic

HUMMUS BI TAHINI

Hard to believe: In 1972, when the first edition of *The Bean Book* came out, hummus was unknown in mainstream America. I wrote then, "It is much better than it sounds, this dish; I probably wouldn't have tried it on the basis of the recipe had I not enjoyed it first at a Middle Eastern restaurant. Now it's a favorite of mine." Now it's a favorite of almost every American . . . so much so that you'd be hard-pressed to find a supermarket in the United States that doesn't stock it.

Why, then, make it from scratch? If you've only had the commercial kind, you'll love the fresh sprightliness of the homemade. You can also tweak it to your taste. Serve it with warmed (not toasted) triangles of soft whole wheat pita bread; crisp vegetables such as celery, radishes, and carrots; and the beet-pinked pickled turnip called *turshi lif't,* much beloved in many Middle Eastern countries and available at Middle Eastern groceries.

This classic is best made several hours ahead of time. Whether you use canned or home-cooked chickpeas, be sure they are very tender (some canned organic brands are a bit firm—great in salads or soups, not so in hummus). Tahini, a paste of ground sesame seeds much like peanut butter, is available in natural foods stores and Middle Eastern markets. You can skip skinning the cooked beans, and I often have: it's time-consuming. But grandmothers throughout the Middle East would be horrified at your laziness; skinning the chickpeas makes much creamier hummus. **Vn** **Gf**

3 cups (two 15-ounce cans) tender-cooked chickpeas, drained (¼ cup liquid reserved), preferably skinned (see Note)

3 tablespoons roasted (not raw) tahini

2 tablespoons extra-virgin olive oil, plus extra for garnish

4 cloves garlic, peeled and quartered

Juice of 1 to 2 lemons, or more to taste

Salt and freshly ground black pepper

Finely minced fresh parsley and/or fresh mint, for garnish

Smoked paprika, for garnish

Toasted pine nuts, for garnish

Sumac (optional, see page 263), for garnish

1 Combine the chickpeas, 2 tablespoons of the reserved chickpea liquid, the tahini, the olive oil, garlic, and juice of 1 lemon in a food processor and buzz until very smooth. Add more bean liquid and buzz until the hummus is slightly thinner than commercial sour cream (thinner, for that matter, than most commercial hummus).

Taste, adding salt and black pepper to taste, and maybe more lemon juice, till it's as you like it.

2 Refrigerate in an airtight container to allow the flavors to meld, at least 2 hours or up to 2 days. Let the hummus come to room temperature before serving. Taste again and re-season if necessary.

3 Spoon the hummus onto plates (salad plates for individual servings, a serving plate or shallow bowl for a larger batch as on a buffet table), smoothing it into thick rounds. Drizzle the top very lightly with a few drops of olive oil, then scatter with a bit of each of the remaining garnishes.

Serves 4 to 6 as an appetizer, more as part of a buffet

Note: To skin the chickpeas, place them in a clean dish towel and rub them gently until the skins loosen and come off. Then pick out and discard the skins.

VARIATIONS

Where hummus in America is concerned, familiarity has bred countless variations.

Olive Hummus: Stir a few finely diced pitted oil-cured olives into the finished hummus. `Vn` `Gf`

Red Pepper Hummus: Add a roasted red pepper, roughly chopped, with the other ingredients in step 1 (omit the chickpea liquid initially, adding it in step 2 as needed). `Vn` `Gf`

Spicy Harissa Hummus: In step 1, add 1 teaspoon to 1 tablespoon prepared harissa, a very hot and wonderful Middle Eastern roasted chile and olive oil paste (see page 266). `Vn` `Gf`

Lemony Hummus: Add the finely grated zest of 1 lemon (preferably organic) in step 1. `Vn` `Gf`

ꙅ ꙅ ꙅ

HILLBILLY HUMMUS

I lived for thirty-three years in Eureka Springs, Arkansas, a small community in the Ozarks. I grew to love the local ingredients, and worked out their translation in hummus: I replace the chickpeas with black-eyed peas, the tahini with peanut butter. The results: improbably toothsome nouveau 'Zarks fare. I get lots of fan e-mail on this one, which first appeared in *Passionate Vegetarian,* and guests at the restaurant I owned raved about it. It's twice leguminous: Beans and peanuts are relatives. `Vn` `Gf`

2 cups (one 15-ounce can) well-cooked black-eyed peas, drained, at least ½ cup liquid reserved

3 to 5 tablespoons natural, unhydrogenated peanut butter (see box, page 323), plus more to taste

2 cloves garlic, peeled

½ teaspoon dried sage, or 1 leaf fresh sage, finely cut up

Dash of cayenne, or to taste (optional)

2 teaspoons to 2 tablespoons cider vinegar, or to taste

Salt and freshly ground black pepper

1 In a food processor, combine the black-eyed peas, 3 tablespoons of the peanut butter, garlic, sage, cayenne, 2 teaspoons of the cider vinegar, and salt and pepper to taste. Buzz until smooth. Begin adding the reserved bean liquid, and, if you like, the additional peanut butter and vinegar. Keep pulsing until the consistency is smooth and velvety and the dip tastes just right.

2 Refrigerate in an airtight container overnight, or for up to 2 days. Bring back to room temperature before serving.

Makes about 3½ cups, serves 4 to 6

ASIAN-FLAVOR HUMMUS

In the Far East, beans are accorded different places of pride on the menu and are used in utterly different ways than in the West. Sprouted, they make their way into stir-fries; fermented, you'll find them in miso and miso soups as well as any dish seasoned with "black bean sauce"; and sweetened, they're part of dessert (ice cream and pastries filled with sweet red bean paste—see page 341). One place you won't find them, though, is in a hummuslike dip.

And yet, why not translate that dish, using an Asian culinary vocabulary? The results are very pleasing, especially when served with crudités and Asian-style rice crackers. I like a combination of tahini and peanut butter here (the flavors of both are authentically Asian), but one or the other also works well. **Vn** **Gf**

3 cups (two 15-ounce cans) well-cooked adzuki beans, drained, ½ cup liquid reserved

1 to 2 tablespoons tahini

1 to 2 tablespoons natural, unhydrogenated peanut butter (see box, page 323)

1 tablespoon toasted sesame oil

2 cloves garlic, peeled

A thumb-size piece of fresh ginger, peeled and coarsely chopped

½ to 1 whole Thai chile pepper, stemmed and coarsely chopped (optional; use the whole thing if you want it kicky in a major way)

1 tablespoon regular or wheat-free tamari soy sauce

1½ teaspoons honey or sugar

1 tablespoon mirin (Japanese rice wine) or sherry (optional)

2 teaspoons to 2 tablespoons rice vinegar, or to taste

Salt and freshly ground black pepper

Minced fresh cilantro, for garnish

Finely chopped roasted peanuts, for garnish

Toasted sesame seeds, for garnish

❶ In a food processor, combine the beans, 1 tablespoon of the tahini, 1 tablespoon of the peanut butter, the sesame oil, garlic, ginger, chile, tamari, honey, mirin, and 2 teaspoons of the rice vinegar. Buzz until mostly smooth. Taste and add salt (begin with the lesser amount, because the tamari is salty) and freshly ground black pepper. Buzz again, pausing to scrape down the sides of the bowl. Begin adding the bean liquid and, if you like, the additional tahini, peanut butter, and rice vinegar. Keep buzzing (adding more salt if necessary) until the dip is smooth and velvety and tastes just right to you.

❷ Refrigerate overnight, or for up to 2 days, and bring back to room temperature before serving. Spread on a plate and sprinkle with cilantro, chopped peanuts, and toasted sesame seeds.

Makes about 3½ cups

WARMED WHITE BEAN & HERB SPREAD

Herbs and aromatics give this lush spread a Provençal twist, and it's not unlike the kind of combination that, chopped rather than pureed, might be served on crisp toasts as bruschetta. But, baked in a pretty, shallow gratin dish and served from it with crisps, toasts, crackers, and a cruet of good olive oil for anyone who wants a little more, it's an easier-on-the-host, serve-yourself offering. An extra tablespoon or so of olive oil drizzled over the top of the beans before baking adds richness and a slight crunchiness: excellent. **Vn** **Gf**

2 tablespoons extra-virgin olive oil, plus extra as needed for greasing the gratin dish and drizzling over the top

1 large onion, chopped

3 cloves garlic, minced

1½ teaspoons dried rosemary leaves (or, in the summer, a tablespoon or so of chopped fresh tarragon leaves or a combo of 1 tablespoon chopped fresh tarragon and 1 teaspoon chopped fresh rosemary)

3 cups (two 15-ounce cans) cooked cannellini, Great Northern, navy, or other white beans, drained

2 tablespoons white wine vinegar

⅛ teaspoon cayenne, or to taste

Salt and freshly ground black pepper

Fresh rosemary sprigs (if using tarragon in the dish, use tarragon sprigs), for garnish

Diced pitted kalamata olives, for garnish

❶ Preheat the oven to 350°F.

❷ Heat the olive oil in a medium-size skillet over medium heat. Add the onion and sauté until soft and limp but not brown, about 6 minutes. Lower the heat slightly and add the garlic and rosemary, sautéing until fragrant, another 2 to 3 minutes. Remove from the heat.

❸ Scrape the onion mixture into a food processor and add the beans, vinegar, cayenne, and salt and black pepper to taste. Buzz until smooth. Taste and adjust the seasonings to your liking.

❹ Oil the bottom and sides of a shallow 1-quart gratin dish (or two smaller shallow baking dishes). Transfer the bean mixture to the oiled dish(es), smoothing its top a little with a spoon. You may drizzle a little extra oil over the top at this point, if you like. Pop it into the oven and bake, uncovered, until good and hot, about 25 minutes. Garnish with rosemary sprigs and a scattering of olives.

Makes about 3 cups

GREEKTOWN DIP

The home version of a beany, feta-cheesy spread, piquant and a little salty, that I enjoyed in Chicago's Greektown on South Halsted Street. Neufchâtel or cream cheese gives the rich smoothness usually supplied by sesame tahini or olive oil in bean dips. Serve this with warm pita bread and cold, crisp crudités—and try to save some for sandwiches the next day. This dip can be made up to three days ahead. **Ve** **Gf**

3 cups (two 15-ounce cans) cooked chickpeas or navy beans, rinsed and drained

4 ounces Neufchâtel or cream cheese, at room temperature

1 ounce feta cheese, well drained

2 cloves garlic

About 2 tablespoons freshly squeezed lemon juice

3 tablespoons chopped sun-dried tomatoes in oil

¼ cup finely chopped fresh parsley, dill, or mint, or a combination

¼ cup chopped pitted kalamata olives

❶ In a food processor, buzz the beans, Neufchâtel and feta cheeses, garlic, and lemon juice until smooth. Transfer to a bowl and stir in the sun-dried tomatoes with a little of their oil, 3 tablespoons of the parsley, and half of the olives.

❷ Spoon into a serving bowl and sprinkle with the reserved chopped herbs and olives. Refrigerate, covered, to let the flavors meld, at least a couple of hours, or ideally, overnight. Bring the dip back to room temperature before serving.

Serves 4 to 6 as an appetizer, 8 to 10 as part of an appetizer spread

---

COOL SUPPER, HOT JULY

Classic Hummus Bi Tahini (page 30) or Greektown Dip, with pita triangles

★

Sliced feta cheese

★

Roasted red and yellow bell peppers

★

Greek-style Green Beans (page 284), at room temperature

★

Barely steamed beets, marinated early in the day with olive oil, honey, soy sauce, and a drop of vanilla extract

★

Cucumber-yogurt soup garnished with dill, walnuts, and pureed green grapes

★

Store-bought stuffed grape leaves, at room temperature

★

Local strawberries over vanilla ice cream, drizzled with rose water and pomegranate syrup

MARRAKECH MELANGE

A sensuous slather, spicy-sweet, redolent of the flavors of the souk, this is my favorite bean-based spread. Anyone who's loved the smooth sensuality of traditional hummus but become a little bored with it will swoon over this. Because of its red kidney beans, I named it for Marrakech, Morocco's Red City; my starting point was a combination of influences from the region. There's the famed North African carrot salad (the carrots, raw or cooked, are dressed with cumin, olive oil, and cilantro or parsley), the smoky-hot chile bite of harissa, the tang of lemon, and an indistinguishable, perfect bit of cinnamon.

Try this with crisp, sturdy sesame-sprinkled crackers, like Ak-Maks, Suzie's Flatbreads, or Mary's Gone Crackers, and crisp vegetables such as celery, carrots, radishes, and pickled turnips (available at Amazon.com, oddly enough). **Vn** **Gf**

½ batch Roasty-Toasty Carrots & Onions (recipe follows)

3 cups (two 15-ounce cans) tender-cooked red kidney beans or pigeon peas, drained, liquid reserved

2 to 3 cloves garlic, peeled, tough ends removed

2 tablespoons extra-virgin olive oil, plus more as needed

2 tablespoons freshly squeezed lemon juice, plus more as needed

1 teaspoon ground cumin

½ teaspoon ground cinnamon

1 teaspoon Harissa (page 266)

Salt, to taste

¼ cup minced fresh cilantro

1 Place all the ingredients except the cilantro in a food processor, adding 2 or 3 tablespoons of the bean liquid. Buzz until smooth and thick, pausing to scrape down the sides of the bowl. Taste, adjust for salt, and perhaps add a little more lemon juice, olive oil, or bean liquid to your liking.

2 Transfer the spread to a bowl, cover, and refrigerate for up to 2 days. Bring back to room temperature and sprinkle with the cilantro before serving.

Serves 4 to 6 as an appetizer, more as part of a buffet

VARIATION

Mélange à l'Orange: It's hard to believe how divine this improbable-sounding combination of ingredients is, but it's right up there—a bit sweeter and more sprightly than the spicier main recipe. Use just 1 clove garlic and just 1 tablespoon lemon juice, omit the cumin, and reduce the cinnamon to ¼ teaspoon. Add the freshly squeezed juice of 1 orange as well as 1 teaspoon finely grated orange zest. If you have it on hand, a few drops of orange flower water (see the note on page 325) may be added, too. Finally, substitute fresh spearmint for the cilantro. **Vn** **Gf**

Roasty-Toasty Carrots & Onions

These intensely flavorful carrots (with potatoes added, as on page 38) were almost always on our dinnertime side-vegetable plates during my years as chef-innkeeper at Dairy Hollow House (RIP). They remain a beloved trope of my kitchen life; the roasting technique, which caramelizes and slightly dehydrates the vegetables, makes them taste like the essence of themselves: earthy, elemental, and primitive.

Be sure to allow the roasty-toasties plenty of air space, essential so they do indeed achieve roastiness rather than steaminess; use a shallow-sided pan that's large enough so the vegetables don't lie on top of one another. The carrots should be dark in spots and a bit shriveled when they come out.

While they make a stellar side dish, roasty-toasties lend their simple brilliance to other dishes, such as Asian-Flavor Hummus (page 33) and seductive Marrakech Mélange (opposite). Always make more roasty-toasties than you think you need (see Cook Once for Two Meals, page 38). **Vn** **Gf**

Vegetable oil cooking spray

1½ pounds carrots (about 9 medium), scrubbed, unpeeled, stem end left on

2 large onions, unpeeled, quartered

1 to 2 tablespoons mild vegetable oil, such as corn, peanut, or canola oil

1 to 2 tablespoons regular or wheat-free tamari or shoyu soy sauce, plus additional to taste

1 Preheat the oven to 375°F. Bring a large pot of water to a boil over high heat. Spray a generous-size baking dish, or dishes, with oil. (Remember, the baking dish(es) should be large enough to accommodate all the vegetables in a single layer.)

2 Drop the carrots into the boiling water and cook until they're bright orange and barely cooked though slightly tender, 4 minutes for long, skinny carrots; 5 to 6 minutes for fatter carrots. Drain well.

3 Transfer the carrots to the prepared baking dish(es) and add the onion quarters. Drizzle the oil over the vegetables, and rub it in a bit with your hands.

4 Bake for about 30 minutes; then drizzle with the soy sauce and toss to coat. Continue baking for 15 to 20 minutes more or until the carrots are very soft and

BEANS IN NORTH AFRICA

Legumes are highly esteemed throughout the Middle East and North Africa. They're used in salads, stews (tagines, often over couscous), soups (including *harira,* the famed potage that breaks each evening's fast throughout the month of Ramadan), and dips, the most widely known of which is hummus (see page 30). But though chickpeas, lentils, and favas are most strongly associated with the region, dried haricot beans, red kidney beans, and pigeon peas are also loved and used. Especially in Morocco, these legumes' natural blandness gives way to exquisite flavors through the addition of fragrant spices, dried chiles, and fruits and vegetables from nearby souks.

shriveled looking and quite brown in places; you should be able to pierce them easily with a fork at their thickest point.

⑤ If using as a side dish, serve at once, hot (although these don't mind staying in a warm place for 30 minutes to an hour before serving). For use in another recipe, let them cool until they're easily handled, then cut off the stem ends of the carrots and onions, and remove the onions' papery skins.

Serves 4 to 6

Note: This cooperative dish is happy to be baked at 350°F for an hour or 325°F for an hour and a half or at 375°F for less time. Whatever else you have going in the oven, at whatever temperature, roasty-toasties will get along with it.

VARIATIONS

Roasty-Toasty Carrots, Onions & Potatoes: Add 2 pounds scrubbed, unpeeled, halved, blanched potatoes (about 8 small boiling or all-purpose potatoes) to the carrots and onions in step 3. If using this variation in another recipe that calls for roasty-toasties, simply serve the potatoes with half the carrots and onions as a side dish, and reserve the remaining carrots and onions for the other recipe. Vn Gf

Cook Once for Two Meals: Double the recipe and eat half as a side dish and reserve the remainder for use in Marrakech Mélange (page 36) or another glorious recipe.

"Although the potato, like man, was not meant to dwell alone, occasionally I have eaten it so perfectly prepared that it asked, and needed, no companion. [In a] cool country kitchen . . . we ate with enormous satisfaction fried potatoes for our supper—an enormous platter of them set in the middle of a table black with a century of polishing. They were fried in butter touched with a breath of garlic that was no more obtrusive than the good smell of cleanliness that hung about the room, and each thin circle was a delicate crisp gold on the outside and melting softness within. There was soup in a white tureen to start, and our supper ended with coffee and a bit of country cheese, but the potatoes were the sacred trick."

—*Sheila Hibben,* A Kitchen Manual

TEX-MEX FRIJOLES DIP/SPREAD

Tex-Mex/Border-style bean dips always start the same way: with mashed cooked beans, either refried (see page 271) or not. They can be beans cooked from scratch or spooned from a can; they can even be dehydrated beans (see page 20) that have been reconstituted. You want them about the consistency of thick mashed potatoes, and they should be either warm or at room temperature when you begin. From there, you simply stir in flavoring ingredients: If the beans will be the base for a multilayer dip, go with the plain beans pureed with their liquid. If they'll be served with simple corn chips, choose any or all of the more expansive elaborations. **Vn** **Gf**

3 cups (two 15-ounce cans) black or pinto beans, heated and mashed with ¼ cup bean liquid or salsa (or use 3 cups amount of canned or homemade refried beans, see page 271)

1 or 2 cloves garlic, quartered (optional)

2 charred poblano peppers, finely chopped (optional)

2 onions, finely chopped and sautéed (optional)

2 whole chipotle chiles in adobo sauce (stems removed), 1 tablespoon adobo sauce reserved (optional)

Salt and freshly ground black pepper

Place the beans, the bean liquid or salsa, and any of the optional flavorings in a food processor and buzz until smooth. Season with salt and pepper to taste. Serve warm or at room temperature, or reheat and serve hot.

Serves 4 to 6 as an appetizer with chips; more as part of a buffet setup

VARIATION

Creamy Tex-Mex Frijoles Dip/Spread: Add about 8 ounces room-temperature cream cheese, Neufchâtel cheese, or farmer's cheese to the processor with the other ingredients and pulse to combine. **Ve** **Gf**

THE NACHO DECONSTRUCTED

A small batch of this is a great solo lunch. Basically, you take most of the stuff you'd put on tortilla chips to make nachos, put it in a small gratin dish, heat under the broiler until the cheese is nice and melty, and serve, hot from the oven, with baked corn chips, such as those made by Guiltless Gourmet. (Baked chips save big-time calorically, plus you really get more corn flavor when the chips are not fried.) Why not just make nachos using baked-not-fried chips instead of traditional ones? Simple: Baked chips get soggy when given the usual nacho treatment.

To make this recipe super-quick, open a can of good, natural foods–brand refried beans—I favor Amy's Traditional. Black or pinto? Spicy or not? Whichever takes your fancy at the market. If you go the canned route, you'll use about a third of the typical sixteen-ounce can per serving. Ve

Vegetable oil cooking spray

About ⅔ cup mashed or refried beans (page 271)

2 to 4 tablespoons sliced pickled jalapeños, or to taste

1 to 2 ounces (about ½ cup) grated sharp Cheddar or Monterey Jack cheese

Fixings to taste: shredded lettuce, diced tomato, salsa or pico de gallo, yogurt or sour cream, diced avocado, minced fresh cilantro, chopped onion

A small bowlful of baked corn chips

1. Preheat the oven to broil.

2. Spray the sides and bottom of a shallow individual-size (about 8 ounces) gratin dish or an ovenproof plate with the oil. Spoon the beans into the dish and spread them to make a reasonably smooth, not-too-thick layer. Sprinkle with the jalapeños and then the cheese, and pop under the broiler until the cheese melts and is bubbly and a bit brown. Keep a close eye on things; if the oven rack is close to the heating element, this could be just a minute or two.

3. Remove the dish from the oven (careful—it's hot!) and top with the fixings of your choice. Enjoy straight from the dish (don't forget the pot holders here), dipping the chips into the beans.

Serves 1 (easily scaled up for as many as you wish to feed)

7-LAYER TEX-MEX MOUNTAIN

A group-size party version of The Nacho Deconstructed (opposite), I first experienced this dish some twenty-five years ago when my friend Gina Meadows brought it to a Mexican-themed Christmas Eve party in Arkansas. It's a festive, almost geological concoction, fantastic then and now. Since then, I've seen this delicious room temperature dip at many potlucks (naturally enough—it's the perfect informal party dish), especially in the South and Southwest. Though it's a familiar player, there's never any left.

It's often served in a glass pie pan, the better to accommodate its mountainousness. **Ve**

3 to 4 soft-ripe Hass avocados, peeled and pitted

Juice of 1 lemon

1 teaspoon salt

2 bunches of scallions, derooted, whites and about 3 inches of green chopped

1 bunch of fresh cilantro, well rinsed, stemmed, and finely chopped

2 to 3 tablespoons sliced pickled jalapeños, minced

2 to 2½ cups refried beans, either homemade (see page 271) or canned (I like Amy's Traditional)

8 ounces (2 cups) shredded sharp cheese, preferably a combination of Monterey Jack and Cheddar

3 large tomatoes, stemmed and finely chopped

1½ cups sour cream or thick, full-fat unsweetened plain yogurt (Greek-style is ideal here)

1 cup sliced California black olives, drained

A few large red-leaf lettuce leaves (optional)

Red, yellow, and/or blue tortilla chips, for serving

1 Place the avocados, lemon juice, and salt in a medium-size bowl and coarsely mash together with a fork. Set aside.

2 In a separate bowl, combine the scallions, cilantro, and minced jalapeño. Set aside.

3 Spread the refried beans on the bottom of a glass pie pan. Spread the avocado mixture on top, then the scallion mixture, then the cheese, and then the tomatoes. Cap the mountain with the sour cream or yogurt, and lastly, sprinkle with the circles of black olives. If you like, poke a few lettuce leaves around the mountain's base to frame it decoratively.

4 Place the tortilla chips in a bowl (or separate bowls, by color) alongside.

Serves 8 to 10 as an appetizer

7-LAYER MIDDLE EASTERN MOUNTAIN

Given the deliciousness and popularity of layered bean dips like the 7-Layer Tex-Mex Mountain on page 41, why not riff on the idea using Mediterranean/Middle Eastern ingredients? This take is a wonderful creation; as a friend tasting it remarked, "This totally puts the 'Bop' in Bosporus." Well, yes, kind of. Another testing-and-tasting compañero called it "Mount Olive." **Ve**

1 very crisp cucumber, peeled, seeded, and chopped

6 to 8 fresh red radishes, tops and tails removed, well washed, and chopped

1 fresh green chile, stemmed, seeds removed for mildness or left in for heat, finely minced

Juice of 1 lemon

¼ teaspoon salt

2 bunches of scallions, derooted, whites and about 3 inches of green chopped

1 bunch of fresh mint or parsley or ½ bunch of fresh dill (or a combination of all three), well rinsed, stemmed, and finely chopped

2½ cups hummus, either homemade (see page 30) or from the market

6 ounces (½ cup) good-quality creamy, tender feta (I like the kind made from sheep's milk)

3 large tomatoes, stemmed and finely chopped

1½ cups sour cream or thick, full-fat unsweetened plain yogurt (Greek-style is great here)

1 cup pitted, oil-cured black olives, minced

A few large red-leaf lettuce leaves or a handful of pretty, well-washed spinach leaves (optional)

Pita chips, such as Stacy's brand, or toasted wedges of pita bread, for serving

1 In a medium-size bowl, toss together the chopped cuke and radishes. Add the chile, lemon juice, and salt and toss to combine. Set aside.

2 In a separate bowl, combine the scallions and mint, parsley, and/or dill. Set aside.

3 Spread the hummus on the bottom of a glass pie pan. Sprinkle the cucumber mixture over it, then the scallion mixture, the feta, and lastly, the tomatoes. "Ice" the mountain you've made with the sour cream or yogurt, and sprinkle with the minced olives. If you like, poke a few lettuce or spinach leaves around the mountain's base to frame it decoratively.

4 Serve with a bowl of pita crisps alongside.

Serves 6 to 8 as an appetizer

Newly Minted
PUREE OF FRESH FAVAS

In spring, fresh favas, fat and succulent in their slightly fuzzy pods, appear in many markets. As with fresh green peas, mint makes their lovely green sweet-starchiness even more sprightly.

Since shell beans are a relative rarity, I generally prefer to eat them whole, not pureed. But each spring make this fava bean puree at least once. As a first course, with aperitifs on the porch on a warm spring night: crisp toasts, steamed-until-tender-crisp fresh asparagus spears . . . perfect, elegant, seasonal simplicity.

The earlier in the season you get your favas, the sweeter they'll be. Later they'll be starchier: fine, but not superlative. If favas are unavailable, make this with cooked frozen edamame. **Vn Gf**

2½ pounds fresh fava beans, shelled, skinned, and cooked (see page 44), or 2½ pounds frozen edamame, cooked according to package directions, pods discarded (1 pound cooked, shelled edamame)

1½ tablespoons freshly squeezed lemon juice

2½ tablespoons finely minced fresh mint, preferably spearmint

2½ tablespoons good, fruity extra-virgin olive oil, plus extra to pass at the table

Salt and freshly ground black pepper

❶ Place the skinned fava beans in a food processor and buzz until smooth. Add the remaining ingredients, with salt and pepper to taste, and pulse-chop. (The idea is smooth favas, but with still discernible bits of mint.) Taste, and add a little more of any of the seasonings until they're about right, bearing in mind that the flavors of the mint, lemon, and olive oil will grow more pronounced over time, while the salt will fade back.

❷ Transfer to a storage container and refrigerate, preferably overnight but at least for a few hours. Let the spread come to room temperature before serving, then transfer to a bowl and serve with a cruet of olive oil for those who want to drizzle on a bit more at the table.

Serves 4 as an appetizer, 6 to 8 as part of a buffet

VARIATIONS

Newly Minted Fresh Lima Bean Puree: Prepare the dip as instructed above, but use limas instead of favas. **Vn Gf**

Fresh Fava or Lima Bean Puree with Dill: Substitute 1 tablespoon minced fresh dill for the mint. This dip is also quite wonderful and springlike. **Vn Gf**

EXCEPTIONAL (FRESH) FAVAS

Every rule has an exception. Leave it to the exceptional fava bean, already immortalized in *Silence of the Lambs,* with its weird Pythagorean associations and its own doppelgänger is cookie form (page 324), to be something of a prima donna both culinarily and phytochemically.

First, phytochemically: Raw favas contain several alkaloids that can bring about anemia in those who have a hereditary condition called—get this—"favism." They're also rich in tyramine, a subcomponent of the amino acid tyrosine. Tyramine interacts badly with the category of drugs known as monoamine oxidase (MAO) inhibitors (sometimes used to treat Parkinson's, and occasionally as an antidepressant of last resort; if you take them, you definitely know it).

Now, moving right along to the quirks of fava preparation. The lease of fresh favas, as Shakespeare said of summer, hath too short a date. Their fleeting seasonality matches their pale spring-green color; you can enjoy them fresh only for a month or so each spring.

The upside of their rarity is that *they are mighty labor-intensive to prepare.*

At market: Purchase way more favas than you think you'll need: Each pound of fava bean pods yields only about *½ cup* of shelled beans. Check the amount called for in your recipe and buy accordingly. (If you're serving straight favas as a sprightly side dish, buy ¾ to 1 pound per person. But remember, and don't say I didn't warn you: labor-intensive).

The steps:

Shell the favas: First, you remove them from their big bulky bright-green pod, splitting said pod with your thumbnail and popping out the pale green favas, discarding the pods.

Blanch the favas: Bring a small pot of water to a hard boil. Dump in the shelled (de-podded) fava beans, each the size of a small, flattened-out lima. Precook for 2 minutes; then drain and rinse them with cold water.

Skin the favas: Now you pop each blanched fava bean from its own individual tough skin. Again using your thumbnail, work bean by bean, slitting the skin and discarding it while keeping the bean (think shelling pistachios, sort of—except the skins don't have a slit and your fingers won't be salty).

Please note that these outer skins are merely fibrous, not poisonous. You don't *have* to skin favas, especially if the beans are on the small side. And, if you don't mind eating fibrous vegetal parts (if, for instance, you eat the skins of winter squashes or sweet potatoes), you won't mind fava skins.

If skinning each individual fava is too fussy for you, go ahead and sauté skin-on shelled beans in olive oil, garlic, salt, and freshly cracked black pepper. Add just a little water and pop a cover on. Steam them for 6 to 8 minutes; then remove the cover and cook to evaporate any water. Serve hot, showing each diner how to squeeze each bean from its skin with fingers and teeth (now you know why you have opposable thumbs). In this case, your fingers *will* get salty. And oily, and garlicky. And you won't care. It's orgiastic spring, and there are fresh fava beans!

Ellen Levine's Vegetarian
"CHOPPED LIVER"
A LA DRAGON

There are countless variations on this much-loved recipe, which has its origins in kosher cooking. By making a meatless (pareve) version of chopped liver, Jews who keep kosher get to enjoy a much-loved dish while sticking to the dietary requirements of nonmeat meals. While this is often served as a Sabbath appetizer, particularly in homes with Ashkenazic roots, and also as a seder dish, novelist Ellen Levine brings it to the annual potluck picnic that gathers together writers and illustrators of children's and young-adult books from all over New England. It's always swiftly scarfed up.

As odd as it may sound to prepare a vegetarian spread whose name references an animal organ, somehow this dish lacks the turn-up-your-nose unpleasantness of many pseudo-meat dishes. Maybe this is because its origins are based in authentic foodways. But it could just as well be because it is very versatile and just plain good. As with all home-style dishes, from bouillabaisse to barbecue to gumbo, there are many versions of pareve chopped liver, and whichever one you grew up with is, to you, the one and only. I've attempted to give at least a nod to some of these variations following the main recipe, but this is my take on Ellen's. Try it as a sandwich spread or with crudités; or serve it with crisp crackers, toasted baguette slices, or, at Passover, matzoh. **Ve** **Gf**

Vegetable oil cooking spray

¼ cup olive oil, walnut oil, or a mild vegetable oil such as corn, canola, or peanut

2 large onions, chopped

3 cloves garlic, peeled and quartered

¼ pound mushrooms, tough ends trimmed and discarded, chopped (about 1 slightly heaping cup)

1½ cups fresh green beans, cooked to tenderness, cooking water reserved (see page 10)

1½ cups lentils, cooked to tenderness (see page 354)

4 hard-boiled eggs, quartered

1½ cups walnuts, toasted (see box, page 50)

1 tablespoon tomato paste (optional; Ellen doesn't use it, I do more often than not)

1 tablespoon mayonnaise

Salt and freshly ground black pepper

2 to 3 tablespoons minced onion (optional)

Minced fresh parsley, for garnish

Paprika, for garnish

1 Spray a large skillet with oil and place it over medium heat. Add 2 tablespoons of the oil, and when the oil thins, add the onions and cook slowly, stirring often. You want them caramelized and golden, so allow 8 to 10 minutes. Lower the heat, add the garlic, and sauté until fragrant, another 2 to 3 minutes. Transfer the onion mixture to a food processor.

2 Heat the remaining 2 tablespoons of oil in the same skillet over medium heat. Add the mushrooms and sauté until they are just limp, about 4 minutes. Transfer them, too, to the processor, along with the green beans, lentils, hard-boiled eggs, toasted walnuts, tomato paste, if using, mayonnaise, and salt and pepper to taste.

3 Buzz the heck out of the mixture, pausing to scrape down the sides of the processor. Taste the mixture and season it again, if needed. If you like, stir in the minced onion.

4 Transfer the spread to a serving bowl, cover it tightly, and let it rest in the fridge for at least 2 hours or overnight. About an hour before serving, remove the spread from the refrigerator and let it come to room temperature. Garnish with minced parsley and paprika, and serve.

Makes about 3½ pints

Note: You may be wondering why I spritz a skillet with oil before adding more oil. It's because I generally use less oil than is traditional, making sautés et al (especially those done in a wok or cast-iron skillet) more prone to sticking.

VARIATIONS

Ellen's version: Omit the cooked green beans, lentils, and mushrooms. Instead, use one 14.5-ounce can French-cut string beans, drained, and one 14.5-ounce can peas, drained. Double the walnuts, and omit the tomato paste. (Sorry, Ellen, I love it when you make this, but I just can't bring myself to do the canned beans and peas in my own kitchen.) **Ve** **Gf**

Cracker version: Omit the mushrooms; increase the cooked lentils to 2 cups. Add 1 board of matzoh or 1 cup crushed crackers (Tam Tams are traditional). This makes a stiffer, thicker dip, but one that's still surprisingly moist. **Ve**

Vegan/Hippie-style Veggie Pâté: Toward the end of sautéing the onion, before you add the garlic, stir in 2 coarsely grated carrots. Use 2 cups each cooked green beans, lentils, and toasted walnuts. Omit the hard-boiled eggs and use an egg-free mayo, such as Nasoya. To the mixture in the food processor, add ⅔ cup cooked brown rice and 1 tablespoon red miso. You'll definitely have to scrape the sides of the processor bowl several times to get the rice pureed. **Vn** **Gf**

CHANUKAH AT BARBARA'S HOUSE

*Ellen Levine's Vegetarian "Chopped Liver"
à la Dragon on leaf lettuce,
with carrots, celery, and cucumber slices*

★

Assorted knishes

★

*Potato latkes galore, with sour cream or
tofu sour cream, and applesauce*

★

*A winter vegetable salad: chilled steamed
carrots, cauliflower, and broccoli in vinaigrette*

★

Sliced beef brisket or brisket-style seitan

★

Carrot, prune, and apricot tzimmes

★

Pear-cranberry strudel

★

Butter cookies

LENTIL TAPENADE

Another retelling of those Mediterranean flavors we can't get enough of, this hearty, addictive spread has olives in it, like classic tapenade. But because they don't serve as the base, it's less salty and less oily. Please note that unlike most of the offerings in this chapter, this spread starts with dry (uncooked) lentils: they must be cooked with several of the ingredients.

Serve this at room temperature with before-dinner drinks, in a bowl with several butter knives provided and a basket of baguette toasts on the side. But before you do, set some aside to use in a next-day sandwich or wrap; if you put it all out, it'll be gone before you sit down to dinner.

Anchovy lovers (I am not one) might enjoy substituting anchovy oil for the extra-virgin, or adding a couple of chopped anchovies to the spread. **Vn** **Gf**

Vegetable oil cooking spray

1 cup lentils, preferably French green lentils (lentilles du Puy), rinsed and picked over

5 cloves garlic, peeled

1 bay leaf

2½ cups vegetable or chicken stock, or water

2 tablespoons sun-dried tomatoes packed in oil, drained, patted dry, and chopped

2 tablespoons extra-virgin olive oil or the oil the sun-dried tomatoes were packed in

2 tablespoons freshly squeezed lemon juice

½ cup coarsely chopped fresh parsley

3 tablespoons capers, drained

½ cup chopped pitted kalamata olives

Salt and freshly cracked black pepper

A few pretty sprigs of fresh parsley or 1 tablespoon minced fresh parsley, for garnish

Lemon wedges, for garnish

1 Spray a large saucepan with oil and in it combine the lentils, 3 cloves of the garlic, the bay leaf, and the stock over high heat. Bring to a boil, then turn down to a simmer and let cook gently for about 20 minutes. Add the sun-dried tomatoes and continue cooking, over medium heat, until the lentils are tender, 30 to 45 minutes. Let the lentils cool slightly, and remove the bay leaf.

2 Transfer the lentil mixture to a food processor and buzz for 30 seconds, scraping down the sides of the bowl a couple of times. Add the remaining 2 cloves garlic, 1 tablespoon of the olive oil, and the lemon juice and buzz a little more, again pausing to scrape the bowl. When smooth, add the chopped parsley and pulse several more times to incorporate. Transfer the mixture to a mixing bowl.

3 Stir in the capers and chopped olives. Taste, and season with salt and pepper. If

you like, you may refrigerate the tapenade for up to 2 days, bringing it to room temperature before serving.

④ When ready to serve, drizzle with the remaining tablespoon of olive oil and garnish with the parsley sprigs and lemon wedges.

Serves 6 to 8 as an appetizer, more as part of a buffet

If by chance you have a few slices of leftover baked or grilled eggplant around, chop it fine and stir it in with the capers and olives. Ah, yes, when you serve it this way—*that* would be a good night to invite me to dinner. Vn Gf

Salt-of-the-Earth
BREAD SPREAD

What do those who don't eat butter spread on their toast? For many vegans, a miso-tahini spread is the answer. It doesn't taste in the least like butter, but its smooth, sweet-salty richness is deeply satisfying. Many nonvegans are astonished by it. It is a spread for bread to go with a savory meal; if you're looking for a vegan spread for, say, toast and jam, go with almond butter, cashew butter, or that old favorite—and from the legume family, too—peanut butter.

I use Roasty-Toasty Carrots & Onions in this, but you could simply sauté the vegetables in oil if you like. Make them the day before if you have time; double the recipe and you can have some with supper one night, and as part of this spread all week long. Vn Gf

1 batch of Roasty-Toasty Carrots & Onions (page 37)

2 cups tahini

1 cup dark or light miso (see page 80)

1 to 3 tablespoons toasted sesame oil

Combine the carrots and onions, tahini, miso, and 1 tablespoon of the oil in a food processor and buzz, pausing often to scrape down the sides of the bowl, until a thick paste forms. You may need to add more of the oil to make the processor buzz, but try to keep it minimal. Store, tightly covered, in the fridge. The saltiness of the miso has a preservative effect; the spread will keep for 1 to 2 months.

Makes about 4 cups

TOFU MAYONNAISE

Throw everything in the processor and *fwhoop!* Done. Easy, delicious, and healthy. I much prefer this to conventional mayonnaise these days; although the flavor and texture are almost identical, traditional mayo tastes too oily to me now. Tofu mayo keeps (refrigerated, of course) for five days to a week . . . a little water will accumulate over time, but just drain it off.

I know the umeboshi plum paste sounds improbable, but trust me on this—its salty, tart notes somehow transform and meld everything into a perfect mayonnaise parallel universe. The other must, besides the umeboshi, is *silken* tofu—you must use silken (it will announce its name right there on the package), which has a smooth, almost custardy texture. The more cottage cheese–like, shaggier tofus *will not work* here.

Check out the variations; just look at all the dips you can make with this as a base! Actually, you can replace any sour cream- or mayo-based dip with tofu mayo and it will work out well. **Vn** **Gf**

1 box (10½ ounces) silken tofu, soft and "lite" variety preferred

1 tablespoon olive oil

½ to 1 heaping teaspoon prepared Dijon mustard

Juice of 1 lemon

1 heaping teaspoon umeboshi plum paste (see Note)

½ to 1 teaspoon salt

A few grinds of black pepper

1 Combine all of the ingredients in a food processor, using the lesser amount of salt. Pulse until smooth, then taste and adjust the seasonings, adding more salt if necessary.

2 Transfer the mayo to a storage container or jar. Use immediately, or refrigerate. This keeps for 5 days to a week. It will thicken and release a bit of water over time, but just drain off any liquid that accumulates.

Makes about 1½ cups

Note: Umeboshi paste is a thick Asian condiment made from pickled plums. When you first taste it, its intensity can be off-putting. But it is exactly that sour-salty-bitter intensity that makes umeboshi a seasoning like no other, adding a just-right piquant, balancing note in many dishes. You can find umeboshi in the Asian or macrobiotic section of large natural foods supermarkets or smaller Japanese groceries. It keeps indefinitely.

VARIATIONS

Herbed Tofu Mayo Dip: To the basic ingredients in the food processor add 2 cloves garlic, quartered; ¼ cup fresh basil leaves; 2 teaspoons fresh rosemary leaves; the leaves from 2 stems of tarragon or Mexican marigold (see page 146); and the leaves from ½ bunch of fresh flat-leaf parsley. `Vn` `Gf`

Dip à la Russe: To the basic ingredients in the food processor add 1 small roasted beet, quartered; 1 clove garlic, pressed; 2 teaspoons tamari or shoyu soy sauce; about ¼ cup plain Greek-style yogurt; and 1 tablespoon chopped fresh dill. A tablespoon or so of finely minced dill pickle is optional—and good. `Ve` `Gf`

Garlic-Tahini-Lemon Dip: To the basic ingredients in the food processor add ½ cup tahini; 3 to 4 cloves garlic quartered; 1 tablespoon tamari or shoyu soy sauce (wheat-free, if desired); 1 to 2 tablespoons additional lemon juice; and 1 teaspoon finely grated lemon zest (preferably from an organic lemon). `Vn` `Gf`

> ### A LARGE NIBBLING PLATTER FOR EASTER EVENING SUPPER
>
> *Parsley-sprigged paprika'd deviled eggs, made with Tofu Mayonnaise and capers, on a bed of vinaigretted shredded cabbage, parsley, and scallions*
>
> ★
>
> *Red-bean Mélange à l'Orange (page 36) garnished with fresh spearmint*
>
> ★
>
> *The season's first asparagus, steamed, chilled, and vinaigretted*
>
> ★
>
> *Toasted multigrain rolls*

HERE'S TO NUTS (AND SEEDS): A TOAST!

Want a more pronounced nutty flavor and extra crunch from a nut or seed? Toast it, just barely browning its outside, before adding it to a recipe.

Spread nuts or seeds in a single layer in a small heavy skillet. Set the skillet over medium-high heat. Don't go anywhere! Shake the pan often to redistribute the portion of nuts in contact with the hot pan.

Your big clue here is going to be aroma. All of a sudden, just before and as the nuts or seeds begin to turn golden, you will smell a deliciously intensified, distinctive toasty-nutty (of course) scent. That is the moment you start to shake the pan continuously. The *second* that most of the nuts or seeds deepen in color, remove the pan from the stove and swiftly transfer them to a plate to cool (if you leave them in the pan, they'll continue to cook: bad idea). Timing is particular to the nut or seed; sesame seeds, say, will take 3 to 4 minutes and walnuts, 5 to 6. This is one instance in which you really must let your eyes and nose tell you what's going on.

You can toast nuts in the oven, and aficionados of the method toast them on a baking sheet at a preheated 375°F, shaking the pan periodically. It's true you can do more nuts at one time this way. It's also true that I have said, "Oh, (expletive)!" more times than I can count because those pecans or walnuts got away from me and went into overtoast.

CHAPTER 3

Soulful Simmer

SOUPS

for

SPIRIT

and

SUBSTANCE

You now know the ancient provenance of beans themselves. But let us pause and consider how long human beings have been making beans into soup. When we drop beans or lentils into liquid (with other good things), place them over heat, and simmer them to tenderness, we're doing something humans have done for twelve thousand years. Twelve *thousand* years: as long as human beings have cooked food, period. Make bean soup, and you take your place in a long line of relationships.

Filling, easy to digest, soup was as inevitable for our early ancestors as it is for us. It makes sense that soup was one of humankind's first dishes (archaeologists and food historians back this up). Cooking foodstuffs in liquid is, was, and always will be the simplest, most forgiving of techniques. Is the bean, grain, or chunk of bread rock-hard? Has the meat been gnawed from the bone? Put these unpromising items in a pot, add water, place over heat. Leave the pot alone to cook.

In a not-too-long time you'll find goodness and edibility, nourishment and flavor, where there was none. (By contrast, other ancient cooking methods—cooking directly in or over fire, or baking—required more skill; turn your back and your flatbread or hunk of animal was burnt.)

Whether your ancestral culture was sedentary or nomadic, primarily carnivorous or mostly vegetarian, soup was on for dinner. But even as human beings developed more complex social structures, economies, medicine, and cuisines, soup remained part of what nourished us. Variations proliferated: While the simpler manifestations remained, countless elaborations reflected human development. As regions developed, so too did signature soups and ingredients. No matter when or where you were born, whether you were rich or poor, kept kosher or halal or fasted for Lent, there was a soup for you. If you were healthy, a good hearty soup kept you that way. When you were ill, soup in its more delicate incarnations, sometimes with

THE BIG CHILL

All finished bean soups, with the exception of those containing dairy products or potatoes, freeze beautifully, holding well for two to three months. Once cooled, they can also be refrigerated for two to three days, and they'll only get better as the flavors merge. Bean soups do get much thicker when they cool, however, so when reheating, add water or stock as needed. (The recipe you want to freeze has dairy or potatoes? Just add the potatoes or cream or yogurt after you've thawed the bean component or base.)

medicinal herbs added, was often part of returning you to health. Some soups were celebratory; some helped human beings to survive.

Perhaps no single ingredient lends itself more naturally to soup than dried beans, since they begin the road to succulence by being cooked in liquid. Add a little extra liquid (water, stock)—or sometimes a lot—to those cooking beans. Add some vegetables, perhaps a chunk of meat or bone, herbs and spices and seasonings, a bit of fat; all natural, inevitable extensions. And that, in stripped-down essence, is bean soup.

But this does not begin to do justice to the world of bean soups, or the bean soups of the world, infinite in their elaborations and kinds of goodness, their positions in, or as, a meal, their soothingness or heat, the way they proclaim a special occasion (Harira, page 66, Fanesca, page 121), or a pure daily sustaining down-homey delicious satisfaction (Elsie's Cuban Black Bean Soup, page 124, U.S. Senate Navy Bean Soup, page 106).

As we inhale our simmering bean soups, as we exhale that almost automatic "mmmm," we go back to the earliest hungers felt by our ancient kin.

Let us feed those hungers again. Spoon by spoon, and bean by bean.

"It is not vegetables which come from a nearby garden which present a problem. It takes a cook with downright homicidal tendencies to do much harm to lima beans or squash or green peas picked within the hour . . . [It is] the cheek of the grocer who asks and gets twice as much for shelled limas as for those in the pod, although every minute out of the shell takes away from what freshness the vegetable might once have possessed."

—*Sheila Hibben*, A Kitchen Manual, *1941*

MIDDLE EASTERN BEAN SOUPS

Lentils are almost certainly the first legume ever cultivated, and their domestication marks the beginning of agriculture itself. They're native to that half-moon-shaped swath of ultrarich Near Eastern soil watered by the Tigris and Euphrates rivers, named the Fertile Crescent around 1900 by archaeologist James Henry Breasted (an almost too-perfect last name for someone whose lifework lay in, as is often said, "the cradle of civilization").

But if the Fertile Crescent cradled humankind, what was its mother's milk? At least in part, the lentil, remains of which have been carbon-dated to ten thousand years ago in Syria—where they're still grown and eaten today.

So, like agriculture itself, let's start there with pots of soup that simmered—an old, old cooking method—on those ancient fires.

Ꭷ   Ꭷ   Ꭷ

SYRIAN-STYLE RED LENTIL SOUP
with Onion & Herbs
(SHAWRBAT ADDAS)

Lovely salmon-colored red lentils cook very quickly, ultimately becoming a duller but still appealing golden-yellow color. Here, we wake them up with garlic and cumin and coriander, a bright spritz of lemon, and a perfect contrast of chopped parsley and cilantro. The slight thickening added by a little flour near the end is traditional (some versions use the more modern cornstarch), but not necessary. Omit it if you like. **Vn**

2½ cups split red lentils, picked over and rinsed

2½ teaspoons salt

Vegetable oil cooking spray

2 tablespoons olive oil

1 large onion, chopped

1 to 3 cloves garlic (more or less to taste), finely minced

1½ teaspoons ground cumin

1 tablespoon ground coriander

2 tablespoons unbleached all-purpose flour

¾ cup finely minced fresh parsley (optional)

½ cup finely minced fresh cilantro (optional)

Lemon wedges, for serving

Extra-virgin olive oil, for serving

① Put the lentils in a large soup pot. Add 10 cups water. Bring the lentils and water to a full boil, then turn down the heat to medium-low and cover partially. Let simmer, giving the occasional stir, until the lentils are a mushy, medium-thick uniform potage, 45 minutes to 1 hour. Add the salt and stir well. Continue to simmer over low heat, uncovered, stirring occasionally to keep the lentils warm while you finish the soup.

② Spray a heavy skillet with vegetable oil (or use a nonstick skillet) and place it over medium heat. Add the olive oil and, when it is hot, add the onion. Cook, stirring, until the onion has softened and is translucent but not browned, 7 to 8 minutes. Then lower the heat slightly and add the garlic, cumin, and coriander. Cook about 30 seconds (make sure not to cook the garlic over high heat; it burns easily). Remove from the heat and stir gently into the simmering lentils. If you like, scoop a little of the lentil soup into the skillet, place it over medium heat, and stir, scraping the bottom of the skillet to get up any last little flavory bits (a process known as "deglazing"). Return this mixture to the soup.

STARRY NIGHT SEPTEMBER SOUP SUPPER ON THE SCREENED PORCH

Syrian-style Red Lentil Soup with Onion & Herbs

★

Multigrain sourdough toasts spread with black olive paste

★

Salad of mesclun greens with sliced garden tomatoes and cukes, chilled freshly steamed green beans, scallions, and feta cheese

★

McIntosh apples and fresh figs

③ Dissolve the flour in ¼ cup water and stir it, too, into the soup. Simmer, stirring often, until the soup loses any raw flour taste, 5 to 7 minutes. Stir in the fresh herbs, if using, and simmer until they wilt, about 5 minutes more.

④ Serve hot, passing the lemon wedges and additional olive oil at the table so each diner can modify his or her own bowl.

Serves 4 to 6

VARIATION

Syrian Fava Bean Soup (*Ful Nabed*): Substitute dried split favas for the red lentils, and cook them with 1 small hot dried chile. To the onion mixture, add a large chunk of peeled fresh ginger (about the size of 2 thumbs), coarsely grated or finely chopped, a few minutes before you add the garlic and spices. In addition to salt, season with at least 1 teaspoon freshly ground black pepper. Use the green herbs and lemon wedges as called for. Dried split favas are available at Middle Eastern or, sometimes, Indian markets, or online at Dayna's Market: www.daynasmarket.com. Vn

SAHADI'S LEBANESE LENTIL SOUP
with Spinach
(Shawrbat Addas B'Sbaanegh)

By age sixteen, I was living communally and happily in the Fort Greene neighborhood of Brooklyn, having adventures right and left (well . . . mostly left). This was 1969, 1970. I think of those days—staying up late with my friends and housemates, drinking herb tea, having impassioned political discussions, reading with a pen in one hand so I could underline and fiercely scribble marginalia—as being the equivalent of my college years, since I never did go to college. One of my favorite things to do, then, was to take the subway a couple of stops to the Middle Eastern section of Brooklyn Heights. I felt perfectly at home in the sense of being comfortable and safe. Yet, the fact that I felt *not* at home (being immersed in another culture) was part of the experience.

Lining Atlantic Avenue were small, inexpensive, family-owned restaurants, the kind where a couple of generations of relatives would sit at a back table snapping the stems off gigantic bowls of green beans, speaking Arabic. Eating there, I felt adventurous and worldly, though I had not then actually traveled beyond U.S. borders. And I loved the food, which was then very exotic: Syrian and Lebanese versions of hummus, stuffed grape leaves, meltingly tender lamb in various formulations.

There were many Middle Eastern markets, too. The largest, most venerable was Sahadi's, still very much in business, as it has been since 1948 (now online at www.sahadis.com). I bought a cookbook there, and although it's long vanished from my library, I still make this lemony lentil-spinach soup, the great-grandchild of the one I learned it from. I think the original used much less spinach than I do, and over the years I've used many other greens instead of spinach; Swiss chard is particularly good. **Vn** **Gf**

½ cup brown lentils, picked over and rinsed

4 cloves garlic

About 1 teaspoon salt (preferably coarse),
    or to taste

⅓ to ½ cup extra-virgin olive oil

1½ to 2 large onions, finely chopped
    (about 2 heaping cups)

⅛ pound (2 ounces) fresh spinach, including
    stems, very well washed, chopped, plus
    a few small, perfect leaves of spinach for
    garnish

½ cup freshly squeezed lemon juice

1 teaspoon cornstarch (optional)

Lemon slices, for garnish

1 Place the lentils in a large soup pot
with 7 cups water and bring to a boil over
high heat. Reduce to a simmer and cook,
partially covered, until the lentils are
tender but still retain their shape, 25 to
30 minutes.

2 Place the garlic on a work surface or
in a mortar and sprinkle it with the salt.
Use the back of a large knife or a pestle to
mash it into a paste. Set aside. (Mashing
the garlic intensifies the flavor, but if you're
in a hurry, just coarsely chop the garlic and
throw it into the skillet in the next step;
salt the soup in step 4.)

3 Heat 3 or 4 tablespoons of the olive
oil in a skillet over medium heat. Add
the onions and sauté until softened,
translucent, and starting to brown lightly
around the edges, about 10 minutes. Lower
the heat slightly and add the spinach and
garlic paste. Cook, stirring often, until the
spinach wilts, about 5 minutes.

4 Add the onion mixture to the lentils,
along with as much of the remaining olive
oil as you like. Bring to a boil, then lower
the heat to a simmer and cook for
5 minutes.

5 Just before you serve the soup, place
the lemon juice in a small bowl and whisk
in the cornstarch until it dissolves. Add this
slurry to the soup, stirring it until the soup
thickens slightly but noticeably and gets a
little glossy, 2 to 3 minutes. Don't overcook
it, or the cornstarch will *un*thicken.

6 Serve immediately with a slice of lemon
and a leaf of raw spinach floating on the top
of each bowl.

Serves 4

THE LENTIL DIASPORA

Lentils and "pulses"
(an archaic term used
for legumes of all kinds,
including peas and beans)
are mentioned four times in
the Old Testament: Genesis
25, Samuel 17, Samuel 23,
and Ezekiel 4. (This is the
passage that spawned the
natural foods company
Ezekiel 4:9, which bakes
many types of bread; ironically,
although their bread itself is
delicious, the biblical verse
mentioning it views the bread
as punishment rations, part
of an elaborate penance meted
out for the sins of the House
of Israel and the House of
Judah.)

Despite the lentil's early
origins in the Fertile Crescent,
today India, Canada, Turkey,
Australia, Nepal, the United
States, Bangladesh, and
China are the world's top lentil
producers.

Of Jacob, Esau, Lentils . . . and Lord Byron

The most famous biblical mention of lentils is in Genesis 25, the story of twin brothers Jacob and Esau . . . and a bowl of lentil soup. Here's the backstory, with a little reinterpretation.

The brothers are born to Rebekah and Isaac (the son of the patriarch Abraham). During Rebekah's pregnancy the two "babies jostled each other within," and she wondered, "Why is this happening to me?" So she went to inquire of the Lord. He tells her this: "Two nations are in your womb, and two peoples from within you will be separated; one people will be stronger than the other, and the older will serve the younger." Thus does it seem the twins' birth—and lifelong sibling rivalry—was preordained.

Esau, the firstborn, was Isaac's automatic heir, by primogeniture or birthright. He wasn't very attractive:

"The first to come out was red, and his whole body was like a hairy garment." But he became his father's favorite, possibly because Isaac had a "taste for wild game" and when Esau grew up he "became a skillful hunter, a man of the open country."

The second-born child, presumably more comely, was Jacob, who emerged from the womb holding on to Esau's heel. He was his mother's favorite, growing up to be "a quiet man, staying among the tents."

In other words, Esau was the hunter-gatherer in the family, the don't-tie-me-down, property-is-a-burden type. Naturally, he would have more kinship with his father (since males, accurately or not, are viewed as more primitive and rootless than females). Jacob, contrarily, was the agriculturalist, to whom land meant everything, who stayed close to home (hence his

mother's affections, women being, in this understanding, the domesticators and civilizers). To Jacob, Esau's notions of freedom from society were incomprehensible.

Historically, hunter-gatherers and farmers *were* indeed two main competing human "nations" as civilization developed. In which direction would humanity go? If we read the story symbolically rather than literally, naturally Esau, the hunter-gatherer, was the firstborn, representative and practitioner of the older, earlier ways. It makes perfect sense that Jacob, the farmer, would follow him. Why was he holding on to his brother's heel? My understanding is that he's holding on *because farmers literally followed in the footsteps of hunter-gatherers.*

And Esau's birthright? Of what use would inheriting property be to a hunter of the open country? To Jacob, it must have seemed manifestly unfair—that his brother, who had no use for the constraints of agricultural life, should receive so much, just by virtue of being born a few minutes earlier. Had he lived his whole life infuriated? Maybe; family dysfunction is an old, old story. For when Jacob saw an angle to get his brother's birthright, he took it: Though aboveboard, his action had an unmistakable taint of underhandedness and hostility. If you understand this, the much-quoted lines make more sense:

Once when Jacob was cooking some stew, Esau came in from the open country, famished. He said to Jacob, "Quick, let me have some of that red stew! I'm famished!"

Jacob replied, "First sell me your birthright."

*"Look, I am about to die,"
Esau said. "What good is the birthright to me?"*

But Jacob said, "Swear to me first."

So Esau swore an oath to him, selling his birthright to Jacob.

Then Jacob gave Esau some bread and some lentil stew. He ate and drank, and then got up and left.

So Esau despised his birthright.

Did Esau mean he was about to die *of hunger*? And if so, did he mean this colloquially, as when we come in famished and say, "I'm starving to death!" One would think so; after all, nowhere does it say anything else about Esau's imminent death; if he was old, ill, or wounded, the Old Testament doesn't mention it.

And he *despised* his birthright. Pretty strong wording—though obviously a translation—for someone who, perhaps, just didn't care much one way or the other. In context, it sounds like Esau

had just never been much concerned about inheriting property. Perhaps he was even relieved to be unburdened of the matter. Esau's feelings were, perhaps, less a despising in the sense of hatred than a deep preference for solitude and the wild, one Lord Byron, many centuries later, would write about:

*There is a pleasure in the
    pathless woods,*

*There is a rapture on the lonely
    shore,*

*There is society, where none
    intrudes,*

*By the deep sea, and music in
    its roar;*

*I love not man the less, but
    Nature more.*

SPICY SYRIAN-STYLE LENTIL SOUP

(SHAWRBAT ADDAS MAJROOSHA)

You'd expect this potage's panoply of spices and chile heat in an Indian lentil soup, but in India, the spices are toasted and sautéed before they're added to the pot. Here, the process is simpler and the results are just as good, though very different.

This soup gains heft first because it simmers with a bit of stale bread or a few tablespoons of uncooked rice, and second, because it's pureed after cooking. You'll find the region's signature sparkle of lemon juice at the end, along with a fresh cilantro garnish that echoes the coriander seed cooked with the lentils. **Vn**

1 cup split red or yellow lentils, picked over and rinsed

2 tablespoons uncooked rice or 1 pita bread, preferably stale, torn into pieces

1 carrot, coarsely chopped

¼ cup olive oil

2 large onions, chopped

1 jalapeño or other fresh chile, stemmed, seeds removed for mildness or left in for heat, chopped

2 teaspoons salt

1½ teaspoons ground cumin

1½ teaspoons ground coriander

½ teaspoon freshly ground black pepper

Pinch of saffron threads

¼ cup freshly squeezed lemon juice

Lemon slices, for garnish

Chopped fresh cilantro leaves, for garnish

1 Combine the lentils, rice, and carrot in a large soup pot. Add 2 quarts (8 cups) water and bring to a boil over high heat.

2 Meanwhile, in a large skillet, heat the olive oil over medium-high heat. Add the onions and cook, stirring often, until they begin to soften, about 5 minutes. Add the chile and continue to cook until the onions are limp and golden, but not brown, about 5 minutes more.

3 When the lentils come to a boil, lower the heat to a simmer and let cook, covered, for about 10 minutes. Then stir in all the remaining ingredients except the lemon juice and garnishes. Cover again and cook for about 15 minutes.

4 Cool the soup to lukewarm-ish, then transfer to a food processor and buzz, pausing to scrape down the side of the bowl, until you have a nice thick puree. Return the soup to the pot and reheat it, stirring in the lemon juice just before serving it. Serve nice and hot with a lemon slice and a sprinkle of cilantro atop each bowl.

Serves 6

VARIATIONS

Syrian-style Lentil-Tomato Soup
(*Shawrbat Addas Maa Banadoura*): The
same basic soup, not pureed and with
tomatoes added, makes for a surprisingly
different outcome. Use ¼ cup uncooked
rice (not the bread) and cut the water back
to 6 cups. When the onions are almost
softened, add 5 cloves garlic, chopped.
When you scrape the onion mixture
into the simmering lentils and rice, add
one 14.5-ounce can chopped fire-roasted
tomatoes. Omit the saffron and skip
pureeing the finished soup, but go ahead
and add the lemon juice before serving, as
well as the lemon-cilantro garnish. **Vn** **Gf**

**Syrian Lentil Tomato–Red Pepper
Soup:** Once, well into the variation above,
I discovered I had only half a can or so
of tomatoes. I did, however, have a jar of
roasted (not pickled) sweet red peppers.
I made about a cup of chunky red pepper
puree in the processor and made up
the difference with that. It was terrific:
complex, sweet-hot, and beautiful. So,
follow the previous recipe variation, but
substitute pureed roasted peppers for
half of the tomatoes. **Vn** **Gf**

ｮ　ｮ　ｮ

SYRIAN
ZUCCHINI-CHICKPEA SOUP
(SHAWRBAT HASA AL-HUMUS)

Simple, satisfying, this soup is of ancient Middle Eastern
lineage, updated somewhere along the line by New
World additions: zucchini and tomato (in the form of
tomato paste). But cooking rests on such fusion, and
soups, like people, adapt easily to new ingredients. Please
feel free to follow suit: Add sun-dried tomato paste or a cup
of diced canned tomatoes instead of the tomato paste, or
substitute two handfuls of thinly sliced green beans or a few
diced potatoes for the zucchini (the latter for a heartier soup). In a pinch, you can
use canned chickpeas, but in this recipe from-scratch is really better (see variation
for the canned chickpea method).

Don't have a chile? Add cayenne to taste, starting with ⅛ teaspoon. Don't like cumin? Omit it. Try adding a few tablespoons of uncooked long-grain white rice with the sauté in step 2, then letting the rice cook in the broth, slightly thickening the soup and making it more substantial. Or cook a finely chopped carrot and/or stalk of celery with the onion. Recipes like this are meant to be played with.

In any iteration, try serving it with a feta-sprinkled salad and hot pita bread: heavenly. **Vn** **Gf**

1 cup chickpeas, picked over, rinsed, and soaked overnight (see page 346)

¼ to ⅓ cup extra-virgin olive oil

2 large onions, chopped

8 cloves garlic, finely chopped

1 jalapeño or other fresh chile, stemmed, seeds removed for mildness or left in for heat, finely chopped

2 teaspoons ground cumin

½ to 1 teaspoon ground allspice

2 to 3 tablespoons tomato paste

2 small zucchini, chopped

2 teaspoons salt, or to taste

1 teaspoon freshly ground black pepper

½ cup finely chopped fresh cilantro leaves, plus 6 to 8 large, pretty sprigs for garnish

Juice of 2 lemons

Lemon slices, for garnish

1 Put the soaked chickpeas in a large saucepan or soup pot, add 2 quarts (8 cups) water, and bring to a boil. Turn down to a simmer, cover, and cook over medium-low heat until the chickpeas are tender but not mushy, 1½ to 2 hours. (Sometimes chickpeas can take as long as 3½ hours; they are the bean most variable in cooking time, I've found.)

2 Toward the end of this period, heat the olive oil in a skillet over medium heat. Add the onions and sauté, stirring occasionally, until they are soft and just starting to turn golden brown, 6 to 8 minutes. Lower the heat slightly, add the garlic and chile, and cook, stirring, until the garlic is fragrant, another few minutes. Scrape the onion mixture into the simmering chickpeas, along with the cumin, allspice, tomato paste, zucchini, salt, and pepper. Cover and continue cooking over medium heat for another 45 minutes.

3 Add the cilantro leaves and simmer to let the flavors meld a little, another 15 minutes. (If you want to stop here, cool and refrigerate the soup overnight, and then reheat it; the flavors will meld even more.) Just before serving, stir in the lemon juice. Serve hot, garnishing each bowl with lemon slices and a cilantro sprig.

Serves 6 to 8

VARIATION

Quick Syrian Zucchini-Chickpea Soup: Substitute 2 cans (19 ounces each) chickpeas, with their liquid, and 2 cans water for the soaked chickpeas. Just put them in a soup pot over medium-low heat, skipping step 1, and pick up at step 2. **Vn** **Gf**

AFRICAN BEAN SOUPS

Moving south and west from the Middle East, we cross the Red Sea into Egypt, where the fava bean rules and the soup seasonings echo those of the ancient Fertile Crescent. But if we continue bowl by bowl across the top of Africa into Algeria, Tunisia, and Morocco, additional layers of spice, sweetness, and surprise await us: The soups of these countries, bordered by the Mediterranean, reflect centuries of trade and a crosswind of influences, from the region we've just left as well as Europe, particularly Spain. Heading south again, we move back and forth across this vast horse head–shaped continent, and country by country, region by region, the flavors—like the climates, crops, and cultures—continue to change.

FAVA BEAN SOUP-STEW
(Ful Medames)

Considered the national dish of Egypt, *ful medames* is eaten in other parts of North Africa, particularly Sudan, as well, and frequently for breakfast. And why not, since it's built around the hearty and proteinacious fava bean?

Much as "couscous" refers to both the grainlike pasta and the completed stew served with it, "ful medames" refers both to the dish and to the fava bean itself. This is a simple dish; the garnishes and spices are what make it. Split, shelled favas, which have the tough outer skin of each bean already removed, are a major time-saver. You could also use canned favas, available in Middle Eastern grocery stores, but cooking the spices in with the beans, as always, deepens the flavor.

Not everyone enriches the dish with tahini toward the end (like so many dishes of this kind, whatever way you grew up with is the *right* way), but I think doing so adds a distinctive creamy richness. As an accompaniment, warm pita bread is de rigueur. To enjoy your *ful* as the Sudanese do: use the pita as an edible spoon, scooping up the thick beans. **Ve** **Gf**

2 cups skinned, split dried fava beans,
   picked over

2 quarts (8 cups) boiling water

1 quart (4 cups) unsalted vegetable broth

1 small fresh or dried chile
   (optional but very good)

2 bay leaves

3 cloves garlic: 1 whole, 2 finely chopped

3 tablespoons olive oil

1 large onion, chopped

1 teaspoon ground coriander

1 teaspoon ground cumin

⅔ cup canned crushed tomatoes
   (I like fire-roasted), or 1 tablespoon
   tomato paste

2 tablespoons freshly squeezed lemon juice

2 tablespoons tahini
   (sesame paste, see Note)

⅓ cup chopped fresh parsley

1½ teaspoons salt, plus more to taste

Freshly ground black pepper

⅓ cup finely chopped fresh cilantro,
   for garnish

4 hard-boiled eggs, quartered lengthwise,
   for garnish

4 whole scallions, derooted and trimmed,
   for garnish

1 Place the favas in a large heat-proof bowl. Pour the boiling water over the favas. Let the beans soak for 1 to 2 hours, then drain them, rinsing well.

2 Transfer the rinsed beans to a heavy soup pot and add the vegetable broth, chile, bay leaves, and the whole clove of garlic. Bring to a boil, then lower the heat and simmer, half-covered, until the beans are tender, about 45 minutes.

3 Toward the end of this time, heat the olive oil in a large, heavy skillet (preferably cast-iron) over medium heat. Add the onion and sauté, stirring, until it is tender and just starting to turn color, 6 to 8 minutes. Lower the heat. Add the coriander, cumin, and chopped garlic and cook for about 2 minutes more, stirring constantly. Transfer the onion mixture to the soup pot, add the crushed tomatoes, and let the mixture simmer together for another 20 minutes. It will, perhaps, look a bit liquidy to your eye at this point, but we're about to fix that.

4 With a slotted spoon, scoop out about half the cooked favas and place them in a large bowl. (Fish out and discard the bay leaves while you're at it. Fish out the chile, too, but reserve it for the next step if you like things hot.)

5 Add the lemon juice, tahini, parsley, salt, and, if you wish, the chile to the favas in the bowl and mash to a rough paste with a potato masher, or even a wooden spoon against the side of the bowl (a food processor would make it too smooth). Stir this mash back into the soup, and simmer over very low heat to slightly thicken and recombine everything nicely, another 5 to 8 minutes. Then add more salt and plenty of pepper to taste.

6 Stir the soup well and ladle it into bowls, sprinkling each bowl with the fresh cilantro. Perch the hard-boiled eggs and scallions along the sides of the bowls (1 scallion, one quartered egg per bowl).

Serves 4 as a light main course

Note: Tahini can be found in the ethnic foods aisle of most supermarkets, or at a natural foods store.

TUNISIAN CHICKPEA & VEGETABLE SOUP

with Harissa

(LABLABI)

Simple, and simply wonderful. Harissa, which is fiery toasted chile paste, heats up this cumin-scented chickpea and vegetable soup, with its familiar Middle Eastern bean enhancers: olive oil and lemon juice. But the crisp baguette slice atop each serving gives a French note. Colonialism, arrogant and regrettable in countless ways, did, at least, expand culinary cross-cultural fertilization from Europe to much of Africa.

Some lablabis are very dense (thickened with mashed chickpeas) and share the egg-scallion garnish common to ful medames (see page 63). This version is hearty, but brothier, the chickpeas swimming in their spicy, savory bath. **Vn**

2 cups chickpeas, picked over, rinsed, and soaked overnight (see page 346)

⅓ cup olive oil, plus extra for the table

1 large red onion, diced

3 carrots, diced

2 stalks celery, diced

4 to 6 cloves garlic, finely chopped

1 tablespoon cumin seeds

1 tablespoon Harissa (see page 266), plus extra for serving

Salt

1 lemon, halved

4 slices French bread, oven-toasted until crisp

Minced fresh parsley, for garnish

Lemon quarters, for serving

1 Drain the chickpeas, rinse them well, and transfer them to a large, heavy pot.

Add 3 quarts (12 cups) water. Bring to a boil over high heat, turn down to a simmer, cover, and let cook until the chickpeas are tender, about 1½ to 2 hours.

2 Toward the end of this period, heat the olive oil in a large skillet over medium heat. Add the onion and sauté, stirring, until it is limp but not brown, 8 minutes. Add the carrots and celery and cook for another 5 minutes. Lower the heat slightly, add the garlic and cumin, and cook for 5 minutes more. Stir the onion mixture into the cooking chickpeas, along with the harissa and salt to taste.

3 Let the chickpeas simmer for another 10 to 20 minutes, or, ideally, remove from the heat, cover, and let sit longer to allow the flavors to blend. (You could refrigerate it overnight, covered, at this point; like most soups, lablabi is even better the next day.)

④ To reheat the soup, place the pot over low heat and bring it to a simmer. Taste the soup and adjust for salt and pepper. Just before serving, squeeze in the juice of the lemon through a small strainer to catch any seeds. Stir well. Serve very hot with a slice of toast and a sprinkle of parsley atop each bowl. At the table, pass the lemon quarters, olive oil, and additional harissa for each guest to doctor to taste.

Serves 4

᧚   ᧚   ᧚

HARIRA

No mention of the cuisine of the Maghreb (the region comprised of Tunisia and Morocco) would be complete without a recipe for this famous soup, which is eaten to break the fast each evening throughout the Muslim month of Ramadan. Although I wouldn't go as far as my friend Daudik, who says that harira "is without question the single greatest soup *in the world,* possibly the universe," well, this is one wondrous potage. With flavorings drawn from an entire casbah's worth of spice stalls and vegetable markets, made hearty by round chickpeas and plump lentils and skinny little noodles and sparkling with fresh herbs, it's sweet and hot, optionally tart, gentle and hearty, sustaining, intriguing, and improbably floral. Most often it's made with lamb, but I've given a vegetarian base recipe, followed by a lamb variation.

This soup can be either a starter or the main course. If you serve it as a main course, couscous is the traditional accompaniment. But it's also satisfying served over steamed brown basmati rice.

Vegans: Use all olive oil instead of half-oil, half-butter, and skip the optional egg thickening, and this soup will make you one wonderfully satisfying exotic bowl.

Vegetable oil cooking spray

½ cup chickpeas, picked over, rinsed, and soaked overnight (see page 346)

1 cup lentils, picked over and rinsed

1½ quarts (6 cups) vegetable stock

2 tablespoons butter

2 tablespoons olive oil

1 large onion, chopped

3 stalks celery, with leaves, chopped

¾ cup minced fresh parsley

¼ cup minced fresh cilantro

2 teaspoons very finely minced fresh ginger

1½ teaspoons ground turmeric

1 teaspoon ground cinnamon

1 can (14.5 ounces) diced fire-roasted
tomatoes, with their liquid

Small pinch of saffron threads

Salt

1 teaspoon freshly ground black pepper

About 4 ounces very fine noodles,
such as vermicelli or angel hair

Thickener for Harira (optional; see page 68)

① Spray a large, heavy soup pot with oil. Drain and rinse the chickpeas. Place them in the pot, add 1 quart (4 cups) water, and bring to a full boil over high heat. Turn down to a simmer, cover, and cook until the chickpeas are barely tender, about 1½ hours.

② Add the lentils and simmer until the chickpeas and lentils are soft, another 45 minutes or so. Add the vegetable stock, bring the mixture back up to a boil, and turn down to a simmer again. Cook, half-covered, for 30 minutes.

③ During the last 30 minutes of simmer, spray a 10- to 12-inch skillet with oil and place it over medium heat. Add the butter and olive oil. When the butter has melted, add the onion and cook, stirring, until the onion is translucent and well on the way to softening, about 7 minutes. Add the celery and cook, stirring, for another 3 minutes. Add the parsley, cilantro, and ginger and cook, stirring, for 3 minutes more. Turn the heat down very low and add the turmeric and cinnamon. Cook, stirring often, until the kitchen is fragrant and the spices have deepened in color, about 10 minutes. Don't let this mixture burn; watch and stir it.

④ Add the onion mixture to the now-tender lentils and chickpeas, along with the tomatoes, saffron, salt, and pepper. Let the whole pot simmer gently, about 15 minutes. (If making this ahead of time, stop here; let the soup cool to room temperature, then cover it, and refrigerate until ready to reheat it. Pick up at this point the next day.)

⑤ Shortly before serving, cook the noodles in boiling salted water according to the package directions until they are barely tender. Drain the noodles into a colander and keep them hot by loosely tenting the colander with foil.

⑥ Five minutes before serving, thicken the soup, if you like, following the directions for the thickener of your choice.

⑦ If you plan on serving all of the soup at once, stir the noodles into the pot. Otherwise, put a scoop of noodles into each bowl and ladle the soup over them.

Serves 4 as a main dish or 6 as part of a larger spread

VARIATION

Harira with Lamb: The lamb simmers to tenderness in the soup, so use ¾ to 1 pound of meat from a tougher cut, such as shanks (bones removed) or stew meat. If there are any bones available, ask the butcher to wrap them up for you.

Start by cooking the chickpeas and lentils through the point in step 2 where they're just short of tender (before the stock is added). As they're cooking, begin the lamb base: Place about ¼ cup olive oil in a large, heavy soup pot over medium-high heat. Add the lamb pieces and bones and cook, turning, until they are fragrant and deeply browned. Add the 1½ quarts stock to the lamb and bones in the pot. (You can use water or canned chicken broth in place of the vegetable broth—your call.) Bring everything to a boil, then turn down the heat to a simmer, cover tightly, and let cook until the lamb is falling apart, about 1 hour. Remove and discard the bones.

Add the cooked chickpeas and lentils and continue with the recipe, picking up at step 3. Me

Thickener for Harira

Sometimes harira is thickened at the end, in one of two ways. The flour method gives the soup a little more body, and is simpler. The egg-yolk method adds a rich, silky-creamy finish as well as thickness but is a bit trickier (and more caloric). Both of them are optional: Use one method or the other, or skip this step entirely if you like.

Flour thickening: Whisk 3 tablespoons unbleached white all-purpose flour into an additional ½ cup vegetable stock. Five minutes before serving the harira, stir a little of the hot harira broth into the flour paste, then dump all of the paste mixture into the simmering soup. Stir like the dickens, and then simmer for a few minutes, stirring now and again, until it thickens slightly. Ready!

Egg-yolk thickening: Lightly beat 3 to 4 large egg yolks in a heat-proof bowl. Ladle out a little of the hot harira broth into the yolks and whisk vigorously. Then add a little more, whisking. In all, you'll want to whisk in 1½ to 2 cups of the hot broth, a little at a time. Then, gently stir the egg-yolk mixture back into the soup, which should just be barely simmering. Cook gently, stirring, 3 or 4 minutes more.

Harira thickened with egg yolk doesn't reheat well, because the yolks get overcooked and are inclined to curdle. The flour-thickened and unthickened versions, however, reheat just fine. Gf

Nigerian Seed-Thickened

BEEF & SHRIMP SOUP STEW

(Egusi)

Just as Creole, Cajun, and French families and communities, respectively, have their very particular ways with gumbos, jambalayas, cassoulets, or bouillabaisses, so each Nigerian and Sierra Leonean family and village makes their egusi with slight differences. And whatever way they make it is *the* way to make it. Almost anything that walks, crawls, swims, or grows might find its way into egusi. Fish or seafood might be fresh or salted; meat might be beef or goat. Beans, when added, are often fermented; greens run the gamut from tender spinach to more assertive mustard greens or collards. But one thing's for sure: All egusi is kick-ass *hot*.

Quite a few Americans are familiar with the African trick of enriching soups and stews with peanut butter, which adds creaminess, richness, and the inimitable flavor of peanut (or groundnut, in some African languages). Throughout Nigeria and Sierra Leone, a similarly rich paste is made with a base of egusi melon seeds. Egusi seeds feature so prominently in the traditional soup-stew that they've lent their name to it. While you can find the seeds at African food stores, or online at www.exceedfoods.com, to simplify matters, I've used pumpkin seeds, botanical cousins that yield similar results. Cowpeas, a native African legume, may be similarly difficult to find; use black-eyes unless you're lucky enough to have cowpeas available. This is my beef-shrimp version of egusi; it uses ingredients available at most American supermarkets but is true to the spirit of the original dish. **Me** **Gf**

⅓ cup peanut oil

1 pound beef stew meat, cut into 1-inch cubes

2 large tomatoes, stemmed and quartered

1 large onion, peeled and quartered

½ to 1 Scotch bonnet or habanero chile, stemmed, seeds removed (or use a whole chile and with seeds for typical West African blow-the-top-off-your-skull heat)

¼ cup tomato paste

1 can (14.5 ounces) black-eyed peas, with their liquid, or 2 cups cooked cowpeas with about ½ cup cooking liquid

2½ quarts (10 cups) beef or chicken broth, clam juice, or vegetable stock

1½ pounds shrimp, peeled and deveined

1 can (14.5 ounces) diced fire-roasted tomatoes

¼ pound green beans, tipped, tailed, and sliced crosswise into ¼-inch pieces

½ pound kale or Swiss chard, cut into ribbons, or spinach or turnip greens, chopped

⅔ cup roasted shelled pumpkin seeds

Salt and freshly cracked black pepper

❶ Heat the oil in a Dutch oven or other large, heavy pot over medium-high heat until not quite smoking. Add the beef and brown it well on all sides, stirring often, about 4 minutes.

❷ Between stirs, combine the fresh tomatoes, onion, chile, and tomato paste in a food processor and pulse several times to chop. Then run the machine until the mixture is almost smooth.

❸ Scrape the tomato mixture into the pot with the beef (stand back because there will be a large, steamy, spicy hiss when the liquid hits the hot oil). Add the black-eyed peas, stir well, and lower the heat to the merest simmer. Cover the pot tightly and let simmer gently until the meat is tender, 30 to 45 minutes. Meanwhile, wash and dry the work bowl of the food processor.

④ Add the broth, shrimp, canned tomatoes, green beans, and greens to the pot. Cover it, and let simmer until the greens are wilted and the shrimp are cooked through, 10 minutes more.

⑤ During this last 10-minute simmer, place the pumpkin seeds in the food processor (or, if you have one, a mini-processor) and pulse a few times. Then run the machine, pausing occasionally to scrape down the sides, until you have a paste similar in consistency to a powdery peanut butter. Add the pumpkin seed paste to the soup, stirring well. Add salt and pepper—get vigorous with the pepper—to taste. Simmer a few more minutes to let the flavors meld, then serve immediately.

Serves 6 to 8 as a hearty main dish

ᔑ   ᔑ   ᔑ

AFRICAN PEANUT & BEAN SOUP
Caribbean Style

I f you get *Afropop Worldwide* on your local NPR affiliate, you have the pleasure of traveling, musically, throughout Africa and along the sound lines of the African diaspora, with the exuberant, honey-voiced Georges Collinet. Georges, aka "Maxi Voom Voom," is a Cameroonian recording artist and filmmaker. In addition to hosting the show and introducing the music, he occasionally intersperses recipes, a step or two between each song, with such enthusiasm you sometimes hear him literally smacking his lips.

In part because I'd followed Georges on these musical and culinary travels, I was not that surprised when, during a visit to St. Lucia, a fiery hot peanut butter–laced bean and vegetable soup turned up regularly at the hotel's lunch buffet. When I asked the waitress about it, she said, "Oh, it's ours" (meaning St. Lucian) "but I think it's really African. I will ask Chef." When she came back and told me more, I took notes on a napkin.

Georges offers a similar soup on the Afropop website (www.afropop.org). There, he describes it as ". . . one of my favorite soups while I lived on the banks of the Kwilu river, in the Congo (ex Zaire)." Several of his recipes—including the soup—use peanuts (groundnuts), a popular ingredient throughout many parts of Africa.

This recipe melds Georges's soup with the one we had in St. Lucia. If you prefer not to use bouillon cubes, instead cook the beans in 1 quart water, and when they're tender, add 2 quarts well-flavored broth. The soup is on the thick side; feel free to add extra broth, tomato juice, or water to thin it down. **Vn** **Gf**

1 cup navy beans, picked over, rinsed, and soaked overnight (see page 350)

1 cup black-eyed peas, picked over and rinsed

2 or 3 vegetable or chicken bouillon cubes (optional; see headnote)

3 tablespoons butter, mild vegetable oil, or coconut oil

1 large onion, finely chopped

1 green bell pepper, stemmed, seeded, and finely chopped

1 Scotch bonnet or habanero pepper, stemmed, seeded, and very finely chopped

2 teaspoons ground coriander

1 large butternut squash, peeled, seeded, and cut into 1-Inch chunks

1 small bunch of hearty greens (kale, collard, turnip, mustard), rinsed and finely chopped (Georges says, "Chop greens to a polite mouth size.")

1 cup roasted, salted, skinned peanuts

Salt, to taste

1 to 2 tablespoons very finely chopped fresh basil

① In a large soup pot, combine the soaked navy beans and the unsoaked black-eyes. Add 3 quarts (12 cups) water, and bring to a boil. Turn down the heat to a simmer, cover, and let cook until both beans are barely tender—not mushy, but not at all hard—about 1½ hours. Add the bouillon cubes, if you wish.

② Melt the butter in a large skillet over medium heat. When the fat has sizzled and then quieted (or if using oil, when it thins and begins to shimmer), add the onion and sauté, stirring, for 5 minutes. Add the green pepper and sauté for another 5 minutes.

Lower the heat, add the Scotch bonnet and coriander, and sauté for 2 minutes more.

③ Scrape the contents of the skillet into the simmering soup, then rinse the skillet with a little of the bean broth to deglaze the last little delicious bits. Add the butternut squash and greens to the soup at this time, and stir well. Bring the soup back to a boil, lower the heat again to a simmer, and let cook, covered, for another 20 minutes.

④ Meanwhile, dump the salted peanuts onto a cutting board, and, using a chef's knife, work back and forth, chopping them fine. For this soup, you don't want a paste (though you can use chunky-style peanut butter if you're in a hurry); you want a fine chop with some texture. Add the chopped peanuts to the simmering soup.

⑤ When the squash is tender, add the salt incrementally (remember the peanuts are salted). Add the fresh basil. (Basil? "He learnt that in chef school," said the St. Lucia waitress.) Stir well and serve hot.

Serves 4 to 6 as a main dish, 8 to 10 as a starter

"Mofere ipa eiye na!"

"Aki ofere li obbe."

"I almost killed the bird!"

"But no one can eat 'almost' in a stew."

—*Yoruba proverb, collected by Richard Francis Burton in* Wit and Wisdom from West Africa: Or, A Book of Philosophy, Idioms, Enigmas, and Laconisms, *1865*

TANZANIAN BLACK-EYED PEA & COCONUT SOUP

with Bananas

This combination might sound unlikely, but it will knock your socks off. Spicy-hot and spicy-complex, the layers of flavor in this creamy coconut milk–enriched potage will almost certainly earn it a spot on your family's list of regularly repeated favorites (that is, unless your family numbers a majority of straight salt-and-pepper, meat-and-potatoes types, with no tolerance for envelope-pushing). You might doubt me when you read the ingredients list, but I promise you, this gets better with every bite and is a meal in itself. The bananas? Wonderfully sweet, slightly starchy, meltingly translucent. Even when this is made with reduced-fat coconut milk, the richness of the luscious liquid comes through clearly, mitigating and blending the spices and peppers.

Tanzania was formed in 1964 when two former British colonies, Tanganyika (on mainland East Africa) and the large island of Zanzibar (and its accompanying archipelago of many smaller islands), joined to become the United Republic of Tanzania. With Africa's highest mountain (Kilimanjaro) and deepest lake (Lake Tanganyika), with coastal areas and a central plateau, the country is diverse geographically, ecologically, and agriculturally. This luscious bowl reflects the coast's coconut palms and banana trees. The seasonings combine indigenous Zanzibar cloves with spices introduced by immigrants from the Indian subcontinent, particularly Goa. The beans are widely grown throughout this still mostly small-farm-based country. **Vn** **Gf**

1 cup black-eyed peas, picked over and rinsed

2 tablespoons coconut oil, or any mild vegetable oil, such as corn, canola, or peanut

Vegetable oil cooking spray

1 large onion, finely chopped

1 large green bell pepper, stemmed, seeded, and finely chopped

1 small hot chile, such as serrano (or if you like extreme heat, Scotch bonnet) seeds left in for heat or removed for mildness, finely chopped

1 teaspoon finely chopped or grated fresh ginger

2 teaspoons curry powder, preferably Zanzibar-style (see Note)

⅛ teaspoon ground cloves

1 cup canned diced tomatoes with juice

1 teaspoon honey or sorghum

1 can (15 ounces) regular or reduced-fat unsweetened coconut milk

Salt and freshly ground black pepper

1 just-ripe banana, thickly sliced

2½ cups cooked white rice, for serving

Toasted unsweetened coconut flakes, for garnish (optional)

Banana chips, for garnish (optional)

1 Combine the black-eyed peas and 1 quart (4 cups) water in a large, heavy saucepan over high heat. Bring to a boil, turn down the heat to a simmer, and let cook, partially covered, until the black-eyes are tender, 45 minutes to 1 hour.

2 Toward the end of this period, when the black-eyes are nearly tender, heat the oil in a large, heavy oil-sprayed or nonstick skillet over medium heat. Add the onion, and let it cook until it begins to soften, about 6 minutes. Stir in the green peppers, chile, and ginger and cook, stirring often, for another 4 minutes. (Mmm! Nice fragrant kitchen!) Lower the heat slightly and add the curry powder and cloves, sautéing until the oil has taken on a yellowish tint, the kitchen is even more fragrant, but nothing's sticking, another 1 to 2 minutes.

3 Stir the onion mixture into the simmering black-eyed peas, along with the tomatoes, honey, and coconut milk. Continue to simmer, gently, to let the flavors meld, 5 to 10 minutes. Salt the soup now—to taste, but generously—and pepper it likewise.

4 Just before serving, add the sliced banana. Serve hot with a scoop of hot rice in each bowl. Garnish each with toasted coconut shreds and a few banana chips if you like.

Serves 4 to 6

Note: The spice mixture that comprises Zanzibar-style curry powder has less turmeric than Indian varieties. It's also distinctly sweet, very hot, and nicely toasty, the result of dry-roasting the spices— among them black mustard seed, fennel, coriander, and cumin—before they're ground. An excellent one can be found at www.seasonedpioneers.co.uk.

VARIATIONS

Tanzanian Black-Eyed Pea, Beef & Coconut Soup with Bananas: Before you begin the vegetable sauté in step 2, brown 8 to 12 ounces (½ to ¾ pound) ground beef, crumbled, in a heavy skillet over medium heat. Remove the browned beef from the skillet with a slotted spoon, and set it aside. Pour off all but 1 tablespoon of the beef fat, and to it, add 1 tablespoon coconut or other mild vegetable oil. Continue with the recipe as written, adding the beef to the black-eyes in step 3. **Me** **Gf**

Vegetarian Tanzanian Black-Eyed Pea, "Beef" & Coconut Soup with Bananas: Before you begin sautéing the vegetables in step 2, place about 1 tablespoon coconut oil in a large skillet over medium heat and in it brown one 8-ounce package "ground-beef-style" soy meat, such as Lightlife's Gimme Lean. Remove the browned soy meat from the skillet, add the remaining 2 tablespoons oil, and proceed with step 2 as written. Add the browned soy meat to the black-eyes along with the other ingredients in step 3. Alternatively, if your soy meat is already "cooked" (that is, firm, and in discrete little crumbles, like sautéed ground beef), skip sautéing it and instead add it directly to the cooked black-eyes in step 3. **Vn**

STOCK ANSWERS

Here's a pop quiz (multiple choice). What's the difference between stock and broth?

> **A.** they're similar
>
> **B.** they're different
>
> **C.** whatever they are, their meaning and definition have changed substantially in recent years
>
> **D.** all of the above

Well, fact is, there are no stock answers about stock (or broth). But as Keats said of truth and beauty, here is "all ye need to know" on the subject:

1. The *similarity* between stock and broth is this: Both are water—(preferably spring or filtered, see page 12) simmered with flavorful ingredients, traditionally meat and/or bones, some vegetables, and maybe a few aromatic herbs. This is

then strained, and the solids are discarded. The flavorful liquid component is the stock or broth, and it's used as a base for soups, sauces, gravies, and, sometimes, either partially or wholly, for cooking soaked dried beans, to add oomph to their agreeable starchy blandness.

2. The *difference* between the two *used* to be this: Stock was made predominantly from animal bones and the minor bits of meat left on them. *Broth* was usually made with pieces of actual meat—for example, a whole chicken was simmered for chicken broth—so the end result was richer, more finished. A cup of broth could be served on its own to start a meal (especially if "clarified," in which case it was called consommé—but because that's a whole other kettle of fish or beef, and wholly irrelevant to beans, let's don't go there).

3. Their respective *meanings*, drawn from classic French cooking techniques, have changed as the world has changed. The way people

eat—especially with more and more people avoiding meat—has changed. Now the flavorful liquid may have been simmered without meat or bones at all, in which case it becomes vegetable stock. What would have been a laughable oxymoron to a French chef a hundred years ago is now a wholly accepted ingredient in the culinary canon.

Thus, the correct answer to the pop quiz is D.

Basic Amped-Up Vegetable Stock

If you want a vegetable stock with real muscle—this is it; it's amazing what a difference intentionality, pre-roasting the vegetables, and nutritional yeast make. (If it's too much trouble to put this together, go ahead and make the variation.) This is delicious stuff, but it's more of a big deal than you'd want to make every day or even every week. **Vn**

> **Vegetable oil cooking spray**
>
> **4 carrots, unpeeled, scrubbed, halved lengthwise**
>
> **3 onions, brown papery skin and all, quartered**

1 bunch of celery, quartered (each quarter will have several stalks attached to the root base)

¼ cup tamari or shoyu soy sauce

3 tablespoons olive oil

1 head garlic, halved crosswise but otherwise left intact

1 to 2 ripe or overripe pears or 2 apples (or a combination), well washed and halved (seeds, core, and all)

½ cup nutritional yeast (see box, page 109)

Sea salt (optional)

1 tablespoon tomato paste (optional)

1. Preheat the oven to 375°F. Spray a large baking dish with the oil.

2. Combine the carrots, onions, and celery in a large bowl. Add the tamari and olive oil and toss well to coat. Transfer these vegetables to the oiled baking dish, stick it in the oven, and bake, uncovered, for 30 minutes. Add the halved garlic and continue baking until the vegetables are well browned, shriveled-looking, and almost but not quite burned, 20 to 30 minutes more. Remove the pan from the oven.

3. Transfer the roasted vegetables to a stockpot. Pour 3½ quarts (14 cups) water over them. Pour 2 cups water into the vegetable-roasting pan and deglaze it: Put the pan on top of the stove or back in the oven for a few minutes and heat until the water simmers, then scrape with the flat end of a spatula to loosen any delicious stuck-on bits. Add this liquid (the "deglaze") to the stockpot along with the pears.

4. Bring the stockpot to a boil over high heat. Cover the pot, turn down the heat to medium-low, and let simmer for 1 hour. Let cool to lukewarm and strain out and discard the solids.

5. Whisk the nutritional yeast, salt to taste, and the tomato paste, if using, into the lukewarm stock. Refrigerate this precious liquid, knowing how much delectability is in store for anything you add it to. It will keep for 4 to 5 days and can be frozen almost indefinitely.

Makes about 4 quarts

VARIATION

Okay, I'm a go-to-any-lengths person in the kitchen. If you,

dear reader, are likewise, stop here and make the stock above. But if *you*, other dear reader, are short on the time (or obsession) it takes to create such a stock, then here's one for you:

MIDDLE PATH SOMEWHAT-AMPED-UP STOCK: Heat two 32-ounce boxes commercially made natural vegetable broth (I like Imagine Foods and Pacific Natural Foods; both are organic). Add one quartered pear, one quartered apple, and one head garlic, unpeeled and halved crosswise. Bring to a boil, turn down the heat to a simmer, and cook, covered, for 45 minutes. Strain. Whisk in the nutritional yeast and tomato paste, and season with tamari to taste. And that'll do you!

ASIAN BEAN SOUPS

From the innumerable influences and ingredients that bubble up in the bean soups of Africa, things *appear* to become simpler as we go east. In Asia the soybean reigns, with adzuki and mung beans playing the part of minor courtiers; and the beans in your soup transform so much as to become unrecognizable. Soy is a shapeshifter, a legumagician. Fermented soybeans become soy sauce, miso (see page 80). Cultured soybeans become tempeh (see page 243). Soaked and processed soybeans become soy milk, tofu.

Add the layers of seasonings specific to each nationality and region—hot currents from Thailand and parts of China; Japan's sea vegetables; coconut milk from Indonesia and Thailand; green herbs from Vietnam, Thailand, Cambodia, and Burma—combine them with other dominant ingredients (chicken, fish, beef, pork, vegetables, including green beans), and it's a whole new world. Then consider the "influenced by" soups, the more Western-style potages that have incorporated Asian flavors and ingredients—it's a whole new universe.

ა ა ა

THAI HOT & SOUR SOUP
Vegetarian Style
(TOM YUM GOONG)

Thai soups with a broth base are usually infused with fresh herbs like lemongrass, kaffir lime leaves, galangal, basil, or cilantro (both the leaves and the stems). These soups are quickly made; as with most Asian cookery, the only time-consuming part is chopping everything beforehand, so that once you start cooking, you're ready to roll. Oh yeah, and the trip to the Asian grocery store before you start.

Healthy, extraordinarily flavorful, almost heady with the perfume of citrus and all those herbs, my personal favorite in this category of soup is this vegetarian version of Thai Hot & Sour. Like the chicken-based variation that follows, it's low in calories, light on the tongue, not too filling, yet also satisfying because of its contrasting, layered flavors. You might think it'd be impossible for soup to be both soothing and exhilarating, but this one, somehow, is. It may be my favorite thing to eat for a light supper after a long day that's run too late: It gives me that restorative, all's-right-with-the-world feeling without getting overly stuffed.

Some of the ingredients—galangal, lemongrass, kaffir lime leaves, fish sauce—may sound obscure, but they should be easily found at an Asian market.

Use the larger amount of broth if you're using a lot of the optional vegetables; in this case you could slightly increase the seasonings, like the galangal and lemongrass, too. **Vn** **Gf** **Me**

4 ounces dried shiitake mushrooms

About 2 quarts (7 to 9 cups) well-flavored vegetable stock

4 to 6 cloves garlic, finely minced (but not put through a press)

2 thumb-size pieces galangal (see note, page 78) or ginger, thinly sliced

3 stalks lemongrass, white part only, sliced on the diagonal in ¾-inch pieces and smashed with the flat side of a knife

2 tablespoons traditional or tamari soy sauce (wheat-free if desired), plus extra as needed

1 tablespoon Thai fish sauce, vegetarian fish sauce, or Amie's Vietnamese Dipping Sauce (recipe follows), plus extra as needed

1 to 2 fresh red or green Thai chiles, stemmed, seeds removed for mildness or left in for extreme heat, finely minced

1 tablespoon freshly squeezed lemon juice, lime juice, or tamarind concentrate

1 tablespoon light or dark brown sugar

2 kaffir lime leaves (fresh if humanly possible, or frozen in a pinch; *not* dried)

4 to 6 ounces firm Thai-style baked—or firm water-packed—tofu, sliced into 1-inch by ¼-inch strips

Any or all of the following vegetables to equal 2 to 3 cups prepared: 1 red or green bell pepper (or half of each), stemmed, seeded, and sliced into thin strips; 3 small baby bok choys, thinly sliced crosswise; 1 carrot, very thinly sliced on the diagonal; 1 small handful of fresh sugar snap or snow peas; 1 small handful of green beans, sliced on the diagonal into ½-inch pieces

A few fresh spinach leaves, a small handful of fresh cilantro (with stems), and/or a small handful of chopped fresh basil leaves (preferably Thai)

1½ teaspoons cornstarch (optional)

Thai red chile paste (*nam prik pao*) or Sriracha chile sauce, for serving

1 A few hours before you plan on making the soup, place the dried shiitakes in a heat-proof bowl. Place 2 cups of the stock in a small saucepan and bring it to a boil over high heat. Pour the hot stock over the mushrooms and let them soak. When you're ready to begin the soup, remove the soaked shiitakes, slice them, and set them aside. Reserve the soaking liquid, straining it if it is at all gritty.

2 Combine the mushroom soaking liquid with the remaining vegetable stock in a large, heavy soup pot and bring to a simmer over medium-high heat. Drop in the garlic, galangal, lemongrass, tamari, fish sauce, chile, lemon juice, brown sugar, and kaffir lime leaves. Bring to a boil (*mmm*—pause to inhale that fragrant steam), then reduce the heat to a simmer.

③ Drop the tofu, mixed vegetables (not the greens), and reserved shiitake slices into the simmering soup and let cook until the vegetables are just barely cooked, still tender-crisp, 3 to 5 minutes.

④ If using the cornstarch, place it in a cup and add 2 tablespoons water or stock, using your fingertips to mush the cornstarch and work out any lumps. Whisk or stir this slurry into the simmering soup, which should almost immediately thicken ever so slightly and grow clear. (You may also omit this step entirely if you like a thinner soup.) Taste the soup, adding more fish sauce or soy sauce if not salty enough, or a little extra broth if you think there's too high a ratio of vegetables to liquid.

⑤ Stir in the spinach, cilantro, and/ or Thai basil (they'll wilt immediately) and ladle the soup into bowls. Serve immediately, steaming hot. Pass the Thai chile paste at the table. Be sure to tell everyone to suck on, but not eat, the kaffir lime leaves, lemongrass, and galangal (they're so flavorful, all of them, but tough). Invite me to dinner for this one, please!

Serves 4 as a starter or 2 as a main course

Note: Galangal is sometimes called Thai ginger because it tastes like—guess what?—a hot peppery ginger, to which it's related. It's available fresh in Asian markets and occasionally natural foods and conventional supermarkets.

VARIATIONS

Tom Yum with chicken and/or shrimp: Many of my non-v friends are as rhapsodic about this as I am about the above. Make the following substitutions:

★ Substitute chicken broth for the vegetable stock

★ Use actual fish sauce (*nam pla,* which is Thai, or *nuoc mam* or *cham,* which is Vietnamese) instead of the vegetarian version

★ Use about half as many vegetables and just 2 or 3 ounces of tofu

★ Have ready two skinless, boneless raw chicken breasts, sliced into thin strips and/or 1 to 2 medium-large shrimp, peeled and deveined, per person

Follow the directions as given above, but at the end of step 2, drop in the sliced chicken breasts. Let the chicken cook until it's white and firm, about 2 minutes. Add the vegetables and the shrimp, if using. Proceed with the rest of the recipe as written. When serving the soup, divide the shrimp among the bowls. **Me** **Gf**

Tom Khaa, either vegetarian or with chicken and/or shrimp: Follow either variation of the recipe above, but use only 1 quart vegetable stock. At the end of step 2, just before you drop in the tofu and vegetables, stir in a can (13.5 ounces) of unsweetened coconut milk (full or reduced fat; your choice). Bring the liquid to a boil, lower to a simmer, and proceed with the recipe as written. **Gf**

Amie's Vietnamese Dipping Sauce
(NUOC CHAM CHAY)

Vn **Gf**

3 to 4 teaspoons freshly squeezed lime or lemon juice

1 tablespoon plus 1 teaspoon tamari or shoyu soy sauce (wheat-free if desired)

1 tablespoon sugar or agave syrup

1 scant teaspoon commercial Asian chile-garlic paste (or pound a clove or two of garlic together with some minced serrano pepper)

Sea salt (optional)

Combine 3 teaspoons of the lime juice with the tamari, sugar, and 2 tablespoons water in a small jar. Tighten the lid and shake the jar until the sugar has dissolved and all the ingredients are well blended. Add the chile-garlic paste and shake again. Taste, and adjust the seasonings with more lime juice, tamari or sea salt, if using, and sugar. This keeps for a week, refrigerated.

Makes about ⅜ cup

NOODLED JAPANESE BROTH
with Tofu & Bean Threads

This is the epitome of quick-to-make, homey comfort food. When I'm too tired to think, feel like I'm coming down with a cold, or am generally dispirited, this soup comes to mind, pot, and bowl.

A bean in any form is a thing of beauty and succulence. Add "surprise" when it becomes a noodle. Cellophane, glass, or bean thread; they're all noodles made of mung bean starch. Members of the infinite family of Asian noodles, all cook quickly, absorbing the flavors of the broth in which they revive. They lend any broth an intriguing, singular soft-chewy texture. Vn

2½ quarts (10 cups) vegetable stock

1 tablespoon peeled finely grated fresh ginger

2 bundles (each about 1½ ounces; 3 ounces total) dry, very thin, fine cellophane noodles

4 large mushrooms, white or shiitake, sliced

2 carrots, sliced on the diagonal into very thin ovals

8 ounces very fresh firm or extra-firm water-packed tofu, diced into ½-inch cubes

4 scallions, derooted, white and tender green portions diced

About 12 spinach leaves (full-size, not baby spinach), washed well

½ cup boiling water

3 tablespoons miso (I prefer white miso, but any type works beautifully here)

1 Place the stock and ginger in a large pot and bring to a boil over high heat. Add the noodles. Drop in the mushrooms, carrots, and tofu and let simmer until the noodles are transparent, about 3 minutes.

2 Meanwhile, divide the scallions and spinach among 4 large soup bowls. In a small heat-proof bowl, whisk together the boiling water and miso.

3 By now the noodles should be done. Quickly stir the miso slurry into the soup, and, just as quickly, ladle the soup into each bowl, which will wilt the spinach. Eat immediately.

Serves 4

Do, Re, *Miso*, Fa, La, Ti, Do

In America, 54 percent of all adults start the day with a cup of coffee. In Japan, 72 percent get rolling with an elixir made not from the coffee bean but the soybean: They have a nice hot cup of miso soup.

Maybe you're long familiar with miso. Maybe you met it the first time you went to a Japanese restaurant and chose what was described on the menu as "bean soup," and were surprised to receive not a thick potage, but a brothy, salty, scaldingly hot flavorful liquid in a lightweight lacquered bowl with its own cover. Brown, a little cloudy, it may have had slivers of scallion floating in it, or a cube of tofu—which, like miso itself, originates with the soybean. That's bean soup, Eastern style.

Readily available in natural foods stores, miso is a highly concentrated paste made of fermented soybeans, salt, and, usually, a grain like rice or barley. Miso is exotic to many Americans, though far more widespread and beloved here than even a decade ago. But it's been used for thousands of years throughout Asia, especially in Japan. It's used most often as we use bouillon cubes: Add it to boiling water, stir, and you have a full-flavored, distinctive broth. But miso's horizons extend further: It's an ingredient in many soups, excellent in salad dressings and dips, and part of countless stews and sauces.

There are dozens of types of miso, all savory, some sweet *and* savory, each individual. The bean used, the fermentation method, and the aging process make each miso as distinctive as vintages from different grapes, hillsides, climates, and years. And like, say, cheese, there are exquisite small-batch artisanal misos which are even more individualized, as well as mass-produced misos that are more standard issue. In general, longer-aged misos are a darker color and stronger, heartier, saltier. They do not require refrigeration and keep indefinitely. Among dark misos made with grains are *mugi* (barley-soy), *kome* and *genmai* (rice), and *soba* (buckwheat). *Hatcho,* probably the most widely available, is made from pure soybeans.

Misos that are more briefly aged are lighter in color (beige, golden, ivory white) and taste. They have a delicate, appealing sweetness and need to be refrigerated. They're generally sold as "sweet miso," "mellow miso," "mellow white miso," or "traditional white miso."

When it comes to fresh miso, I prefer the taste of the light young misos to that of the older, dark ones; however, I use both and always have a tub of at least one of each kind on hand. To approximate the difference between the two main types in very loose culinary equivalencies, you could say the dark misos are "beefy," while the light are "chicken-y."

And I'd be remiss if I didn't mention the instant dried misos, such as (my favorite) Miso-Cup. I can't tell you how often half an envelope of Miso-Cup with a pour of boiling water from a flight attendant or server at a hotel restaurant has brought me back to myself. Miso, restorative in that way you feel almost down to your cells, is the vegetarian's chicken soup.

INDIAN BEAN SOUPS

We've now seen, and tasted, the Indian-via-British influence in Africa, taken there by Indian immigrants. Now let's follow the immigrants back to their own home continent. You'll find more on the infinity and subtle variation of Indian spicings in "Superior Stews, Companionable Curries," which is where the majority of the Indian recipes in this book are located (see page 185). For now, let's just say how particularly astonishing it is that this variety is possible in a country where there are vast numbers of poor people who exist primarily on grains (rice or wheat, in the form of chapattis) and beans, including lentils and peas. Beans, grains, vegetables: Because of the huge spectrum of spices and cooking methods used on the Indian subcontinent, these simple basic foods transform over and over again.

DAHL

Every day in India, and among immigrant Indian communities around the world, millions of people eat dahl, a thin, soupy mixture of tender-cooked lentils or peas, made plush with spices and served over rice or, sometimes, with warm whole wheat chapattis. Dahl is one of the basic components of almost every India meal, simple or elaborate.

"Dahl," also spelled "daal" and "dal," refers both to the legumes themselves and to this ubiquitous but always unique dish made with them. If you go to an Indian market and check the dahl aisle, you will find variety upon variety of beans and peas, whole and split.

But here is a recipe for dahl, the soup, which you make from dahl, the legume. It's a staple in my house, but an ever-changing one, as you'll see from the numerous variations that follow. Mix and match them to your heart's content. Vn Gf

1 cup split mung beans (*moong dahl*), yellow lentils (*thoor dahl*), or red lentils (*masoor dahl*), picked over, rinsed, and drained well

Vegetable oil cooking spray

3 to 4 cloves garlic, chopped

2 large onions, sliced into thin crescents

1¾ teaspoons ground turmeric

2 teaspoons ground cumin

¼ to ½ teaspoon cayenne, more or less to taste

1½ teaspoons salt, or to taste

3 tablespoons ghee, butter, coconut oil, or any mild vegetable oil, such as corn, canola, or peanut

1½ teaspoons cumin seeds

2½ teaspoons ground coriander

Hot steamed rice, for serving

Chopped fresh cilantro leaves, for serving

1 Place the beans in a large, heavy oil-sprayed (or nonstick) saucepan. Add 3 cups water, the garlic, half of the sliced onions, the turmeric, ground cumin, and cayenne. Bring to a boil over high heat, then cover partially and lower the heat to a simmer. Simmer the lentils until they're tender but not mushy, about 30 minutes. Add the salt and stir well.

2 When the lentils are nearing tenderness, place an oil-sprayed 10- to 12-inch skillet over medium-high heat and add the ghee. You want to get the skillet hot enough that if you flick a drop of water into the pan, it will immediately sputter and sizzle dramatically. However, the line between this point and burning is close, so be attentive.

3 At this point, add the remaining onions and, stirring almost constantly, let them sauté for about 2 minutes. Then add the

cumin seeds, cook for 30 seconds longer, and lower the heat to medium. Add the ground coriander and continue cooking, stirring frequently, for 6 to 8 minutes, until the onions are soft and evenly well browned: They should be sweet and caramelized.

4 When the lentils or split peas are thoroughly cooked (but not overcooked), stir in the onion-spice mixture. At this point, you can turn off the heat and let the dahl sit at room temperature for a few hours to develop its flavor more fully, or refrigerate it covered overnight for the same purpose, and reheat it later. Or, you can serve it right away, piping hot.

5 When you do serve the dahl, serve it with rice. Either place a few tablespoons of steaming hot rice in the bowl (if you are serving the dahl as a soup) or ladle the dahl over a nice big mound of the rice if you're using it as a sauce. In either case, top with a generous shower of cilantro just before serving.

Serves 6 to 8 as an accompaniment

VARIATIONS

Dahl-Vegetable Soup: When the lentils are almost done, add 2 cups to 1 quart vegetable or chicken stock. Bring to a boil and add 2 to 3 sliced carrots, 1 to 2 diced fist-size potatoes, and, if you like, a small diced zucchini or summer squash and/or a cup or so of diced winter squash and/or a cup or so of thin-sliced-crosswise green beans. Add the onion-spice sauté and turn the heat down to a simmer, cover partially, and let cook slowly for 25 to 35 minutes, giving the occasional stir. **Vn** **Gf**

Tomato-Ginger Dahl or Dahl-Vegetable Soup: When the lentils are just about tender, scoop out a ladleful or two into the food processor. Add 1½ cups canned fire-roasted tomatoes, a hunk of ginger about the size of your thumb, coarsely chopped, and an extra clove or two of garlic. Buzz all to a texture-y smoothness. Return this mixture to the soup, and then either add the vegetables and stock as in the variation above or leave as is, stirring the onion sauté in either case. **Vn** **Gf**

Seasoning options: In addition to these longer variations, you can fool around with different spices and different methods of using them. Any of these small changes will vary the final dahl.

★ Dry-toast whole coriander seeds in a small skillet and grind them in a spice grinder. Use the resulting ground toasted coriander (in place of preground coriander) in the sauté. **Vn** **Gf**

★ Omit the cayenne, or cut it back, and instead sauté a minced serrano or other green or red chile with the onion. Leave the chile seeds in for heat or omit them for mildness. **Vn** **Gf**

★ Add 2 teaspoons black or brown mustard seeds at the same time as the cumin. **Vn** **Gf**

★ Add 1 teaspoon to 1 tablespoon finely chopped fresh ginger, either directly to the simmering dahl, or to the onion-spice mixture (add the ginger when you add the coriander). **Vn** **Gf**

★ Toss a pinch of ground cloves, either solo or with an even tinier pinch of cinnamon, into the simmering dahl. **Vn** **Gf**

ə ə ə

PANCH DAHL

This nubbly, thick dahl, cooked with layers of aromatics, is another of the thousand permutations of dahls that are served daily throughout the Indian subcontinent, providing protein to a largely vegetarian population. One could say this is the Indian equivalent of an American many-bean soup, but where American many-bean soups are usually flavored with a ham hock and may contain ten, twelve, even fourteen kinds of beans, panch dahl has fewer types of legumes—five, to be exact—and far more seasonings.

Panch is Sanskrit for "five"; for example, the group of five musicians who play ancient instruments at any auspicious occasion are *panchavarum.* The beverage that we call "punch" was an anglicization of both the word and the five-ingredient, fruit juice–based beverage that the British found when they colonized India. Here the five refers to five types of pulses (small legumes, such as peas and lentils).

Fresh ginger is the only seasoning actually cooked with the lentils. The transformative alchemy takes place at the moment when the spices—the holy trinity of cumin, turmeric, and coriander—are sautéed in oil, and then a moist, gingery tomato-onion-chile buzz is poured over them. The aromatic steam is almost unbearably, salivatingly piquant. And when it hits those lentils, oh my! **Ve** **Gf**

1 cup yellow split peas

½ cup brown or green lentils

¼ cup red lentils (*masoor dahl*)

½ cup split white gram beans (*urad dahl*)

¼ cup yellow mung beans (*moong dahl*)

2-inch chunk of fresh ginger, unpeeled

½ to 1 teaspoon salt

1 large onion, peeled and quartered

2 to 3 cloves garlic, peeled and halved

2 fresh tomatoes, stemmed and quartered
   (or ⅔ cup canned diced tomatoes)

1 small green chile, stemmed, seeds left
   in for heat or removed for mildness

1 to 2 tablespoons mild vegetable oil or ghee

1½ teaspoons cumin seeds

½ teaspoon ground turmeric

½ teaspoon ground coriander

Hot steamed rice, for serving

Chopped fresh cilantro leaves, for garnish

Plain yogurt, for serving

Lime pickle (see Note), for serving

1 Combine all the lentils and beans with 1½ quarts (6 cups) water in a large, heavy saucepan and bring to a boil over high heat. Finely chop about half the ginger and add it, too. Let the beans simmer until they are tender (some will disintegrate), 30 to 45 minutes. Add the salt to taste. If the dahl is looking too thick for your taste and you'd like it a bit soupier, add 1 to 2, even 3 more cups of water.

2 While the beans and lentils cook, coarsely chop the remaining ginger and place it in a food processor with the onion, garlic, tomatoes, and chile. Pulse until all is buzzed into a thick, slightly chunky puree. Set aside.

3 Toward the end of the bean cooking time, heat the oil in a separate skillet over medium-high heat and then add the cumin seeds. When the seeds begin to sizzle and splutter, in no more than 30 seconds if the pan and skillet are hot, add the turmeric and coriander, stirring constantly. Sauté for about 30 seconds, then add the puree from the processor, which will go in with a great and aromatic, steamy hiss. Sauté until the mixture dries out a bit, a few minutes longer. Stir this spice paste into the simmering beans.

4 Let the beans and spices cook together for 1 minute. You can eat the dahl immediately, or stop here and either let it sit for a few hours or refrigerate it, covered, overnight and reheat it just before it's time to eat. Serve it over or alongside rice, garnished with the cilantro, a dollop of yogurt on the side, and lime pickle passed at the table. Like all such soups, a little wait is beneficent in terms of amping up flavor.

Serves 6 to 8 as part of an Indian dinner

Note: Lime pickle—sour, pungent, salty, hot, powerful with spice, not sweet—is made from chopped whole lime pieces (tastewise, no shrinking violets themselves), which are further sharpened with a combination that usually includes mustard, chile, ginger, fenugreek, and asafetida, among other spices, all in an abundant bath of oil. One widely available brand is Patak's, which comes in several iterations: Lime Pickle, Lime Relish, Hot Lime Relish Spicy & Fruity Extra Hot (www.pataks.co.uk). They're available in the Indian or ethnic foods section of most large natural foods stores or even conventional supermarkets, as well as at Indian markets (where you'll find easily half a dozen varieties in addition to Patak's).

VARIATION

Kerala-style Panch Dahl: This version is slightly modified by the delicious and distinctive seasonings of southern India. In step 2, add to the ingredients in the processor ¼ to ⅓ cup dried, unsweetened coconut flakes. In step 3, substitute coconut oil for the oil, and add 2 teaspoons black or brown mustard seeds, sautéing them with the cumin seeds. Watch out—they pop! Ve Gf

KERALA-STYLE DAHL

The cooking of Kerala, the South Indian state whose name means "land of the coconut palms," differs notably from the northern style, the one much more generally familiar to American restaurant-goers. The use of coconut oil as a cooking fat, as well as grated coconut itself, with black mustard seeds a frequent addition to a slightly different combination of spices, make this one almost wholly distinctive from the other dahls. It is served at a late lunch, the main meal of the day, with a huge mound of rice, an amazingly refreshing yogurt-buttermilk mixture referred to as "curd," a couple of spoonfuls of various vegetable preparations, and a few crunchy things—a papadum (a fried bread, also made of lentil flour, so crisp it shatters) and maybe some circles of fried bananas. After a Kerala lunch, you are ready to toddle off for a deep, deep siesta. When you awake, perhaps it will be a bit cooler. . . . Vn Gf

1 cup split yellow lentils (*toor dahl*)

Cooking oil spray, preferably coconut

2 teaspoons ground turmeric

A thumb-size chunk of ginger, peeled and finely chopped

3 tablespoons coconut oil

1 teaspoon black mustard seeds

2 dried red chiles

2 shallots, chopped, or 1 small onion, chopped

2 to 3 cloves garlic, coarsely chopped

½ teaspoon ground cumin

1 teaspoon ground coriander

⅛ teaspoon cayenne, or more or less to taste

¼ to ⅓ cup grated unsweetened coconut (preferably fresh, but unsweetened dried is okay, too)

Salt, to taste

1 heaping tablespoon tamarind concentrate (see page 304)

1 Rinse and pick over the lentils, then drain them well.

2 Transfer the lentils to a large, heavy, oil-sprayed (or nonstick) pot. Add 3 cups water and the turmeric and ginger. Bring to a boil over high heat; then partially cover, lowering the heat to a simmer. (Start on step 3 as the lentils continue to cook, which will be in toto about 30 minutes, or until they're tender.)

3 As soon as you've got the lentils going, begin the spice sauté: Heat the coconut oil in a small skillet over medium-high heat. Add the black mustard seeds and the red chiles, cover the pan, and shake it like the dickens until you hear the seeds beginning to pop. Lift the lid (stand back; the fumes will be pungent), and add the shallots. Lower the heat and cook, stirring, until the shallots are nicely brown but not burned, 3 to 4 minutes.

4 Lower the heat and add the chopped garlic and the ground cumin, coriander, and cayenne. Cook, stirring constantly, while you count to 20. Then add this spice mixture to the simmering dahl, to cook together.

5 When the lentils are tender and mushable (after about 30 minutes), stir in the coconut and salt. At this point, you can turn off the heat and let the dahl sit at room temperature for a few hours to develop its flavor more fully, or refrigerate it overnight, to be reheated before serving.

6 Serve the dahl hot, and just before you serve it, stir in the tamarind concentrate.

Serves 6 to 8 as part of an Indian meal

> ### ON A BANANA LEAF PLATE
> ─────────────
> *Large mound of basmati rice*
> ★
> *Kerala-style Dahl*
> ★
> *Papadums*
> ★
> *Green Beans T'horin (page 287)*
> ★
> *Lime pickle*
> ★
> *Buttermilk*

SAMBAR

Sambar, sometimes spelled with an h (*sambhar*), is a South Indian lentil-based, vegetable-enhanced soup-stew, quite thin, that is never served by itself but is always served as an accompaniment. Throughout the states of Karnataka, Tamil Nadu, and Kerala, it's one of two saucelike breakfast condiments universally served with *idli* (steamed sourdough rice-lentil dumplings) or *dosa* (crisp, paper-thin lentil–and–rice flour pancakes). A bright yellow-brownish-gold, and a tiny bit sour (from the addition of tamarind), sambar is always made with the same near-identical combination of spices that verges on the acrid side. For South Indians residing abroad, sambar is a true taste-of-home food. For Americans, it provides an occasional exotic zing. **Vn Gf**

1 cup red lentils (*masoor dahl*), picked over and rinsed

¾ teaspoon ground turmeric

About 1 tablespoon any mild vegetable oil (or coconut oil, to make it Kerala-style)

Salt

Vegetable oil cooking spray

3 to 5 small dry red chiles (or to taste), stemmed and broken in half

1 teaspoon brown or black mustard seeds

½ teaspoon fenugreek seeds

8 fresh curry leaves, if available (see Notes)

1 onion or 3 to 4 shallots, finely chopped

1 tablespoon seedless tamarind paste (see page 304), stirred into ½ cup hot water

⅛ to ¼ teaspoon asafetida (optional)

1 large tomato, chopped, or 1 cup canned diced tomatoes with juice

1 cup vegetables (any or all of the following): thinly sliced green beans, okra, carrot, finely chopped potato, or butternut squash (optional)

2 tablespoons sambar spice mix (see Notes)

¼ cup cilantro leaves, finely chopped, for garnish

Cooked rice, for serving

1 Bring 2 cups water to a boil in a large, heavy saucepan over high heat. Add the dahl, turmeric, and 1 teaspoon of the oil and bring everything back to a boil, skimming off and discarding any foam that rises to the top. Turn the heat down some and continue cooking, half-covered, at a hard simmer, adding a little water if needed (you want it thin, but not watery), until the dahl is soft and starting to disintegrate, about 25 minutes. Mash the soft dahl coarsely by mushing it against the side of the pot with the back of a wooden spoon. Add salt to taste.

2 Meanwhile, spray a small skillet with oil and place it over medium-high heat. Add the remaining oil, and when it is hot (it will begin to liquefy and shimmer), add the chiles and let them brown—they can get almost black, which is fine, and if your oil's hot enough, they will—stirring, for about a minute. Add the mustard and fenugreek seeds and sauté them for about 1 minute; they should sizzle and begin to pop. Lower the heat slightly, add the curry leaves and onion, and continue sautéing, stirring until very fragrant, with the onion slightly colored but not yet translucent, another 3 or 4 minutes.

3 Pour the tamarind-water mixture into the spices, and stir; it will immediately bubble up and boil. If it starts to stick, add a little more water and cook, stirring, 30 seconds to 1 minute more. You want enough liquid to be able to cook the onions just a little further.

4 Transfer the sauté to the dahl along with the asafetida, tomato, vegetables, if using, and sambar spice mix. Cook the mixture at a hard simmer, stirring often, until the vegetables are tender, 5 to 10 minutes more. Transfer the sambar to a serving dish, sprinkle with the cilantro, and serve with a spoon alongside the rice: Each person helps him- or herself.

Serves 6 to 8 as an accompaniment

Notes: Curry leaves, the lovely and aromatic leaves of a tree native to India, are found in many South Indian dishes and are always used fresh (bay leaves are sometimes used in their place, though they're not remotely the same); you can find them at Indian markets (sometimes sold as kari or karry leaves).

Sambar spice mixtures, often sold as sambar powders, are available in any Indian grocery or online. The MTR brand is a good one, but most are quite similar. The ingredients are toasted and ground, and usually include coriander seeds, dried red chiles, kala gram (small Indian chickpeas) and sometimes *urad dahl* (Indian black lentils), cumin, black pepper, and just a little mustard seed, cinnamon, clove, and turmeric.

EUROPEAN BEAN SOUPS

Hard to imagine, but not so long ago, Italy was without tomatoes, France and Switzerland without chocolate, Hungary without paprika, and a vast expanse, the entire continent, without beans. Not green beans; not, more importantly, all varieties of dried beans except the chickpea, lentil, and fava. This is because these foodstuffs, and many others, were the gifts of (or, depending on how you look at it, appropriations from) the New World. These new crops changed the Old World dramatically. It was not just that these new arrivals meant there was more food available; it was the type of nourishment both people and the land could derive from them. The bean's contribution was notable and unique.

While beans and their New World vegetable kin may have revolutionized Europe, European cooking methods, ingredients, and tastes infinitely expanded the ways this new bounty was prepared. Thousands of regional ingredients and dishes came to incorporate beans and their American agricultural compatriots. Bite by bite, dish by dish, bean by bean, country by country, America and Europe met at the table and shared a bowl of soup.

FRENCH GREEN BEAN SOUP
Ville-Preux Style

This very simple French soup is, like most light, smooth soups, best as a starter rather than a main dish. If you have a surfeit of green beans from the garden and it's that just-starting-to-turn-cold point in the fall harvest, you could have no better beginning to a meal than this. If you don't care for (or don't have) tarragon, use basil, savory, a little rosemary, a combination of herbs, plain old parsley, or even no herbs at all. You can also jazz it up by adding a little grated lemon zest to the garlic butter, and squeezing the juice of a lemon into the soup before serving.

I like this pretty straight-up and vegetable-centered, but if you want it richer or more multilayered, use chicken broth instead of vegetable, and stir in ½ cup of cream at the end. **Ve** **Gf**

3 tablespoons butter, at room temperature

5 cloves garlic, pressed

1 tablespoon finely minced fresh parsley

1 tablespoon mild vegetable oil, such as corn or canola

1 large red onion, chopped

2 stalks celery with leaves, chopped

2 quarts (8 cups) vegetable stock, plus extra as needed

½ pound potatoes, peeled and coarsely chopped

1½ pounds green beans, tipped and tailed

1½ to 2 tablespoons tarragon leaves, stripped from tough stems

Salt and freshly ground black pepper

1 In a small bowl, smooth together the butter and pressed garlic with a spoon. Stir in the parsley, and set aside.

FROM A FRENCH COUNTRY KITCHEN IN OCTOBER

Bright green salad with mustard vinaigrette and loads of minced parsley

★

Roasted beets, grated and tossed with the same vinaigrette

★

French Green Bean Soup, Ville-Preux Style

★

Crusty French bread

★

Grilled lamb chops or grilled marinated tempeh

★

Potato-mushroom gratin

★

Tarte Tatin

② Heat the oil in a large soup pot over medium-high heat. Add the onion, lower the heat to medium, and sauté, stirring, until the onion has softened slightly, about 6 minutes. Add the celery, and continue sautéing until the celery is slightly softened and its leaves are wilted, another 5 minutes.

③ Add the stock, potatoes, green beans, and tarragon. Bring to a boil, turn down to a brisk simmer, cover, and let cook until the potatoes and green beans are soft and very tender, 10 to 12 minutes.

④ Using a slotted spoon, transfer the solids to a food processor and buzz until they're absolutely smooth. Taste the puree; season it with salt (a good bit) and pepper (not much). Stir the puree back into the broth, and reheat it to piping hot, adding extra broth if you want to thin the soup a little. Serve in cups with a rounded teaspoon of the garlic-parsley butter on top.

Serves 4 to 6 as a starter

ᘒ   ᘒ   ᘒ

SOUPE PRINTEMPS VILLE-PREUX

Herewith my imagined version of what the rich green bean soup would have been, had we been in Ville-Preux in spring (see page 91). The greens are a bit sprightlier, the flavors a bit sweeter. I doubt my old friend the innkeeper would have used mint, but you never know. For a richer version of this delicious but light vegetarian soup, feel free to fancy it up by using chicken stock and adding ½ cup of cream at the end.

If you can get nice sugar snap or snow peas, or have some growing in your garden, substitute ¾ pound of them, trimmed, for the zucchini and frozen peas. **Ve** **Gf**

¼ cup (½ stick) butter, at room temperature

1 small bunch of garlic chives or chives, very finely minced

1 tablespoon mild vegetable oil such as corn or canola

1 large red onion, chopped

1 stalk celery with leaves, chopped

1 carrot or tender parsnip, chopped

2 quarts (8 cups) vegetable stock, plus extra as needed

½ pound potatoes, peeled and coarsely chopped

1 small zucchini, quartered lengthwise

¼ cup fresh mint leaves

2 cups frozen peas or fresh shelled peas (taste the fresh peas to make sure they are young and sweet), or 2½ cups sugar snap or snow peas

1 teaspoon honey or sugar

Salt and freshly ground black pepper

Chive blossoms (a lovely lavender color),
for garnish (optional)

A few tender pea tendrils, for garnish
(optional)

Tender mint leaves, the prettiest you can
find, for garnish (optional)

1 In a small bowl, smooth together the butter and garlic chives. Set aside.

2 Heat the oil in a large soup pot over medium-high heat. Add the onion, lower the heat to medium, and sauté, stirring, until the onion has softened slightly, about 6 minutes. Add the celery and carrot and sauté until they are slightly limp and starting to color, another 5 minutes.

3 Add the stock and the potatoes. Bring to a boil, turn down to a brisk simmer, cover, and let cook for about 6 minutes. Lift the lid and drop in the zucchini and mint. Cook for another 5 minutes. Add the peas and honey and cook until the peas are heated through but still bright green, just 2 to 3 minutes more, no longer.

4 Using a slotted spoon, transfer the solids to a food processor and buzz until they're absolutely smooth. Taste the puree and season it with salt and pepper. Stir the puree back into the broth you scooped it from, and reheat to piping hot. Serve in cups with a rounded teaspoon of the chive butter melting on each cup and garnish(es) of your choice on top.

Serves 4 to 6 as a starter

PEAS ON EARTH: VILLE-PREUX REMEMBERED

The international study group to which I belonged met, a couple of decades ago, in a large private home on a wooded hilltop a few kilometers outside the French village of Ville-Preux, about an hour from Paris. The group got together every few years somewhere in the world, for ten days to two weeks. Virtually everyone, it seemed, was on a budget. When our joinings-together took place in the United States, it was usually in a large college town, where there were plenty of lodging and eating options. Abroad, our group tended to be more on our own as far as food and lodgings were concerned. That year in France, I stayed in a room above, and I mean directly above, the village bar. Eventually, growing tired of living on fruit, cheese, French bread, and single-serve cups of yogurt, I negotiated supper with the owner of the room above the bar. This supper was generally soup, sometimes with a small salad; the soup was, generally, a puree of a single fresh cooked vegetable, dolloped with a big honkin' spoonful of butter, served with a baguette from the bakery around the corner and more butter. The meal was hot, simple, good, and much less expensive than the everything-dripping-with-vinaigrette dishes that were the only other affordable vegetarian bistro options in that town.

The green bean soup on page 89 was, along with one made of pumpkin and another of tomato, in regular rotation on the menu. In my version, I've jazzed it up a little, but not much.

MINESTRONE

Minestrone means "big soup," and indeed, that's what this generous Italian potage of beans and vegetables is. It's big enough to capture a thousand variations (of which I've offered five), none the same, yet each recognizably and satisfyingly minestrone. It's big enough to include almost every vegetable the garden or farmer's market has to offer, big enough to serve as dinner, big enough to encompass dried beans (most often cranberry or borlotti beans, sometimes cannellini beans, a portion of which are most often pureed as the soup's base) as well as fresh green beans. It's big enough for dinner, big enough to satisfy hunger, nourish, and give pleasure. It's just one heck of a big-hearted soup, and it's loved the world over in a big way.

To my mind, what makes minestrone recognizably minestrone is its bean base and some configuration of green beans, tomatoes, garlic, onions, basil, olive oil, and cabbage or greens. Most versions include some form of small pasta, but some use potatoes instead, or both. Though many people swear by the addition of salt pork or bacon, just as many insist it must be meatless. The latter camp includes Irma Goodrich Mazza, an American woman married to an Italian, whose 1937 cookbook *Herbs for the Kitchen* was probably the first to awaken Americans to the wonders of the Italian kitchen and its herb garden. Of minestrone, she noted, "Dished piping hot, it melts the shower of grated Romano cheese into just one more bit of assembled deliciousness to make a superlative meal. A plate of this potage . . . served with crisped and garlicked French bread, a salad, and a glass of wine, and we have dined."

Even better, as soups and stews so often are, is minestrone reheated the next day, or the following. Ve

1 pound dried cannellini, borlotti, or cranberry beans, soaked overnight (see page 346)

Salt

⅓ to ½ cup extra-virgin olive oil (the more oil, the tastier—though more caloric)

2 large onions, diced

1 carrot, quartered lengthwise and then finely chopped crosswise

1 stalk celery, quartered lengthwise and then finely chopped crosswise

2 cloves garlic, finely chopped

3 cups canned diced tomatoes with their juice (from about two 28-ounce cans)

About ½ pound fresh green beans, tipped, tailed, and cut crosswise into ¼-inch slices (or thinner)

2 small to medium zucchini, quartered lengthwise and then chopped crosswise

2 tablespoons finely minced fresh Italian (flat-leaf) parsley

1 teaspoon finely minced fresh rosemary needles

3 tablespoons minced fresh basil leaves (preferably globe basil, if it's available)

2 quarts (8 cups) water or vegetable stock

About ⅛ head savoy (curly) cabbage, slivered (roughly 2½ cups)

Freshly ground black pepper

About ⅔ cup frozen peas

About 2 cups cooked small pasta, such as small shells, ditalini, or broken linguini, for serving

Grated Parmesan and/or Romano cheese, for serving

1 Rinse and drain the soaked beans. Cook them according to the method of your choice (see page 18) until very tender, adding 1½ teaspoons salt in the last 30 minutes. (If you like, start cooking the vegetables while the beans are cooking; see step 3.)

2 Using a slotted spoon, transfer about half the cooked beans to a food processor and buzz to a puree. Stir this puree back into the whole beans and their cooking liquid, and set aside.

3 Heat the oil in a large, heavy soup pot or Dutch oven over medium-low heat. Add the onions and cook, stirring occasionally, until they are limp but not browned, about 8 minutes. Add the carrot, celery, and garlic and cook, stirring, until fragrant, another 3 or 4 minutes. Add the tomatoes, cover, and let simmer for 10 minutes more.

4 Lift the lid of the soup and add the green beans, zucchini, parsley, rosemary, 1 tablespoon of the basil, and the water. Bring to a boil, turn down the heat to a simmer, cover, and let cook until the vegetables are tender and your nose follows the fragrant steam back to the kitchen, 45 minutes to 1 hour.

5 Lift the lid again and add the reserved beans and the cabbage, stirring well. Cover and let simmer for another 30 minutes. (By this time family members will be sniffing their way hungrily into the kitchen.) Lift the lid and taste for salt (you'll need quite a bit). Add the remaining basil, black pepper to taste, and the peas. (At this point, if you're planning to serve it right away and don't have leftover cooked pasta in the fridge, you'll need to get the pasta cooking.) Let simmer for another 10 minutes.

6 Divide the pasta into bowls and ladle the hot soup on top. Serve with grated cheese alongside, for each person to sprinkle or shower, as they wish.

Serves 6 to 8

VARIATIONS

Minestrone Ligurian Style: Place a good dollop of homemade or purchased pesto on top of the pasta, then ladle the hot minestrone over it. Tell each diner to stir before eating. Ve

Minestrone with Salt Pork: You'll need about a 2-inch square of salt pork. Rinse it, dry it, and dice it fine. Cut the olive oil back to 1 to 2 tablespoons. Before you start sautéing the onion, slowly cook the salt pork in the oil, stirring often, over low heat until all the fat has rendered out and the bits of pork are crisp, 8 to 10 minutes.

Remove and discard the pork, leaving the fat and oil in the pot. Add the onions and proceed with the recipe as directed. Some use chicken or a light meat stock with this version instead of water. **Me**

Summer Minestrone: Substitute 4 to 5 cups fresh, cooked fava beans (see page 44 for cooking instructions) for the dried beans, and instead of 2 zucchini, use 1 zucchini and 1 yellow summer squash. Add 4 to 6 medium potatoes, peeled and diced into ½-inch cubes, with the zucchini. Omit the pasta. **Ve** **Gf**

Fall Minestrone: Omit the carrot; add an extra 2 to 3 cups water or stock. When you add the zucchini in step 4, add 1 potato, peeled and diced into ½-inch cubes, and half a peeled butternut squash, also cut into ½-inch cubes. Then, when you stir in the cabbage in step 5, add a cup or so of very

small cauliflower florets and a few slices of finely ribboned black kale (also called Lacinato, Tuscan, or dinosaur kale). **Ve**

Quick(er) Minestrone: Instead of the soaked, cooked dried beans, use 2 cans (25 ounces each) pinto or navy beans. Puree 1 can of the beans with their liquid, transfer them to a heavy soup pot, and stir in the remaining can of whole beans. Use the lesser amount of olive oil, even as little as 1 tablespoon, and just 1 onion. Instead of the canned tomatoes, use 3 cups of the very best quality jarred (not canned) Italian-style tomato sauce with herbs and garlic. This means you can omit the parsley, rosemary, and basil. This version, when made with plenty of fresh green beans and zukes, is more than acceptable. Just make sure you go easy on the salt, since both the canned beans and the tomato sauce are already salted. **Ve**

ง   ง   ง

TUESDAY FAVA BEAN & RICE SOUP
alla Romana

In many parts of the world where food is taken seriously, there is a conservative loyalty not only to certain dishes, but to the days of the week on which they're traditionally served. For instance, it wouldn't be Monday in New Orleans without the beloved bowl of red beans and rice. And in Rome, it wouldn't be Tuesday without this soup, primarily fresh favas, rice, and olive oil. Like much of true Italian food, it's rooted in deep, close-to-the-earth simplicity. (Just so you know, in Rome you should look for gnocchi on Thursdays and tripe on Saturdays.)

You'll get three very different soups from this, depending on whether you use beef broth, vegetable stock, or water: all very good. With water, the beans really come across with clarity and deliciousness—a pleasing purity.

Shell, blanch, and hull the fresh favas before starting (see page 44). You'll need to allow about a pound of favas in the pod per cup of shelled and hulled beans. **Vn** **Gf**

¼ cup olive oil, plus extra as needed

1 large onion, chopped

2 to 2½ cups fresh fava beans (shelled, blanched, and hulled—from about 2½ pounds favas in the pod)

2 cloves garlic, chopped

⅓ cup Arborio rice

2 tablespoons tomato paste or ⅓ cup diced canned plum tomatoes with their juice

1 quart (4 cups) boiling water, vegetable stock, or beef broth

Salt and freshly ground black pepper

1 Heat the olive oil in a large soup pot or Dutch oven over medium heat. Add the onion and sauté until it's limp but not browned, about 5 minutes.

2 Add the favas, garlic, and rice and cook, stirring constantly, for 1 minute more (add a little extra olive oil if it starts to stick).

3 Add the tomato paste and pour in the boiling water. Bring the whole pot to a boil, then lower the heat to a brisk simmer and cook until the favas and rice are tender, about 30 minutes. About halfway through, add salt and lots of pepper to taste; taste and season again before serving.

4 Serve the soup very hot in warmed bowls, garnished with another grind of pepper and a thin trickle of olive oil.

Serves 4

"Of all fresh and dried vegetables, the fava bean is queen, sovereign of all, soaked in the evening, cooked in the morning."

—*Italian folk saying*
(Pugliese region)

PASTA E FAGIOLI

Pasta e fagioli: simply "pasta and beans" in Italian. But for satisfying, earthy dishes easily and inexpensively made, this traditional peasant dish is hard to beat. Originally prepared as a homey way to use up leftovers, this typically meatless soup can range from a flavorful broth studded with small pastas and cannellini or borlotti beans, to a heartier soup-stew. The longer it sits, the thicker it gets. **Ve**

1½ cups dried white beans, such as cannellini or Great Northern, soaked overnight (see page 348) and rinsed

2 onions, 1 coarsely chopped, 1 finely chopped

½ cup extra-virgin olive oil, plus extra for serving

1 carrot, diced

1 stalk celery with leaves, diced

2 to 3 garlic cloves, minced

⅔ cup canned diced tomatoes with their juice

1 sprig of fresh rosemary, needles stripped from the stem and finely chopped

About 5½ cups boiling water or vegetable or chicken stock, or a combination

½ cup minced fresh Italian (flat-leaf) parsley

Salt and freshly ground black pepper

About 6 ounces ditalini, small shells, elbows, or ziti (roughly one third of a 1-pound package)

Freshly grated Pecorino Romano and/or Parmesan cheese, for serving

1 Place the beans in a large, heavy saucepan, add water to cover to a depth of 1 inch, and set over high heat. Add the coarsely chopped onion, bring the pot to a boil, and then turn down to a simmer and let cook until the onion has almost disintegrated and the beans are almost tender, about 1 hour.

2 Drain the beans and onions, reserving the cooking liquid. Transfer about a cup of the liquid and about a cup of the beans (with some of the cooked onions) to a food processor. Buzz smooth and set aside.

3 Toward the end of the bean cooking time, heat the oil in a large, heavy soup pot or Dutch oven over medium heat. Add the finely chopped onion and gently sauté it until it begins to get limp but not brown, about 5 minutes. Add the carrot and celery, and sauté until slightly tender, another 5 to 8 minutes. Add the garlic and sauté until fragrant, 1 minute more.

4 Add the beans and their cooking liquid to the vegetables in the soup pot. Then add the tomatoes, rosemary, and pureed beans, as well as about 3 cups of the boiling water. Bring the pot to a boil, turn down to a simmer, and let cook, covered, until the beans are fully and meltingly tender and everything has gotten to know each other cozily, about another hour. Lift the lid from time to time, both to stir (the pureed beans may want to stick) and to add more boiling water as needed. The beans should be covered by 1 to 3 inches of simmering liquid at all times. (This range is so large because, as noted, the amount of liquid depends on whether you prefer a brothy or thick soup. Remember, too, that the pasta will cook in the liquids, thickening them.)

5 When the beans are pillowy and soft, add half the minced parsley, salt and pepper to taste, and another cup of boiling water to the pot. Bring back to a boil, uncovered, add the pasta, and cook, stirring frequently, until the pasta is tender, about 10 minutes. Remove from the heat. Taste again, adding more salt and pepper as needed.

6 Serve, hot, in warmed bowls. Garnish each bowl with a thread of olive oil, a shower of the remaining parsley, and some cheese. Pass additional cheese and a cruet of olive oil at the table.

Serves 4 to 6

VARIATION

Sardinian Chickpea & Fennel Pasta e Fagioli: Substitute chickpeas for the cannellini, but in step 1, let them cook for 2½ hours instead of 1 hour. In step 3, the vegetable sauté, replace the carrot and celery with 1 large bulb fennel, halved and very thinly sliced (remove and discard the stalk, stem, and most of the fronds; mince a few fronds to yield 2 to 3 tablespoons; set them aside). Sauté the sliced fennel and onion over low heat until the fennel starts softening, about 8 minutes. In step 4 add 4 or 5 peeled and diced small potatoes and the reserved minced fennel fronds to the soup pot along with the other ingredients. Proceed with the recipe as directed. Ve

FOOLING, DROOLING, PASTA FAZOOLING

Pasta e fagioli has humble origins, but this unassuming soup is a celebrity featured in the lyrics of not one, not two, but *three* popular American songs. The first was "Pastafazoola," by the vaudeville duo Van and Schenck in 1927 ("Please take my advice / If you wanna eat something nice / don't be a fool, eat pasta fazool"). The second was Cab Calloway's recording of "Everybody Eats When They Come to My House," which was written in 1947 by Jeanne Burns. In it, an ebullient Cab invites friends to sample various foods: "Have a banana, Hannah . . . Pasta Fazoola, Tallulah!" The third mention is "That's Amore," made famous by Dean Martin in 1952. The song (composed by Harry Warren, born Salvatore Guaragna, and lyricist Jack Brooks) explains that you know that you're really, truly in love "When the stars make you drool just like pasta fazool . . ."

Hungarian

GREEN BEAN SOUP

(ZÖLDBABLEVES)

Mellifluously creamy, this is a rich Occasion-with-a-capital-O soup, plush with those so-good Hungarian tropes: onions slowly sautéed, paprika, butter, and thickened sour cream. My Vermont neighbor, Gaelen, lived as an au pair in New York during her teens and remembers learning this style of cooking from one of her early families; she, like me, still returns to it periodically and fondly.

If Hungarian wax peppers—long, yellow-green, sometimes called "banana peppers" or "Italian frying peppers"—are not available, use half a red bell pepper and half a green bell pepper instead. Also, you can prep this soup ahead of time if you wish; just be sure not to add the sour cream until the soup is already piping hot and you are two shakes away from serving. The soup must not boil after the sour cream is added, or the cream will curdle. **Ve**

Vegetable oil cooking spray

3 tablespoons butter

1 medium onion, finely chopped

2 Hungarian wax peppers, stemmed, seeded, and finely chopped

2 quarts (8 cups) vegetable stock or chicken broth

1 tablespoon tomato paste

1 pound fresh green beans, tipped, tailed, and cut diagonally into ¼-inch pieces

3 tablespoons unbleached white flour

2 teaspoons smoked sweet Hungarian paprika

1 bunch of parsley, leaves only, finely chopped

½ cup sour cream, reduced-fat (*not* nonfat) sour cream, or 2% Greek-style yogurt

½ teaspoon vinegar (preferably white wine vinegar)

Salt and freshly ground black pepper

1 Spray a large skillet with oil and place it over medium heat. Add half the butter. When the butter has melted, sizzled, and stopped sizzling, add the onion and sauté, stirring, until softened, about 5 minutes. Add the peppers, lower the heat slightly, and continue sautéing until everything is very soft and the onions are deeply golden, another 8 to 10 minutes.

2 Place 6 cups of the stock in a large soup pot set over medium-high heat. Swirl 1 cup of the remaining stock into the skillet with the sautéed vegetables, stirring with a wooden spoon to get every bit of flavory glaze, then add the contents of the skillet to the soup pot. Add the tomato paste and green beans and bring the soup to a boil, then turn down the heat and let simmer, half-covered, until the green beans begin to grow tender and the ingredients get to know each other, 15 minutes.

❸ Meanwhile, wipe the skillet clean, set it over medium-low heat, and melt the remaining butter in it. Stir in the flour and carefully cook it until it browns just a little, about 3 minutes. Whisk in the remaining cup of stock, the paprika, and the parsley. Turn down the heat to the lowest possible simmer and let cook, half-covered, while the green beans finish cooking.

❹ When the green beans are tender, whisk the sour cream and vinegar into the flour mixture, and gently transfer this to the soup pot. Stir a few times, season with salt and pepper, and serve immediately.

Serves 4 to 6

VARIATIONS

Hungarian-style Mushroom–Green Bean Soup: These ingredients are not traditional in this soup but are right at home: Sauté ¼ pound or so chopped mushrooms in butter, then add them to the pot in step 2. Ve

Gaelen's Slightly Simplified Method: Use all of the butter to sauté the vegetables in step 1. Skip step 3, instead stirring the parsley, paprika, and remaining cup of stock into the simmering green beans. Just before serving, whisk together the flour and the sour cream in a medium bowl, then whisk in a cup of the hot soup. Then, with the green beans at a low simmer, stir the flour mixture into the soup pot. Cook, stirring often, until the soup has heated through and thickened slightly, 3 to 5 minutes, tasting to make sure there is no hint of raw flour (if there is, just give it a few more watchful minutes of cooking and stirring). Ve

A Vanished World, Remembered

I count eating at a wondrous Hungarian restaurant, now long-vanished (and not a trace of it to be found), called Berry's as one of the three or four childhood experiences that imprinted on me the ideal of what a restaurant is, can be, or should be. A small husband-and-wife-owned establishment, it was very quiet, oddly formal, but serene and welcoming. Fragrant with the odors of good food cooking, tables set with immaculate white tablecloths and heavy silverware, a glass pastry case just inside the door: I'd say, from my current perspective, that it must have been as literal as possible a transplanting of the couple's Old World experience, presumably from somewhere remembered from before the war that had expatriated them to Westchester County, New York. At Berry's, each bite was so good that you just wanted to stop, put down your fork, and experience the veal and noodles, the goulash, the delicate, barely sweet cheesecake.

I never tasted *zöldbableves* there, but every Hungarian, and every Hungarian cookbook, has a version. I combined several of them to come up with this one, and each time I eat it I raise a cup to toast Berry's. How very glad I am to have this memory of the place, since the place itself is gone.

GREEK GIGANDES OR WHITE BEAN SOUP-STEW
(FASOLADA)

Some consider this beloved Greek soup—the name of which is pronounced *fah-so-LAH-thah*—the national dish, as Egyptians do *ful.* It is similar to ful both in nomenclature and in makeup: Its main ingredient is beans (in Greek, *fassoli,* in Egyptian Arabic, *ful,* in Italian, *fagioli*). Greeks eat fasolada year-round, hot or at room temperature. But since it is meatless as well as hearty, sustaining, and full of flavor, Greek Orthodox Christians often associate it with Lent (which is held to with particular rigor—the garnish of fried *haloumi* cheese, which takes the dish from very good to over the top, is forgone in Lenten weeks).

Fasolada's provenance is ancient: Plutarch mentioned it (as an aphrodisiac!) back in the first century. Then, it would have been made with the amazing *gigandes* or even larger *elephantes.* These legumes are very large white or buff-colored beans shaped like large, flattened lima beans (which they are often, wrongly, called; they're actually in the family Phaseolus coccineus, and native to Greece). They are giants in the bean world, at least four or five times as large as a navy bean. Gigandes are still sometimes used to make the soup (you can find them online at www.kalustyans.com). They also commonly appear as a mezze or side dish, merely cooked and marinated in olive oil and lemon. Though less showy, any one of several more readily available and less expensive New World white beans will do just fine, including Great Northern, navy, cannellini, or large limas. Tomatoes are another New World addition to the soup, and they're now universally used (they provide a flirt of tartness, which originally was probably given, in amplified form, with lemon juice). I've cut back the tremendous amount of olive oil typically called for, but a good glug is still essential because (a) the beans are cooked in water, not stock, and thus the olive oil is a major flavor component, and (b) it's part of what makes the dish distinctively Greek. Ve

1½ cups white beans such as gigandes, Great Northern, navy, cannellini, or large limas, picked over, rinsed, soaked overnight (see page 348), and well drained

2 bay leaves

2 carrots, sliced into ½-inch-thick rounds

1 large onion, chopped

1 to 2 cloves garlic, chopped

4 stalks celery with leaves, chopped (or 2 stalks celery and 1 stalk lovage)

1 can (14.5 ounces) chopped plum tomatoes with juice

1 tablespoon tomato paste

1 to 1½ teaspoons dried oregano, preferably Greek (optional)

1 to 2 teaspoons dried mint (optional)

⅓ cup extra-virgin olive oil, plus extra for serving

Salt and freshly ground black pepper

About 3 tablespoons minced fresh parsley leaves, for garnish

Sautéed Haloumi Cheese (recipe follows), for serving

Crusty bread, for serving

1 Place the beans, bay leaves, and 2 quarts (8 cups) water in a large soup pot over high heat. Bring to a boil, reduce the heat to low, cover, and simmer for 30 minutes. Remove the bay leaves.

2 Add the carrots, onion, garlic, and celery and simmer for another 30 minutes.

3 Add the tomatoes, tomato paste, oregano and/or mint (I like both), olive oil, and plenty of salt and pepper to taste (I usually start with 1 teaspoon salt). Simmer until the beans are soft and creamy, but not quite disintegrating, 30 minutes more.

4 Remove the soup from the heat and let it cool slightly. Adjust the seasonings to taste and serve warm or at room temperature, with the parsley and a drizzle of extra olive oil on top.

Serves 4 to 6

Sautéed Haloumi Cheese

Haloumi (sometimes spelled with two l's) cheese is something like a cross between provolone and low-moisture mozzarella. Kashkaval, very similar, can also be used here. Haloumi is traditionally made with a combination of sheep's and goat's milk and is stored in a light brine with its own liquid (as feta and mozzarella are). It's widely eaten throughout Greece, Cyprus, and Turkey. Because it is heated, shaped, and pressed before being brined, it doesn't melt to gooey-ness but can actually be browned in a skillet or on a grill—oh, lovely! When served with fasolada, placed on top as one might place a crisp toast, its firm, browned saltiness and texture set off the slightly sweet, soft starchiness of the beans to perfection. Ve Gf

½ pound haloumi or Kashkaval cheese

Olive oil

Cut the cheese into ⅓- to ½-inch-thick slices (you'll have about six). Brush a skillet with olive oil and place it over high heat. Pan-fry the cheese slices for 3 to 5 minutes on the first side, peeking after 3 to see that the cheese is nicely browned. When it is, flip with a spatula to brown the other side. Serve hot, one slice per bowl of fasolada. As mentioned, haloumi can also be cooked on a medium-hot grill, which gives you those always-appealing brown grill marks.

Serves 4 to 6

CALDO VERDE

This is Portuguese soul food: healthy, hearty, garlicky. A bowl—which, with bread, is a very full meal indeed—will get you through any literal or figurative stormy weather. I found my way to my own take on caldo verde when working on my previous cookbook, *The Cornbread Gospels*; the soup is a classic go-with for the Portuguese-style yeast-risen cornbread called *broa*. For this recipe, I combined a dozen different versions with my own memory of a caldo verde eaten many years ago in Martha's Vineyard. This rich, heady, and complex version—made with meat—is the result. It is followed by a variation for vegetarians.

Did I say this soup is garlicky? Yes, I did—and restoratively so. The recipe calls for 1 cup of garlic cloves. Since garlic heads, and individual cloves, vary greatly in size, you are probably looking at 3 to 4 heads of garlic to get the requisite cup. Although I'm usually fanatical about peeling my own garlic right before use, caldo verde requires so much that using the pre-peeled garlic available in the refrigerator case at the supermarket makes sense. You can make even quicker work of things by chopping the garlic in a food processor. I've simplified the recipe with the use of canned beans, but, of course, you know enough by now to easily substitute soaked and cooked dried beans, right? **Me** **Gf**

Vegetable oil cooking spray

2½ quarts (10 cups) vegetable, beef, or chicken stock, or water

6 to 8 medium potatoes (about 2 pounds), peeled and coarsely chopped

2 bay leaves

¼ teaspoon ground cloves

1 apple (preferably Golden Delicious or Gala), peeled, cored, and halved

About 1 cup peeled garlic cloves (yes, you read this right), finely chopped

3 to 4 tablespoons olive oil

2 onions, chopped

¾ pound fresh chorizo sausage, removed from its casing and crumbled

½ to 1½ teaspoons crushed red pepper flakes, or to taste

1 to 2 teaspoons Hungarian paprika (preferably smoked)

1 pound kale, tough center ribs removed, cut crosswise into thin ribbons

1 can (10 ounces) diced tomatoes in juice

2 cans (15 ounces each) white beans, either navy or Great Northern

Salt and freshly ground black pepper

2 to 3 lemons, quartered lengthwise

1   Spray a large, heavy soup pot with the vegetable oil, add the stock, and set it over high heat. Bring it to a boil, turn down the heat to medium, and drop in the potatoes, bay leaves, cloves, apple, and about half the garlic. Let simmer, half-covered, until the potatoes and apple are fairly soft, about 20 minutes.

2   Meanwhile, heat the olive oil in a skillet over medium heat. Add the onions and sauté, stirring, until softened, about 5 minutes. Add the chorizo, lower the heat slightly, and continue sautéing until the chorizo is browned and has rendered most of its fat (which you may drain off if you like), a few minutes more. Add the remaining garlic, the crushed red pepper, and the paprika and cook, stirring, for 1 minute more. Turn off the heat.

3   Back at the soup pot, scoop out about half of the cooked potatoes and some apple pieces (much of the apple may simply have dissolved into the soup) and transfer them to a heat-proof bowl. Mash these together using a potato masher or the back of a wooden spoon.

4   Scrape the chorizo mixture into the soup pot. Spoon a little of the simmering potato broth into the skillet, set it over high heat, and bring the broth to a boil. Scrape the bottom of the skillet with a wooden spoon to loosen any browned bits, then pour this into the soup pot.

5   Add the kale to the soup pot and simmer, giving the occasional stir, until it is nice and tender, about 15 minutes. Stir in the mashed potato-apple mixture and

the tomatoes and beans. Bring to a full boil, then turn back down to a slow simmer.

6   Let the soup simmer another 15 minutes, then season it with salt and pepper to taste (lots and lots of black pepper; in my view, the more the better), and serve. If you eat it right away, it'll be great; cool it overnight and reheat it the next day, and it'll be even better. Pass the lemons at the table; some like to squeeze a little lemon juice into the soup.

Serves 6 to 8

VARIATION

Vegetarian Caldo Verde: I can almost hear the Portuguese fishermen snorting, but this is great. Follow the recipe above, using vegetable stock or water as the cooking liquid and substituting vegetarian chorizo, such as Field Roast, Lightlife, or Tofurky Chorizo, for the traditional meat sausage. Sauté the soysage separately in olive oil until browned; then slice it and add it just before serving. Vn

A RESTORATIVE PORTUGUESE REPAST

Grilled fresh sardines

★

Caldo Verde with crusty corbread

★

Rice pudding with cinnamon

★

Black coffee, Madeira

Spanish-style

SPLIT PEA SOUP

(Potage de Guisante Barcelona)

An old favorite with a lot of personal history. Back in the days when I lived in Arkansas and owned an inn, Dairy Hollow House, we had an annual staff holiday party, usually on Christmas Eve or the evening before (which we began calling "Christmas Adam"). Each year, we chose a different nationality and everyone scurried to the cookbook section of the Carnegie Library, did their research, and brought a dish from the chosen country. In 1989, the feast was Spanish.

This soup had its starting point with a recipe in Myra Waldo's *International Encyclopedia of Cooking,* but went on to be influenced by Colman Andrews's description of techniques in his then just-published *Catalan Cuisine.* I can't vouch for its authenticity, but as I wrote in *Dairy Hollow House Soup & Bread,* "It was extremely popular: Two cooks, four inn guests, and most of the party attendees requested the recipe."

The relatively large number of onions—one cooked with the peas, three sautéed *sofrito*-style—is a big part of what makes this soup so special. Why frozen spinach? It's easier. I've made it with fresh, and you know, you can't even tell the difference in the completed soup. `Vn` `Gf`

Vegetable oil cooking spray

2 cups dried split peas

2 quarts (8 cups) well-flavored vegetable
  stock or chicken broth

4 large onions: 1 sliced, 3 chopped

2 carrots, sliced

5 cloves garlic: 2 whole, 3 minced or pressed

2 bay leaves

1 box (10 ounces) frozen chopped spinach,
  thawed

Salt

¼ cup olive oil

6 fresh tomatoes, stemmed and chopped
  (or 2½ cups canned diced tomatoes,
  preferably fire-roasted, in juice)

2 tablespoons thinly sliced fresh basil leaves

2 tablespoons minced fresh parsley,
  plus extra for garnish

Freshly ground black pepper

1. Spray a large, heavy soup pot with oil and set it over high heat. In it, combine the peas, stock, sliced onion, carrots, the 2 whole cloves garlic, and the bay leaves. Bring to a boil, lower the heat to a simmer, and cook, partially covered, for 1 hour. Add the spinach and season with salt (I recommend at least 1 teaspoon). Continue simmering for another 30 minutes, then let cool slightly. Remove the bay leaves and, in batches, buzz the soup in a food processor until smooth. Transfer the pureed soup back to the pot and keep warm, covered, over low heat.

2. Meanwhile, heat the olive oil in a large skillet over medium heat. Add the chopped onions and sauté, stirring, until they start to soften, 3 to 4 minutes. Turn down the heat to medium-low and continue sautéing until the onions are wilted, another 6 to 8 minutes. Turn the heat down and continue cooking, stirring often, until the onions are meltingly soft and caramelized, about 10 minutes more. (Watch the onions closely and stir often during the last 10 minutes to make sure they don't burn.)

3. Add the tomatoes to the onions and, increasing the heat to medium-low, cook, stirring often, until the liquid is reduced and the mixture is very thick and almost pastelike (you may need to reduce the heat as the liquid evaporates). Depending on how juicy the tomatoes are, this could be 8 to 12 minutes. Turn off the heat.

4. Add the minced garlic, basil, parsley, and plenty of black pepper to the onion mixture and stir to combine. Stir this mixture (called *sofregit,* and a seasoning staple of Spanish cuisine) into the pureed split pea soup.

5. Serve the soup at once, piping hot and garnished with additional parsley, or refrigerate it overnight for next-day reheating (it's hard to imagine, but it will taste even better).

Serves 6 to 8

"The anxiety to eat [peas], the pleasure of having eaten them and the desire to eat them again, are the three great matters that have been discussed by our princes for the past four days."

—Marquise de Maintenon, belle lettriste and mistress of Louis XIV, 1696

BEAN SOUPS OF THE AMERICAS

I t is a marvel to consider the plump lima bean; the shiny black bean; the cream-colored soldier bean with its yellow eye; the Holstein-like spotted black-and-white anasazi bean; the pied, speckled pinquito, pinto, nightfall, and rattlesnake beans; the plain-Jane navy bean; as well as fresh green (string) beans, which may be not just green but yellow and even a deep purple-black (a hue they shed, reverting to green during cooking). All of these are in the same vast, friendly, common family, Phaseolus. That family's antecedents grew wild, from what's now northern Mexico clear south to the Peruvian Andes, and over time evolved and were developed into all these variations. Why the multiplicity of forms? Because of bean plants' own adjustments to differing soils and climates, and because of alterations humans made by carefully selecting, over generations, the seeds of those plants that most suited their purposes in terms of yield, flavor, growing habit, ability to be stored, and so on.

The wonder that is Phaseolus is only one prize in a treasure chest of New World ingredients, including tomatoes, squashes, peppers, chiles, potatoes, and corn. Any and all of these often, and satisfyingly, find their way into bowls of soup in North, South, and Central America and the Caribbean, too.

ↄ ↄ ↄ

U.S. Senate
NAVY BEAN SOUP

D o you ever get cravings for a particular dish, only to discover you don't have the ingredients in your cupboard, or that the restaurant to which you've come with high expectations has taken it off the menu? If so, you can relate to the outburst of Speaker of the House Joseph G. Cannon (R, Illinois; 1903–11). One hot, damp summer day, the cooks at the Senate restaurant (yes, in addition to great health care, the senators have their own restaurant, with eleven dining rooms) understandably decided to nix the hot, damp navy bean soup that had *usually* been served there since an Idaho senator, Fred Dubois, had expressed a fondness for it during his term, which ran from 1901 to 1907.

"Thunderation!" Cannon is said to have expostulated that warm and hungry noon. "I had my mind set for bean soup. From now on, hot or cold, rain, snow, or shine, I want it on the menu every day." And so it has been for more than one hundred years: A 1907 resolution introduced by Minnesota's senator Knute Nelson states that while the Senate is in session, bean soup *must* be served daily, regardless of weather. Was Nelson trying to suck up to Cannon? Was he, too, a bean soup fan? And what of the contribution of that earlier Idaho senator who suggested the humble soup in the first place (with the addition of mashed potatoes, of course)?

Of these apocryphal stories "none," says the Senate's website primly, "has been corroborated." Here's the official recipe with one change: soaking the beans overnight (if they did this in the Senate kitchen, perhaps some of the discussions might be less windy). **Me** **Gf**

2 pounds dried navy beans, picked over, rinsed, and soaked overnight (see page 380)

3 to 4 quarts hot water

1½ pounds smoked ham hocks, rinsed

2 tablespoons butter

1 onion, chopped

Salt and freshly ground black pepper

1 Rinse and drain the beans. Place them in a large, heavy soup pot over high heat and add 3 quarts of the hot water and the ham hocks. Bring to a boil, then turn down the heat to low and simmer, covered, stirring occasionally, until the beans are very soft and the mixture is quite thick, 2 to 3 hours.

2 Fish out the ham hocks and set them aside to cool a bit. Meanwhile, melt the butter in a large skillet over medium heat. Add the onion and sauté, stirring, until it is limp but not brown, about 6 minutes. Scrape the onion and any residual butter into the still-simmering bean soup. Let cook for another 30 minutes.

3 When the ham hocks have cooled to where you can handle them, pick the meat from the bones (discard the bones) and dice it into bite-size pieces. Return the meat to the soup. Taste, seasoning with salt and pepper. The soup can be served at once, kept warm in a slow-cooker, or cooled and refrigerated, to be reheated the next day.

Serves 8

VARIATIONS

Slightly Jazzed-Up Senate Bean Soup: As you can see, the above recipe is plain as plain can be. Even when I still ate meat, I could hardly bring myself to eat it as is. I'd add a bay leaf or two, maybe a dried chile, to the simmering beans; I'd add a few sliced carrots and some celery and garlic to the sauté. That made me and my guests happy, as we are today with my vegetarian version, below.

Vegetarian Jazzed-Up Senate Bean Soup: Omit the ham hocks (duh), use vegetable stock instead of water, and add 1 to 2 bay leaves and a dried chile to the simmering beans. Sauté 2 chopped carrots and 2 chopped celery stalks in the butter (or olive oil, if you prefer) along with the onion. Stir in the sauté with 2 cloves pressed garlic and a heaping tablespoon of golden miso toward the end. A small shake of liquid smoke or Bacon Salt (see box, page 112) is optional but good. Another way to go: Sauté some vegetarian sausage, dice it, and stir it in last. **Ve**

Senate Bean Soup à la Fred Dubois: Follow either of the two variations above, using a little extra liquid to simmer the beans. At the end, stir in a cup or so of leftover creamy mashed potatoes. This, with the vegetarian version? Now we're talking! **Ve**

Locro: This is an Argentinean navy bean soup with a lot of wallop, but it begins like the plainer Senate soup. Use ¼ pound smoky bacon (*not* rinsed), diced, in lieu of the ham hocks. When the beans have cooked for 2 hours, stir in a peeled, seeded, diced butternut squash and the kernels cut from 3 ears of corn (or 1½ cups frozen corn kernels). At about this point, sauté 8 ounces fresh or smoked spicy chorizo (reserve the rendered fat in the pan), let it cool slightly,

slice it, and stir it into the soup. In step 2, sauté the onion in the same pan in which you sautéed the chorizo, using the rendered chorizo fat and 2 tablespoons vegetable oil in place of the butter. After the onion has started to soften, add 1 large diced red bell pepper. When it, too, is limp, stir in 1 teaspoon smoked sweet Hungarian paprika, ¾ teaspoon cayenne, and ½ teaspoon ground cumin. Scrape the onion mixture into the simmering locro, then swirl a little water in the sauté pan to deglaze it; pour this liquid into the soup. Let the soup simmer for at least 40 minutes after adding the seasonings, then serve sprinkled with a little minced scallion on top. Some also cook locro with browned stew beef, simmering in the pot alongside the beans. **Me Gf**

Vegetarian Locro: Omit the meat and use veggie chorizo, sautéed, sliced, and added at the end. Double the onion, bell pepper, and spices. **Vn**

Jerry Stamp's Great Bean & Corn Chowder: My old friend Jerry was Eureka Springs's beloved pharmacist for many years and also a fine home cook with a wicked laugh. He made the wedding cake for me and my late husband, Ned, too. This soup was one of his specialties. In the last hour of simmering the beans, add a bay leaf and a good pinch of cayenne, plus a teaspoon each of the following dried herbs: basil, oregano, rosemary, thyme, and savory. Sauté ¼ pound or so sliced mushrooms with the onion in step 2, and add them to the soup along with the onion. In that last 30 minutes of simmering in step 3, stir in 1 can (15 ounces) diced tomatoes and their juice, 1 to 2 cups corn (fresh or frozen niblets), 2 cloves pressed garlic, and, if you like, ½ pound or so very thinly sliced summer sausage or sautéed vegetarian sausage. **Ve** or **Me Gf**

(Re)name that Ingredient!

Back when I ran the Restaurant at Dairy Hollow, I'd "make the rounds," as my late husband used to put it, after dessert went out. This meant going from table to table, having changed into a clean chef's jacket, and visiting briefly with the guests at each table. Guests told me what they'd liked, where they were from, how they'd heard of the inn. Sometimes they asked me to sign one of their books. Though I always dreaded switching gears—a restaurant kitchen and the front of the house are two different planets—once I'd actually landed, I thoroughly enjoyed these conversations, which occasionally were very funny.

One night, a well-dressed woman from Little Rock looked up at me and said, with some awe, as if recounting a conversion experience, "You know, because of you, *I have nutritional yeast in my kitchen.*"

Nutritional yeast needs a name makeover in the worst way. First off, it's *not* the type of yeast you use to leaven bread or ferment beer; though related botanically to the latter, brewer's yeast, it's deactivated (nonleavening). It has a taste and savor somewhat akin to that of Parmesan cheese (though a wholly different texture) and is a golden-brown, flaky powder that easily dissolves in liquids.

Now, its predecessor was deactivated brewer's yeast, a nutritional powerhouse that tasted terrible. Some blessed chemist or scientist must have decided *there had to be a better way*. And there was, and is: today's nutritional yeast, the yeast whose Latin name is *Saccharomyces cerevisiae.* It is grown specifically for culinary use. Cultured on a mixture of sugarcane and beet molasses, it's harvested, rinsed, dehydrated, and packaged. By this time, it's become those dry golden flakes, familiar and loved by those of us who know and use them, available at most natural foods supermarkets. Red Star is one widely available brand, and it is very, very good.

The whole thing sounds surpassingly strange, I know, until you remember that yeasts are part of so many of our well-loved foods. Wine, beer, bread (especially sourdough), vinegar, cheeses, miso—yeasts make them what they are. And yeasts are fungi; think of the savoriness of, for instance, shiitake mushrooms. It doesn't strike us as strange that we'd add wine to a soup or sauce that needed a little something, and that that wine would not only supply a flavor of its own but meld with and amplify the other ingredients.

Because nutritional yeast is so flavorsome but not animal-derived, vegans and vegetarians are often special fans. But truly, anyone who gets to know it will be happy with the discovery. A few quick ways to use it:

★ in almost any broth or sauce that needs some oomph; it gives a loosely chicken-y taste

★ sprinkled over salted, buttered popcorn (I knew I was living where I belonged when I saw that the Latchis Theatre, Brattleboro's downtown movie venue, had a container of nutritional yeast out for customer use)

★ in cooked oatmeal served in a savory style, almost risotto-ish, doctored with butter, tamari, nutritional yeast, and Parmesan

★ in macaroni & cheese; you can use much less cheese and still have as much or more flavor

DEE'S LUMBERJACK SOUP

A potent potage, deeply hearty, this lives up to its name. It's a *very* meaty soup containing ham, chicken, and Polish sausage. A bowlful is easily a filling meal, especially with a side of bread or maybe corn muffins. A vegetarian version follows; though meatless, it, too, is plenty hearty.

This is also a soup of two Eurekas. How's this for provenance? It was given to me, handwritten on a file card, by Delphine (Dee) Mulvahill. Dee's the mother and mother-in-law, respectvely, of King (RIP) and Grace Gladden, friends from back in my old hometown, Eureka Springs, Arkansas. Dee, in turn, was given the recipe back in the 1980s, by Fern, an old friend of hers who for many years lived and taught school in Eureka, California. Think how many miles this soup traveled to reach you, and how many friends it linked along the way! Think, too, of Fern, who would be more than a hundred years old now if she were still alive. Perhaps some bit of her spiritual DNA comes to life with each batch of this soup, the steam reaching up toward heaven, a nourishing, useful, earthy incense.

According to Dee, Fern's original recipe made "a vat." I have cut it down to a more manageable size and tweaked it a bit. The soup takes a while to cook, so get started early in the day. **Me** **Gf**

½ cup navy beans, picked over, soaked overnight (see page 350), and rinsed

½ cup kidney or pinto beans, picked over, soaked overnight, and rinsed

½ cup lentils, picked over and rinsed

½ cup split peas, picked over and rinsed

1 smoked ham hock, rinsed

1 dried chile pepper

1 can (14 ounces) diced tomatoes in juice

2 stalks celery, diced

1 large onion, diced

2 cloves garlic, pressed

Salt and freshly ground black pepper

2 boneless, skinless chicken breasts, diced into ½-inch pieces

¼ pound Polish sausage (kielbasa)

¾ cup hearty red wine, such as Beaujolais or Bordeaux

Chicken broth, vegetable stock, or water (optional)

½ cup minced fresh Italian (flat-leaf) parsley

1 Combine the navy beans, kidney beans, lentils, split peas, ham hock, chile, and 1½ quarts (6 cups) water in a large, heavy soup pot over high heat. Bring to a boil, then reduce the heat to low and simmer, covered, stirring occasionally, until the beans are

very tender, about 3 hours. Remove what's left of the ham hock (some of the meat will have fallen off the bone) and set it aside.

2 Add the tomatoes, celery, onion, and garlic. Cover and cook for 30 minutes more, then lift the lid and season with salt and pepper to taste. Pick off any meat remaining on the ham hock (discard the bone), chop it, and stir it back into the soup. Add the chicken, stir well, cover, and simmer for another 30 minutes.

3 Meanwhile, during this last simmer, sauté the Polish sausages in a skillet over medium heat until they're well browned on all sides. Remove the sausages from the skillet, slice them, and add to the simmering soup along with the red wine. If the soup seems too thick, dilute it to your liking with a little chicken broth, vegetable stock, or water.

4 At the end of this final simmer, stir the soup well and add the fresh parsley. Folks are probably congregating hungrily in the kitchen by now, drawn by their noses. You may feed them immediately, serving the soup hot in heated bowls.

Serves 10 to 12

VARIATIONS

Dee's Version: "I always add a tablespoon of diced fresh ginger to all dried bean soups," writes Dee, "to minimize flatulation." She puts it in right at the start, as the beans begin cooking. **Me** **Gf**

Vegetarian Lumberjack Soup: Cook the beans as directed in step 1, but omit the ham hock. Use a dried chipotle pepper for the chile, to add smokiness. In step 2, add ⅓ cup good-tasting nutritional yeast (see box, page 109) along with the vegetables; it will dissolve into the broth deliciously. Omit the chicken and replace the meat sausage with 1 pound vegetarian kielbasa (Tofurky makes a good one): Brown the sausage, slice it, and after the wine is added, stir it into the soup. **Vn**

ჟ   ჟ   ჟ

Ruth's Southern Country-style
GREEN BEAN SOUP

Ruth Eichor was a tiny lady, and there was definitely more mischief in her than that little body could have held. She lived in a stone house tucked away in the trees at the curvy, hidden-away, far dead-end of an unpaved street in the city of Eureka Springs, Arkansas. Unless you were told that that house existed and were given directions, you would never have believed there was anything there. Ned, my late husband, met Ruth through the Preservation Society and was delighted to discover that she was the ultimate "primary source":

an enthusiastic very old storyteller, sharp as a push-pin and gifted with a long memory. In her mind (and mouth), events of fifty years earlier were as gossip-worthy and scandalous as if they'd taken place the day before.

Long before I knew her, Ruth had run a small café. She was still an excellent cook, and she told me about her habit of fixing supper at home by basically putting everything compatible on hand into a skillet or casserole dish, heating it up with cheese or breadcrumbs on the top, and serving it. Her children and grandchildren loved these concoctions and would periodically beg her to remember how she'd done a particular one. "'But what *is* it?' they'd ask and I'd say, 'Oh, I don't know, just what we had,' and they'd roll their eyes and say, 'Oh, it's one of Mother's Messes again.'"

This potato-thickened, slow-cooked green bean soup is one of Ruth's honest-to-goodness recipes, too simple to be so very good. It's a homey, end-of-summer supper, just made for the moment when your garden or local market overflows with green beans. Evaporated milk gives richness while keeping it relatively low in fat (well, if the recipe didn't also include bacon and butter). It's affordable and fairly easy to pull together from fridge and pantry staples. Ruth made it for her family with bacon and butter, but for Ned and me, I made it with butter only. I later amended this vegetarian version with Bacon Salt (see below) for a bit of smokiness. **Me** **Gf** or **Ve**

1½ pounds fresh green beans, tipped, tailed, and sliced into ⅔-inch pieces

1½ pounds potatoes, cut in medium-size chunks (Ruth peeled hers; I never do)

¼ pound bacon, chopped (optional)

1 large onion, chopped

1 stalk celery, chopped

1 tablespoon butter (use 3 tablespoons or more if you omit the bacon)

Salt and freshly ground black pepper

Bacon Salt (optional)

1 can (12 ounces) evaporated whole or skim milk

No-Bacon Bacon Salt

Bacon Salt is a seasoned salt that's meatless (though it does contain wheat) and adds just the right smoky touch. It's available at www.baconsalt.com; I use the hickory flavor.

1 In a large, heavy soup pot, combine the green beans, potatoes, bacon (if using), onion, and celery. Add 2 quarts (8 cups) water—it will just barely cover the ingredients—and set over high heat.

Bring to a boil, then turn down to a simmer and cook, covered, until the beans are very soft and the potatoes are on the edge of disintegrating, about 1 hour.

2 Using a potato masher, coarsely mash up some of the green beans and potatoes. You certainly don't want this smooth, but you want enough of it mashed so the consistency is soupy but thickened. Season to taste with the salt and pepper, and, if you omitted actual bacon, some Bacon Salt.

3 Just before serving, make sure the soup is nice and hot, pour in the evaporated milk, and stir well. Heat through, mindfully; don't let it boil (the milk will curdle). Serve hot, right away. (If you have leftovers, or want to do the soup ahead of time and reheat it the next day—Ruth felt it got even better on the second day, as do many soups, and she was right—remember to reheat carefully, adding the milk at the end.)

Serves 6 to 8

VARIATIONS

Ruth's Southern Country-style Green Bean Soup by Slow Cooker: This is a perfect candidate for the slow-cooker. Follow the directions for the recipe, cooking the soup on high for about an hour, even two. About 1½ hours into the cooking, do the mashing described in step 2. Turn the heat to low and let cook 2 to 3 hours longer. Me or Ve Gf

Ruth's Southern Country-style Squash, Green Bean & Potato Soup: About 30 minutes into step 1, add 2 cups peeled, diced butternut squash; delicious. Me or Ve Gf

Ruth's Southern Country-style Butter Bean & Green Bean Soup with Potatoes: Heartier, more main-dishy. The night before, pick over, rinse, and soak

(see page 350) ½ cup dried lima beans. The next morning, drain and rinse them and place them in a large, heavy soup pot with 3 cups water or unsalted vegetable stock or chicken broth. Bring to a boil, turn down to a simmer, and let cook, covered, until the beans are pretty close to tender, about 1 hour. At this point, add the green beans, potatoes, et cetera, and follow the directions as given. Me or Ve Gf

Ruth's "And if you have people drop in at supper" Southern Country-style Soup: "I just throw in an extra can of evaporated milk and a whole stick of butter. Yes, even if I've used that bacon. I didn't grow up worrying about cholesterol, Crescent, and I'm not going to start now." Me or Ve Gf

Crescent's Vegan Take on Ruth's Southern Country-style Green Bean Soup with Potatoes: Omit the bacon. Substitute vegan margarine or your favorite oil for the larger quantity of butter. Season with the Bacon Salt and use ¾ cup plain, unsweetened soy milk or oat milk instead of the evaporated milk. Brown up a package of Lightlife's Fakin' Bacon Smoked Tempeh Strips in a skillet. Dice 'em up, then add them after you've mashed up the vegetables in step 2. Vn

REMEMBERING RUTH

Sliced tomatoes from the garden

★

Ruth's Southern Country-style Green Bean Soup

★

Dairy Hollow House Skillet-Sizzled Buttermilk Cornbread biscuits (page 167)

★

Butter, blackberry jam

★

Baked apples

My Mother's 1950s-Elegant
BLACK BEAN SOUP

T imeless ingredients though they are, beans have traveled up and down the ladder of social acceptance in America. In the 1950s, they were decidedly déclassé; it was an era when "gourmet" and "continental," not "fresh, local, seasonal," were the calling cards of discerning diners. It was a time when beef Stroganoff, steak Diane, tidbits rumaki, lobster Thermidor or Newburg—high-fat, fancied-up dishes—were de rigueur for dinner parties. Beans? Definitely out.

Unless they were black beans, that is, in black bean soup, with sherry. This unlikely potage gained prestige by appearing for forty-four years on the menu of the Coach House, Leon Lianides's famous four-star restaurant, a New York institution that opened in 1950. My mother, inspired by the Coach House, came up with her "company" black bean soup, which she also sherried and then dressed up with two of her favorite ingredients, lemon and minced fresh parsley. It was and is seriously good! **Ve** or **Me**

FOR THE BEANS:

1 pound dried black beans, picked over, rinsed, and soaked overnight (see page 344)

1 quart (4 cups) *unsalted* chicken broth or vegetable stock

1 large onion, skin and all, studded with 4 whole cloves

¼ teaspoon ground allspice

¼ teaspoon dried thyme

2 cloves garlic, finely chopped

1 bay leaf

FOR THE SAUTÉ AND THICKENING:

¼ cup (½ stick) butter

1 large onion, finely chopped

1 to 2 stalks celery, finely chopped

2 tablespoons unbleached all-purpose flour

2 to 3 tablespoons ketchup (optional)

FOR THE GARNISH AND FINISHING TOUCHES:

Salt and freshly ground black pepper

⅔ cup dry sherry or Madeira

2 lemons (preferably organic), thinly sliced and seeded, for serving

3 hard-boiled eggs, sliced, for serving

About ¼ cup finely chopped fresh curly parsley

1 Prepare the beans: Drain and rinse the black beans well. Transfer them to a large, heavy soup pot and add 1 quart (4 cups) water, the stock, whole onion, allspice, thyme, garlic, and bay leaf. Bring to a boil, then turn down the heat to a simmer and let the beans cook, covered, until they are almost tender, 1½ to 2 hours. Check them once in a while, perhaps adding a little more water or stock if they look too dry.

2 Toward the end of this period, melt about 2 tablespoons of the butter in a large skillet over medium heat. Add the chopped onion and sauté, stirring until it is soft and translucent but not browned, about 5 minutes. Add the celery and sauté for another 3 minutes, then scrape the sauté into the beans and let cook until the beans are quite tender, another hour or so. Don't wash the sauté skillet just yet.

3 Turn off the heat under the beans and let them cool to lukewarm. Fish out the whole onion with its cloves, as well as the bay leaf; discard. Strain off and reserve most of the bean liquid. Transfer the cooled beans, in batches, to a food processor. Adding a little bean liquid as needed, buzz them until smooth. Return the pureed beans and all but 2 cups of the bean liquid to the soup pot.

4 Now, in the sauté skillet, melt the remaining butter over medium-low heat. Whisk in the flour and cook slowly, stirring often, until it is a light toasty brown. Gradually whisk in the reserved bean liquid and cook, stirring, until slightly thickened, about 3 minutes. Transfer this mixture to the puree in the soup pot, along with the ketchup, if using. (The ketchup gives a tiny hint of sweetness and deepens the color, but some prefer the soup without it.)

5 Reheat the bean soup over low heat, and when it is hot, taste it for salt and pepper. It will need quite a bit of salt, since the beans were cooked without it. Good, eh?

6 The soup is now ready to serve, ideally in warmed bowls or soup cups. Pour a tablespoon or so of sherry in the bottom of each bowl and add a slice of lemon and a couple of slices of hard-boiled egg. Ladle the piping-hot soup over this, and top with another lemon slice and a sprinkle of parsley. Pass the remaining sherry at the table, for each person to doctor his or her own bowl.

Serves 6

VARIATION

Coach House–style Black Bean Soup (meatist): Omit the thyme. Follow step 1, boiling the beans, stock, cloved onion, allspice, and garlic for 1½ hours. At this time, add both a hefty beef bone and a smoked ham hock. Continue to cook for another 30 minutes. In step 2, fry 5 slices bacon over medium heat. Drain the cooked bacon on paper towels, making sure to leave some bacon fat in the skillet. Instead of using butter, sauté the chopped onion in the bacon fat. As in the original recipe, add the celery, cook it, and scrape it into the bean pot. Add 2 chopped carrots and 1 chopped parsnip directly to the pot as well. Continue simmering the beans, covered, for another 30 minutes.

After you turn off the heat under the beans in step 3, remove the whole cloved onion *and* the meat and bones. Chop the ham fine. Crumble the bacon from step 2 and combine with the ham. Strain and reserve the cooking liquid, but puree about half of the beans in the food processor, instead of all of them. In step 4, whisk the flour into the remaining bacon fat, and thicken with the reserved bean stock. Add the thickened liquid back to the bean pot, along with the processed beans. Omit the optional ketchup, but add the bacon and ham mixture. Use salt sparingly; the meat will already contain quite a bit. Finish the soup in the same way, but omit the lemon in step 6. **Me**

New South–style

SPICY COLLARD & BLACK-EYED PEA SOUP

Traditional Southern bean soups are usually pretty plain and simple; basically, they're ham hock–enriched soups (like the U.S. Senate Navy Bean Soup on page 106) made with black-eyes, crowder peas, or other favored legumes. These soups have their partisans, especially among those who grew up on them. But I prefer this spicy potage, which weds many beloved Southern vegetables with comforting black-eyed peas and a slight chile kick and has, to my taste, more verve than the standard. If you care for still more kick, either toss a dried chile in with the beans while they cook, sauté a fresh one with the bell pepper and celery, or add cayenne to taste at the end. Serve the soup with cornbread, or stir a few tablespoons of cooked rice into each bowlful, and you'll have very happy diners. **Vn** **Gf**

2 cups dried black-eyed peas, picked over and rinsed

1½ quarts (6 cups) water or unsalted vegetable stock or chicken broth

3 tablespoons mild vegetable oil (such as corn, peanut, or canola) or butter

2 onions, coarsely chopped

2 stalks celery, coarsely chopped

1 green bell pepper, coarsely chopped

3 to 4 cloves garlic, minced

1 can (14.5 ounces) diced tomatoes with green chiles (preferably fire-roasted), with their liquid

1 large or 2 medium sweet potatoes (preferably Red Garnets), peeled and diced

1 teaspoon salt, plus extra as needed

Freshly ground black pepper

½ pound collard greens or kale, tough center stems removed, halved lengthwise and then cut crosswise into very thin ribbons

Minced fresh parsley, for garnish

Vinegar-y commercial hot sauce, such as Tabasco or Frank's RedHot, for serving

1 Place the beans and the water or stock in a large soup pot over high heat. Bring to a boil, then turn down to a medium simmer, cover, and cook until barely tender, 45 minutes to 1 hour.

2 Meanwhile, toward the end of the cooking time, heat the oil in a large skillet over medium-high heat. Add the onions and cook, stirring, until softened but not browned, about 5 minutes. Add the celery and green pepper and sauté for about 8 minutes more. Add the garlic and cook until just becoming fragrant, 1 minute. Stir in the tomatoes and heat through, scraping the bottom of the skillet with a wooden spoon to mix any little flavory bits into the tomato.

3 Add the onion mixture to the beans along with the sweet potato, 1 teaspoon salt, and pepper to taste. Raise the heat to a boil again, then turn it down to a medium simmer and cook, covered, until the sweet potato starts to soften, 10 minutes. Add the greens, re-cover, and cook until the greens are wilted and somewhat tender, another 10 to 15 minutes.

4 Taste for seasonings; you may well need a bit more salt, and be generous with the black pepper, too. Serve hot, or let cool, refrigerate, then reheat and eat the next day, when it'll be even better. Garnish the soup with parsley, and pass hot sauce at the table.

Serves 6 to 8

Day-After-Thanksgiving
TURKEY, WILD RICE & RATTLESNAKE BEAN SOUP

Similar to pintos, the heirloom rattlesnake bean is a variety that's been grown in the Southwest since time out of mind. The two beans look similar, but where the pinto has a pinkish background, the rattlesnake is more golden or buff, with its striations and mottling a deep reddish brown. Some hypothesize that it got its name because of its twisty vining habit, but most pole beans are also twisty and vining, so that seems like a stretch. What's not a stretch is that the rattlesnake is a nicely tender, plump bean, with a flavor some describe as pintolike, but a little more intense. That's about right, though you could certainly substitute pintos for rattlesnakes.

I confess part of the reason I like this bean is for its looks and captivating name. But it's more than that: In this robust potage—so soul-satisfying at the dark, gray time around Thanksgiving—it meets up with two other American natives, wild rice and turkey. The result is something rich, dark, unusual, fragrant, and deeply flavorful—unforgettable, inn guests used to tell me.

If you make this around Thanksgiving time, I suggest you make a good, rich turkey stock with the turkey carcass, onions, and carrots (you can buy turkey stock, too, if that's easier). And, when you're packing up the leftovers from the feast, save one or two (or more) cups of turkey gravy—the soup's secret ingredient—and some turkey fat if you have it. If there's leftover turkey, you can dice it and add at the end to make this soup even heartier. **Me**

---

2 cups rattlesnake beans, picked over, rinsed, and soaked overnight (see page 352)

2 quarts (8 cups) turkey stock (preferably homemade)

¾ cup wild rice

2 to 3 tablespoons congealed turkey fat, if available, or butter

1 large onion, coarsely chopped

2 carrots, coarsely chopped

2 tablespoons tomato paste

About 3 tablespoons port or dry sherry

1 to 2 cups turkey gravy (preferably homemade)

Salt and freshly ground black pepper

Minced fresh parsley, for garnish (optional)

---

1 Drain the beans, place them in a heavy soup pot, and add water to cover to a depth of 1½ inches. Set the pot over high heat, bring it to a boil, then turn down the heat to a simmer, cover tightly, and cook until the beans are barely tender, about 1 hour and 15 minutes. Check periodically to see if you need more water; you want enough water to keep the beans cooking and certainly to prevent them from burning, but less than usual. The turkey stock is yet to come, and it will supply more liquid (and flavor).

2 When the beans are done, but only just, lift the pot lid. Add the turkey stock and the wild rice, and bring everything back up to a boil. Again turn it down to a simmer, cover tightly, and cook until the rice is tender, about 45 minutes.

3 While the wild rice is cooking, heat the turkey fat or butter in a large skillet over medium heat. Add the onion and sauté, stirring often, until it is very limp and golden but not browned, about 8 minutes. Add the carrots and sauté for 3 minutes more. Scrape the onion mixture into the soup pot, along with the tomato paste. Deglaze the skillet with the port, scraping the bottom of the skillet with a wooden spoon to loosen any browned bits. Pour this liquid into the soup along with the turkey gravy.

4 By this point the rice is probably half-cooked, so let everything cook together until it's done. Then add salt and pepper to taste and cook until all the flavors blend, about 15 minutes more.

5 Taste the soup one more time. So much here depends on the quality of your turkey stock and how much gravy you have. It should be full-flavored and thick but not stewlike. You might want to amp up the flavor, if it's not already there, with a little more tomato paste or port, or to thin it with a little extra turkey stock (okay, chicken stock if you've used up all the turkey). Serve the soup with a little minced parsley to add some green, and get ready for the compliments and swoons.

Serves 8 to 10

CD's Very, Very Best
LENTIL, MUSHROOM & BARLEY SOUP

This is my pizzazzed version of the old Eastern European Ashkenazic favorite, and is it ever *good*. With lentils (or yellow split peas, or dried baby limas), and dried and fresh mushrooms of several varieties, it is easily a meal. It's dark, flavorful, and robust, with a broth thickened by cooked-in grain. But its herbal note (fresh dill), interesting sprightliness (white wine), and an indefinable touch of sweetness (the parsnip), besides the fact that it's meatless, make it wholly different. I underline the mushroominess by using mushroom stock, too; you can buy it, boxed, at your local supermarket or natural foods store. Imagine Foods makes a delicious one.

Since this soup is so hearty and brown, try it with something lighter (in texture, not calories) than your classic good crusty bread: warmed brioche, perhaps, or popovers. Add a simple green salad with some bitter greens, very lightly dressed with an assertive vinaigrette . . . when winter seems to have gone on too dishearteningly long, this is the dinner to have. Ve

1 cup lentils, yellow split peas, or quick-soaked baby lima beans (see page 350)

¾ cup pearled barley

1 bay leaf

1½ quarts (6 cups) mushroom stock (you can use vegetable or chicken stock in a pinch)

2 ounces mixed dried porcini and shiitake mushrooms

Boiling water, to rehydrate the dried mushrooms

2 to 3 tablespoons butter

1 large onion, coarsely chopped

2 stalks celery with leaves, coarsely chopped

1 carrot, coarsely chopped

1 small parsnip, peeled and finely chopped

3 to 4 cloves garlic, chopped

2 cups crisp, dry white wine, such as Sauvignon Blanc

1 tablespoon tomato paste

1 pound fresh mushrooms (I usually use about ⅔ pound button mushrooms, the remainder a mix of shiitake, oyster, maitake, baby bellas, or whatever else is available), tough stems removed, coarsely chopped

½ bunch of fresh dill, tough stems removed, chopped, plus a few sprigs for garnish

1 teaspoon salt, or more to taste

Freshly ground black pepper

❶ In a large, heavy soup pot, combine the lentils with 1 quart (4 cups) water, the barley, and the bay leaf. Bring to a full boil, then turn down the heat to a companionable simmer and cook, covered, until the legumes and barley are almost tender; this will take 45 to 50 minutes for lentils, 25 to 30 minutes for yellow split peas, and 50 minutes to 1 hour for baby limas.

❷ Stir in the mushroom stock, bring to a boil, then bring down to a simmer and cover tightly. Continue to cook slowly.

❸ While the lentils and barley are continuing to cook, place the dried mushrooms in a heat-proof bowl, pour in enough boiling water to barely cover them, and set them aside to soak.

❹ Meanwhile, get out a good-size skillet, put it over medium heat, and, when hot, whomp the butter into it. When the butter has melted, lower the heat slightly, add the onion, and cook, stirring often, until the onion is limp and golden but not browned, about 8 minutes. Add the celery, carrot, and parsnip and sauté for 3 minutes more. Turn the heat to low, add the garlic, and sauté for 1 minute. Add the wine and tomato paste and heat, stirring and scraping with a wooden spoon to loosen any browned bits. Stir this onion mixture into the simmering legume-barley mixture.

❺ Carefully strain the dried mushrooms through a coffee filter–lined sieve set over a bowl; reserve both the mushrooms and their soaking liquid (discard the filter and any grit in it). Coarsely chop the rehydrated mushrooms and add them and the reserved soaking liquid to the pot. Add the fresh mushrooms, dill, salt, and black pepper to taste. Stir well, cover, and continue cooking over very low heat until the lentils and barley are very tender, the soup thick, and the ingredients cozy together, about 1 hour. Discard the bay leaf.

❻ When the cooking time is up, you'll have a wonderful thick potage and a steamy kitchen probably full of people wandering around saying, "Is it going to be ready soon?" Oblige them by serving the soup hot, in warmed bowls, with a sprig of dill atop each one.

Serves 4 to 6 as a main dish

"The wise man acts always with reason, and prepares his lentils himself."

—Hardwick's Science-Gossip, *1875*

The Caribbean and Points South

When we consider the leguminous wonders of the soups of South and Central America, Mexico, the Caribbean—goodness, what a lot of ingredients go into the broth! There are foods native to the Americas, treasures far greater than those sought by Cortez's men: tomatoes, peppers, chiles, cocoa, potatoes, corn, quinoa, avocado, squashes, and, of course, beans. And side by side with these ingredients are the effects wrought by Cortez and his fellow conquistadores, which also find their way into the pot: slaughter, pillage, subjugation, and much intermingling of Spanish and indigenous languages, cultures, and religions. With slight variation, the story is the same in every South and Central American country except Brazil (which was colonized by Portugal), with, additionally, the importation of Catholicism as well as slaves.

All this in a bowl of bean soup? Oh, yes—and more. Take the example of Fanesca (below). The beans, the avocado, and quinoa, the annatto-tinted oil: indigenous. The milk and cheese: Well, the foreigners brought dairy cows, as well as salt cod, another prominent ingredient in the soup. Peanut butter? The contribution of Africa, which is to say, slavery. And the fact that it is a once-a-year specialty, eaten at Lent? Catholicism.

So, every bite contains the whole of the world, its good and bad, its contradictions, its nourishment, its confusion, and its fusion: in other words, life, itself.

FANESCA

There's nothing else quite like this multilayered, golden Ecuadorian soup, traditionally made only during Lent. It's meatless, like many traditional Lenten recipes. (Though most versions do contain salt cod, I've given a basic recipe that's vegetarian and offered salt cod as a variation.) But Fanesca is hardly self-denying: It's a rich cream soup made even richer with the addition of cheese and just a tad of peanut butter, and a garnish of avocado and hard-boiled egg. The cream is tinted with annatto oil, and swimming in that creamy orange-gold liquid are a market's worth of green vegetables zip-zapped with Latin spices, made hearty by the addition of a little cooked grain. While fresh shell beans are a constant—usually favas, although baby limas or edamame (my choice) are also delicious—sometimes it also contains cooked dried beans and/or lentils. It's often made with twelve different kinds of beans and grains, representing the twelve apostles. And it's sometimes made with potatoes instead of or in addition to corn. Fanesca is usually pretty thick, but some thin it down with milk or stock (I like it on the thin side myself).

The largesse and complexity of this potage may explain why Ecuadorians make it only once annually, and anticipate it highly. This recipe makes a huge batch; it's enough of a big deal, and contains so many ingredients, that it just doesn't work as a small recipe. Nor does it freeze well. I suggest having a lot of people over for dinner and farming out the traditional accompanying dishes—empanadas, fried plantains, thin-sliced onions marinated in fresh lime juice, sliced chiles, or Ecuadorian hot sauce—to your guests. Fanesca is one of those meals that can hardly be called "light," yet is full of delight. **Ve** **Gf**

FOR THE GRAIN:

About 6 cups milk (preferably whole)

1 cup quinoa or long-grain white rice

1 teaspoon salt, plus more to taste

FOR THE SEASONING SAUTÉ:

3 tablespoons annatto oil
  (see box, page 315)

2 medium onions, coarsely chopped

2 cloves garlic, coarsely chopped

1 teaspoon dried oregano

½ teaspoon ground cumin

1 teaspoon cumin seed

¼ teaspoon cayenne

1 bay leaf

3½ to 4 cups water or vegetable stock

FOR THE VEGETABLES AND BROTH:

3 small or 2 medium-size zucchini, coarsely
  chopped

½ pound green beans, tipped, tailed,
  and cut crosswise in ⅓-inch pieces

1½ cups fresh or frozen corn kernels
  (if fresh, sliced from 2 to 3 ears corn)

⅛ head green cabbage, cored and very
  thinly sliced

1½ cups shelled frozen or fresh edamame

1 cup frozen or hulled fresh green peas

1 cup heavy (whipping) cream, light cream,
  or half-and-half

FOR THE FINISH:

⅓ cup creamy, natural, unhydrogenated
  peanut butter (see box, page 323)

6 ounces queso blanco or Muenster cheese,
  grated (about 1¼ cups)

½ cup fresh cilantro leaves

Freshly ground black pepper

FOR THE GARNISH:

3 hard-boiled eggs, sliced

2 ripe avocados, sliced

① Prepare the grain: Bring 1 cup of the milk and 1 cup water to a boil in a medium saucepan over medium heat. Stir in the quinoa or rice and 1 teaspoon salt, and the second it comes back to a boil, lower the heat to a simmer, cover the pan tightly, and let cook until the grain is tender, 12 to 15 minutes for quinoa about 20 minutes for rice. Turn off the heat and set the cooked grain aside.

2 Make the seasoning sauté: Heat the annatto oil in a large, heavy saucepan over medium heat. Add the onions (they will immediately take on the red-orange annatto coloring) and cook, stirring, until soft, about 5 minutes. Add the garlic, oregano, ground cumin, cumin seed, cayenne, and bay leaf, and sauté for 1 minute. Add 3 ½ cups of the water or vegetable stock and bring to a boil.

3 Stir in all of the vegetables except the peas. Cover, turn the heat down to low, and simmer for 15 minutes.

4 Stir in the peas, cooked grain, the remaining 5 cups milk, and the cream.

(If the soup is too thick for your liking, feel free to add a little extra water, stock, or milk.) Turn up the heat to medium-low and, stirring often, bring up the heat to just under a boil.

5 Finish the soup: Stir in the peanut butter, about a tablespoon at a time, smoothing it in vigorously with a spoon, and smushing any clumps of peanut butter against the side of the pot. Add the cheese, cilantro, and black pepper to taste, and stir well. Discard the bay leaf.

6 Serve hot, in warmed cups or bowls, garnishing each with sliced egg and avocado.

Serves 8 to 10

"When my teachers heard during afternoon classes that after having a *fanesca* for my midday meal I intended to have another one for dinner that evening— at El Maíz, a restaurant that describes its food as Cuencan rather than Ecuadoran—they looked at me the way an American might look at someone who had just announced that he intended to have two Thanksgiving dinners. In a Cuencan home on Good Friday, they explained, a bowl of *fanesca* is a meal in itself, except for something like fruit for dessert, and supper that evening tends to be light. It's true that when I was about halfway through the *fanesca* at Ceres—I'd calculated that I could finish the bowl if I paused for a moment to get my second wind—it occurred to me that this couldn't have been what my mother had in mind when she told me to finish my vegetables. On the other hand, my window of opportunity was not wide. I thought about saying to my teachers, 'So many *fanescas,* so little time,' but by the time I had constructed that in Spanish the moment had passed."

—Calvin Trillin in "Speaking of Soup," an article about fanesca, Cuenca, Equador, and very remedial Spanish, published in The New Yorker, *September 5, 2005*

VARIATIONS

Fanesca with Baccalà: Baccalà, or dried salt cod (available at Sam's Caribbean, www.sams247.com), is very hard and must be soaked before it is used. Begin the night before: Soak 1 pound of salt cod in enough cold water to cover for at least 12 hours (at room temperature) or up to 24 (under refrigeration); change the water every few hours, at least 4 times. (Some use whole milk for the last soaking for extra mildness and a creamy note; soaking tames the saltiness and bitterness of the fish.) Drain the soaked fish and place it in a saucepan with enough fresh water (some use milk here, too) to cover. Bring it to a boil and then lower the heat to a simmer and cook until the fish is tender, 10 to 15 minutes. Reserve the cooking liquid and use as much as you like in the soup (to replace either the water or milk). When the fish is cool enough to handle, remove and discard any bones or skin and cut it into ½-inch pieces. Divide the fish among the bowls, then ladle the soup on top. **Me** **Gf**

Apostolic Fanesca: The idea here is to have a total of 12 beans and grains (as in the twelve apostles). My basic version has 2 grains (corn and quinoa or rice) and 3 beans (the nontraditional edamame, green beans, and peas). So, you'll need 7—yes, 7—other types of beans. Soak together overnight (see page 15) ½ cup chickpeas, ½ cup pinto beans, and ½ cup lima beans. In the morning, drain and rinse them, cover with 1 quart fresh water, bring to a boil, turn down the heat, and simmer for 1½ hours until everything is not quite tender (the chickpeas will still be firmish). Stir in ¼ cup black-eyed peas and ¼ cup pigeon peas and let simmer for another half hour. Lastly, add 2 tablespoons each brown and red lentils to make essentially a big pot of cooked mixed beans. Combine this with the spice-vegetable mixture in step 2. Since at least six of the apostles were fishermen (before they became "fishers of men"), this version is always done with baccalà. **Me** **Gf**

HOLY WEEK FANESCA FEAST

Fanesca

★

Fried plantains

★

Onions marinated in lime juice

★

Sliced queso fresco

★

Sweet empanadas, sprinkled with confectioners' sugar

★

Fresh papaya slices with lime wedges

Elsie's Cuban

BLACK BEAN SOUP

This gorgeous, simple black bean soup came from a dear friend, the late watercolorist/jewelry maker Elsie Freund, who fed it to me countless times. It has been one of my favorite soups for almost forty years: Ned and I served it at our wedding dinner, and I included it in both the *Dairy Hollow House Cookbook* and *Dairy Hollow House Soup & Bread*. It's even better when reheated the next day. The more olive oil you add, assuming it's good, fresh, and extra-virgin, the better it will be.

Serve the *Couve a Mineira* as a perfect salad partner.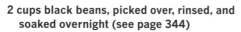

- 2 cups black beans, picked over, rinsed, and soaked overnight (see page 344)
- 2½ quarts (10 cups) well-flavored vegetable stock or water
- 2 bay leaves
- 1 fresh jalapeño pepper, stemmed, seeds removed for mildness, or left in for heat, chopped
- ¼ to ½ cup extra-vigin olive oil
- 3 large onions, chopped
- 2 green bell peppers, stemmed, seeded, and coarsely chopped
- 4 to 6 cloves garlic, finely minced
- Salt
- 2 cups cooked long-grain white rice, for serving
- 1 red onion, finely chopped, for serving
- *Couve a Mineira* (recipe follows), for serving (optional)

1 Drain and rinse the beans and place them in a large, heavy soup pot with the stock. Bring to a boil, then turn down the heat to a simmer and drop in the bay leaves and jalapeño. Cover tightly and cook, stirring occasionally, until the beans are tender, 1½ to 2 hours.

2 Toward the end of this period, heat the oil in a large, heavy skillet over medium heat. Add the onions and sauté, stirring, until they begin to become translucent, about 3 minutes. Add the green peppers and continue sautéing for another 3 minutes, then stir in the garlic and cook for another minute. Turn off the heat.

3 When the beans are tender, stir in the onion mixture, add salt to taste, and simmer, slowly, uncovered, to let the flavors meld, at least 20 minutes and longer if you like. Discard the bay leaves and jalapeño.

4 Place some rice and a good sprinkle of red onion into the center of each bowl and ladle the soup over top. It's even better the next day.

Serves 6 to 8

Note: For another South American bean soup, see Locro, given as a variation of U.S. Senate Bean Soup on page 106.

Brazilian Collard Green Salad
(Couve a Mineira)

It was love at first bite for me and *Couve a Mineira,* a salad traditionally served with feijoada (see page 45). Though most often collard greens are cooked (simply steam-sautéed or slow-simmered), they're sometimes served raw, like this, as a salad. That's the way I like them best. In fact, I love them, and not just with feijoada. Here they're cozied up to Elsie's Cuban Black Bean Soup, to which they are a perfect companion. This is my interpretation of the greens served at Café Bossa Nova, my favorite place to eat in Little Rock, Arkansas. Thank you, Rosalia, for introducing me to them.

Raw collard greens may be hardly comprehensible to American Southerners, but these energetically green ribbons and couldn't-be-simpler dressing will convert you. If you can't get collards, use kale. And make sure your knife is good and sharp: The only trick is slicing the greens very, very thin. It is the almost threadlike thinness of the cut that makes this so fresh and vibrant it almost leaps into your mouth. Vn Gf

2 large bunches of collard greens or kale, washed well, dried, tough center stems removed

2 tablespoons extra-virgin olive oil

Coarse sea salt and freshly ground black pepper

1 to 2 lemons, halved

1 Stack the collard leaves and roll them up tight the long way, making a firm cigar-shaped roll. (You may have to do this in batches.) On a cutting board, with your sharpest knife, cut as narrow as possible across the greens to make narrow ribbons. This can be done up to two days in advance; store the cut greens in zip-top bags and refrigerate them.

2 Up to one hour before serving, put the greens in your largest salad bowl. Drizzle the oil over them, then salt and pepper them well, and finally, squeeze the lemons over them (if the lemons have a lot of seeds, squeeze them through a strainer directly onto the greens).

3 Toss well. That's it!

Serves 4 to 6 as a side salad

CHAPTER 4

Cool Beans

SALADS
FOR EVERY
SEASON

Beans chill out in infinitely variable ways. A bean salad can start, accompany, or be a meal; it can be sophisticated (French green beans, cooked tender-crisp, chilled, and splashed with vinaigrette, on creamy butterhead or limestone lettuce leaves) or down-home (the bean salad someone brings to every neighborhood potluck, six different beans swimming in tart-sweet dressing). We'll discover new twists on both: adding tarragon or basil and Dijon mustard to the vinaigrette, or letting the multibean salad kick up its heels with a light toss in less dressing with bigger flavors, like the Honey-Cilantro Vinaigrette on page 154. Another new and oooh for tried-and-true: a chicken salad enlivened with green beans, yellow wax beans, a rainbow of cherry tomatoes, and a creamy Thai basil mayo.

Some offerings I'm pretty sure will make you wholly re-imagine beans in salad. I love the Three Sisters Salad with Fresh Corn & Zucchini Ribbons (page 133)—the perfect light start to any heavier Tex-Mex meal.

The piquant sweet-hot Thai-style Green Bean & Carrot Salad with Lime & Peanuts (page 140) is another winner, too easy to be believed. And just think of the color, textures, and flavors on parade in Marinated Lentilles du Puy with Greens, Baked Beets, Oranges & Walnuts (page 144).

Possibly my favorite are the healthy, grain-and-legume, full-meal salads, the ones that are summer on a plate and ready when you are. In warmer months, having such a salad in the refrigerator, amiably on call for a quick lunch several days running, is an easy way to be good to yourself (and any others you may feed). The one in my fridge right now has chilled cooked barley; chilled sliced steamed beans (both green and yellow); cooked kidney beans; a shower of parsley, thyme, dill, and tarragon—a garden full of vegetables. My partner, David, and I had it for lunch yesterday (the height of summer as I write this) and will again today; I'm already looking forward to it.

Please look forward to this array of bean salads, too, with happy anticipation.

STARTER SALADS

Though we began our luminous, leguminous journey with spreads, dips, and nibbles, there's more than one way to pod a bean—or to commence a meal. These days, more and more of us begin with a salad. And any good salad can be made that much better by the addition of beans. Leading the list of possibilities are eleven simple variations on a theme: that of greens (and sometimes other vegetables) tossed or overlaid with cooked, chilled green beans, the whole made sprightly and piquant with an appropriate dressing, one that might be classically French or Asian or might take its cue from America's Southwestern flavors. Most of these are very light and simple, but, for instance, the Deconstructed Niçoise Still Life (page 131) is a pretty major first course, and the Three Sisters Salad with Fresh Corn & Zucchini Ribbons (page 133), a personal fave, although light, does take a bit of prep. But browse among them, and you'll find a just-right salad that will make you as happy as that naughty Peter Rabbit . . . for whom one of our starter salads is named. Hippity-hop!

꒰   ꒰   ꒰

Simplified
GREEN BEAN SALADS

The simplest way to bean up a salad—that is, by using fresh green beans—is more of a strategy than a recipe as such.

It begins with cooking once for two or three meals—deliberately cooking extra beans (or any other central ingredient of choice) with several future meals in mind. This saves energy in several ways and makes good sense. When you have good precooked ingredients at hand, ready to be turned into dinner or lunch by nothing more than being combined and seasoned, it's easy to eat healthfully and deliciously, within one's caloric and fiscal budget.

I always advocate doing the "cook-once-for-several-meals" thing with dried beans, whole grains, and pasta. But in the warmer months, summertime especially, when fresh beans are inexpensive, bursting out of farmer's markets and gardens from coast to coast, and organics are widely available, I urge you to extend this wise and generous strategy in their direction, too.

Here's how: Purchase (or harvest) *way* more fresh green or yellow beans than you'll need for a single meal. When you are ready for your first meal, blanch them all, by either the steam version or boiling water version of the Basic Green Bean Cookery method (page 10). Drain the cooked beans well, then rinse them immediately in a colander with cold water, repeatedly, until they are cooled to room temperature. Drain them again, very well.

This is where the cook-once-for-several-meals piece comes in. Divide the cooked beans. Some, eat right away in any form you like; this book is full of ideas. But save the rest for later. Right now, we're concerned with these set-aside-for-later cooked green beans: They are the stuff of déjà food, deliberate planned-overs ready to be turned into perfect salads with easy, expeditious culinary sleight of hand.

Here's how to treat the set-asides: Blot dry the remaining cooked green beans, and refrigerate them. Once chilled, these cooked green beans have the potential to go in multiple directions . . . but let's look at them here plainly as salads to be, your refrigerated vegetable mad money. (Do people still keep mad money, as my mother used to? A twenty-dollar bill stashed here and there and then deliberately half-forgotten for the sheer pleasure of later rediscovery and utilization?) Cooked green beans are your in-fridge equivalent.

1. **Dressed for Success:** Serve the chilled, cooked green beans cold, as is or on lettuce leaves (or your choice of greens), drizzled with whatever vinaigrette strikes your fancy and fits the meal: My Basic Feisty Vinaigrette (page 132), the dressing for Gingered Asian Green Bean Salad (page 132), Citrus-Mint Vinaigrette (page 135), Honey-Cilantro Vinaigrette (page 154) . . . ad infinitum. **Vn** **Gf**

2. **Summer Simplicity:** Overlap sliced fresh summertime tomatoes (several different varieties, if you can get your hands on them, such as stripey green-gold Green Zebras, pinkish orange Brandywines, deep-red meaty Japanese black trifeles, gorgeous golden Big Rainbows, their centers veined pink and red—any of the sensual, surprising heirlooms that strut their stuff now at farmer's markets).

"First he ate some lettuces and some French beans; and then he ate some radishes; and then . . . he went to look for some parsley."

—*Beatrix Potter,*
The Tale of Peter Rabbit

Top this succulent spectrum with a small pile of cooked whole vinaigretted green beans. There you go: as much a first course as a salad, sophisticated in its simplicity. You can even forgo the dressing, adding the merest shake of coarse sea salt and a few grinds of black pepper. **Vn** **Gf**

3. Mediterranean Mood: Add greens to the above, along with olives (kalamata or oil-cured, preferably pitted) and roasted peppers (fresh or out of a jar). **Vn** **Gf**

4. Mediterranean Mojo: Same, with a little feta or ricotta salata sprinkled over the top, and/or half a cold cooked artichoke (or bottled marinated artichoke hearts). **Ve** **Gf**

5. Deconstructed Niçoise Still Life: To the Mediterranean Mojo (minus the feta) add, per person: a small piece of grilled fresh tuna steak; a halved, barely hard-boiled egg; and a few cooked potatoes tossed with the same vinaigrette you used on the green beans. Though in a classic Niçoise all the ingredients are usually tossed together, I think it's more gorgeous and satisfying when each component is in its own pile and you can pick among the ingredients, varying each bite slightly. One mouthful might be tuna and potato; another, green bean, tomato, and olive. **Me** **Gf**

6. Two- or Three-Bean Salad: Slice the chilled, cooked beans into ½-inch lengths and toss them in vinaigrette with any cooked or canned beans (such as kidneys or chickpeas, or one of the more exotic legumes, like nightfall, rattlesnake, or anasazi beans), a little chopped celery, and some diced onion or scallion. Use about 2 parts green beans to 1 part cooked dried beans. Of course, your green beans could also include some yellow wax beans. **Vn** **Gf**

7. Citrus-Sparkled Bean Salads: Do any of the above, but instead of vinaigrette, use just the merest drizzle of your favorite extra-virgin olive oil, the squeeze of half a lemon (catch any seeds), a little coarse sea salt, and a few grinds of black pepper. If you've never had one, a non-sweet two- or three-bean salad made this way is a revelation. **Vn** **Gf**

8. Raffa's Mother's Green Beans: Do the olive oil, lemon, s-and-p treatment described above, tossing together those chilled, cooked green beans with some raw fennel, sliced paper-thin. Too good to be so easy! **Vn** **Gf**

9. Bean Salad in an Avocado Boat: Halve a perfectly ripe avocado, remove the pit, and leave its skin on. Balance a half in a nest of greens or shredded cabbage (you can drizzle the other half with lemon juice and save it for later: or eat it right away, scooping out the flesh with a spoon, or make a second salad for a friend). Fill the cavity of the avocado with the Two- or Three-Bean Salad described above, or simply with diced, chilled cooked green beans, lightly dressed (try the Honey-Cilantro Vinaigrette on page 154); mound the filling a bit and let it flow generously over the sides of the avocado and onto the bed of greens. Garnish the whole thing with a shower of finely minced parsley, cilantro, or mixed fresh herbs. I serve this with the bamboo-handled serrated-tip grapefruit spoons handed down to me from my aunt, which practically invites eaters to scoop a little avocado with each bite of beans; but if the avocado is ripe, any teaspoon is fine. **Vn** **Gf**

10. Gingered Asian Green Bean Salad: Slice the chilled, cooked green beans into 1- to 2-inch lengths. Just before serving, toss them with a tablespoon or so of finely minced fresh ginger; 1 clove garlic, pressed; and 3 or 4 trimmed scallions, the whites and a few inches of green thinly sliced. Whisk together (or shake in a jar) 2 tablespoons tamari soy sauce (wheat-free if desired), 1 tablespoon honey or agave syrup, 1 tablespoon each peanut and toasted sesame oil, 2 to 3 tablespoons rice vinegar, and 1 teaspoon dry mustard. Toss the dressing over the green beans just before

serving. I sometimes add coarsely grated carrots or a handful of bean sprouts to this, and I often gild the lily with a tablespoon or so of toasted sesame seeds or toasted finely chopped peanuts. (This, with some cooked cold spaghetti and a little chopped baked tofu, is a very nice main-dish salad, perfect for lunch on a hot summer day.) **Vn** **Gf**

11. Peter Rabbit's Salad: Slice the chilled, cooked green beans on an angle into ¾-inch lengths. Toss together with very fresh sliced radishes and a dash of coarse salt. Optional: Add a little grated carrot, a couple of sliced scallions (whites and a few inches of green), and a few tablespoons of minced parsley. Mound this mixture onto leaves of limestone, buttercrunch, or red-leaf lettuce. Drizzle with a little dressing, such as My Basic Feisty Vinaigrette (below), or pass really good olive oil and lemon halves or white wine vinegar at the table. **Vn** **Gf**

MY BASIC FEISTY VINAIGRETTE

I've made this somewhat classic, you-can't-go-wrong vinaigrette for more years than I can count. What makes it feistier than average is the amount of garlic and the Dijon mustard. You can cut these back, or vary the herbs or the type of vinegar; this basic is infinitely versatile.

This will keep in the fridge, stored in a glass jar, for a couple of months. Because olive oil solidifies when chilled, let it sit out at room temperature for an hour or so before you need it, then give it a good shake. **Vn** **Gf**

½ cup vinegar (my faves are cider, red wine, or sherry; freshly squeezed lemon juice is also a refreshing substitute)

2 to 3 tablespoons good grainy Dijon mustard

½ teaspoon salt

4 to 6 cloves garlic, peeled

5 to 6 good grinds black pepper

1 to 3 large fresh basil leaves (optional)

1 cup extra-virgin olive oil

In a food processor, combine the vinegar, mustard, salt, garlic, black pepper, and basil. Start the machine buzzing, and gradually drizzle in the olive oil through the hole in the pusher tube until all is emulsified.

Makes about 1½ cups

THREE SISTERS SALAD
with Fresh Corn & Zucchini Ribbons

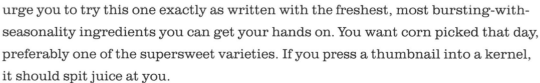

Corn, beans, and squash, those Native American staples that indigenous people called the Three Sisters, are codependent in the most positive way. They are literally and figuratively beautiful together, in the garden and on the plate. Here, in almost pristine purity, they taste absolutely themselves.

You could fancy this up in all kinds of ways, including adding garlic and/or scallion, flavors I usually love; but I urge you to try this one exactly as written with the freshest, most bursting-with-seasonality ingredients you can get your hands on. You want corn picked that day, preferably one of the supersweet varieties. If you press a thumbnail into a kernel, it should spit juice at you.

Fixing the zucchini in barely cooked ribbons makes all the difference in the taste, appearance, and unusualness of this salad. I wait all year for this one. **Vn** **Gf**

¼ pound fresh green beans, tipped, tailed, and cut into ¾-inch lengths

1 to 2 long, tender zucchini, ends trimmed

2 ears very fresh raw corn, kernels cut from the cob (about 1 cup)

1 large garden-fresh tomato, cut in large dice (optional)

1 tablespoon extra-virgin olive oil

Juice of ½ lemon

Salt and freshly cracked black pepper

Medium to large lettuce leaves (preferably buttercrunch), for serving

1 Bring a large pot of water to a boil. (Use plenty of water, more than you'd normally use for cooking the beans.) Drop the beans in. Let them cook to just a hair past tender-crisp, 2 to 5 minutes depending on the diameter and age of the beans.

2 While the beans cook, use a vegetable peeler to cut the zucchini, skin and all, into wide, thin, ribbon-like strips. If the seeds in the center seem overly firm or the core fibrous, save those strips for another recipe (you can use them in soup or ratatouille). You just want those tender ribbons, some green and some white. Pile the cut zucchini in a colander.

3 When the beans are cooked, drain them over the zuke ribbons. This pour-over cooks the zucchini very, very slightly. They'll remain a little crisp, but they won't taste raw, and I guarantee they'll be unlike any zucchini you've ever had before in your life.

④ Run or spray cold water over the zuke ribbons and green beans to cool them, then drain them very thoroughly (I use a salad spinner to get the zucchini as dry as possible). This is essential to keeping things crisp-fresh, not sodden.

⑤ Place the corn and the tomato, if using, in a large serving bowl, and add the beans and zukes. Toss well. Add the olive oil, lemon juice, and salt and pepper to taste, and toss well again. Serve immediately, each portion cupped in a lettuce leaf.

Serves 4 as a starter or 6 as a side

ↄ   ↄ   ↄ

SUGAR SNAP PEA, ORANGE & SPINACH SALAD
with Citrus-Mint Vinaigrette

There are two types of fresh edible-pod peas, also called *mange-touts* ("eat-alls"). Snow peas are the flatter of the two, with barely developed peas. Somewhat sweet, they often show up in Chinese stir-fries. Sugar snaps are rounder, with plumper peas, and, as you'd think from their name, they're markedly sweet. They are a definite seasonal treat, and this sprightly salad shows them off. Bright green and orange, with alternating currents of crisp, tender, juicy, and a slight sweetness modulated by mint, this almost sparkles on the plate. It pairs nicely with a chicken salad sandwich for lunch, or with chicken or tofu teriyaki plus any cooked grain for dinner.

A ripe avocado, peeled and cubed and scattered over the top of the tossed salad, is an excellent addition. **Vn** **Gf**

1 pound sugar snap peas, stemmed

2 oranges, preferably seedless navel oranges, peeled and sectioned

3 scallions, derooted, whites and about two inches of green sliced

½ pound fresh baby spinach, well washed and dried

1 recipe Citrus-Mint Vinaigrette (recipe follows)

Coarse salt and freshly cracked black pepper

1 Bring a large pot of water to a full boil (you want the quantity of water large enough so that it doesn't stop boiling when you add the sugar snaps) and set a colander in the sink. Drop the snaps into the boiling water and watch them closely. When they turn an exquisitely bright green, after about a minute, drain them immediately into the colander and rinse them with very cold water. Blot them dry, treat yourself to one (crispy, sweet, tender), and put the rest in the fridge until you're ready to complete the salad. (You may refrigerate the cooked sugar snaps for as long as overnight.)

2 Combine the sugar snaps, orange sections, scallions, and spinach in a large bowl. Drizzle with about half the vinaigrette and toss well. Taste a leaf, and sprinkle with the salt and pepper. Add more vinaigrette if you like (I personally prefer under-dressing a salad and passing extra at the table) and serve immediately.

Serves 4 as a starter

Citrus-Mint Vinaigrette

Technically not a vinaigrette since it is made not with vinegar but with lemon and orange juice, but "citrusette" is too coy for something so good. **Vn Gf**

- 1 orange, preferably organic
- 2 lemons, preferably organic
- 1 teaspoon honey or sugar
- 2 tablespoons finely chopped fresh mint
- ½ teaspoon salt
- ¼ cup extra-virgin olive oil

Using the finest grater you have, grate the zest of the orange and one of the lemons, and place the grated zests in a medium jar with a screw-top lid. Now halve the citruses and squeeze their juice into the jar, catching and discarding any seeds. Add the remaining ingredients to the jar, and shake well. This vinaigrette will keep in the refrigerator for up to 2 days.

Makes about ½ cup

HARICOTS VERTS & ROASTED TOMATO SALAD
with Roasted Garlic Cream

Those contrary French and their conundrums: Say all you want about the French paradox, there's still something perverse about the home of haute couture being the world's culinary capital for all-butterfat-all-the-time. But heavy cream and skinniness—in beans, at least—find delectable expression in this elegant starter: Tender-crisp haricots verts, slender little green beans sometimes called French beans and sometimes fillets (see box, opposite), are given the unctuousness that only full fat confers.

This recipe is admittedly fussy to make; I myself do it only once in a while, when I happen to have all the ingredients on hand, usually left over from other meals (why else would you happen to have a third of a cup of heavy cream around?). But the lusty, earthy sweetness of the roasted garlic (whisked into the cream), and the roasted plum tomatoes, chewy and concentrated in flavor, are quite special. (Be sure to roast the garlic *before* you begin the recipe.)

If you grow your own chives—and they are one culinary plant that almost grows itself, very ambitiously—you know they flower like crazy, sometimes three times in a single season if you keep them cut back. These tiny garlicky pale lavender fireworks make a splendid additional garnish, one blossom per plate. Ve Gf

1 pound haricots verts (fillet green beans), stemmed and tipped

1 tablespoon olive oil

10 plum tomatoes, quartered lengthwise

Coarse salt

1 teaspoon red wine vinegar or freshly squeezed lemon juice

⅓ cup heavy cream

⅓ cup Greek-style yogurt

2 heads Roasted Garlic (recipe follows), cloves squeezed from their skins and mashed (about 2 tablespoons mashed roasted garlic)

Freshly cracked black pepper

Medium to large lettuce leaves (preferably buttercrunch), for serving

Fresh chives, finely chopped (or chive blossoms, if available), for garnish

1 Blanch the haricots verts: Bring a medium-large pot of water to a boil. Submerge the haricots verts in the boiling water until their color brightens but they are still on the crisp side of tender-crisp, about 1 minute. Immediately rinse the beans in cold water, then blot dry and refrigerate them.

2 Preheat the oven to 450°F. Coat a rimmed baking sheet with 1 teaspoon of the oil or line it with a silicone baking mat.

3 Toss the tomatoes with the remaining oil and a little coarse salt. Spread the tomatoes on the prepared baking sheet, and roast them until deepened in color and somewhat shriveled, 20 to 25 minutes. Let cool to room temperature.

4 In a small bowl, briskly whisk together the red wine vinegar, heavy cream, yogurt, and mashed roasted garlic.

5 Combine the roasted tomatoes and chilled haricots verts in a large bowl and season them with coarse salt and plenty of

black pepper. Pour the garlic cream over the vegetables and toss gently. Put a few leaves of lettuce on each plate, and divide the salad among the plates. Scatter the chopped chives over each, and serve.

Serves 4 as a starter or 6 to 8 as a side

Roasted Garlic

As it cooks, garlic sweetens and grows mild. I usually prefer it raw, lusty, and odiferous, but sometimes tame is what you need. The deli counters at many natural foods markets have preroasted garlic, but doing it yourself is easy. **Vn** **Gf**

> 10 heads of garlic, skin on, pointy end of each head sliced off so tops of cloves are barely exposed
>
> 1 tablespoon olive oil

Vegetable oil cooking spray (optional)

1 cup vegetable stock

1 Preheat the oven to 325°F.

2 Rub the garlic heads with the olive oil. Place them in a nonstick 13 x 9-inch baking dish, or one that has been sprayed with cooking spray, and pour in the stock.

3 Roast until the garlic is very soft, 1 to 1¼ hours. Let cool slightly.

4 Serve warm, in the skin, for guests to squeeze out on their own, or squeeze out the cloves yourself. Reserve any liquid in the pan; it's an extra-flavorful addition to the stockpot.

Makes ½ to ⅔ cup roasted garlic cloves

THIN, GREEN, THRICE-NAMED

The very, very thin green beans known as fillet green beans, French beans, or haricots verts are actually not French in origin. Fillets are various varieties of our good old American friend Phaseolus, but picked at a young and tender age and therefore very thin. While any green bean can be picked young and thus be a fillet, uncurved varieties such as Burpee's "La France," or "Rolande" or "French Duet" (the latter two from www.reneesgarden .com), grow with the pencil-straightness that fillet lovers prize. Do these varieties taste better than their plumper, curved, older kin? I don't think so myself, though they're undoubtedly more tender and usually are sold at a hefty uptick in price. But it may be a case of "you can never be too thin or too rich"; these beans do have cachet and elegance. And yes, they are much loved by the French.

Thai-style
SUMMER ROLLS

Okay, so these don't qualify as "salad" in the traditional sense. But since they're essentially crisp, clean, delectable salads in a wrapper, I'm including them here.

Why the heavy, deep-fat-fried versions of these are called "spring" rolls is beyond me; something which burns your fingers and leaves grease on the napkins when you wipe your hand does not bring delicate April or May to mind. To my eye and taste, these "summer" rolls are more springlike: poetic, the ghosts of fillings shyly half-visible through the delicate, translucent, veil-soft, white rice paper that encases them. Inside, a layered, saladlike spiral of tofu, green aromatics, and lettuce, maybe a few carrot shreds. And, naturally, some bean threads—another poetic food, very thin transparent noodles made from mung bean flour.

These rolls are dazzling in their delicious simplicity, especially when topped with a bit of crunch from a sprinkle of sesame seeds or chopped toasted peanuts. Their mild freshness is complemented by a fiery sweet-hot garlicky sauce like Thai Crystal (page 200). Or try version 3 or 4 of the stir-fry sauces following Basic Asian Tofu Stir-Fry on page 294. **Vn** **Gf**

5 leaves crisp romaine lettuce, cut crosswise into ¼-inch slices

2 scallions, derooted, whites plus 3 inches of green cut crosswise into paper-thin slices

½ to ⅔ cup fresh mint leaves

½ to ⅔ cup fresh cilantro leaves

½ to ⅔ cup fresh basil leaves (preferably Thai basil)

12 to 14 ounces New Wave–New Fave Baked Tofu or Tempeh (page 249), or 1 batch Traditional Asian-style "Crisping" Marinade & Method for Oven-Baked Tofu (page 250), or commercially made Thai-style tofu

12 ounces rice-paper wrappers (see Note)

3 ounces very thin dried bean-flour noodles, cooked (see box, opposite)

1 carrot, peeled and coarsely shredded or julienned (optional)

¼ cup toasted unsalted peanuts, chopped (optional)

Dipping sauce of choice (see headnote)

❶ Combine the romaine lettuce, scallions, mint, cilantro, and basil in a medium-size bowl. Toss very well to combine thoroughly.

❷ Cut the tofu into 12 long ¼-inch-wide strips (reserve the remaining tofu for another use, such as the Basic Asian Tofu Stir-Fry, page 294).

❸ Set out a tray and on it assemble all the remaining ingredients (except the dipping sauce and salad greens) and place beside them the lettuce-herb bowl and prepared tofu. In addition, you'll need a pie pan or skillet filled with very warm water, a cutting board (a plastic one works best) as work space for rolling up the rolls, and a plate to place the finished rolls on. Okay, now you're literally ready to roll.

④ Submerge 1 rice wrapper in the warm water, and hold it down for 20 to 25 seconds. Gently lift it from the water and place the now-pliable rice sheet on your work surface. (It's okay if it's a bit softer at the edges and firmer in the middle; it'll soften all the way through on its own.) Let it sit there once removed from the water for another 20 or 30 seconds to further soften a bit.

⑤ Fill the wrapper: Starting about a third of the way from the bottom edge of the wrapper (that is, the edge closest to you), lay out a thin horizontal row of noodles. Top it with some of the lettuce-herb mixture, some carrot, and lastly, placed end to end, a few strips of the tofu. Sprinkle with some of the toasted peanuts, if you like (I think you will).

⑥ Finish the rolls: Fold the wrapper edge nearest you up and over the filling, then tuck it under firmly, compressing the filling tightly. Roll the wrapper away from you once to enclose the filling completely, then tightly fold in the right and left ends and continue rolling it up until the summer roll is compact. Press the seam at the end to close; the damp rice paper will stick to itself agreeably. It's a tamping-down, compressing, tight-rolling movement, similar to rolling a burrito, in case you've ever done that.

⑦ Set the finished roll aside on the plate, seam side down. Repeat with the remaining wrappers and filling.

⑧ Slice the rolls in half or into thirds, and serve with individual bowls of sauce.

Makes about 12

Note: Rice-paper wrappers are available at Asian food markets.

BEAN-FLOUR NOODLES

Just when you thought you were starting to know everything there was to know about beans, the legumes' versatility delivers another knock-out surprise: bean pasta, a standard part of Asian cuisine. Sometimes called "glass noodles," these thin noodles are made from mung bean flour and are widely available at Asian foods stores, traditional supermarkets, and food co-ops. Sometimes they come nested in a snarled-up, twisted tangle, sometimes they're straight as boxed spaghetti. Usually, the packaging has writing in several languages. The package I just pulled from my pantry, for instance, describes them as BEAN FLOUR NOODLE, JAPANESE STYLE ALIMENTARY PASTE, H'U TI EU DAI, NOUILLES DE FARINE EN HARICOT VERT, plus a couple of names in Asian characters that I can't decipher.

White when raw, the noodles turn transparent when cooked. And cooking them is ridiculously easy, though contrary to everything Americans know about typical noodle cooking. Just do this: Soak the bean threads in a bowl of hot water for 10 minutes or drop them into boiling water for 1 to 2 minutes, then drain and rinse (or, in other recipes, add them to a stir-fry and toss). That's it!

THAI-STYLE GREEN BEAN & CARROT SALAD
with Lime & Peanuts

The fresh interplay of sweet, tart, fiery-hot, herbal, and often citrus that is Thai cooking surprises and delights the mouth. I especially love the Thai way with grated salads, many of which include green papaya or mango. No oils or heavy dressings are used, so the salads are lively enough to jump off the plate and spit in your eye.

This is my own take on those gorgeous, vivid flavors and crispy textures. I make this frequently or try variations, and I'm never disappointed. **Vn** **Gf**

¾ pound cooked, chilled green beans (see page 10)

2 or 3 carrots, scrubbed but not peeled, coarsely grated

3 scallions, derooted, whites and 2 inches of green sliced

5 cups very fresh Asian salad greens, such as baby tatsoi, well washed and dried, or 3 cups thinly sliced Chinese or napa cabbage

1 recipe Thai-Style Dressing (recipe follows)

¼ to ⅓ cup finely chopped peanuts (or Gotcha-Hotcha Sweet-Smoky Cocktail Peanuts, page 28), for garnish

2 to 4 hot Thai peppers, very thinly sliced and chopped (optional)

Toss all of the vegetables with the dressing in a large bowl, and taste; you might want to add more of any one of the dressing ingredients to get the sweet-sour balance just right. Serve ASAP, sprinkling the chopped peanuts and peppers over each portion. And that's it!

Serves 4 as a starter

Thai-style Dressing

3 tablespoons freshly squeezed lime juice

1½ tablespoons sugar

1 tablespoon tamari soy sauce (wheat-free if desired)

Combine all of the ingredients in a jar with a tight-fitting lid and shake well.

Makes about ¼ cup

FULL-MEAL SALADS

These salads are perfect for making in quantity in summertime and nibbling your way through. You'll almost always find a container of one of the grain-based bean salads in my fridge during warmer months. Such salads, with a side of a chilled soup (cucumber yogurt, say, or sorrel) are pretty much the summer luncheon chez Dragonwagon-Koff. And although I probably shouldn't admit it, there are times when I am so busy, and those already-there grain-and-bean salads and the chilled soups are so inviting, so ready and willing, that this combo is pretty much the breakfast, lunch, *and* dinner chez Dragonwagon-Koff.

Though I have been a vegetarian for many years, and most of the salads in this chapter reflect that, my mother, who is ninety-five at this writing, has always been a devotee of chicken salad. I developed the one on page 149—with cooked green beans and a creamy Thai basil dressing—for her. She loves it!

ɔ ɔ ɔ

Bountiful, Beautiful
BEAN & BARLEY SALAD

Although tabbouleh, made with cracked wheat, is the most widely known grain-based salad, with few exceptions (see variations) almost any grain can be used as a base, and this category of salad is one of the very best ways to discover the true pleasure of whole grains. They're texture-y and nutty, and we're always being told we "should" eat them, given that they're little gift-wrapped packages of good nutrition and fiber. Well, for me, my partner, David, and most of my pals, there's no "should" to it—we just like 'em. Barley, especially in the form of this salad, is a staple that never fails to satisfy. Use pearled or hull-less barley for this (the inedible hull of the grain has been removed from both); pearled cooks more swiftly.

Treat this as a mistress (as opposed to master) recipe, using different grains and beans as you fancy. I never make it exactly the same way twice. Some variations follow, but please don't stop there. Ve

1 cup frozen peas (do not thaw)

2 to 3 carrots, scrubbed and chopped into ¼-inch dice

½ pound chilled, cooked green beans (see page 10)

1½ cups cooked or canned beans (preferably chickpeas or kidney beans; canned beans should be rinsed well and drained)

4 cups pearled barley, cooked and chilled (see Note)

3 scallions, derooted, whites and 2 inches of green sliced

1 small unwaxed cucumber, quartered lengthwise and sliced

½ to ¾ cup minced fresh herbs (see box, page 146)

About 3 tablespoons extra-virgin olive oil

1 to 2 lemons, halved

Coarse salt and freshly cracked black pepper

Lettuce leaves, for serving

Red and yellow cherry tomatoes, for serving

Crumbled feta or ricotta salata cheese, for serving (optional)

❶ Bring a medium-size pot of water to a boil. Place the peas in a colander in the sink, then drop the carrot pieces into the boiling water and cook briefly, until their color brightens, about 30 seconds. When the carrots are ready, drain them over the peas (if you like, place a bowl beneath the colander to trap the carrot cooking water for a stock). Rinse the carrots and peas with cold water, and drain well.

❷ In a large bowl, combine the carrots and peas with the green beans, chickpeas,

barley, scallions, cucumber, and herbs. Toss together well.

❸ Drizzle with the olive oil and squeeze the lemons over the salad (through a strainer to catch the seeds, or pick them out if you don't mind fiddly work). Season with salt and pepper, toss again, and add more oil, lemon juice, salt and pepper to taste—whatever you think it needs. But the beauty of this dish is that it is not swimming in dressing; the good grainy flavors and the vegetables are not obscured.

❹ Serve the salad on lettuce leaves, surrounded by cherry tomatoes and sprinkled with crumbled feta, if you like.

Serves 6 to 8

Note: If you buy your pearled barley in a box, simply prepare it according to the package directions. If you purchase it in bulk, however, follow these basic cooking instructions: Combine 1 cup pearled barley and 2 cups water in a medium-size pot and bring to a boil. Reduce the heat to a simmer, cover, and let cook for 30 minutes. After the time is up, turn off the heat and let the barley sit, still covered, until the grain is soft and tender, another 10 minutes.

VARIATIONS

Mixed Wholegrain Rice & Bean Salad: Start with 4 cups cooked mixed-variety rice blend (I've used several from Lundberg Family Farms, available at www.lundberg .com; their Wild, Countrywild, and Jubilee blends are all terrific). Add 1 finely diced medium zucchini to the cooking water with the carrots, draining both over the peas.

Use cooked edamame instead of chickpeas. Add 1 or 2 stalks diced celery with the scallions. Omit the cucumber. **Ve** **Gf**

Sweet-Savory, Somewhat Asian Bean & Barley Salad: Add ½ cup raisins (or diced dried pineapple) and an extra scallion. For the herbs, use equal parts parsley, cilantro, and mint, and add about 1 tablespoon very finely grated fresh ginger. Use 2 tablespoons peanut oil and 1 tablespoon toasted sesame oil instead of the olive oil; you can stick with the lemon juice or use rice vinegar instead. Omit the optional cheese at the end; instead, scatter with toasted sesame seeds and chopped roasted peanuts. I love this one! **Vn**

Week-After-Thanksgiving Grain Salad: Use cooked barley or one of the cooked rice mixtures above. Omit the cucumber, tomatoes, and cheese. In step 2, add ⅓ cup dried cranberries; 1 to 2 cups cooked, diced turkey (or baked tempeh or tofu); 1 small bulb fennel, very thinly sliced (optional); and 1 apple, cut in small cubes. For the herbs, use ½ cup minced parsley, 2 or 3 finely minced sage leaves, and 2 tablespoons finely minced celery leaves. Use canola oil and sherry vinegar instead of the olive oil and lemon juice; garnish with toasted pecans. **Me**

Forbidden Rice Salad: Forbidden Rice, with its mysterious dark purple-black color and slightly sweet flavor, makes a marvelous grain salad. (It can be purchased at LotusFoods.com or in bulk at Whole Foods.) Start with 4 cups cooked rice. I choose bright, crisp vegetables to contrast with the dark rice. Omit the cuke and tomatoes, double the carrots, and use equal parts cooked green beans and yellow wax beans. In step 2, add ½ cup golden raisins and a finely chopped red bell pepper. Omit the cheese. **Vn** **Gf**

Asian Flavors Forbidden Rice Salad: Begin with 4 cups Forbidden Rice. Substitute blanched snow peas or sugar snap peas for the green beans; omit the tomatoes and cheese. In step 2, add ½ cup golden raisins, a finely chopped red bell pepper, and 1 good, juicy orange, carefully sectioned and pitted. Whisk together a dressing from the following: ¼ cup peanut oil, 2 tablespoons freshly squeezed lime juice, 1 tablespoon tamari or shoyu soy sauce (wheat-free if desired), 1 tablespoon toasted sesame oil, 1 clove pressed garlic, 1 to 2 teaspoons finely grated ginger, and 1 teaspoon sugar. **Vn** **Gf**

Quinoa Salad with Corn and Peppers: Use 4 cups cooked quinoa. Omit the carrots and peas. Add an extra scallion; the raw kernels from 2 ears fresh corn, preferably a picked-that-morning supersweet variety (about 1 cup); and a small zucchini, sliced and blanched. Use cooked lima beans instead of chickpeas, and just before serving, stir in a few diced garden tomatoes (instead of the cherry tomatoes). A good herb mix here is equal parts parsley, cilantro, and basil, and an optional garnish is sliced avocado. Omit the cheese. **Vn** **Gf**

Yin-Yang Salad: A showstopper at a potluck, and a great do-ahead dish for crowds. Make two versions: the original, pale barley salad and the dark Forbidden Rice salad. Using your hands, fill one side of a large bowl with the barley version and the other side with the Forbidden Rice version (the mixtures are sticky enough that you can get everything in place nicely). The contrast in colors and flavors is something else. **Vn**

Tabbouleh: Start with 4 cups cooked cracked wheat. Use chickpeas, of course, for your cooked dried beans. Increase the herbs to 1½ cups, using a full cup minced parsley and ½ cup finely chopped mint. Add a little extra lemon juice and olive oil. Use chopped tomatoes, stirred into the salad, rather than cherry tomatoes. Cheese is not traditional, but it's a nice option sprinkled on top. **Ve**

ᕧ   ᕧ   ᕧ

MARINATED LENTILLES DU PUY
with Greens, Baked Beets, Oranges & Walnuts

A perfect main-dish salad for a late-fall lunch or dinner. Start with a cup of creamy tomato, red pepper, or squash soup, accompanied by crisp croûtes smeared with goat cheese. Pears, perhaps with gingersnaps, for dessert. **Ve**

Vegetable oil, for greasing the baking dish

3 medium red beets with fresh, vibrant greens

2 cups dried lentilles du Puy (French green lentils)

2 cloves garlic, peeled

1 bay leaf

1 cinnamon stick

2 quarts vegetable stock, chicken stock, or water

1 large red onion, thinly sliced

1 recipe Orange Vinaigrette (recipe follows)

Salt and freshly cracked black pepper

1 large or 2 small heads romaine lettuce, leaves washed and dried

3 medium oranges, peeled, seeded, and sectioned

About ½ cup toasted walnuts, coarsely chopped

1 baguette (preferably wholegrain), sliced and toasted, for serving

1 log (4 ounces) plain or herbed goat cheese, for serving

1 Preheat the oven to 350°F. Coat the bottom and sides of a shallow baking dish with oil.

2 Trim the leaves from the beets, discarding any bruised or rotten ones. Set the greens aside. Scrub each beet, and place them in the prepared baking dish. Cover tightly with aluminum foil and bake until the beets are fork tender, 1 hour. Let the beets cool to room temperature; then slip them out of their skins and slice them into ¼-inch-thick rounds.

3 Meanwhile, cook the lentils: Combine the lentils, garlic, bay leaf, cinnamon stick, and stock in a large pot over high heat. Bring to a boil, turn down to a simmer, and let cook, covered, until the lentils are *almost* tender, 30 to 40 minutes.

4 Trim away and discard the tough stems from the beet greens. Stack the leaves, roll them into a tight cylinder, and cut them crosswise into ¼-inch ribbons (you'll want to use a good sharp knife). Add the sliced beet greens to the lentils, and continue cooking until the lentils are fully tender but still hold their shape, about 10 minutes more. Drain off the excess liquid (reserving it for a soup stock, if you like). Fish out and discard the bay leaf and cinnamon stick. Transfer the lentils to a large bowl and let them cool to room temp.

5 Toss the red onion into the lentils. Shake the dressing and add about two thirds of it, tossing well to coat. Season the lentils to taste with salt and pepper, then cover them and place them in the refrigerator.

6 In a separate bowl, toss the beets with the remaining dressing. Chill them, too. You can prepare the recipe, up to this point, up to 2 days before serving.

7 About an hour before serving, bring both the beets and lentils to room temperature. When ready to serve, place the romaine lettuce leaves on one large or several small serving plates. Overlap the beets on top of the romaine, mound the lentil salad over that, and scatter with the orange sections and toasted walnuts. Put the toasted bread slices ("croûtes") in a basket and pass with the goat cheese on a small cutting board at the table.

Serves 4 as an entrée, with accompaniments

Orange Vinaigrette

It doesn't get easier than this. Taste your olive oil; you want it fruity and fresh, with just a tiny hint of pleasing bitterness. **Vn** **Gf**

Juice and grated zest of 1 orange (preferably organic)

⅓ cup extra-virgin olive oil

2 tablespoons red wine vinegar

1 clove garlic, pressed

1 teaspoon coarse salt

1 teaspoon honey or maple syrup, or a little more to taste

Combine all of the ingredients in a small jar with a tight-fitting lid and shake the heck out of it. It'll keep, refrigerated, for up to 10 days.

Makes about ¾ cup (enough for 1 to 2 salads)

A Note on Fresh Herbs

A little alteration in your choice of herbs makes each salad distinctive. Some work well as a single herb, lending their one-of-a-kind flavor to the whole dish; others are better partnered. If you don't have your own herb garden, use what's available at the market.

Parsley is the little black dress of herbs: always appropriate. It adds a bright but nondominant note of freshness and verve (tabbouleh, the grain salad made with cracked wheat, is, in the Middle East, actually more of a parsley salad, with just a little cracked wheat). Most food people will tell you to use Italian, or flat-leaf, parsley; I happen to like both the flavor and look of curly parsley better.

Dill, Basil, Mint, and **Cilantro** are all much more dominant and distinctive in flavor than parsley, but can be used in quantity. They are each good soloists (if the eaters like dill, say, or cilantro—about the latter, folks tend to be love-it-or-hate-it). And they can also do well with just parsley, or in combination with others, in a mix. Try, for instance, ¼ cup minced parsley with ½ cup minced dill, or ¼ cup minced parsley with ½ cup minced basil. Or go all mint, all cilantro, or use 2 tablespoons of each plus ¼ cup minced parsley. Basil comes in dozens of varieties, each with its own distinctive zing; my special favorites are Thai, holy (tulasi), globe, spicy, and lemon. Lime basil doesn't do much for me (it has a grassy taste) and the ruffled purple basil is ornamental; its taste is rank and weedy. Mint also comes in many varieties; my favorites are spearmint (rather than peppermint), lemon mint, and the sweetly fragrant pineapple mint.

French Tarragon and **Mexican Marigold** (a tarragon taste-alike) are terrific, underused in most American kitchens. Their elusive tone is sweetish, with a very slight lemoniness and an almost aniselike flavor. For grain and bean salads, like those on pages 141–144, these are too strong to be soloists. You can use one or the other in a duet with parsley, but since tarragon and marigold are more decisive, try just 1 or 2 tablespoons, finely chopped, to ½ cup or so of minced parsley. They're also appealing in a mix of fresh herbs. Gardeners, avoid Russian tarragon; it is pretty flavorless.

Oregano, Marjoram, Savory, and **Thyme,** all high in aromatic oils, are great team players, but they are too strong to work as soloists or duet partners. Use even less of these; a teaspoon or more, up to but no more than a tablespoon of each (we're talking smallish, sometimes tiny, leaves here, stripped from their stems).

Sage and **Rosemary** are marvelous, very resinous, strong herbs. Use them with constraint: 1 smallish sage leaf in an herbed vinaigrette or as part of the fresh herb mix, and just a few needles of rosemary. More is just too pungent.

A good herb mix for grain or bean salads: Here's approximately how my own ¾ cup of minced herbs often breaks out (measurements after stripping herbs from stems and finely chopping): 5 tablespoons parsley; 3 tablespoons assorted basils; 2 tablespoons tarragon; 1 tablespoon dill or mint (maybe, maybe not); ½ teaspoon each thyme, marjoram, and oregano; 4 or 5 small needles of rosemary; 1 sage leaf. (To see how to go about all this mincing, visit www.dragonwagon.com.)

DRAGON-STYLE DAN-DAN NOODLES
with Baked Tofu, Bean Sprouts & Crisp Vegetables

This is my version of the classic, much-loved peanut-sesame noodles that every Chinese restaurant and food co-op in America offers (for better, and sometimes, for much, much worse). For the story of this dish's migration, see "The Streets are Alive . . . with the Sound of Dan-Dan" (page 149): There are countless themes and variations.

No matter which you make, mix the dish just before serving it: It's infinitely better than the sesame noodles in the deli's prepared food case. (Once the noodles absorb the sauce, as they do if everything is mixed up ahead of time, they grow sticky, not satisfyingly slippery-slithery.) The other thing is, don't overdress the noodles with the peanut sauce. Serve this cold, at room temperature, or slightly warm—not hot.

Look at all the legumes quietly shining here. Peanuts. Sprouts. Soy sauce. Tofu.

Serve extra bowls of the individual sauce components, so each diner's dan-dans can be personalized. This also truly tastes better eaten with chopsticks. **Vn**

FOR THE SALAD:

2 cups fresh mung bean sprouts

2 carrots, coarsely grated

¼ cup very thinly sliced napa cabbage

1 cucumber, peeled, quartered lengthwise, seeded, and then sliced crosswise into ¼- to ⅓-inch-thick slices

5 scallions, derooted, whites and 2 inches of green sliced

1 to 2 tablespoons chopped commercially made kim chi (spicy Korean pickled vegetables) (optional)

FOR THE PASTA:

½ pound spaghetti

1 teaspoon toasted sesame oil

1 teaspoon chile oil (optional, see Note)

1 recipe Dan-Dan Peanut Dressing (recipe follows)

FOR SERVING:

¼ cup minced fresh cilantro leaves, for garnish (optional)

6 to 8 ounces Basic Oven-Baked Tofu, either homemade (see page 247) or commercial (I like Wild Wood Organic's Aloha Baked Sproutofu), cut into bite-size pieces, for garnish

Condiment tray: Sriracha sauce, chile oil, or minced chiles; soy sauce; sesame oil; rice vinegar

1 No more than 1½ hours before serving, make the salad: Combine the bean sprouts, carrots, napa cabbage, cucumber, scallions, and kim chi in a large bowl and toss well. Set aside.

2 Make the pasta: Bring a large pot of unsalted water to a boil and cook the spaghetti according to the package directions until it is al dente. Pour the spaghetti into a colander, drain it well, and rinse it thoroughly with cool water to remove all surface stickiness. Drain the spaghetti very well again, transfer it to a large bowl, and toss it with the sesame and chile oils. Set aside.

3 When ready to serve, pile the pasta onto individual plates. Top each pasta pile with some salad, dividing the salad evenly among the plates. Now, drizzle a *little* of the dan-dan dressing on each salad and scatter cilantro over each, along with chunks of tofu. Instruct each diner to toss the salads together with their chopsticks. Pass the extra dan-dan dressing at the table, as well as the condiment tray, so everyone can achieve their own dan-dan perfection.

Note: If you don't have chile oil on hand or would like to omit it, simply use 2 teaspoons of the toasted sesame oil.

Serves 4

Dan-Dan Peanut Dressing

The orange zest is my addition to this dressing, and it is, I think, terrific . . . but definitely not traditional. Omit it if you like. The dressing can be made several days in advance. For ease of serving, transfer the completed dressing to a plastic squeeze bottle with a tip, so you can just zigzag it straight onto the salads. **Vn** **Gf**

⅓ cup creamy, natural, unhydrogenated peanut butter (see box, page 323)

2 tablespoons toasted sesame oil

2 tablespoons rice vinegar

Finely grated zest of 1 orange (preferably organic)

2 cloves garlic, coarsely chopped

A large chunk of ginger (about the size of 2 thumbs), peeled and coarsely chopped

2 tablespoons tamari or shoyu soy sauce (wheat-free if desired)

2 tablespoons honey

Chile to taste, either fresh chile (jalapeño, Thai chile, or part of a habanero or Scotch bonnet); a shot of Sriracha or similar chile sauce; a pinch of cayenne; or a few teaspoons chile oil

Combine all of the ingredients in a food processor and buzz until just about smooth and well incorporated, pausing to scrape down the sides. Transfer to a lidded container.

Makes about ⅔ cup

"A 4,000-year-old bowl of noodles unearthed in China is the earliest example ever found of one of the world's most popular foods, scientists reported today. It also suggests an Asian—not Italian—origin for the staple dish.

The beautifully preserved, long, thin yellow noodles were found inside an overturned sealed bowl at the Lajia archaeological site in northwestern China. The bowl was buried under ten feet of sediment . . . "

—National Geographic News, *October 12, 2005*

THE STREETS ARE ALIVE . . . WITH THE SOUND OF DAN-DAN

Dan-dan noodles, popular now and a staple at most co-op delis and American Chinese restaurants, have made a long journey, according to Jung-Feng Chiang of *Mrs. Chiang's Szechwan Cookbook.* This is a book that certainly rocked my culinary world when it first came out, back in 1976, at the dawn of hot-and-spicy foods' general popularity in America. The first few restaurants featuring Szechuan cuisine were opening; Thai was to follow. "This is the most famous street food of Szechwan [sic]," wrote Mrs. Chiang and her co-author, Ellen Shrecker. "Its name echoes the hollow, clunky sound of the two sticks hit together by the itinerant vendors who hawked it through the streets." The vendors, she explained, sold individual portions of cold, cooked noodles over which they would ladle out the sauce ingredients separately: tahini, soy sauce, hot peppers, scallions, raw garlic, ginger. "The buyer mixed the noodles and condiments together himself. Nothing could have been simpler, cheaper, or more delicious." Over time, *dan* became the colloquialism for the bamboo carrying pole with which the on-foot noodle vendors portaged their ingredients, cookware, and serving accoutrements. And the peanuts that, to Americans, are essential to the dish? They didn't become part of dan-dan until migrant Szechuan noodle-hawkers reached Taiwan, in the last five or six decades.

∂ ∂ ∂

CHICKEN SALAD
with Green Beans, Yellow Beans & Creamy Thai Basil Dressing

While lovers of chicken salad won't say no to the basic old-fashioned version—cooked chicken, celery, mayo, maybe onion—it's a little plain for contemporary tastes. These days, chicken salads are often dressed up with the addition of fresh fruit and/or nuts (green grapes, fresh pineapple, and almonds were the combination I used in my innkeeper days). But even this has become commonplace, plus sometimes you just don't want a sweet note in your main dish.

This version is contemporary: savory, not sweet, nonfruited but with plenty of color and juicy textural contrast. Its ingredients—including fresh green and yellow beans—are recognizable, pleasing, yet unexpected. A scoop of this, atop a pile of perfectly fresh spinach, arugula, spring mix, or romaine, served with crisp wholegrain toast or a baguette with serious crust, strikes a delicious balance between tried-and-true and brand-new.

Cook the chicken yourself, or purchase it precooked (a roasted chicken can serve double duty as dinner one night and lunch, in the form of this salad, the next day). Make the dressing before you begin. And please, don't refrigerate the cherry tomatoes; the cold changes their cellular structure, making them cottony. Rinse them and have them ready, but toss them in only at the last minute. **Me** **Gf**

1 pound cooked chicken, diced

5 scallions, derooted, whites and 2 inches of green sliced

¾ pound fresh green beans, tipped, tailed, blanched (see page 10), chilled, and sliced into 1-inch lengths

¾ pound fresh yellow wax beans, stemmed, tipped, blanched, chilled, and sliced into 1-inch lengths

1 stalk celery, chopped

1 recipe Creamy Thai Basil Dressing (recipe follows)

Salt and freshly ground black pepper

About ½ pint yellow cherry tomatoes, such as Sun Golds, larger tomatoes halved, plus extra whole tomatoes for serving

About ½ pint red cherry or grape tomatoes, larger tomatoes halved, plus extra whole tomatoes for serving

Salad greens (see headnote), for serving

Any very good extra-virgin olive oil (optional; use lemon-infused if you like), for serving

Sprigs of fresh Thai basil (optional), for garnish

Roasted red bell pepper strips (optional), for garnish

1 Combine the chicken, scallions, green and yellow beans, and celery in a large bowl and toss well to combine. Add the dressing, starting with about ¾ cup and adding more until it's dressing-y enough for your taste. Season with salt and pepper to taste. This can be done, and stored in the fridge, a day or two ahead of time.

2 Right before serving, add the ½ pint of tomatoes to the chicken salad and toss well.

3 Line a platter with the salad greens. Mound the chicken salad onto the greens. Do any or all of the following as final touches: Drizzle with a tiny bit of olive oil, poke in a few basil sprigs, drape a few slices of roasted red bell pepper here and there. Surround the finished work of art with the additional cherry tomatoes. Serve immediately.

Serves 6 to 8

VEGAN VARIATION

Use chilled savory baked tofu, store-bought or homemade (see page 247), instead of the chicken, with Tofu Mayonnaise (page 49) as the base for the dressing. **Vn** **Gf**

Creamy Thai Basil Dressing

Although Thai basil adds a very special note to this rich dressing, it is also good made with the more readily available Italian basils, such as globe, or a mix of, say, spicy, Thai, lime, purple, and globe. **Vn** **Gf**

1½ cups commercial mayonnaise or Tofu Mayonnaise (page 49)

1 tablespoon olive oil

1 bunch of fresh Thai basil leaves, stripped from the stems and thinly sliced (about ½ cup packed)

Juice of ½ lemon

1 clove garlic, pressed

Combine all of the ingredients in a small bowl, whisking together well. That's it! This will keep for 3 or 4 days in the fridge; if you use homemade tofu mayo, pour off any liquid that accumulates on top.

Makes about 2 cups

WARM DAY, COOL LUNCH BUFFET

Thai-Style Green Bean & Carrot Salad with Lime & Peanuts (page 140)

★

Dragon-Style Dan-Dan Noodles with Baked Tofu, Bean Sprouts & Crisp Vegetables (page 147)

★

Chicken Salad with Green Beans, Yellow Beans & Creamy Thai Basil Dressing

★

Iced green tea

★

Lemon thin cookies

SIDE SALADS

C hacun à son goût—everyone to his taste—especially when it comes to classifying a particular dish in a particular category. Any of the following bean-participatory salads could be served as a first course or even a main . . . but to me, they just *feel* like side dishes. Some contain potatoes. Several are slightly sweet and to my taste are better suited to accompany rather than begin a meal. So take a look, take a bite, and then place them wherever they belong in your menu.

੭   ੭   ੭

German-style
GREEN BEAN, POTATO & BACON SALAD

A s a child I *loved* Grand Central Station, the getting-off place for fascinating New York City, where my mother and sometimes my father worked—much more exciting than the Westchester suburbs where we lived. Grand Central was (and is) vast, with a huge vaulted dark-blue ceiling studded with constellations. And if by any chance you got lost, all you had to do was look for the clever octagonal Information booth, its small clock tower pinpointing its central location, and ask for help.

My mother and I, on our New York excursions, often began or ended by taking the escalator to the adjacent building (then the Pan Am building, now MetLife) and having lunch at the Zum Zum, a slightly upscale German luncheonette (I think it was a small local chain), whose name I loved to say—my mother and I called it the Zum Zum Room. There I always had the exotic (to me) potato salad. It was warm! It didn't have mayonnaise! It had bacon! It was a little sweet and sour! We were in New York City!

Herewith, my green-beaned take on the remembered Zum Zum's potato salad (a delicious vegetarian version follows). Green beans, it turns out, are a traditional addition to many German potato salads. Although the German way is to peel the potatoes, I prefer 'em unpeeled; and I like to use half red-skinned and half brown-skinned. **Me**

6 slices bacon

2 tablespoons unbleached white flour

3 tablespoons sugar

⅓ cup white wine vinegar

2 pounds steamed or boiled small potatoes, unpeeled, cut into ½-inch slices, warm or at room temperature

¾ pound fresh green beans, tipped, tailed, cooked tender-crisp (see page 10), and cut into 1-inch lengths

4 scallions, derooted, whites and 2 inches of green sliced

2 tablespoons finely minced fresh parsley (or, if you prefer, fresh dill)

Salt and freshly ground black pepper

1 Line a plate with paper towels. Cook the bacon in a large, deep skillet over medium heat, turning it frequently, until it's nice and brown, 7 to 9 minutes. Remove the bacon to the plate to drain and cool. Set aside the skillet with the bacon fat. Crumble the bacon and set it aside, too.

2 Place about 3 tablespoons of the bacon fat in a small bowl, and whisk the flour into it. Return the skillet with the remaining bacon fat to medium-low heat and whisk in the flour slurry. When the flour mixture is smoothly incorporated, whisk in the sugar, ⅓ cup water, and the vinegar. Turn up the heat to medium and cook, stirring, until the

dressing thickens and there's no raw flour taste, about 5 minutes.

3 Add the potatoes and green beans to the skillet and stir well, coating the vegetables with the dressing. Cook until the potatoes and green beans are heated through, then turn off the heat and add the scallions, reserved bacon crumbles, and parsley. Season to taste with salt and pepper, and serve warm.

Serves 4 to 6 as a side dish

VARIATION

German-style Green Bean, Potato & Tempeh Salad: Omit the bacon. Instead, sauté 1 package (8 ounces) smoked tempeh strips (such as Lightlife's Fakin' Bacon) in 2 tablespoons any mild vegetable oil, such as corn, canola, or peanut, until it is browned on both sides, allowing 2 to 3 minutes per side. Set aside the cooked tempeh to cool, then dice it. Add an additional ⅓ cup oil to the skillet (needless to say, in either variation, this is not what you could call a light recipe) and proceed with the directions except (a) whisk the flour directly into the oil in the skillet, and (b) obviously, add the diced tempeh instead of the bacon at the end. You can also add a shake of Bacon Salt (page 112) if you like. **Vn**

BLACK BEAN & SWEET POTATO SALAD

with Honey-Cilantro Vinaigrette

When you next bake some sweet potatoes, do the cook-once-for-two-meals thing and bake a few extra. Then, especially if you use canned black beans (or if you have them, too, on hand as planned-overs), this Halloween-colored side salad is done in a flash. The optional green beans add a bit of time, but they're worth it and with a little thinking ahead, they too can be on hand as planned-overs.

The dressing is so good it'll make your toes curl. This extremely pleasing salad is perfect for pairing with a spicy main dish (like jerk-style chicken, tofu, or eggplant). **Vn** **Gf**

3 cups (two 15-ounce cans) tender-cooked black beans, drained well and rinsed

4 scallions, derooted, whites and 2 inches of green sliced

About ⅓ pound chilled, cooked green beans (see page 10), sliced into 1-inch lengths (to equal 1 to 2 cups; optional)

1 recipe Honey-Cilantro Vinaigrette (recipe follows)

2 or 3 large sweet potatoes, baked, peeled, and chunked

Salt and freshly cracked black pepper

1 Combine the black beans, scallions, and green beans, if using, in a large bowl and toss with about ½ cup of the dressing. Add the sweet potatoes and toss very, very gently to keep the tender sweet potato pieces somewhat intact.

2 Taste. Correct the seasonings with salt, pepper, and additional dressing if you like. Pass the remaining dressing at the table. Dig in, and get ready for the compliments; act modest.

Serves 4 to 6 as a substantial side dish

Honey-Cilantro Vinaigrette

Sweet but not overly sweet, with that lovely cilantro kick. You'll find many happy uses for the extra you'll have left over, including CD's Five-Bean Salad Southwestern Style on page 156. My friend Chou-Chou once, not realizing it was salad dressing, spooned a half-cup or so over some enchiladas; she was so rapturous over the flavors I wouldn't have dreamed of stopping her.

If your honey is thick and crystallized, warm it by submerging the jar in a large pot full of very hot water. **Vn** **Gf**

2½ cups fresh cilantro leaves
   (about 1 bunch)

½ cup cider vinegar

⅓ cup honey, warmed if not very liquid

4 cloves garlic, diced

1½ teaspoons salt

Plenty of freshly ground black pepper

Dash of Tabasco or similar hot sauce

1 cup olive oil

Combine all of the ingredients except the oil in a food processor and buzz smooth. You may need to scrape the processor sides once or twice. If your machine's pusher tube has a little hole, pour the oil into the tube in two batches and let the oil drip in as the machine runs. Otherwise, drizzle in the oil by hand. Taste for seasonings, then transfer to a lidded container or jar and store in the refrigerator for up to a week.

Makes about 1¾ cups

ﾜ   ﾜ   ﾜ

Almost Classic

FIVE-BEAN SALAD

This is a freshened-up version of the well-known multibean salad with its very sweet dressing. I can live with canned dried beans, but not canned green or yellow beans; hence I cook those up nice and fresh for this one. **Vn** **Gf**

¼ pound green beans, tipped, tailed, cooked tender-crisp (see page 10), and cut into 1-inch lengths

¼ pound yellow wax beans, tippeded, tailed, cooked tender-crisp, and cut into 1-inch lengths

1½ cups (one 15-ounce can) tender-cooked black beans, very well drained

1½ cups (one 15-ounce can) tender-cooked chickpeas, very well drained

1½ cups (one 15-ounce can) tender-cooked kidney beans, very well drained

1 red onion, sliced paper thin

1 red bell pepper, stemmed, seeded, and minced

1 stalk celery, chopped

1 recipe Mariam's Sweet-and-Sour Dressing (recipe follows)

Salt and freshly ground black pepper

Place the beans and veggies in a large bowl, add the dressing, season with salt and pepper to taste, and toss to combine. Cover and refrigerate for at least 12 hours or up to 2 days. Serve with a slotted spoon to drain off the dressing. Pretty durned simple, yes?

Serves 6 to 8 as a side dish or 8 to 10 as a buffet item

Mariam's Sweet-and-Sour Dressing

Still plenty sweet but way less so than some of the traditional bean salad dressings, this is from Mariam, an old friend of my mother's. For extra sprightliness, replace the vinegar with freshly squeezed lemon juice, or go east with rice wine vinegar and a little grated fresh ginger. **Vn** **Gf**

1 cup packed dark brown sugar

1 cup cider vinegar

1 cup any mild vegetable oil, such as corn, canola, or peanut

1 tablespoon prepared yellow mustard (preferably American-style "ballpark," not Dijon)

1½ teaspoons salt

1½ teaspoons celery seed

Combine the brown sugar and vinegar in a 1-quart jar with a tight-fitting lid. Shake well and let stand for 10 to 15 minutes. Shake again; the sugar should dissolve into the vinegar. Add the remaining ingredients, shake well again, and serve over mixed beans.

Makes about 2½ cups

VARIATIONS

CD's Five-Bean Salad Southwestern Style: A little less sweet, a little more herbal; I like this even better than the classic. Follow the recipe above but omit the celery seed. Dress the beans with Honey-Cilantro Vinaigrette, page 154. Just before serving, add ¾ cup or so peeled, diced jicama. Garnish with sliced ripe avocado. This, with a simple cheese quesadilla made on a whole wheat tortilla, is pure wonderful. **Ve**

Almost Classic Five-Bean Salad Plus: Nominally more main-dishy, this is a version I "developed" (the quote marks because "developed" is just too high-falutin for how this came about) when I had some leftover Five Bean and . . . well, if you cook regularly, you know how this works. Place ½ to 1 cup frozen green peas in a strainer and run under hot water to thaw, then toss them into the salad along with the kernels cut from 2 to 3 ears raw fresh corn, preferably a supersweet variety. Sprinkle each serving with a little feta or ricotta salata cheese. **Ve** **Gf**

CHILI WEATHER

Spicy, Steamy Simmerings

What we call "chili" today isn't much like the simple chuckwagon cowboy food that originally went by that name. One of America's first fusion dishes, chili was created on the fly when beef-rich Anglo cowboys, ranchers, settlers, and camp cooks came in contact with the chile (with an e) peppers and vibrant seasonings of the American Southwest. Combine the beef on hand, the local seasonings, and the austere working and cooking conditions that life in that time and place offered, and you got chili, a dish that was unfussy, stripped-down, nourishing, and heavy. With mostly unattended simmering yet palatable ready-when-you-are results, chili ruled. These same qualities also made chili a natural part of the army diet in the American West, sustaining troops during both the Mexican War (1846–48) and the Spanish–American War (1898). The first written chili recipes appeared between the two wars, entering the *Manual for Army Cooks* in 1896.

These original chilis contained no tomatoes and few if any of the "secret ingredients" that proud winners of today's countless chili cook-offs brag about. (All such events, by the way, are spawned by the first and most famous, the Original Terlingua International Championship Chili Cookoff, a South Texas charity event held in Terlingua, Texas, and founded in 1966.) Beef, and pork, too, were imports—no more native to America than chili powder, or, for that matter, cowboys.

To our palate today, chili powder (chili with an i)—made of powdered chile peppers, cumin, garlic, oregano, usually salt, and sometimes allspice—is the standard and dominant seasoning mix for any "bowl of red." Yet it was invented by a German immigrant to New Braunfels, Texas, William Gebhardt, in 1890; he began marketing it in 1894.

And beans? Strangely, this native ingredient didn't enter into the picture until quite a bit later, colloquially around

1895 to 1900, finally showing up in army cookbooks around 1910.

My chilis are more freewheeling and expansive, and come more from the garden than the hoof. If untraditional by contemporary chili standards, their roots are ancient, relying on ingredients native to the New World. Beans, tomatoes, corn, potatoes, peppers of all kinds, occasionally unsweetened chocolate, but always and especially chile peppers, with their range of heat levels, colors, and subtle undernotes that simmer beneath the burn—all these are true native American foodstuffs, part of any chili I make. And I make plenty of chili, in a whole palette of colors, as you'll see.

And again, my present-day chilis always, *always* have beans.

Now, by this point in our meanderings, it's true we've acquainted ourselves with the world's beans: China's soybean, India's lentil and split pea, the Middle East's chickpea and fava. But for sheer numbers and staggering diversity, no part of the world comes close to America's abundance and variety: kidney and black beans, navy and cranberry, limas, white runners, scarlet runners, brown teparies and white teparies, calico, eye-of-the-goat, nightfall—

even fresh green beans. (The latter, after all, are just the immature pods of the kidney beans.)

Of the chilis that follow, I've included one classic Texas beef bowl-of-red: Genie's Mother's Homegrown Texas Chili (page 160), which I used to make back when I was a meat-eater. It does not contain beans, but beans served alongside it were an essential part of the experience. I've also included a vegetarian white chili. The rest are highly seasoned stews—some red, some green, some brown—in which chile peppers play a major role. They're deeply rooted in American soil (a soil that was, after all, tilled by successive waves of immigrants as well as many native inhabitants). To me, they are every bit as satisfying as— though different from—the chili you may be familiar with.

One essential practical Chili Truth: All chilis bloom, magically, a day or two after they're made. Not only can chili be done ahead of time, it really *should* be. I always make huge batches and freeze some; it's even better made ahead, frozen, and reheated. Most of these recipes are generous in yield, but you can't go wrong doubling 'em.

Genie's Mother's

HOMEGROWN TEXAS CHILI

T his was the first chili I ever made, back in 1969 when I was a wild child of sixteen and living in New York with my West Texan now-long-since ex. His best friends, a then-couple named Ray and Genie Reece, were also Texans, and they patiently initiated me into spicy food, chili, and Tex-Mex. Genie taught me how to make her mama's chili, gifting me with a handwritten recipe, on which I noted then, "Exact quantities of spice cannot be given for it is strictly to taste." Strange it is to consider how widely accepted these once-exotic flavors have become since those days, and certainly since the '40s, the days when Genie would have been a little girl. "I remember," she wrote on the recipe in her rather elegant handwriting, "this used to be an all-day process. We would go to this fantastic spice shop to buy the ingredients for it. "

In its original version, it was probably pretty close to the earliest chilis; it was centered around beef right down to rendered beef fat, rather than oil, for cooking. Though beanless, it is served with a generous side of what Genie then called "real imported Mexican chili beans:" pinto, cooked with salt pork or bacon.

I still think of Genie every time I make chili of any kind. **Me** **Gf**

¼ cup bacon fat, vegetable oil, or olive oil

2 pounds beef chuck or round steak, cut into ¼-inch dice—not ground

Freshly ground black pepper

Salt

2 cloves garlic

1 dried whole pasilla chile (see box, page 162)

1 tablespoon ground cumin, or to taste

1 tablespoon ground red chile powder (*not* chili powder, the spice mix), or to taste

1½ teaspoons ground ancho or pasilla chile powder, or to taste

1½ teaspoons dried oregano

3 cans (6 ounces each) tomato paste

Genie's Mother's Beans for Chili (recipe follows), for serving

Dairy Hollow House Skillet-Sizzled Buttermilk Cornbread (page 167), corn tortillas, or cooked brown or white rice, for serving

❶ Heat the bacon fat in a large, heavy skillet over medium-high heat.

❷ Add the beef and cook, stirring frequently to break it up, until it has become grayish brown, 8 to 10 minutes. Stir in the pepper (grind vigorously and "use lots!" as Genie counseled). Salt lightly. Keep stirring and cooking until the beef is grainy and brown, 3 to 5 minutes more. (At this point you can drain off some of the fat if you wish—as much or as little as you like. It's a matter of taste—Genie and her mother didn't.) Scoop out the browned meat and set it aside.

③ Add the garlic, whole chile, ground cumin, chile powders, and oregano to the fat in the skillet. Turn the heat to medium-low and cook, stirring, until the spices are toasty and fragrant and the whole pasilla is slightly darkened, 3 to 5 minutes.

④ Take the reserved browned meat and transfer it to a Dutch oven, along with the spice sauté. Open the cans of tomato paste, and scrape their contents into the pot, too. Fill each can with water, stirring to get any remnants of tomato paste dissolved, and add the 3 cans of water.

⑤ Bring to a boil, then lower the heat. Simmer, half-covered, for about 45 minutes, giving it a stir now and then. You can serve it right away, let it sit a few hours and then reheat it, or chill it overnight and then reheat it the next day. (If you chill it, you have the option of lifting off and discarding the fat cap that will rise to the top.) Either way, serve the chili hot, with beans and cornbread alongside.

Serves 6 to 8 generously, when served with beans and cornbread or rice

Genie's Mother's Beans for Chili

This is a simple, classic bean preparation from the American Southwest (or, if done with navy beans, the South). Leftovers of these beans, or any red, brown, or green chili, or any other spicy bean stew can be used to fill Tamale Pie Delahanty (page 236) or Cornbread Pie à la Hippie (page 239). (Why not white chili, you ask? Its dairy-based sauce doesn't work well tastewise or functionally in corn-topped or -bottomed casseroles.) **Me** **Gf**

> **3 cups dried pink beans, small red beans, or, if unavailable, pinto beans, soaked overnight (see page 352), drained, and rinsed**
>
> **¼ pound slab bacon or rinsed salt pork, quartered**
>
> **Salt and freshly ground black pepper**

① In a large, heavy pot, cover the beans with fresh water to a depth of about 1½ inches and bring to a boil. Remove from the heat and let stand for 1 hour, then drain and rinse again.

② Cover the beans a second time with water, this time to a depth of ¾ inch. Bring to a boil, turn down the heat to a simmer, and let cook until the beans are just barely starting to soften, 45 minutes to an hour.

③ Add the bacon and continue to cook, stirring occasionally, until the beans are fully tender and the ingredients have had a chance to know one another for 45 minutes at least—but a longer, slower simmer, up to an hour and a half, won't hurt at all. Add salt and pepper to taste.

Serves 6 to 8

VARIATION

CD's Long-Ago Version: Genie's mom didn't do this, but in the old days when I cooked these beans with salt pork, I always added a bay leaf and a dried ancho chile to the beans in step 1. Remove the bay leaf and the ancho stem before serving.

CHILL OUT (AND HEAT UP) WITH CHILES

Chiles—their varieties, their usages, their varying degrees of heat, sweetness, and distinctive flavors, their history, their nutritional value, even their pharmacological effects—one could probably write a book at least as long as this one on that subject. Here, a few background chile facts:

★ Chiles were named by the Nahuans, an Aztec tribe living in Central America since at least the seventh century A.D. Chiles are in the same spooky-fascinating family as deadly nightshade, along with tomatoes, potatoes, eggplant, and tobacco.

★ A single variety of chile has many personalities, depending on whether it is picked green or allowed to ripen to red or golden, used raw, cooked, dried, or pan-toasted in either raw or dried whole form. Chiles also appear as a powdered spice, which may be pan-

toasted or not . . . an infinity of possibilities, given the uncountable varieties of chiles.

★ The seeds and the white fibrous interior ribs are responsible for most of the heat in hotter chiles. If you want things a little milder in a recipe, remove the seeds and fiber; or, for extra heat, leave 'em in.

★ The **poblano** pepper, one of my faves, has a mellow, gentle heat and a sweet undernote that is, to me, vaguely reminiscent of chocolate. When fresh, it's a flattened heart shape, and a much darker green than a bell pepper. Poblanos are deliciously piquant sautéed fresh and used in chilis and stews, stuffed, or fire-roasted and skinned as a seasoning.

★ When dried, poblanos are called **anchos.** They have a leathery texture that softens up and half-disintegrates (except for the tough stem)

during a long, slow cooking in a pot of beans. I often use them just this way. Toward the end of the cooking time, I poke around in the bean pot with a spoon, locate the stem, scoop it out, and discard it. Then, almost always, I scout around again for any large chunks of the ancho itself. These I mash or puree and return to the bean pot.

★ **Pasilla chiles,** called for in Genie's Mother's Homegrown Texas Chili (page 160) and Lisa Esposito's Soul-Soothing

Vegetarian Black Bean Chili (page 168), are the dried version of the skinny little chiles called *chilacas* or *chiles negros.* One rarely sees chilacas fresh in American markets, but pasillas are easy to find. They are quite dark and shriveled-y looking; in fact, the name *pasilla* translates as "little raisin"; *negro* refers to their near-blackness when dried. They are most often used toasted, to add flavor to sauces or chilis. They are mildly hot and have a distinctive smokiness; to me, they taste the way wood smoke smells.

★ Bright green and plumply triangular, **jalapeños** are currently the most easily available and widely recognized fresh hot chile pepper in U.S. supermarkets. Their heat varies widely jalapeño to jalapeño, and I know of no way to tell, until you cut a particular one open, whether you have a relatively mild one or a singeingly hot one. Sliced and pickled, they are now a familiar topping for nachos, pizzas, and other dishes that have become part of America's culinary lingua franca.

★ If young jalapeños that are fully grown (to a length of two to three inches) are allowed to remain on the plant until fully matured, they eventually turn red and, after that, dry out a little and start to wizen. At this point they are picked and are ready to be turned into that delectable darling, the **chipotle:** a smoked, red, dried jalapeño. One can buy chipotles as a dried whole pepper, a powder, or canned in **adobo sauce.** Adobo sauce is typically made of tomato puree, paprika, salt, onions, oil, vinegar, garlic, bay leaves, oregano, and sugar. No big deal, until you add the elements of hot and smoky from the chipotles, which partially rehydrate in the sauce. One bite of that combo and you understand why this product now flavors a wide variety of mayos, barbecue sauces, marinades, salsas, and more.

CD's Neo-Traditional
RED CHILI

The vegetarian equivalent of basic traditional red chili, this is a dish I've been making ever since I outgrew the meat-centric version and began moving toward a plant-centered, eventually vegetarian, diet. Good Lord, that's more than forty years now!

I make this and CD's Chili Mole (page 170) several times each winter. No two batches are quite the same, though the enthusiasm with which they're greeted at the table is always high. And though this has way more vegetables and seasonings, and no meat at all, my sense of it, in a way maybe no one but I could understand, remains rooted in the previous recipe, given to me by my old friend Genie Reece. My idea of what the *feel* of chili is was formed by that one. If I've wandered far afield from it over the years, the pleasure and satisfaction derived from these two very different bowls of chili are identical. **Vn** **Gf**

1 pound dried pinto beans, picked over, rinsed, and soaked overnight (see page 16) or quick-soaked (see page 17)

About 3 quarts any well-flavored vegetable stock (or a 12-ounce bottle of beer plus enough water to make up the difference)

2 bay leaves

1 ancho chile, whole (see Note)

1 jalapeño pepper, stemmed, seeds removed for mildness or left in for heat, coarsely chopped

Freshly ground black pepper

Vegetable oil cooking spray

¼ cup olive oil

2 large onions, chopped

3 green bell peppers, stemmed, seeded, and chopped

1 tablespoon cumin seeds

2 teaspoons ground cumin

2 teaspoons ground coriander

¼ teaspoon cayenne, or to taste

2 teaspoons sweet Hungarian paprika

½ teaspoon smoked sweet Hungarian paprika

1 tablespoon hot chili powder

½ teaspoon dried oregano

3 cloves garlic, coarsely chopped

1 can (16 ounces) chopped tomatoes in juice (preferably fire-roasted)

¼ cup tomato paste

1 to 2 tablespoons Pickapeppa sauce or vegetarian Worcestershire sauce

1½ teaspoons tamari or shoyu soy sauce (wheat-free if desired)

Salt

1 to 3 teaspoons honey or Succanat

Truman Capote's Family's Cornbread (page 166), for serving

Chili Fixins (page 173), for serving

① Drain the soaked beans and rinse them well. Put them in a large, heavy soup pot, add enough stock to cover the beans to a depth of 1½ inches, and add the bay leaves, ancho chile, jalapeño pepper, and lots and lots of freshly ground black pepper (you can hardly add too much). Bring to a boil, then turn down to a simmer and cook, covered, over low heat until the beans are nearly tender, 1½ to 2 hours.

② When the beans are tender-ish but still holding their shape, about 1¼ hours into their simmer, spray a large, heavy skillet with oil, add the olive oil, and place it over medium heat. Add the onions and cook, stirring, until they start to soften, 3 to 4 minutes. Stir in the bell peppers and cook for another 2 minutes. Then add all of the remaining spices and the oregano, lower the heat slightly, and cook, stirring constantly, for 1 to 2 minutes. Add the garlic and cook, stirring, until it just becomes fragrant, about 30 seconds. Remove the onion mixture from the heat.

③ Scrape the onion mixture into the simmering beans. Deglaze the pan with a little bean stock, stirring to loosen any browned bits from the bottom of the pan. Return this liquid to the beans.

④ Stir the tomatoes, tomato paste, Pickapeppa, tamari, salt—it will take quite a bit—and honey into the beans. Continue to simmer, partially covered, until the seasonings are well blended and the beans are fully tender, 30 to 45 minutes.

⑤ Just before serving, pick out the bay leaves and the stem from the chile. Mash a couple of ladlefuls of the beans against the sides of the pot to thicken the chili slightly. While you *can* serve it hot, right away, it's much better if brought to room temperature then covered and refrigerated overnight, and reheated the next day. Whenever you serve it, accompany it with cornbread and any or all of the Fixins, making dinner an interactive affair.

Serves 8 to 10 generously, with Fixins and cornbread

Note: Ancho chiles are dried poblanos (see page 162). They are dark in color and triangular in shape, and can be found packaged in the Mexican foods aisle of most supermarkets or at any natural foods store where spices are sold in bulk.

VARIATIONS

Kachina's Chili: Substitute black beans for the pintos. Vn Gf

Charlotte's Chili: Charlotte, my mother, is ninety-five as of this writing. She amped up her mild ground-beef-and-bean chili when I got together with my Texan then-husband, Crispin. To Crispin's amusement and wonder, however, she could not be broken of the habit of serving chili over cooked macaroni. So, to do chili Charlotte-style, serve this (or any other chili) over cooked elbow macaroni. Vn

Chou-Chou's Chili: My friend Chou-Chou puts cinnamon—⅛ to ¼ teaspoon per batch—in her chili. It gives the simmering pot an exotic, hard-to-place sweetness reminiscent of some Moroccan and Greek dishes. Very nice. Add the cinnamon when you add the other spices. Vn Gf

Truman Capote's Family's
CORNBREAD

The brilliant Truman Capote, that ultimate demi-monde insider-outsider, grew up in Monroeville, Alabama, eating this unpretentious cornbread. A classic Southern-style cornbread, this version, which appeared in my previous cookbook, *The Cornbread Gospels,* is unsweet (the teaspoon of sugar is only to aid the browning), free of flour, and intentionally a bit dry. That's because many Southerners use it to sop up pot likker (the juice left over from cooking greens) or to crumble directly into soupy beans or chili. People who grew up on very sweet, cake-y, Yankee-style cornbread often find it incomprehensible at first bite, but as a onetime Yankee, I can promise you the pristine purity grows on a person in a big way. **Ve** **Gf**

1 tablespoon butter or bacon drippings

2 eggs

2 cups buttermilk

1 teaspoon sugar

1 teaspoon salt

1 teaspoon baking soda

2 cups stone-ground white cornmeal

1 Preheat the oven to 450°F.

2 Place the butter or drippings in a 10-inch cast-iron skillet, and place it in the hot oven.

3 Combine the eggs and buttermilk in a small bowl or measuring cup, whisking together well with a fork.

4 In a medium-size bowl, combine the sugar, salt, baking soda, and cornmeal, stirring well to combine.

5 Stir the egg mixture into the dry ingredients, beating just until the dry ingredients are moistened, no more.

6 Pull the skillet from the oven. It should be good and hot, with the fat sizzling. Swirl the pan to coat it. Quickly transfer the batter to the hot skillet and return the skillet to the oven.

7 Bake until the cornbread is browned and pulling away from the skillet, 20 to 25 minutes. Serve, hot, in wedges from the pan.

Makes 8 wedges

Dairy Hollow House Skillet-Sizzled
BUTTERMILK CORNBREAD

For eighteen years, I owned and ran a country inn and restaurant with my darling late husband, Ned. Many things changed over those eighteen years, but one that didn't was this, our acclaimed house cornbread. It is a basic African American–style cornbread: not strictly Southern or Northern, but taking the best notes from both. I was taught to make it by Viola, a Georgia ex-pat whom I met in the Fort Greene section of Brooklyn, New York (now gentrified, then—1969—not). I used to say that this cornbread was "the sun around which the other planets of the menu revolved."

It's the first recipe in my previous cookbook, *The Cornbread Gospels,* and more than one person has written to me saying, "I really want to cook my way through the whole book, but the DHH Skillet-Sizzled is so good I just keep making it!" Ve

Vegetable oil cooking spray

1 cup unbleached white flour

1 cup stone-ground yellow cornmeal

1 tablespoon baking powder

¼ teaspoon salt

¼ teaspoon baking soda

1¼ cups buttermilk

2 tablespoons sugar

1 egg

¼ cup mild vegetable oil

2 tablespoons butter or mild vegetable oil

❶ Preheat the oven to 375°F. Spray a 10-inch cast-iron skillet with oil and set it aside.

❷ Sift together the flour, cornmeal, baking powder, and salt into a medium-size bowl.

❸ In a smaller bowl, stir the baking soda into the buttermilk. Whisk in the sugar, egg, and the oil.

❹ Put the prepared skillet over medium heat, add the butter, and heat until the butter melts and is just starting to sizzle. Tilt the pan to coat the sides and bottom.

❺ Pour the wet ingredients into the dry and combine them quickly, using as few strokes as possible. Scrape the batter into the prepared pan and bake until it is golden brown, about 20 minutes. Let cool for a few moments, and slice into wedges to serve.

Makes 8 wedges

"Chili is not a dainty dish, and I believe it should be made in quantity and served to a boisterous crowd."

—Sarah Leah Chase,
Cold-Weather Cooking

VEGETARIAN BLACK BEAN CHILI

It was my pleasure to have poet/caterer/yoga teacher Lisa Esposito in the class I taught on culinary memoir in Key West in the winter of 2008. It was also my pleasure to have her heartwarming, exotic black bean chili at a chili-cornbread reception held in my honor the night I arrived at the Studios at Key West. How good a writer is Lisa? Let's just say that she made the mouth of this long-time vegetarian water with her remarkable description of carnitas, tiny pork squares cooked, as I recall, in rendered pork fat. And how good a cook? Let's just say that I went back for thirds of this rich, smoky, dark chili the night of the party, and took some leftovers home to the studio where I was staying.

I remain grateful to Lisa for the recipe. Its technique and flavors are one of a kind, as is the language with which she gave it to me—and now, generously, to you. Oh, and those toasted pasilla and New Mexico chiles . . . wow! They are the huge difference-makers here. Thanks, Lisa!

Please note this recipe calls for Lisa's Black Beans, so you need to get 'em going before you begin the recipe proper. Lisa does mention that "Canned beans work just fine, but if using them, add an additional 2 tablespoons coriander and 3 tablespoons cumin to the chili." Do this when you add the first go-around of spices to the onions and potatoes. **Vn** **Gf**

½ cup mild vegetable oil, such as canola, corn, or peanut

1 large onion, coarsely diced

3 medium-size russet potatoes, peeled, rinsed, and finely diced

8 pasilla chiles (see Note), stemmed, seeded, and broken into pieces

8 dried New Mexico green chiles (see Note), stemmed, seeded, and broken into pieces

1 tablespoon kosher salt

3 tablespoons ground coriander

2 tablespoons ground cumin

4 cups canned diced tomatoes (preferably fire-roasted), with their juice

5½ cups Lisa's Black Beans (recipe follows)

Chili Fixins (page 173)

Coarsely crushed yellow corn tortilla chips, for garnish (optional)

Minced fresh cilantro leaves, for garnish (optional)

① Place the oil in a Dutch oven over medium-high heat, and heat until "fragrant and rippling." (I told you Lisa was a poet. I love "rippling"!) Add the onions and potatoes, reduce the heat to medium, and cook, stirring occasionally, until the onions are translucent and the potatoes are easily pierced with a knife, about 15 minutes.

② While the onions and potatoes are cooking, toast the chiles: Place a dry, heavy skillet over high heat, add the chile pieces, and toast, stirring often, until fragrant, about 10 minutes. (If you love chile as much as I do, you will find the aromas intoxicating.) Remove the toasted chiles from the pan and place them in a bowl. Add hot water to barely cover, and let them soak until softened, 15 to 20 minutes.

③ Meanwhile, back at the onion-potato mixture: Once the onions are translucent and the potatoes tender, add the salt, coriander, and cumin and stir to coat the vegetables with the spices. Sauté for about 1 minute, then add the tomatoes and black beans. Stir to combine and let cook, half-covered, giving the occasional stir, for a few minutes while you return to the chiles.

④ Remove the softened chiles from their soaking liquid (reserve it). Transfer them to a blender or food processor with a bit of their soaking liquid and puree them to a nice, smooth, fairly thick consistency, about that of, say, ketchup. Stir this puree into the pot of chili and reduce the heat to a simmer.

⑤ Cover the chili and let it cook on very low heat, stirring occasionally, until the flavors have mingled nicely and the potatoes are very, very disintegratingly tender, about 1 hour. Serve immediately, hot, or make it in advance and enjoy it the next day, when, impossible though it is to imagine, it's even better. Pass the Fixins alongside, and, if desired, garnish as Lisa does: with a good sprinkle of crushed-up tortilla chips and chopped cilantro on top.

Serves 8 to 10 with Fixins

Note: Dried pasilla and New Mexico chiles can be found in the Mexican foods section of many supermarkets, in natural foods stores and specialty foods markets, and at www.thechileshop.com.

Lisa's Black Beans

You can prepare these beans a day or two before the chili if you'd like, storing them, covered, in the fridge. They're also good in and of themselves, or as a base for most Southwestern dishes and many curries. **Vn** **Gf**

> 2 cups dried black beans, picked over, rinsed, and soaked overnight (see page 344)
>
> 2 tablespoons ground coriander
>
> 3 tablespoons ground cumin
>
> 2 tablespoons salt

① Drain and rinse the soaked beans, then place them in a large, heavy pot and cover with cold water to a depth of 3 inches. Bring to a boil over high heat, reduce the heat to medium-high, and cook, half-covered, until the beans begin to get tender, about 1 hour.

② Add the coriander, cumin, and salt, and cook until the beans are tender and the liquid has become dark and fairly thick, 1 to 1½ hours more. The bean liquid will thicken more as the beans cool.

Makes 5½ cups cooked beans (sufficient for one batch of chili)

CD'S CHILI MOLE

I f you've gotten a little bored with the regular old bowl of red, try this. It's pronounced "MO-lay," as in the famed Mexican sauce, not "mole" as in little pesky animals who leave holes in your lawn. This is a superb chili. Its taste is indefinable and elusive, its texture decidedly rich. Although you can certainly serve Chili Mole with all the traditional Fixins, it also works beautifully served in a more minimalist style, the better to approach the complex parade of flavors that rolls over your tongue with each bite.

Please promise me you won't be put off by the length of the ingredients list—it's mostly spices—or the seeming peculiarity of some of the ingredients: This is one you will not want to miss.

Note: I adore the crunch of the occasional whole coriander seed in the finished chili. If you don't, omit the coriander seeds, or use 1½ teaspoons ground coriander instead. **Vn**

FOR THE BEANS:

1 pound dried black beans, picked over, rinsed, and soaked overnight (see page 16) or quick-soaked (see page 17)

2½ to 3 quarts any well-flavored vegetable stock (or a 12-ounce bottle of beer plus enough water or vegetable stock to make up the difference)

2 bay leaves

1 ancho chile, stemmed (see box, page 162)

1 jalapeño pepper, stemmed

Freshly ground black pepper

⅓ cup dark raisins (I like monukkas)

FOR THE SAUTÉ:

Vegetable oil cooking spray

¼ cup olive oil

2 large onions, chopped

1 green bell pepper, stemmed, seeded, and chopped

1 jalapeño pepper, stemmed, seeds left in for heat or removed for mildness, chopped

1 poblano pepper, stemmed, seeded, and chopped

1 tablespoon cumin seeds

2 teaspoons coriander seeds

2 teaspoons ground cumin

2 teaspoons ground coriander

½ teaspoon dried oregano

¼ teaspoon cayenne, or to taste

¼ teaspoon aniseed

⅛ teaspoon ground cinnamon

Tiny pinch of ground cloves

2 teaspoons sweet Hungarian paprika (if desired, ½ teaspoon can be smoked)

1 tablespoon hot chili powder

3 cloves garlic, coarsely chopped

FOR THE FINISH:

1 can (16 ounces) chopped tomatoes in juice

¼ cup tomato paste

1 to 2 ounces unsweetened chocolate, diced

2 tablespoons creamy, natural,
     unhydrogenated peanut butter
     (see box, page 323)

1 tablespoon tahini (or 2 tablespoons freshly
     toasted sesame seeds)

1 chipotle chile in adobo, stemmed,
     with 2 teaspoons adobo sauce

Salt

1 teaspoon to 1 tablespoon agave syrup
     or honey (optional)

Chili Fixins (optional; see page 173)

1 Drain the soaked black beans and rinse them well. Place them in a large, heavy pot and add enough stock to cover them to a depth of 1½ inches. Add the bay leaves, ancho chile, jalapeño, and lots and lots of freshly ground black pepper (you can hardly add too much). Bring to a boil, then turn down to a simmer and cook, covered, for 1 hour. Lift the lid and add the raisins. Continue cooking until the beans are nearly tender and the raisins have more or less disintegrated, 30 to 60 minutes more.

2 Meanwhile, about 20 minutes or so before the beans are done, spray a large, heavy skillet with oil. Place it over medium heat, add the olive oil and, when it's hot, the onions. Sauté the onions until they start to soften, 3 to 4 minutes. Stir in the bell pepper, jalapeño, and poblano and sauté for another 2 minutes. Then add all the remaining spices, lower the heat slightly, and cook, stirring constantly, for 1 to 2 minutes. Add the garlic and cook, stirring, until it just becomes fragrant, about 30 seconds. Remove the sauté from the heat.

"The kitchen is no place for fretting!"

—*Lisa Esposito*

3 Scrape the sauté into the simmering beans. Deglaze the pan with a little bean stock, stirring to loosen any browned bits from the bottom of the pan. Return this liquid to the beans.

4 Add the tomatoes and the tomato paste to the bean pot, and stir well. Simmer for another 10 minutes, then maintain at a low simmer while you continue with the recipe.

5 Place the chocolate, peanut butter, tahini, and chipotle in adobo in a food processor. Add a generous ladleful of the simmering beans (including the whole ancho and jalapeño, if you can find them), and buzz to make a thick, highly seasoned paste. Scrape this into the bean pot, turn the heat down as low as possible, and add salt to taste—it will take quite a bit. Simmer slowly, partially covered, until the seasonings are well blended, about 20 minutes longer.

6 Just before serving, pick out the bay leaves and the ancho stem. If you like, mash a couple of ladlefuls of the beans against the sides of the pot to thicken the chili slightly. Taste for seasonings: You want heat (perhaps a little more cayenne or adobo), richness (more chocolate), a little sweetness (add agave syrup as needed). Serve, with the optional Fixins, right away, or let it come to room temperature, then refrigerate it, covered, overnight and reheat it very, very gently (or in a slow-cooker) the next day. (It's much better after an overnight in the fridge.)

Serves 8 to 10 with Fixins

Chou-Chou's Brother David's
PETALUMA CHILI

This one, essentially a chili-flavored vegetable stew, will shock the purists. But it was a mighty fine welcome when my dear friend Chou's late brother, Dave, and his wife, Betty, brought some over to my partner David and me. It was the holidays, 2002, and David and I, newly involved, had driven up the West Coast beside the Pacific on Highway One. We crowned our first extended period of time together with several quiet, mostly rainy days in Petaluma, a sweet northern California town. We happened to be staying in a home across the street from Dave and Betty. The chili, then, was seasoned with love both romantic (David, the starting-to-be-permanent boyfriend), and fraternal: Dave, the brother of my old friend, saying affectionately as he handed me the quart Mason jar of chili-red vegetable stew, "Oh, I always make this for Chou-Chou, too," knowing that she, like me, is a vegetarian, though he was not.

Did all these circumstances make that chili even better? No doubt; don't fortuitous circumstances, kindness, and new love add illumination to everything on which they shine? Surely. The skies were gray, the air damp, the glow as bright as the rain-spattered lemons on the large, shiny-leafed shrub right in Dave and Betty's yard (to which we were also invited to help ourselves, and did). But even under less benign circumstances, this chili is very good. The green olives make it particularly interesting and one of a kind. Dave, a musician, carpenter, and environmentalist, was also one of a kind.

This is my interpretation of what they brought over that wet night. **Vn** **Gf**

Vegetable oil cooking spray

4 cans (15.5 ounces each) pinto or pink beans, with their liquid

1 bay leaf

2 carrots, scrubbed and cut into large, thick chunks

2 fist-size potatoes, scrubbed, peeled, and cut into large chunks

¼ cup olive oil

2 large onions, chopped

2 green bell peppers, stemmed, seeded, and chopped

1 stalk celery, sliced

1 jalapeño pepper, stemmed, seeds left in for heat or removed for mildness, chopped

2 teaspoons ground cumin

1 teaspoon ground coriander

1 to 2 tablespoons hot chili powder

½ teaspoon dried oregano

3 cloves garlic, chopped

1 can (16 ounces) chopped tomatoes in juice

¼ cup tomato paste

1 teaspoon honey or brown sugar
   (light or dark), or to taste

Salt and freshly ground black pepper

½ to 1 cup coarsely chopped pimento-
   stuffed green olives

Chili Fixins (below), for serving

Cornbread, for serving

1 Spray the inside of a Dutch oven or large, heavy stew pot with oil. Add the beans, bay leaf, and 2 cups water and place over high heat. When the beans come to a boil, add the carrots and potatoes. Turn down the heat to a simmer and let the vegetables and beans cook, half-covered, for about 20 minutes.

2 Meanwhile, spray a large, heavy skillet with oil and place it over medium heat. Add the olive oil and, when it's hot, the onions. Sauté the onions until they start to soften,

3 to 4 minutes. Stir in the bell peppers, celery, and jalapeño and sauté for another 3 or 4 minutes. Add the cumin, coriander, chili powder, and oregano, lower the heat slightly, and cook, stirring constantly, for 1 to 2 minutes. Add the garlic and cook, stirring, until it's just fragrant, 30 seconds.

3 Scrape the sauté into the simmering beans and stir in the tomatoes and tomato paste. Deglaze the sauté pan with a bit of the liquid from the beans, stirring to loosen any browned bits from the bottom of the pan. Return this liquid to the beans.

4 Add the honey, and salt and pepper to taste. (Use a little less salt than you think you need; the canned beans are salted.) Simmer, partially covered, until the seasonings are well blended and the vegetables are tender, about 20 minutes more. Stir in the olives. Serve hot, with your choice of Fixins, right away, or let it come to room temperature, then refrigerate overnight, covered, and reheat gently the next day.

Serves 4 to 6, with Fixins and cornbread

CHILI FIXINS

Set out bowls of as many of the following as you can muster, and let your guests doctor their bowls of chili as they like. To my taste, the Fixins are essential with all red chiles except mole; with mole or chilis of other colors, they're optional. **Gf**

★ Grated sharp Cheddar and/or Monterey Jack cheese

★ Sour cream, plain Greek-style yogurt, or tofu sour cream

★ Guacamole, or sliced ripe Hass avocados sprinkled with lime juice

★ Salsa

★ Pico de gallo

★ Diced raw onion

★ Pickled jalapeños

★ Chopped fresh cilantro

★ Chopped chipotle chiles in adobo

★ Tabasco or other hot sauce

★ Cornbread (see page 166 or 167), corn chips, or warm corn tortillas; or rice

New Mexico–style
GREEN CHILE STEW VERDURA

Given how vivid and vast the rainbow of New World flavors is, it's hard to pick favorites. But those of New Mexico stand out. The heart and soul of their spirited bite is the distinctive New Mexican green chile—both the pepper itself and the sauce/stew/gravy made from it, also called green chile (see box, page 177). If you prepare this dish, or the sauce that is at its heart, with any other type of green chile, you'll be underwhelmed. But with New Mexico dried green chiles, you'll be floored at how astonishingly good it is.

This simple vegetable stew, built around our native cornucopia—and posole puts the "corn" in "cornucopia"—showcases the green chile-ness succulently. What's posole? It's corn whose pH has been altered from acid to alkaline, a process called nixtamalization. The change this renders in flavor (think of the taste of corn tortillas versus cornbread) and in nutritional value (way more available nutrients post-alkalinizing) is profound.

To make this chili even more New Worldish, add some peeled, finely diced butternut squash. Ve

1 recipe New Mexico–style Green Chile Sauce (recipe follows)

1 can (1 pound 13 ounces) white hominy (posole), well drained

2 cans (30 ounces each) black beans, well drained

½ pound green beans, tipped, tailed, cut into 1-inch pieces, and blanched (see page 10)

4 cups cooked white or brown rice (or try one of the white-brown-red–wild rice mixes, such as those grown and sold by Lundberg Family Farms), for serving

Grated sharp Cheddar or Monterey Jack cheese, for garnish (optional)

Minced fresh cilantro leaves, for garnish

1 Place the green chile sauce in a large, heavy pot over high heat. Bring it to a boil, then turn it down to a simmer.

2 To the simmering sauce, add the posole, black beans, and blanched green beans. Simmer all together, over very low heat, for about 30 minutes. Serve hot, over rice, with grated cheese, if desired, and a generous scatter of cilantro.

Serves 4 to 6, with rice

Note: Posole, also called hominy, can be bought at any Latin American grocery. It's also often available at the supermarket in the ethnic foods aisle. Be sure to purchase plain posole—corn, lime, salt, water—not the posole stew with tomatoes and meat.

New Mexico–style Green Chile Sauce

A sauce like no other. People who don't eat much spicy food say it's hot; those who eat spice often consider it mild. Either way, it's one of the greats. **Vn**

2 tablespoons olive oil, or any mild vegetable oil, such as corn, canola, or peanut

1 small onion, diced

4 to 6 cloves garlic, diced

3 tablespoons unbleached white flour

1 quart (4 cups) water, heated to a near-boil

About 1½ ounces dried New Mexico green chiles, stemmed and crumbled (to equal about 1 cup)

½ to 1 teaspoon salt, or to taste

½ to 1 teaspoon dried oregano, preferably Mexican, or marjoram

❶ Heat the oil in a large, deep skillet (preferably nonstick) over medium heat. Add the onion and sauté until translucent, about 5 minutes. Add the garlic and sauté for 1 minute more, then sprinkle with the flour.

❷ Reduce the heat slightly and, stirring near-constantly, let the flour cook until it starts to color to a shade slightly deeper than parchment, but not quite caramel, 5 to 7 minutes. Whisk in the water a little bit at a time. When all the water has been added and the mixture is smooth, raise the heat to medium-high and cook until it thickens slightly, 3 to 5 minutes more. Add the green chiles, salt, and oregano.

❸ Let the mixture simmer uncovered, stirring occasionally, over medium-low heat, until the chiles are rehydrated, the sauce is thickened slightly, and the kitchen is aromatic, about 45 minutes. This is your New Mexico–style Green Chile Sauce. You can stop right here, remove it from the heat, and incorporate it into another dish or serve it at once as a condiment. Or let it come to room temperature and then cover and chill it; it keeps for 2 to 3 days in the fridge (you can also freeze it for up to 6 weeks).

Makes 2½ to 3 cups

CLASSIC GREEN CHILE STEW

Meaty, spicy but not take-the-top-of-your-head-off hot, the flavors here are rich and seductive, redolent with green chile, and just perfect for a wintry night. You can almost smell the sage and piñon as it simmers.

Not traditional but very good is the addition of a cup or two of fresh green beans, tipped, tailed, and sliced; throw 'em in at the same time as the potatoes. And if you have a cup or two of leftovers, extend it with a can of fire-roasted tomatoes with green chiles and serve it over rice, with beans on the side, of course; the dish will have a whole sparkling new lease on life.

If you use commercially made green chile sauce, this is pretty durned quick to put together. If not, make sure you have your green chile sauce made before you start. **Me**

6 strips bacon

1 pound cubed stew beef or pork butt

1 large onion, diced

4 cloves garlic, chopped

3 cups beer

Freshly ground black pepper

2 to 3 fist-size potatoes, peeled or not, diced

1 recipe New Mexico–style Green Chile Sauce (page 175), or 1 quart best-quality commercial green chile sauce, such as 505 Southwestern

Salt

Genie's Mother's Beans for Chili (page 161), ideally made with tepary rather than pinto beans, for serving

1 Place a large Dutch oven or heavy stew pot over medium heat, add the bacon, and cook it until crisp, 5 to 6 minutes. Remove the bacon to a paper-towel-lined plate and set it aside. Leave the drippings in the pot.

2 Brown the beef in the bacon fat over medium-high heat. Then lower the heat slightly, add the onion, and cook, stirring, until it begins to soften, about 3 minutes. Add the garlic and sauté for 1 minute more, then add the beer and lots of black pepper.

3 Bring the stew to a boil, then turn the heat down to the lowest possible heat, and let cook, tightly covered, for about 40 minutes. Lift the lid, add the potatoes (and a little water if you think it's needed to keep things from sticking; it probably won't be, and remember you don't want much liquid since the chile sauce is coming). Cover again, and let simmer for another 20 minutes.

④ Stir in the green chile sauce and simmer, half-covered, for 10 minutes, then taste for salt and pepper. Serve hot, or, even better, let it sit for a few hours (or refrigerate it, covered, overnight) and gently reheat it. Either way, ladle up Genie's Mother's Beans for an accompaniment, and remember to crumble up that crisped bacon from step 1 and sprinkle it over the top of each serving.

Serves 4 to 6

Note: Leftovers of this or any other chili or spicy bean stew (as long as it doesn't have a creamy base, like the White Chili) can be used to fill Tamale Pie Delahanty (page 236) or Cornbread Pie à la Hippie (page 239). The feijoada on page 245 can also be used this way, but it will probably need to be thinned down a bit with stock or canned tomatoes with green chiles (such as Ro*Tel); you want the chili filling to be substantial but also a bit juicy.

THE NEW MEXICO CHILE: OTHERS ARE GREEN WITH ENVY

That the New Mexican green chile pepper is one of a kind is a sacred mystery to chile devotees.

It's not strictly their type—the New Mexico chile botanical family, to which the 3- to 4-inch-long medium-hot fruits belong includes many named varieties: Española improved, New Mexico 6-4, Big Jim, chinmayo, and on and on. It's their habitat, their *terroir,* the soil and climate conditions under which the New Mexican chiles are grown.

Grow these same varieties in your own garden, and they'll taste distinctly different from those grown and harvested in New Mexico (unless, of course, you live in New Mexico). This is especially true of the green pods cultivated in Hatch, New Mexico, a community that is, as I said in *Passionate Vegetarian,* "Mecca to those who worship the great god Chile." New Mexico's soil, rainfall, and geographic felicity combine to give New Mexico–grown—and particularly Hatch-grown— green chiles a complexity of flavors unmatched elsewhere, flavors that deepen further when the chiles are dried.

Green chile (the sauce) made with dried New Mexico green chiles (the peppers) is an intensely, intoxicatingly soulful dish, whether used as a condiment or added to green chili (the stew). You can order the key ingredient at the Chile Shop, a mail-order and retail outlet in, naturally, Santa Fe (visit www.thechileshop.com or call 505-983-6080).

The time-pressed with a green chile hankering can indulge in 505 Southwestern Green Chile Sauce, an Albuquerque-made product that is almost as good as the from-scratch version. Go to www.505chile.com or call 1-888-505-CHILE (2445). The 505 sauce may also be found at your local natural foods or gourmet foods market, or, if you're really lucky, at the supermarket.

A PARALLEL UNIVERSE: MEAT ANALOGS

Would I love my warm fuzzy Polartec jacket less if it were labeled "imitation wool"? Quite possibly; I don't think of it as synthetic anything, but real Polartec. We need that kind of drastic renaming for those cunningly seasoned ingredients made of plants (usually soy and wheat) that are shaped and textured in such a way that they can play the role meat typically plays in a meal.

These plant-based "meats" have a lot going for them. They're healthier: lower in calories, lower in fat, and easier on both the planet and the human being eating them.

As a real-everything, imitation-nothing kind of person, I can well understand why the idea of "meat substitutes" might give you heebie-jeebies. I, too, cringe at the phrase. I don't cringe at the ingredients, though; I'm glad to have them ready to draw on and use, for in some dishes they're just perfect. To my mind, these foodstuffs are less a substitute, more a parallel universe.

Just as Polartec, though a created or man-made substance, is warmer, lighter, and less itchy than wool and would never be mistaken for wool, so too do these plant-based "meats" have a lot going for them. They're healthier: lower in calories, lower in fat, and easier on both the planet and the human being eating them. But if health were all there was to it, I wouldn't eat them, and neither, probably, would you. So, take it from me: Some of them I find utterly satisfactory from a culinary perspective, too. Here are some you should know about.

Seitan (SAY-tan) is made from gluten, the protein component of wheat. This gluten is poached in savory liquid to make a firm ingredient that can be cut up and baked or simmered in any number of sauces. Prepare seitan in any sauced dish, from Irish stew to goulash, and it's a dead ringer for beef. Now, seitan will never be equivalent to, say, a stand-alone steak; but it's just beyond terrific when gravied or stewed. And although new to Americans, it's been used in China for thousands of years. When you need big, hearty, chewy, proteinaceous chunks in chili, as in the Brown Bean Chili with Sweet Potatoes (page 180), and you don't want meat, seitan's the way to go. Since it's already cooked, you need only rinse it, cut it into appropriately sized pieces, and add it in the last 10 to 15 minutes of cooking time.

Ground Round: You use this where you'd use ground beef. Some "ground rounds" parallel ground beef in its raw form; you can use Gimme Lean Ground Beef Style, for example, just as you'd use ground beef to form meatballs or meat loaf; its texture in your hand is almost identical to its cow-derived counterpart. Other versions, like Tree of Life's Ready-Ground Tofu and Lightlife's Smart Ground, mimic ground beef that has already been browned; these are a super-easy way to get a jump on pasta sauces, tacos, and the like. Add this type when cooked ground beef is called for in specific recipes.

Soysage: Look at it this way: Pork or beef sausages don't appear in nature any more than their veggie doppelgängers do. Perhaps this is why the various "soysages" are so successful: They can follow the characteristic seasonings of meat sausage more or less precisely. These days, in the refrigerator case at your local co-op or natural foods supermarket, you'll find Italian sausage, kielbasa, bratwurst, vegetarian chorizo (one brand is called Soyrizo, which is moist and unshaped, like bulk sausage; I prefer Lightlife's chorizo-style "smart sausages" or Field Roast's Mexican Chipotle version), and many other varieties. I don't use them as stand-alones (though I know some who swear by a sub sandwich of Tofurky or Lightlife Italian sausage and sautéed peppers and onions). But in sauces or stews, they can be terrific. Brown them in a skillet, and serve whole as part of a bean and vegetable dinner, or slice them thick and stir into any simmering pot of chili or stew, adding them in the last few minutes.

TVP: Chili is one of the few things I sometimes make with TVP—textured vegetable protein—a soybean product processed to have the texture of ground beef. It differs from the "ground round" mentioned earlier in that it is dry, not moist, and does not require refrigeration. You can buy it in bulk at your local natural foods market; it keeps indefinitely on the shelf. It has generous amounts of protein (though very little flavor), and while it's not an ingredient I use often, I got into the habit of employing it in chilis years ago. It really works well this way: Pour 1 cup boiling vegetable stock over 1⅓ cups TVP, and let soak for 15 minutes to rehydrate; its texture will be fluffy. Season with 2 teaspoons salt and ½ teaspoon freshly ground pepper. Stir the rehydrated TVP into the onion-pepper sauté that is almost always part of a chili; do this when you add the spices.

A Note to Gluten-Intolerants: Some meat analogs contain wheat and other glutenous ingredients; always read the label.

BROWN BEAN CHILI
with Sweet Potatoes

Okay, traditional chilis are red, or, in New Mexico, green. There are even, as we'll see, white chilis. Is there *brown* chili? Well, not as such. But why not extend the range? Though if you'd rather call it a stew, be my guest. You see, there are some lovely brown beans out there—brown teparies, Swedish brown beans, and a few that turn a creamy brown while cooking, like yellow-eyes. Like all beans, these do well when swimming in a chile-scented gravy, and this one, enriched with a few dark secrets, is complex, hot but not searing, and with a faint undernote of sweetness. It moves the chili color-wheel from deep tomato-and-chili-powder maroon to an equally rich, deep golden-brown, with bright chunks of sweet potato that are as uplifting visually as they are pleasing to bite into. Try to get the brilliant, very sweet garnet yams if you can—and enjoy the lush, plush fall colors of every bite.

As you'll see, there are two ways to go with the nonmeat protein component. (To understand the differences, see A Parallel Universe: Meat Analogs, page 178.) I prefer to serve this chili over brown rice, rather than with cornbread. **Vn**

2 cups brown tepary beans, Swedish brown beans, or yellow-eye beans, picked over, rinsed, and soaked overnight (see page 352)

Vegetable oil cooking spray

2 whole ancho chiles (dried poblanos)

2 ounces dried porcini or shiitake mushrooms, crumbled into smallish pieces

1½ teaspoons cumin seeds

2 tablespoons olive oil

1 large onion, chopped

1 red bell pepper, stemmed, seeded, and diced

4 cloves garlic, sliced

½ teaspoon smoked sweet Hungarian paprika

2 teaspoons unsweetened cocoa powder

¼ to ⅛ teaspoon chipotle chile powder (not the wet, canned kind; you want the dried, ground chipotle peppers themselves)

Pinch of ground cinnamon

2 large sweet potatoes, peeled and cut into 1-inch chunks

1 tablespoon sun-dried tomato paste

1 package (8 to 12 ounces) traditionally seasoned seitan, drained and cut into 1-inch chunks, or 1 package (12 ounces) ground soy-wheat based "crumble" or "ground," such as Lightlife's Smart Ground Original or Tree of Life's Ready-Ground Tofu

1 tablespoon honey

2 teaspoons dark or blackstrap molasses or dark brown sugar

1¼ teaspoons salt, or to taste

Freshly ground black pepper

Cooked brown rice, for serving

Mixed Fruit Salsa (recipe follows) or tomato salsa, for serving

1 Drain the soaked beans and rinse them well. Place them in an oil-sprayed Dutch oven or heavy soup pot with the ancho chiles, mushrooms, and 1 quart (4 cups) water. Bring to a boil, then lower the heat to a simmer. Let cook, covered, over very low heat until tender, about 1½ hours.

2 Meanwhile, in a small, dry, heavy skillet, toast the cumin seeds over medium heat, stirring frequently, until they darken and grow fragrant, about 3 minutes. Set aside.

3 Heat the oil in a large skillet over medium heat. Add the onion and sauté until wilted, about 4 minutes. Add the bell pepper and sauté for 3 to 4 minutes more. Lower the heat, add the garlic, and sauté until fragrant, 1 minute more. Remove the skillet from the heat and add the reserved cumin seeds and the paprika, cocoa, chipotle powder, and cinnamon. Scrape this mixture into the bean pot and stir.

4 Bring the beans to a boil. Stir in the sweet potatoes, sun-dried tomato paste, seitan, honey, molasses, salt, and a generous amount of black pepper.

5 Lower the heat to a simmer and cook, half-covered, stirring occasionally, until the potatoes are tender, 20 to 25 minutes. If you can find the anchos, fish them out of the chili, remove and discard their stems, and transfer them to a food processor, along with a generous ladleful of beans (beans only—no seitan or sweet potato, which you want to keep in big, serious hunks). Buzz the chiles and beans to make a smooth, thick paste, and return the puree to the chili. Stir it in well; it thickens the mixture. Serve hot, accompanied by or scooped over the rice and with the luscious crunchy-sweet-hot fruit salsa.

Serves 6 to 8 when accompanied by rice

Mixed Fruit Salsa

This sprightly fiesta of a recipe, on which many changes can be rung, proves that the elements of salsa—hot, juicy, soft, crunchy, acid, sweet, colorful, herbal—can be continually reinvented. You'll note flavor breezes not only from the American Southwest (and points below), but from Thailand, too. **Ve** **Gf**

> 2 oranges, peeled, sectioned, seeded, and diced
>
> 1½ cups finely chopped pineapple, mango, papaya, or peach
>
> 1 cup medium-diced jicama
>
> 1 medium red onion, finely diced
>
> ½ teaspoon salt, or to taste
>
> 2 serrano chiles, seeds left in for heat or removed for mildness, minced
>
> ¼ cup finely minced fresh cilantro
>
> Juice of 1 lime or lemon, or to taste
>
> 1 to 2 ripe Hass avocados

1 Toss together the oranges, pineapple, jicama, red onion, salt, chiles, cilantro, and lime juice in a medium bowl, cover, and refrigerate for up to 2 days.

2 When you're about ready to serve, taste the salsa; you may wish to add a little more salt or lime juice. Then peel, pit, and cut the avocado(s) into ½-inch dice, and gently stir them in. Get ready for raves!

Makes 3½ to 4½ cups

VARIATION

Substitute 2½ cups finely chopped Asian apple-pear, Granny Smith apple, or Anjou pear, or a combination of these fruits, for the pineapple, jicama, and avocado. You may also substitute finely chopped mint for the cilantro, or include both herbs.

WHITE CHILI
with White Beans, Poblanos & Hominy

T hough still not extremely common, about fifteen years ago white chilis began to enjoy great popularity: ground turkey or diced chicken replaced the higher-fat ground beef; and stock, milk, evaporated skim milk, or cream replaced the tomatoes. This vegetarian take starts with white beans, such as navy beans. Then comes hominy—whole nixtamalized white corn, much larger than plain corn kernels, starchy, slightly unsweet—which adds an addictive texture and flavor unlike anything else.

This is a favorite of mine, though its hue is more peachy than truly white and it still isn't what I think of first when I say "chili." But its subtle bite, which begins mild, warms up to suffuse the eater with gentle heat and pleasure. The chile heat capers along, somewhere between barely there (especially if you seed the chiles) and emphatic. The small amount of grated Monterey Jack that's stirred into the stew brings it all together. If you're making this ahead—and, like all chilis, it really is best made ahead—don't add the cheese until the next-day reheat. Serve with a good cornbread made with white cornmeal; I'm partial to Truman Capote's Family's (page 166), which is intentionally dry and on the unsweet side, the better to go with chili and stew.

Molho à Campanha, traditional with feijoada, will add a colorful—and tart—jolt of red. **Vn Gf**

2½ cups white beans, such as navy, white tepary, Great Northern, or pea beans, picked over, rinsed, and soaked overnight (see page 16) or quick-soaked (see page 17)

Vegetable oil cooking spray (optional)

2 bay leaves

About 8 cups well-flavored vegetable stock

1 tablespoon olive oil

2 large onions, chopped

10 cloves garlic: 6 chopped, 4 whole

3 poblano chiles, stemmed, seeds and fiber left in for heat or removed for mildness, chopped

1 to 2 serrano chiles, stemmed, seeds and fiber left in for heat or removed for mildness, chopped

2 teaspoons ground cumin

2 teaspoons dried oregano

1⅓ cups rehydrated TVP (see box, page 179)

Salt and freshly ground black pepper

1 can (10 ounces) tomatoes with green
   chiles, such as Ro*tel or Cascadian Farms
   fire-roasted, with their liquid

1 tablespoon tomato paste

1 can (10 ounces) white hominy (posole),
   drained very well (about 1¼ cups;
   see Note, page 175)

1 cup (4 ounces) grated Monterey Jack
   cheese

Chili Fixins (page 173), for serving

Cornbread (optional), for serving

Molho à Campanha (recipe follows),
   for serving (optional)

1 Drain the soaked beans and rinse them
well. Place them in a large, heavy soup pot
or a large pressure cooker sprayed with
oil over high heat. Add the bay leaves and
enough stock to cover the beans to a depth
of 1 inch. If using a conventional pot, bring
the beans to a boil, then lower the heat to
a simmer, cover tightly, and let cook until
the beans are meltingly tender, 1 to 1½
hours. If using a pressure cooker, cover
the beans and let the pressure come up to
high, then lower the heat until the gauge
is at medium, and let cook for 18 minutes.
Turn off the heat and let the pressure come
down gradually; the beans will be perfectly
tender.

2 Meanwhile, heat the olive oil in an
oil-sprayed or nonstick skillet over medium
heat. Add the onions and sauté until
softened, about 5 minutes. Add the chopped
garlic, poblanos, and serranos, and sauté
for 2 minutes more. Add the cumin and
oregano, and sauté for 1 minute more. Add
the TVP and cook, stirring, until all the
ingredients are combined and the TVP is
just heated through, about 1 minute.

3 When the beans are done, scrape the
aromatic sauté into the bean pot. Fish out

and discard the bay leaves. Deglaze the
sauté skillet with a little of the vegetable
stock, stirring to loosen any browned bits
from the bottom of the pan. Pour this liquid
into the beans. Bring the beans to a boil,
then turn down to a simmer, and add lots
of salt and freshly ground pepper to taste.

4 Remove 3 or 4 ladlefuls of the beans
with a little of their cooking liquid from
the pot, and place them in a food processor
with the canned tomatoes with green chiles,
tomato paste, and reserved whole garlic.
Buzz to a thick puree, and set aside.

5 Add the hominy to the bean pot. Simmer,
half-covered, stirring occasionally, for 7 to 10
minutes. Add the pureed bean mixture and
let simmer, stirring occasionally, over very
low heat, for another 5 to 6 minutes.

6 Taste again to correct the seasonings.
Serve the chili hot, at once, with half of
the cheese stirred in, or let it come to
room temperature, then cover, refrigerate
overnight, and gently reheat it the next day,
stirring in the cheese just before serving.
Pass the remaining cheese, the Fixins, the
cornbread, and Molho, if you like, at the
table.

Serves 8 to 10

Molho à Campanha

Call it what you will—condiment, salsa,
vinaigrette, salad—all apply to its
combination of elements: hot, fresh, tart,
unctuous, tomato-y, herbal. Whatever
you decide it is, it's another piece of the
magic that makes Black Bean Fauxjoada
Vegetariana (page 196) so irresistible. But
why stop there? Since a small but vocal
contingent of eaters loathe cilantro (I am
not among them, but the late Julia Child

was), you can be kind and offer this as a non-cilantro'd salsa with any chili, burrito, enchilada, or bean soup that needs a little exclamation point.

If possible, assemble this an hour or two before serving, to give the flavors time to bloom and develop. In summer, try using a mixture of yellow, deep wine red, and green tomatoes (such as Green Zebra) as well as the typical bright reds. **Vn** **Gf**

> ½ cup extra-virgin olive oil
>
> 1 cup apple cider or white wine vinegar
>
> 1 teaspoon salt
>
> 1 cup finely minced fresh parsley
>
> 4 large fresh tomatoes, halved (or quartered if extra-large) and thinly sliced
>
> 1 large onion, finely chopped
>
> 2 fresh cayenne peppers, stemmed, seeds left in, very finely chopped

Combine all of the ingredients in a large bowl. Stir well, cover, and let stand at room temperature to develop the flavors. Serve at room temperature.

Makes about 3¾ cups

VARIATION

Fast-on-the-Draw "Brazilian Salsa": This is what I used to make in the inn days, before I'd had actual molho. I have to say, it's very good, though inauthentic. Simply combine ½ cup Tabasco sauce or Frank's RedHot Xtra Hot Sauce (or any very spicy vinegar-based hot sauce) with 1 large red onion, halved and very thinly sliced, 1 teaspoon salt, 2 tablespoons extra-virgin olive oil, and 2 tablespoons cider vinegar. **Vn** **Gf**

A CHILI RECEPTION

Chili is my traditional night-before-Thanksgiving dinner if out-of-town company is due. First, it's hassle-free as far as last-minute prep: You can, indeed should, make it ahead of time (if you freeze it, you can make it a month or two ahead). Second, it can be reheated or kept warm in a slow-cooker; it will wait amiably as guests begin arriving—invariably later than expected, and never all at once. Third, chili's rousing flavors and colors, its gently glowing heat on the tongue, are so very decisively *not* the tastes of the feast to come the following day.

I put out a buffet of Chili Fixins (page 173) and a pan of cornbread (pages 166, 167) or tortillas; and as folks drift in, it's an easy serve-yourself thing. We gather in the kitchen, feeding, greeting, catching up. There's a selection of local beers in a big bowl of crushed ice, and a pitcher of water (guests are always dehydrated when they arrive: this I know from my inn days). Sliced pears and quartered oranges with gingersnaps for dessert. It's an evening of quiet, low-key sweetness, food, and friends, including—as often as we can manage it, now that we live across the country from each other—Starr Mitchell, and George, Cane, and Logan West, with whom I've spent most Thanksgivings since 1976. In their company, I find myself just sort of thrumming with contentment and joy, feeling "this is the best, the very best, of life."

CHAPTER 6

Superior
STEWS,
Companionable
CURRIES

When in Rome, it's said, one should do as the Romans do. But you might especially want to do as one particular Roman, the poet Marcus Valerius Martialis (c. 41 to c. 102 A.D.) did, no matter where you are. A friend of Pliny the Younger and Juvenal, he's known as the father of the epigram. In one famous couplet, he wrote, "If pale beans bubble for you in a red earthenware pot / You can oft decline the dinners of sumptuous hosts."

We have already visited beans, pale and otherwise, bubbling away as soups and chilis. Now we'll let the bountiful, obliging bean bubble as stew. Here beans again showcase their versatile, amiable, amendable nature. We'll dip our spoons, forks, and/or chopsticks into stews from the East, such as Extra-Green Thai Green Curry of Green Beans, Green Pepper & Tofu (page 201), with its own homemade From-Scratch Green Curry Paste (page 202). We'll taste stews from the American South (Brunswick Stew, page 192) and from South America (Black Bean Fauxjoada Vegetariana, page 196). We'll sample stews that are tapestries of redolent spice (Ethopian Lentil Stew, page 207), and some that are quietly, modestly seasoned (Dorothy Read's Yellow-Eye Beans Redux, page 190). We'll consider vegetarian stews, and those incorporating meat, fish, or fowl as well as legumes. When in a hurry, we'll turn to more easily done stews (Jennifer's Spiced Red Beans in Coconut Milk, page 211). When we've got time and are in a cooking mood, we'll explore more complex stews (Black-Eyed Peas and Corn in Tomato Masala, page 204).

The lines of categorization do blur: Some bean-based soups in this book might pass as stews, as could many chilis. But rather than fuss over nomenclature, let's lean in toward the steamy kitchen. There, some combination of beans, vegetables, and aromatics is creating slow, vaporous fragrances, which rise through the house or apartment, sneaking under doorways and up stairs, fogging windows, reminding us, inviting us, to partake of life and stew: thick, hearty, and filled with ingredients that appear contradictory but seduce us nonetheless.

Gigi Hamilton's Really Hot, Really Delectable
MIXED BEANS
with a Lot of Ginger

My dear old Arkansas friend Susan Sims Smith was a Jungian therapist when I first knew her; she's now an Episcopalian minister. Her friend Gigi gave her this recipe, which she served and then passed on to me, and I've modified the method over time.

Although I can't imagine a grain dish that wouldn't be honored to accompany it, I always serve it the way I first had it at Susan's: with a gigantic, fresher-than-fresh mixed green salad; a pile of fluffy polenta topped with sautéed spinach, grilled portabello mushrooms, garlic, and tarragon; a good loaf of crusty bread alongside . . . and chocolate for dessert.

Please note that all the beans are drained of their liquid, which gives the finished dish a special lightness and makes the seasonings sparkle—but do save all that drained-off liquid for moistening the beans, if necessary, or for another stock pot. It's good, hearty, flavorful stuff.

This makes a rather large batch, but it freezes well. **Vn** **Gf**

Vegetable oil cooking spray (optional)

3 tablespoons olive oil

2 large onions, chopped

¼ cup loosely packed grated fresh ginger (Yes, ¼ cup—I wasn't woofin' when I said a lot of ginger! To get this amount, start with a root about half the size of your palm.)

5 cloves garlic, chopped

1 small fresh hot chile, such as serrano or jalapeño, stemmed, seeds removed for mildness or left in for heat, diced

1 can (10 ounces) diced tomatoes with green chiles (preferably fire-roasted), with their liquid

1 can (15 ounces) chickpeas, drained well

1 can (15 ounces) black beans, drained well

2 cans (15 ounces each) white or navy beans, drained well

2 cans (15 ounces each) kidney beans, drained well

1 can (15 ounces) white hominy (posole), drained well

1 bunch of fresh cilantro, stems chopped, leaves reserved for garnish (optional)

Hot cooked polenta or brown basmati rice, for serving

① Spray a large Dutch oven with vegetable oil (if it is not nonstick), add the olive oil, and place it over medium heat. Add the onions and sauté until slightly softened but not browned, about 4 minutes. Add the ginger, garlic, and the hot chile, if using, and continue to sauté, stirring often, until everything has wilted slightly and is fragrant, about 5 minutes more. Add the diced tomatoes and heat through.

2 Add all the beans plus the hominy, bring to a boil, turn down to the lowest possible simmer, and let cook over very low heat, stirring occasionally, to blend the flavors, about 20 minutes. Remember, there's not a lot of liquid here; if the heat's too high or if you forget to stir, you could burn it, which would be such a pity. (If you must, add back a little of the bean liquid you drained off, but this is not a soupy dish; add just enough to prevent burning or sticking.)

3 Add the cilantro stems and cook for 3 minutes more. Serve hot, accompanied by the cooked polenta and sprinkled liberally with the cilantro leaves, if using. Bow modestly when praised.

Serves 6 to 8 amply

ꙍ   ꙍ   ꙍ

Four-Star From-the-Cupboard
RED BEAN STEW

By March, a Vermont winter starts to feel very long. And when it snows, yet again, the last thing you want to do is head out in the car. Beans, that cupboard staple of sustenance and style, always come through. But, if you're also inclined to keep a few pantry exotics—sun-dried tomatoes, dried mushrooms—on hand, the beans not only come through, but do it like the culinary equivalent of a Fourth of July marching band. Yes, I know there are some to whom this preparation might seem overly fussy or complex. But the finished dish is *so* worth it, and if you're snowed in anyway, why not experiment?

Enjoy this as is, with toast and salad, on a Monday; on Wednesday, use the leftovers as a base for what may be the most delicious shepherd's pie you've ever had. **Ve** or **Vn**

3 cups dried red beans, picked over, rinsed, and soaked overnight (see page 350)

2 ounces dried shiitake mushroom caps

5 or 6 sun-dried tomato rounds (not packed in oil)

1 cup mushroom or vegetable stock, boiling

2 to 3 fist-size potatoes, peeled and cut into 1-inch cubes

3 carrots, peeled and sliced into ¾-inch rounds

4 cloves garlic, coarsely chopped

1 or 2 fresh jalapeños or other green chiles, canned chiles in adobo, or whatever pickled hot peppers your pantry yields

¾ cup nice hearty red wine

Vegetable oil cooking spray

¼ cup butter or olive oil

1 very large onion, diced

3 stalks celery, finely chopped

3 tablespoons unbleached white flour

1 Rinse the beans, drain them well, and put them in a Dutch oven or other large, heavy pot with enough water to cover them to a depth of about 2 inches. Bring to a boil, turn down the heat to a simmer, cover, and let cook until the beans begin to get tender, about 1 hour.

2 Meanwhile, during the early part of the beans' simmering, place the shiitake mushroom caps and sun-dried tomatoes in a small, heat-proof bowl. Pour the boiling stock over them, and let them sit to rehydrate.

3 Add the potatoes to the almost-tender beans, cover the pot, and let simmer for 15 minutes. Remove the rehydrated mushrooms from the liquid—you can use them whole, halved, or quartered: your choice—and add them to the pot along with the carrots. Let the mushrooms and carrots simmer with the beans until the carrots are tender, 15 minutes more.

4 Remove the sun-dried tomatoes from the soaking liquid, reserving the liquid (strain it if you see any grit). Transfer the soaked tomatoes to a food processor along with the garlic, jalapeño, and wine, and pulse-chop a few times to loosely combine. Leave the mixture in the processor; its moment will come.

5 Spray a large, heavy skillet with oil, add about 1 tablespoon of the butter, and place it over medium heat. When the butter has melted, add the onion and sauté until it loses its rawness, 3 to 4 minutes. Add the celery and sauté until softened slightly, another 3 minutes. Scrape the sauté from the skillet into the pot of simmering red beans, and stir it in well. Wipe out the skillet with a clean towel.

6 Add the remaining butter to the skillet, melting it over medium heat. Stir in the flour and cook, stirring almost constantly, until the flour has browned to a nice golden caramel color, 6 to 8 minutes. Whisk in the reserved mushroom-and-tomato-soaking water and cook for a minute or so, scraping and whisking in the flour to make a thick, flavorful paste.

7 Scrape this paste into the mixture waiting in the food processor. Pulse a few more times to combine everything, but leave it texture-y. Then transfer the paste into the simmering red beans and stir very well.

8 Serve right away, or let sit for a few hours (or refrigerate, covered, overnight) and reheat just before serving.

Serves 4 to 6

VARIATION

Scoot over to Bountiful Bean Bakes, Comforting Casseroles, and see the general directions for Summer Garden Potpie with Cheese-Herb Drop Biscuits (page 240). Four-Star From-the-Cupboard Red Bean Stew makes a superb base for that biscuit topping.

Dorothy Read's
YELLOW-EYE BEANS REDUX

It's pretty easy to spot the Reads's house when you drive into Bellows Falls, Vermont. It's the big pale pink Victorian with the enthusiastic garden . . . and, oh yes, the large gargoyle on the roof. Don't be afraid: He's safely enclosed in the widow's walk, and he's got his nose buried in a book (*Grimm's Fairy Tales,* as it happens). If it's late June, and you're driving with the windows open, you can't help but breathe in: More than fifty varieties of roses are in bloom, and you'll probably wish you could linger there a bit. Oh wait, you can: Dorothy and Stewart's home is also the Readmore Bed, Breakfast and Books.

Dorothy grew up not too far away, in Spofford, New Hampshire, and one of the best-loved dishes of her growing-up years was her mother's yellow-eye beans, a New England favorite. Dorothy's mom cooked them slowly, with an onion and salt pork, and served them with a pitcher of whole milk or cream, warmed, to pour over them at the table, along with "baking powder biscuits so flaky they almost fell apart on the way to your mouth." Although Dorothy serves meat at Readmore's breakfasts unless requested otherwise, she, herself, is quietly vegetarian (as I was when I was an innkeeper). So she makes "what is still one of my absolute favorite dishes, sans salt pork." This is very simple, almost plain. The smoked paprika and the cream pour-over at the end are essential. **Ve** **Gf**

1 pound dried yellow-eye beans

2 to 3 tablespoons butter

1 "whopping" onion or 2 large onions, diced

1 heaping teaspoon smoked sweet Hungarian paprika, plus more to taste

Salt and freshly ground black pepper

1 to 2 cups heavy cream, whole milk, or half-and-half, warmed, for serving

1 Place the yellow-eyes in a large pot and add water to cover. Soak them overnight, then drain and rinse them well.

2 In a large Dutch oven, heat the butter over medium heat. When the butter melts, sizzles, and then stops sizzling, add the onions. Sauté them slowly until very soft, limp, and slightly browned, about 10 minutes. Add the beans and water to cover them to a depth of about 2 inches.

3 Bring to a boil, turn down to a simmer, and let the beans cook, covered, at the lowest possible heat, "all day" says Dorothy; I cook them for at least 4 hours, but longer won't hurt them.

4 When the beans have been cooking for at least 2 hours, stir in the paprika and cover them again.

5 When the beans are very, very tender, check the consistency of the stew: The liquid in which the beans have cooked should be quite thick. Raise the heat a little if needed to evaporate a bit of the cooking liquid, stirring to make sure that the beans don't stick to the pot in the process. Season generously with salt and pepper.

6 Serve in big bowls, passing around the warmed cream to pour over the beans.

Serves 4 to 6 with accompaniments

A SPOFFORD SUPPER AT READMORE

Jacob's Coat Salad: a bed of baby spinach and mesclun greens with sliced purple cabbage; grated carrots; slivered red, green, and yellow bell peppers; diced baked beets; and sliced avocado

★

My Basic Feisty Vinaigrette (page 132), with a touch of maple syrup

★

Dorothy Read's Yellow-Eye Beans Redux

★

Extra-flaky from-scratch biscuits

★

Butter and blackberry jam

★

Apple cider sorbet, sliced Honeycrisp apples, and warm walnuts in the shell

★

Gingerbread

"So many things were foods cooked out of necessity. They were cheap, but they were always delicious and filling and, it turns out, pretty darn nutritious as well. This is a dish that is best made simply. We always had the milk on the side because my brothers didn't like it; the cream came in later, in more abundant years. It's better with cream, but you don't need a lot; it's not bad with soy cream or fat-free half-and-half either. But it is the one dish that I overload with salt, to make up for the absence of the salty pork fat! I've been a happy camper since I found smoked paprika. Its strength does vary, though, so start with a good heaping teaspoon of the paprika and then add more as needed to get the good subtle smokiness."

—Dorothy Read, innkeeper at
Readmore Bed, Breakfast and
Books (www.readmoreinn.com)

BRUNSWICK STEW

Did Brunswick Stew originate in Brunswick, Georgia, or in Brunswick County, southern Virginia? Both claim it. My mother, a native of Norfolk, Virginia, used to make it, and it's a staple of the Southeast: an unpretentious thick succotash-like vegetable mix slow-simmered in a tomato-based sauce with big hearty chunks of beef, pork, game, or chicken (my mother used the latter, the preferred Virginian way, with a bit of smoked ham or bacon for flavor).

When, in 1971, I spent a year in the rural Missouri Ozarks, as part of a self-sufficiency-based commune, I made it, too—with squirrel and rabbit, also traditional, more favored by the Georgia contingent. (Like all such dishes, each variation of Brunswick Stew has its partisans who claim that theirs is *it*.) These days I try not to roll my eyes when, as often happens—still!—people, especially in the culinary world, imply that we vegetarians are dainty, unadventurous wusses. I wonder how many of *them* have skinned and cleaned a rabbit or a squirrel (which also requires removing its musk glands)—then cooked and eaten it.

But I digress. Today, Brunswick Stew is one of those regional dishes that is often made in enormous quantities for church and community fund-raisers, as Boiled Dinner is in New England. But it's still made, and loved, at home. Mine has a little more kick than the traditional; in my commune days I lived with a long, tall Texan and those Texans do like their foods hot, a position to which I was swiftly converted, and which has remained in my life far longer than did most other details of that phase.

A not-sweet skillet-sizzled cornbread like the Truman Capote's Family's (page 166) is just about perfect with this. And, if you can't get fresh okra, omit it. Frozen okra is just plain nasty, in my view. **Me** **Gf**

2 tablespoons vegetable oil, such as corn, canola, or peanut (or, if you prefer, bacon fat), plus more if needed

1 large onion, diced

1 smoked ham hock

1 fryer chicken (3½ to 4 pounds), cut up, excess fat removed

1 quart (4 cups) homemade or canned chicken stock (or 2 cups stock plus 2 cups water)

1 cup any mild, not-too-herbal tomato sauce, or canned stewed tomatoes

1 can (14.5 ounces) diced tomatoes, preferably fire-roasted

½ to ⅓ cup commercial barbecue sauce (see box, page 195)

¼ to ⅓ cup vinegary hot sauce, such as Tabasco, Frank's RedHot, or Crystal

1 to 2 tablespoons Worcestershire sauce

½ to 1 tablespoon honey or brown sugar (light or dark)

2 fist-size russet or Yukon Gold potatoes, peeled and cut into ¾-inch dice

1 bag (10 ounces) frozen lima beans

1 bag (10 ounces) frozen corn kernels

½ pound fresh okra, stemmed and cut into ½-inch slices

Salt and freshly ground black pepper

1 Make the chicken base: Place a large, heavy skillet over medium heat and add the oil. When the oil is hot and shimmering, add the onion and ham hock and cook, stirring, until the onion is softened and you smell the hammy, smoky fragrance of the hock, about 6 minutes. Transfer the onion and hock to a large Dutch oven or other heavy stew pot.

2 Return the skillet to medium heat and, working in batches, brown the chicken pieces, adding more oil or bacon fat if needed. When the underside of each piece is golden, use tongs to flip it; allow about 5 minutes for each side. Transfer the browned pieces to the Dutch oven.

3 Pour about ¾ cup of the chicken stock into the skillet, stirring to loosen any browned bits from the bottom of the pan. Pour this liquid and the remaining stock into the Dutch oven.

4 Set the Dutch oven over high heat and bring it to a boil. Cover it, then lower the heat to the merest simmer and let cook for 45 minutes. At this point, either skim the fat from the top of the stew and discard it, or remove the stew from the heat, let it come to room temperature, cover it, and chill it overnight; in the morning, remove the fat cap on the surface.

5 When the stew has been defatted (and brought back to a simmer, if you went the chilling route), add the tomato sauce, diced tomatoes, barbecue sauce, hot sauce, Worcestershire sauce, honey, and all of the vegetables to the pot. Season with salt and plenty of pepper to taste. Simmer, covered, until the potatoes are fork-tender and the chicken and ham are almost falling off the bone, 20 to 30 minutes.

6 Fish out the chicken and the ham hock. Let them cool slightly, and then pull the meat from the bones and into big chunks. Return the meat to the pot, heat the stew through, taste again for seasonings, and serve.

Serves 6 to 8

"Brunswick stew is what happens when small mammals carrying ears of corn fall into barbecue pits."

—*Roy Blount, Jr.*

CD'S BRUNSWICK NEW-STEW

Obviously this is not traditional, but it takes many licks from the classic Brunswick stew flavors. A nice gutsy vegetable stew, it's particularly excellent when you've got good fresh okra. I add fresh green beans, too, which are always so appealing when slow-cooked with potatoes. The stew is given meatiness by nutritional yeast (see box, page 109)—don't knock it till you've tried it—and baked tempeh stirred in at the last. The Bacon Salt, a vegetarian product that realio, trulio tastes like bacon (you can find it at www.baconsalt.com), plus the smoked paprika, get the smoky note just right.

Get the Basic Oven-Baked Marinated Tempeh going in the oven before or while preparing the stew component. **Vn**

2 tablespoons any vegetable oil, such as corn, canola, or peanut

1 large onion, diced

2 carrots, scrubbed and diced

1 stalk celery, diced

1 quart (4 cups) vegetable stock

1 cup any mild, not-too-herbal tomato sauce, or canned stewed tomatoes

1 can (14.5 ounces) diced tomatoes (preferably fire-roasted)

½ to ⅓ cup commercial barbecue sauce, to taste (see box, opposite page)

¼ to ⅓ cup vinegary hot sauce, such as Tabasco, Frank's RedHot, or Crystal

1 to 2 tablespoons vegetarian Worcestershire sauce or Pickapeppa sauce

½ to 1 tablespoon honey or brown sugar (light or dark)

½ teaspoon smoked sweet Hungarian paprika

2 fist-size russet or Yukon Gold potatoes, peeled and cut into ¾-inch dice

1 bag (10 ounces) frozen lima beans

1 bag (10 ounces) frozen corn kernels

⅓ pound fresh green beans, tipped, tailed, and sliced into ½-inch rounds

½ pound fresh okra, stemmed and cut into ½-inch rounds

¼ cup nutritional yeast (see box, page 109)

Salt and freshly ground black pepper

Bacon Salt (see box, page 112)

2 tablespoons cornstarch or arrowroot (optional)

2 batches Basic Oven-Baked Marinated Tempeh (page 244), cut in good-size triangles or rectangles

① Place the oil in a large, heavy skillet over medium heat. Add the onion and sauté until fragrant and slightly soft, about 4 minutes. Add the carrots and celery and sauté for another 3 minutes, then transfer the vegetables to a large Dutch oven or another heavy stew pot.

② Return the skillet to medium heat and pour about ¾ cup of the stock into it, stirring to loosen any browned bits from the bottom of the pan. Pour this liquid along with 3 cups of the remaining stock into the Dutch oven.

③ Place the pot over high heat and bring it to a boil, then stir in the tomato sauce, diced tomatoes, barbecue sauce, hot sauce, Worcestershire sauce, honey, paprika, and all of the vegetables except the okra. Bring to a boil again, then turn down the heat to a medium simmer, cover, and let cook for about 20 minutes. Stir in the okra and let cook until the potatoes and green beans are tender and the okra is starting to disintegrate a bit. Stir in the nutritional yeast and season to taste with salt, pepper, and Bacon Salt.

④ If you want the stew a little thicker, place the remaining stock in a cup and stir the cornstarch into it, smushing it with your fingers to make a smooth paste. Stir this into the stew, which should thicken and grow glossy almost immediately.

⑤ Stir in the tempeh, and let it cook for a minute to heat through. Serve right away.

Serves 4 to 6

VARIATIONS

Soysage Brunswick Stew: Omit the tempeh, replacing it with 1 pound browned vegetarian chorizo or Italian sausage (I like the ones made by Lightlife, Field Roast, and Tofurky). After you've browned the soysage, cut it into thick slices and stir it into the stew during the last 5 minutes. **Vn**

Sweet Potato Brunswick Stew: Replace the white potatoes with 1 large peeled, diced sweet potato or yam. **Vn**

BBQ, ASAP

But . . . *barbecue sauce,* you say, as you survey the Brunswick New-Stew ingredients list? Well, no, it's not traditional, but it's here because the smokiness plays up the heat, the sweet balances the tomato acidity, and it's the perfect touch—which in my view, makes the stew much more interesting. Of the relatively easy-to-find brands of commercial sauce, I'd go with Bone Suckin' Sauce (a macabre name for vegetarian sensibilities) or Trader Joe's Bold and Smoky Kansas City Style Barbecue Sauce; both have the critical sweet-smoky balance, and neither is loaded up with preservatives or high-fructose corn syrup.

BLACK BEAN FAUXJOADA VEGETARIANA

The national dish of Brazil is traditionally a pot of black beans made savory by herbs, spices, a touch of orange, and, in its classic formulation, with cow and pig in many forms—chorizo sausage, beef tongue, salt pork, and whatever else the home or restaurant cook has on hand and can afford. The stew has many fans when made this way—it's the national dish for a reason—but when I make it, by my long-time personal preferences, I omit the meat. Anyone who deems this a loss has not tasted my version: different, but easily as good, and likely to help you live long enough to enjoy it many more times than the other. I've amped the seasonings way up, added some savory sautéed vegetables, and made a few other changes. The orange, rind and all, cooked with the beans is traditional, and I do love the subtle flavor it gives—so much so that I sometimes make it less subtle by using *two* oranges. Your call; one is standard operating procedure.

Chipotle peppers and smoked paprika give it that nice woodsy, wild flavor reminiscent of the meats. I probably prefer the bean-only variety, but every so often, as a nod to tradition, and also to add texture and further layers of flavor, I incorporate several varieties of soysage. I like this, too, and I must say, many guests have raved about it. Either way, serve it *completa* (see the box on page 198, and be sure to include the sliced oranges, which are essential: because their fruity, juicy, acidic-sweet tang perks up the whole dish). I promise that when you eat either version you won't be saying "Well, not bad for vegetarian," but simply "Wow." Highly satisfactory all around. **Vn** **Gf**

FOR THE BEANS:

3 cups dried black beans, picked over, rinsed, and soaked overnight (see page 344)

2 bay leaves

1 tablespoon dried oregano

1 onion, unpeeled, stuck with 4 cloves

1 whole head garlic, unpeeled

½ teaspoon chipotle chile powder

1 orange (preferably organic), well washed, halved

FOR THE SAUTÉ AND SEASONING:

¼ cup vegetable oil such as olive, coconut, or canola

2 large yellow onions, chopped

6 cloves garlic, crushed

1 dried red cayenne pepper, stemmed and chopped

1 to 2 teaspoons salt

1½ teaspoons smoked sweet Hungarian paprika

2 tablespoons tomato paste

1 tablespoon white miso paste (see page 80)

FOR SERVING:

Cooked white rice

Completa components (see box, page 198)

① Make the beans: Drain the soaked beans and rinse them well. Place them in a Dutch oven and add water to cover by about 1½ inches. Add the bay leaves, oregano, clove-studded onion, whole garlic, chipotle powder, and orange. Bring to a boil, then turn down to a nice low simmer and let cook, covered, until the beans are yielding but still a little firm, about 1 hour.

② While the beans continue to simmer, scoop out the onion and discard it. Scoop out the garlic and reserve it. Press the orange halves against the sides of the pot with a wooden spoon to help extract any residual oils from the rind.

③ Make the sauté: Heat the oil in a large, heavy skillet over medium heat. Add the chopped onions and sauté until slightly softened, about 5 minutes. Lower the heat, add the garlic and the dried cayenne, and sauté for 2 minutes more. Scrape this mixture into the simmering beans. Deglaze the skillet with a little of the bean liquid,

scraping with a spatula, and add the glaze to the beans.

④ Let the beans cook over very low heat, half-covered, until they are tender, another 30 minutes. Add the salt to taste, paprika, tomato paste, and miso. Squeeze the cooled, softened garlic cloves out of their papery skins and stir them into the beans. Let cook over very low heat for 15 minutes more.

⑤ Serve the fauxjoada hot, over or with rice, and with the Completa components any time from here on out. (It doesn't hurt a bit to wait; it only gets better. Reheat, of course—you want it steaming hot.)

Serves 6 to 8 with Completa components

VARIATION

Fauxjoada Vegetariana with Soysage: Meaty, and yet, of course, not, this is a heartier version of the above. After you've sautéed the onion mixture and deglazed the skillet, wash and dry it. Add another 2 or 3 tablespoons oil to the skillet, and place it over medium-high heat. Add 1 to 3 packages (12 ounces each) commercially prepared vegetarian sausage links (soysages)—1 package each Italian, chorizo, and Polish flavors, or just one variety if you prefer—and cook, in batches if necessary, until brown on all sides, about 6 minutes total per batch, adding a little more oil if necessary. Remove the soysages from the pan, and let them cool to the touch. (If you like, again deglaze the skillet with a little of the bean cooking liquid, stirring to loosen any browned bits from the bottom of the pan: extra tastiness. Return this liquid to the pot.) Slice the soysages into 2-inch chunks (you can slice them thinner if you prefer) and add them to the beans when you add the squeezed-out garlic cloves. **Vn**

Completa? Perfecta!

Feijoada Completa is complete feijoada . . . with all the fixings, as we might say, on one plate. Just as feijoada has infinite variations, so do its accompaniments. Like feijoadas themselves, they differ from region to region within Brazil. But here's what *more or less* constitutes the whole thing:

★ Feijoada

★ Cooked white rice

★ *Couve a Mineira* (raw collard greens, page 126, or cooked collards)

★ *Molho à Campanha* (a cross between salsa, tomato slaw, and vinaigrette, page 183)

★ *Farofa* (recipe follows)

★ Sliced fresh oranges

And, on the side: *pan de quiejo* (chewy-puffy tapioca-flour cheese rolls) and *piri-piri* (tiny, very hot triangular hot peppers preserved in oil). One last optional addition: fried plantain slices.

Farofa

Toasted tapioca flour, also called manioc meal or cassava flour, is often served as part of a feijoada completa. Sometimes it's just toasted in a dry skillet over medium heat until golden brown, and then sprinkled over the top of the feijoada. More often, it's made as a kind of quick pilaf, characteristically golden-yellow. To carb-averse Americans, rice *and* farofa might seem like starch overload, but some of each is the way in many Brazilian families.

The fats (plural; two kinds) in which you sauté the onion and then the tapioca flour are all-important: They give flavor, moisture, and color. This last is traditionally provided by dende oil (palm oil, beloved in Africa and Brazil, but hard to find in the United States and highly saturated, too) or annatto oil (not traditional, but often used because it's easier to come by and more healthful; see www.deepfeast.com for a photo essay on making annatto oil). Both the dende and tapioca flour are available at Afro-Caribbean markets, and online at www.amigofoods.com/brazilianfood.html.

Use a very large skillet or wok to prepare the farofa. Make it the day you serve the feijoada; leave it at room temperature and sprinkle it over the steaming hot stew at serving time. Gf Ve or Vn or Me

1/4 to 1/3 cup butter, olive oil, or bacon fat

1 large onion, chopped

1 tablespoon dende oil or annatto oil (optional, but necessary for color)

3 cups manioc meal or coarse tapioca flour (same thing) but *not* finely ground tapioca starch or tapioca granules

About 1 teaspoon salt, or to taste

1. In a large, heavy skillet over medium heat, melt the butter. Add the onion and sauté, stirring, until it is softened but not browned, about 3 minutes. Drizzle in the dende or annatto oil, if using, and stir again.

2. Add the manioc meal and salt and cook over low heat, stirring constantly until the farofa is golden, savory, and heated through, 3 to 5 minutes.

NOTE: In Brazil farofa is often used to stuff roast chicken, too, with dried fruit tossed in. Sometimes garlic is sautéed with the onion; and those who like bacon fat's salty-smokiness often add in crumbled cooked bacon at the end (in which case, reduce the salt).

BHUJIA

This kicky curry of green beans, backed up with potatoes and spinach, has been part of my repertoire since the days of the first edition of *The Bean Book* (this book's predecessor). It's still a winner, though rather on the dry side, hence a great addition to a dinner that includes a nice soupy dahl, such as any of those on pages 81–88. And if you choose coconut oil as the cooking fat, it's vegan.

To make prep simpler, pull all the spices from your cupboard before you begin. Lay them out to your left. Open each jar one at a time, measure its spice into a small dish (in this curry, you can combine all the spices in one dish), move it to the right, and screw on the lid. Continue, jar by jar. Put the spice jars away again before even starting the recipe. Your kitchen will be much tidier and more restful to work in and if the phone rings midway you won't be asking yourself, "Wait, did I put the cayenne in or not?" **Gf** **Ve** or **Vn**

1 pound green beans, tipped, tailed, and sliced into ½-inch lengths

3 fist-size potatoes, peeled or not according to your taste, cubed

½ to 1 teaspoon salt

8 ounces fresh spinach, well washed, tough stems removed, any large pieces torn

2 to 3 tablespoons ghee or coconut oil

2 onions, sliced

1 serrano chile, stemmed, seeds left in for heat or removed for mildness, minced

A chunk of fresh ginger (about the size of a thumb), peeled and finely chopped

1½ teaspoons ground turmeric

1½ teaspoons ground coriander

1½ teaspoons ground cumin

¾ teaspoon ground fenugreek seeds

1 teaspoon black mustard seeds

1 teaspoon paprika (or ½ teaspoon smoked sweet Hungarian paprika)

½ teaspoon ground cardamom

¼ to ½ teaspoon cayenne

½ teaspoon freshly ground black pepper

2 cloves garlic, pressed or finely minced

1 Bring about 2 cups water to a boil in a large, heavy saucepan and drop in the green beans, potatoes, and salt. Lower the heat slightly, cover the pot tightly, and let the vegetables cook at a brisk simmer until the beans are done—past tender-crisp, but not mushy—and the potatoes are not quite tender, 12 to 15 minutes. Add the spinach (you may have to pack it down to fit it all), cover, and continue cooking. The spinach will quickly wilt down. When it does—1 to 2 minutes—lower the heat slightly.

2 While the vegetables cook, prepare the sautéed seasoning mix (called a *baghar*): Heat the ghee in a large skillet over medium-high heat. Add the onions and sauté until they have wilted slightly, 2 to

3 minutes. Lower the heat a little, add the serrano and ginger, and continue stir-frying for about a minute. Then add all the spices at once. Cook, stirring almost constantly, until the spices darken slightly and grow fragrant, 3 to 5 minutes. Add the garlic, stir a few times, and remove from the heat.

3 By this time, the green beans and potatoes should be fully tender and the spinach well wilted. Scoop them out of whatever cooking liquid is left, and toss them thoroughly with the baghar in the skillet. Add a few tablespoons of any residual vegetable cooking water to aid in scraping up the spicy bits from the bottom of the skillet; remember, this is a dryish curry.

4 Reheat through in the skillet if needed, and serve with your favorite curry accompaniments.

Serves 4 to 6 with rice, dahl, and yogurt or raita

THAI CRYSTAL

Go to an Asian market, and you can probably buy a brand of *nahm jeem gratiem,* a Thai condiment: a red-tinged, transparent, glassy (hence "crystal") thick syrup in which float tiny pieces of garlic and flakes of dried chile. But the homemade version is so much better. My friend Nancie McDermott (who lived in Thailand while in the Peace Corps, and is herself a great cook and cookbook writer) translates its name as Sweet-Hot Garlic Sauce. But this true-enough summation doesn't do justice to its four-note flavors (sweet, hot, sour, garlicky), a chord so irresistible your mouth will not be able to get the music out of its mind. Make it once and you will never *ever* let your refrigerator be without a jar.

Other than peeling and dicing all that garlic, this classic is easy to make. I learned it from Nancie's fine book *Real Thai,* making only one change: rice vinegar instead of white.

If you don't want to deal with mucho garlic peeling, buy commercially peeled garlic cloves and go from there, using a food processor to help with the mincing. Don't, however, use a bottle of commercially prepared minced garlic; it often contains preservatives and/or has an off flavor—understandable, as the volatile oils that make garlic emphatic get released the second a clove's cut into.

2 cups sugar

½ cup rice vinegar

About 40 cloves fresh garlic, peeled and finely minced (about ¼ cup)

2 teaspoons salt

2 tablespoons coarse dried red chile flakes (with seeds)

1. Combine 1 cup water with the sugar, vinegar, garlic, and salt in a heavy, medium-size saucepan and bring to a rolling boil over medium heat. Stir to dissolve the sugar and salt, turn the heat to low, and simmer until the liquid reduces to a light syrup, about 20 minutes. Turn off the heat.

2. Stir the chile flakes into the liquid. Let cool to room temperature, then transfer to a clean jar. Thai crystal will keep indefinitely in the refrigerator. Shake well before using.

Extra-Green
THAI GREEN CURRY
of Green Beans, Green Pepper & Tofu

O h, the sweet–searingly hot happy havoc Thai green curries work! Their tingling combination of fresh herbal notes, chiles, often fruit, and creamy, dreamy unctuous coconut milk enchants my palate every single time. I've learned to make them at home, because most Thai restaurants use a splash of fermented fish sauce (*nam pla*), a salty flavoring sauce similar to soy sauce but derived from fish. Nam pla is the one typically Thai flavor note *not* to my liking; to me, it's sort of spoiled-tasting (though if you grew up with it, I understand, nothing Thai tastes quite right without it). Although most dishes on a Thai menu can be made without nam pla (even though the waiter may roll his or her eyes), green curries usually can't be, because the sauce is made, nam pla and all, in advance.

A superb recipe for homemade green curry paste follows. It puts the commercially made curry pastes to shame. However, when I'm jonesing for Thai and in a hurry or short on ingredients, I'm glad to have a jar of the commercial stuff in the pantry (which I always do). But I'm even gladder when I have homemade in the freezer.

Once the curry paste is made, this dish, with its rich, satiny, deeply creamy coconut milk, is a quick business. **Vn** **Gf**

Vegetable oil cooking spray

3½ cups regular or reduced-fat unsweetened coconut milk

¼ cup From-Scratch Green Curry Paste (recipe follows) or a commercial variety, plus extra as needed

1 pound green beans, tipped, tailed, and cut on an angle into 2-inch pieces

1 package (8 ounces) traditional water-packed extra-firm tofu, well drained and cut into bite-size dice

2 tablespoons tamari or shoyu soy sauce, plus extra as needed

1 tablespoon dark brown sugar, plus extra as needed

2 teaspoons grated lime zest

1 green bell pepper, stemmed, seeded, and sliced into thin strips

½ cup loosely packed fresh basil leaves, preferably Thai basil

½ cup frozen green peas (unthawed)

¼ to ½ teaspoon salt (optional)

Chopped cilantro leaves, for garnish

Fresh hot green chile, sliced into rings, for garnish

Steamed jasmine rice or rice noodles, for serving

Thai Condiment Tray (page 203), for serving (optional)

1 Spray a medium-large saucepan or small Dutch oven with oil (if it is not nonstick), add the coconut milk, and bring it to a gentle boil over medium heat. Let simmer for 5 minutes, stirring occasionally, then add the curry paste, whisking to dissolve it into the coconut milk. Continue cooking for 2 more minutes.

2 Add the green beans, tofu, soy sauce, brown sugar, and lime zest. Let cook at a gentle boil, stirring occasionally, until the green beans are tender-crisp, 8 to 10 minutes. Add the bell pepper and half of the basil leaves and stir to wilt the basil.

3 Take the green peas straight from the freezer, pour them into a strainer, and run hot tap water over them briefly. Stir them, barely thawed, into the curry.

4 Taste and adjust the seasonings, adding salt if necessary, as well as perhaps a little more brown sugar, curry paste, or soy sauce.

5 Transfer the curry to a serving bowl, and sprinkle with the reserved basil, the cilantro, and the green chiles. Serve very hot, with rice or noodles and the Thai Condiment Tray, if using, on the table.

Serves 6 to 8, when accompanied by rice or noodles

From-Scratch Green Curry Paste

Yes, I know: Making your own curry paste is a big hassle and will probably require a trip to an Asian market. But make it at least once in your life—it's that good. I use fermented black beans instead of the traditional shrimp paste or nam pla, but you can use either. This recipe makes enough for four full batches of the green curry above, but stirring a tablespoon or two into any stir-fry quickly moves it from ordinary to off the charts.

Once the ingredients are combined and ground, the flavors start losing their mojo. To prevent this, scrape the mixture, in ¼-cup portions, into small zip-top bags, place these in a large zip-top bag, place that in a second big zip-top bag, and then freeze the lot. (This triple-bagging not only provides ready-to-go portioning but also prevents the bag of frozen peaches nestling beside the curry from tasting startlingly of cilantro and garlic.)

Lemongrass, available at Asian food markets and easily grown, is a sturdy, tough, reedy seasoning, which doesn't look at all herbal. It has a magical lemony-floral taste unlike anything else. If you can't get fresh lemongrass, don't bother making this green curry paste. Period.

> 2 tablespoons coriander seeds
>
> 2 teaspoons cumin seeds
>
> 10 whole peppercorns
>
> 6 stalks fresh lemongrass
>
> 1 cup coarsely chopped fresh cilantro, including washed roots and stems if possible
>
> 2 tablespoons peeled, finely grated fresh ginger

2 teaspoons finely grated lime zest

About 4 heads (not cloves, we're talking whole heads here) fresh garlic, cloves peeled and coarsely chopped (to equal ⅓ cup chopped)

¼ red onion or 1 to 2 small shallots, coarsely chopped (about ⅓ cup chopped)

1 cup coarsely chopped fresh green serrano or jalapeño chiles (about 6 to 7 serranos, 5 to 6 jalapeños)

2 teaspoons fermented black beans, or fermented black bean and garlic sauce, or shrimp paste

2 teaspoons salt

1 In a small, dry, heavy skillet over medium heat, toast the coriander and cumin seeds until browned and fragrant, stirring or shaking the skillet often to prevent burning, 3 to 5 minutes. Transfer the toasted spices to a mortar and pestle or a small spice grinder, add the peppercorns, and crush to a fine powder. Set aside.

2 Prepare the lemongrass: Cut away and discard the grassy tops of the stalks as well as any tough root sections, leaving a piece about 3 inches in length with a clean, smooth, flat base at the root end below the bulb. Peel off and discard the tough outer leaves to reveal a softer, pale yellow stalk; thinly slice crosswise what is left.

3 Combine the crushed spices and lemongrass in a food processor along with the remaining ingredients. Buzz, pausing several times to scrape down the sides of the processor. When the paste is thick, fragrant, and fairly smooth—you may wish to add just a little water—it's ready for use. Use as much as you need, then freeze the rest as described in the headnote. It will keep, frozen, for up to 6 months, though it starts losing a little pungency after 3 months.

Makes about 2 cups

THAI CONDIMENT TRAY

You've probably seen this on the table at Thai restaurants—a tray full of little dishes of lots of good things with which to amend your food. This is standard operating procedure in Thailand, where the individuality of taste for *kreung broong,* seasonings, is respected and catered to as a matter of course (kind of like in China with dan-dan noodles, see page 147). Put out a tray with as many of the following as you can manage, each in its own little dish:

★ tamari or shoyu soy sauce

★ coarse-grained sugar, such as turbinado

★ finely chopped roasted peanuts

★ wedges of fresh lime

★ dried red chile flakes

★ Thai-style chile vinegar sauce or pickled chiles

★ Sriracha chile paste

★ Thai Crystal (page 200)

★ rings or strips of fresh red or green chiles

★ coarsely chopped cilantro leaves and/or Thai basil

★ *nam pla* (Thai fish sauce)

BLACK-EYED PEAS & CORN
in Tomato Masala

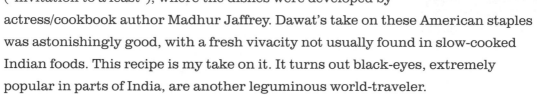

You'd think, given its main ingredients—black-eyed peas and corn—the day's special must have been on the menu at a Southern restaurant. Not so: My friend Sukie and I were at one of New York's first and best white-tablecloth Indian restaurants, Dawat ("invitation to a feast"), where the dishes were developed by actress/cookbook author Madhur Jaffrey. Dawat's take on these American staples was astonishingly good, with a fresh vivacity not usually found in slow-cooked Indian foods. This recipe is my take on it. It turns out black-eyes, extremely popular in parts of India, are another leguminous world-traveler.

You can either use canned black-eyed peas or cook up about a cup of dried beans (see page 15) beforehand to yield the necessary 3 cups cooked. As the dried beans cook relatively rapidly and it's easier to get them to the perfect texture for this—tender but not mushy, holding their shape—I recommend going with them.

Fresh corn is essential for the sweetness and freshness it gives the dish. Use oil as the cooking fat to make the dish vegan. **Gf** **Ve** or **Vn**

1 teaspoon cumin seeds

½ teaspoon ajwain seeds (see Notes)

3 tablespoons ghee or any mild vegetable oil, such as corn, canola, or peanut

2 medium onions, finely chopped

1 to 2 fresh tomatoes, cored and quartered

A chunk of fresh ginger (about the size of a small thumb), peeled and coarsely chopped

2 cloves garlic, halved

¾ teaspoon ground turmeric

1 teaspoon ground coriander

½ teaspoon red chile powder (cayenne if you'd like it stronger, New Mexican if you'd like it milder)

3 cups cooked black-eyed peas

2 cups fresh raw corn kernels (cut from about 4 ears of corn)

Salt

1 tablespoon chopped fresh cilantro or ½ teaspoon *kasuri methi* (see Notes)

½ teaspoon garam masala (see Notes)

1 Place the cumin and ajwain seeds in a heavy skillet over medium heat and toast them, stirring or shaking the pan often, until they are fragrant, about 1½ minutes. Add the ghee and then, immediately, the onions. Sauté until the onions are softened and starting to brown, 5 to 6 minutes.

2 Meanwhile, combine the tomatoes, ginger, and garlic in a food processor and buzz to a not-quite-smooth paste. Add this to the onions, and sauté for another 2 to 3 minutes.

3 Add the turmeric, coriander, and chile powder and sauté until most of the tomato liquid has evaporated and the oil begins to break out and rise to the surface of the sauce, 5 to 7 minutes (depending on the juiciness and size of the tomatoes).

4 Stir the black-eyed peas into the sauce and heat through. Add the corn, stir thoroughly, and cook just until the corn, too, is hot. Taste, and add salt until it's just right. The curry should not be too saucy but you can add a little water if you like.

5 Serve right away, sprinkled with the cilantro and garam masala—quick, while the corn is only slightly cooked and all is hot.

Serves 4 to 6 with rice, yogurt, or raita, and ideally a second vegetable curry

Notes: **Ajwain,** a spice native to India, is also known as ajowan, caraway, and carom seed. Raw, it smells like a pungent version of thyme; cooked (and in India it's almost always either dry-toasted or sizzled in oil, ghee, or coconut fat), it's caraway-ish. You can omit it or approximate it with ¾ teaspoon caraway seeds and ¼ teaspoon thyme leaves for 1 teaspoon ajwain.

Garam masala, like *berberé* (page 209), is not a single spice but a combination of many, some toasted, some not, typically sprinkled on a curried dish just before it is served to add yet one more layer of spice. *Garam* means hot, but the powder is pungent-and-flavorful hot, not chile hot; *masala* means mixture.

Kasuri methi is fenugreek, used often in both leaf and seed form in many Indian dishes. As with the herb *Coriandrum sativum,* which is generally referred to as coriander when in seed form and cilantro when in leaf, fenugreek seems to be known as such when sold as seed (trapezoidal, golden-brown) or powder, but as kasuri methi in fresh or dried leaf form. Its flavor is a slightly bitter combination of celery and fennel, with a maple note—unsweet, but maple-y, hard as that may be to wrap your mind around.

Ajwain seeds, garam masala, and kasuri methi can be found at Indian markets or at www.kalustyans.com.

MUMBAI MUDRA

Bhel of the Ball (page 29)

★

Kingfisher beer

★

Black-Eyed Peas & Corn in Tomato Masala

★

Steamed brown basmati rice

★

Salad of cucumber, yogurt, and cilantro

★

Lime pickle

★

Pistachio ice cream

★

Fresh mango sprinkled with rosewater

MELLOW COCONUT-TEMPEH CURRY
with Spinach, Zucchini & Sweet Potatoes

G entle, satisfying, and slightly sweet, this yellow curry is ultra-mild if you seed the chiles. It captures flavor notes from India, the West Indies, and Thailand. It's a good early-fall dish: Your farmer's market will still be overflowing with zucchini, the fall spinach should be in, and the first sweet potatoes will be arriving. Pretty locavoracious—until you get to the spices and the canned coconut milk.

Don't forget: You must marinate and bake off the tempeh first. The sauce is thin; if you'd like it thicker, simply draw off a bit of the liquid, dissolve one or two teaspoons cornstarch in it, and whisk the slurry back into the hot, finished curry. I like this with tempeh, but you could also do it with tofu. And a meatist might enjoy it with diced chicken breast or shrimp. **Vn** **Gf**

Vegetable oil cooking spray

1 tablespoon mild vegetable oil, preferably peanut

1 onion, chopped

6 cloves garlic, minced

2 teaspoons peeled, minced fresh ginger

1 to 2 serrano peppers, stemmed, seeds left in for heat or removed for mildness, diced

1½ teaspoons to 1 tablespoon curry powder

Tiny dash of ground cinnamon

Dash of ground cloves

⅔ cup canned diced tomatoes (preferably fire-roasted) or 2 large tomatoes, cored and chopped

1 large sweet potato or yam, peeled and cut into ½-inch cubes

½ teaspoon salt

1½ cups vegetable stock

⅓ cup raisins or currants

2 medium zucchini, halved lengthwise and cut into ½-inch-thick crescents

About 10 ounces fresh spinach, well washed, coarsely chopped (about 4 cups loosely packed)

¾ cup regular or reduced-fat unsweetened coconut milk

1 to 2 tablespoons honey, light or dark brown sugar, or agave syrup

1 recipe Basic Oven-Baked Marinated Tempeh (page 244), cut into bite-size pieces or left in large triangles for diners to knife-and-fork at the table

Cooked white rice or another grain, for serving

Minced fresh cilantro and mint, for garnish (optional)

Finely diced red bell pepper, for garnish (optional)

Chopped roasted peanuts, for garnish (optional)

1 Spray a large skillet with oil (if it is not nonstick), place it over medium heat, and add the oil. Add the onion and cook, stirring often, until it starts to soften, about 4 minutes. Add the garlic, ginger, and serrano, and let cook for about 2 minutes more. Add the curry powder, cinnamon, and cloves, and cook, stirring, for 1 minute.

2 Add the tomatoes and sweet potato and stir well to coat the vegetables with the spices. Add the salt, cover, and let steam for 3 minutes. Add the vegetable stock, raisins, and zucchini, cover again, lower the heat slightly, and let simmer for about 20 minutes.

3 Add the spinach, coconut milk, and honey and let cook, covered, until the spinach wilts, about 3 minutes. Stir well,

NIPPY NIGHT IN THE NEIGHBORHOOD

Thai-style Green Bean & Carrot Salad with Lime & Peanuts (page 140)

★

Mellow Coconut-Tempeh Curry with Spinach, Zucchini & Sweet Potatoes

★

Brown & wild rice pilaf

★

Fresh pineapple upside-down cake

add the tempeh, and stir again. When the tempeh is heated through, 2 to 3 minutes more, serve hot, over rice, sprinkling each serving with the garnishes, if using.

Serves 6 to 8, with rice

ↄ ↄ ↄ

ETHIOPIAN LENTIL STEW
(YEMISIR WOT)

Ethiopian cuisine is exotic, seductive, earthy, and unpretentious. It surprises your mouth the first time you taste it—the flavors chile-hot, with layers of spices both pungent (turmeric) and sweet (cinnamon, cloves), the textures usually moist, soft, and stewlike. You may be reminded more of Indian cuisine than of others you might logically expect, given the country's geographic position; Ethiopian food doesn't taste African, North African, or Middle Eastern. But Indian-like doesn't quite describe it either; its tastes are distinctive. It's not just that instead of rice, the Ethiopian staple accompaniment is Injera (page 209)—a soft, pocked, pancakelike sourdough bread made of teff flour that drapes a communal platter and on which the various dishes, shared by all, rest. No, it's the way technique (slow-simmering of stews in

which vegetables mix with legumes, meats, and grains) stacks up with seasonings (the essential components are *berberé,* a spicy red-pepper paste, and *niter kibbeh,* a spice-infused ghee). These tributaries—the country's exceptionally diverse population groups (each of whom has a particular dietary code), its radically different bio-regions (high plateaus, low-lying plains), and its relative poverty—flow into a unique culinary current.

The traditional stews fall into two categories: *alicha* (also spelled *aleecha*), or mild; and *wot* (also spelled *wat*), spicy and berberé-hot. This stew is one of the latter. I use less ghee than is traditional.

Like all Ethiopian dishes, this must be served with injera bread. Though easy to make, injera batter takes a couple of days to ferment, so don't forget to get it going well in advance. **Gf** **Vn** or **Ve**

2 cups green lentils

2 large or 3 medium red onions, chopped

¼ cup ghee or mild vegetable oil, such as corn, peanut, or canola

5 to 7 cloves garlic, chopped

1 tablespoon finely grated fresh ginger

Small pinch of caraway seeds

½ teaspoon ground coriander seeds

½ teaspoon black mustard seeds

⅛ teaspoon ground turmeric

1 carrot, scrubbed and diced

2 to 3 poblano peppers, stemmed, seeded, and diced

3 tablespoons tomato paste (or ½ cup diced tomatoes in juice)

¼ to 2 teaspoons berberé, either commercial or from scratch (see Note); start with ¼ teaspoon and work up to 2 if you like it truly hot-hot

Salt and freshly ground black pepper

Injera bread (recipe follows), for serving

1 Combine the lentils and 1½ quarts (6 cups) water in a large, heavy saucepan and bring to a boil. Turn down the heat to a simmer and let cook until the lentils begin to get mushy, about 20 minutes.

2 While the lentils simmer, heat a large, heavy skillet—a well-seasoned cast-iron skillet is ideal here—over high heat. When the skillet is very hot, lower the heat slightly and add the onions (you're dry-toasting them). Cook, stirring constantly, until the onions are slightly scorched and begin to soften, about 3 minutes. Lower the heat to medium, add the ghee, and stir in the garlic and ginger. Sauté, stirring constantly, for 1 minute, then add all the seeds and spices and sauté for another minute. Add the carrot and peppers and sauté 1 minute more, inhaling to enjoy the redolent combination of cooking aromas.

3 Ladle about ⅔ cup of the lentil cooking water into the skillet with the onions, spices, carrots, and peppers. Stir in the tomato paste, berberé, and salt and pepper to taste. Let this seasoning liquid simmer for 5 minutes, then stir it into the lentils.

④ Let the lentils simmer, half-covered, until they are quite tender and the sauce has thickened a bit, 30 to 40 minutes. Serve hot or warm, with injera bread.

Serves 4 with injera bread

Note: Berberé is not a single spice but a combination. Berberé differs from region to region and ethnicity to ethnicity in Ethiopia. To make Berberé, dry-toast together, over medium-low heat, in a small heavy skillet, watching and shaking the pan constantly, 2 teaspoons cumin seed, 1 teaspoon ground turmeric, ¾ teaspoon cardamom seed, ¾ teaspoon whole black peppercorns, ½ teaspoon fenugreek seed, 4 whole cloves, and 6 dried red chiles, stemmed. When their color deepens and the mixture grows fragrant, and the chiles are blackened here and there, 3 to 4 minutes, immediately remove the skillet from the heat and pour the toasted spices and chiles onto a plate to cool slightly. Buzz the warm but not hot toasted mixture in a spice grinder with half a small stick of canela cinnamon, a few gratings of fresh nutmeg, and 1¼ teaspoons ground ginger. Transfer this mixture to a small bowl, and stir in, using a fork, 1 tablespoon smoked Hungarian sweet paprika, 1 tablespoon smoked Hungarian hot paprika, and 2 tablespoons red chile (not chili) powder. Transfer to a tightly lidded jar. This keeps for 1 to 2 months on the shelf, 4 to 6 if stored in the freezer.

VARIATIONS

Alicha: To make the milder version of the stew, add a couple of peeled, diced potatoes to cook with the lentils. Omit the caraway, coriander, black mustard, and turmeric, as well as the poblanos (or just use one) and the berberé. Instead, in step 3 stir the following sweet spices into the lentils: ⅛ teaspoon each ground cinnamon and grated nutmeg, and a dash of ground cloves. **Gf** **Vn**

Alicha or Wot with Eggs: In Ethiopia, this is company fare or served on special occasions. Peel 4 to 6 hard-boiled eggs and poke each one 10 or 12 times with a toothpick, going in about ¼ inch deep. When the stew is almost ready to serve, add the eggs and spoon the sauce over them, folding them in gently to let the sauce penetrate a bit. **Gf** **Ve**

Injera

A large flat cake of injera bread serves as both platter and utensil for eating wot and alicha: Scoops of both are placed in the center of the bread, and diners tear off pieces of it, scoop up the stews, and pop both into their mouths. Mmmm!

Some Ethiopian immigrants have modified their injera after moving to the States, where wheat flour is more widely available and cheaper, but injera made in Ethiopia and neighboring Eritrea is always made with teff alone. If you're avoiding gluten, know that the injera in many East African restaurants may include some wheat flour along with the teff; make sure to ask.

Though this recipe is quick and easy in terms of hands-on prep, allow time for the batter's unattended fermentation (overnight or so), which gives the finished pancakes their classic tang and bubbles. Wait to cook the pancakes until you're ready to eat. **Vn** **Gf**

1 cup teff flour (see Note)

1 teaspoon active dry yeast

½ teaspoon salt

Vegetable oil cooking spray

1 Whisk the teff flour, the yeast, and 1½ cups warm water together in a medium-size bowl. The batter will be thin.

2 Cover the bowl loosely with a clean kitchen towel and let stand for a minimum of 12 hours or a maximum of 48 hours at 75°F to 80°F (in cold weather, a turned-off gas oven with a pilot light is ideal; in the summer, your countertop should be fine). You're looking for pancake-batter thickness, a pleasantly sour, yeasty smell, and bubbles.

3 Some liquid may have accumulated on top. Pour it off, and stir in the salt.

4 Heat your largest, heaviest skillet over medium-high heat. If it's nonstick, you need not add oil. Otherwise, give a spritz of vegetable oil cooking spray (you don't want the batter to stick, but in no way should it be fried).

5 When the skillet is hot, pour between ¼ and ½ cup batter—depending on how big your skillet is—to cover the surface. Cook, watching closely, until holes appear, polka-dotting the surface of the bread, and the top surface is dry, 2 to 3 minutes. Do not flip over! Injera is cooked on one side only. Immediately remove the bread from the pan, let it cool slightly, and repeat with the remaining batter. Serve the warm injera with the lentil stew.

Makes 3 or 4 large (dinner plate–size) or 6 or 7 small (salad plate–size) injera

Note: Teff is a small high-protein, gluten-free grain, available in most natural foods markets and online through Bob's Red Mill.

"The General . . . invited me to his home where dinner was already prepared for us. We sat on spread carpets and in front of us servants stretched a wide curtain that hid us from outside eyes. One of the ashkers brought a copper wash-stand of intricate form . . . in accordance with Abyssinian custom, [we] washed our hands before the meal. One of the cooks, a beautiful young Galla girl, having washed her hands and having rolled the sleeves of her shirt to the elbow, kneeled . . . and from little pots began to take out slices of injera (a flat cake) and all kinds of foods and to put them on the bread. What an array: hard-boiled eggs cooked in some unusually sharp sauce . . . ragout of mutton with red pepper . . . chicken gravy with ginger—all abundantly seasoned with butter . . . pepper and spices. We ate with our hands, tearing off little petals of injera and collecting with them large amounts of [the] foods. My mouth burned from the quantity of pepper. Tears came to my eyes . . . we devoured everything indiscriminately, cooling our mouths, from time to time, with sour cream or by drinking a wonderful mead— tej—from little decanters wrapped in little silk handkerchiefs."

—*Alexander Bulatovich,* With the Armies of Menelik II *(1896)*

JENNIFER'S SPICED RED BEANS

in Coconut Milk

(MAHARAGWE)

When I mentioned on Facebook that I was working on *Bean by Bean,* my friend Jennifer Yankopolus, an Atlanta-based architectural historian who was a Fearless Writing student in 2008, e-mailed me. "I'm so excited about this!" she wrote. "Do you have a recipe for the African red bean dish Maharagwe?" She explained that she'd seen the Kenyan dish referenced in a legume cookbook, but "no recipe was given, and it sounded so appealing that I had to track it down." She found several recipes online, combined them, and tweaked them to her own taste ("I spice it up or down depending on my guests—and for myself I add more cumin, lots"). Jennifer kindly shared her recipe, adding: "True confessions: I've only made this with canned beans. This is my I'm-too-tired-to-cook backup recipe."

I've left the recipe true to Jennifer's stylings, but you know enough about from-scratch bean cookery by now to switch if you like (see Basic Dried Bean Cookery, page 15). Jennifer loves it served over a bed of rice or pasta, or on a bed of steamed Swiss chard, or (her favorite) topped with a fried egg. The coconut milk, the almost-but-not-quite curry spices . . . this stew is *so* good and satisfying, in that I-could-live-on-this-for-a-week way.

You can see its family relationship to the Tanzanian Black-Eyed Pea & Coconut Soup with Bananas (page 72), but it's Kenyan in origin: In fact, *maharagwe* simply means "beans" in Kiswahili. It's also sometimes served with flat wholegrain bread, such as chapatis or whole-wheat tortillas. Vn Ve Gf

1 to 2 tablespoons coconut or peanut oil

2 medium yellow onions, chopped

1 to 2 jalapeño peppers or chile of choice, stemmed, seeds left in for heat or removed for mildness, finely chopped

2 teaspoons ground turmeric

1 tablespoon plus 1 teaspoon ground cumin

2 teaspoons ground coriander

2 teaspoons sugar

Salt

2 cans (15 ounces each) red kidney beans, drained and rinsed

1 can (14.5 ounces) chopped tomatoes (preferably fire-roasted), with their juices

1 can (15 ounces) full- or reduced-fat unsweetened coconut milk

Cooked rice or pasta, for serving (optional)

Steamed Swiss chard, for serving (optional)

Fried eggs, for serving (optional)

1 Place the coconut oil in a large skillet over medium heat. Add the onions and sauté until they are translucent, about 4 minutes. Add the jalapeño, turmeric, cumin, coriander, sugar, and salt to taste and stir until combined and slightly darkened, about 30 seconds.

2 Add the beans, tomatoes, and coconut milk, lower the heat, and simmer, stirring occasionally, until the beans are heated through and the sauce is slightly thickened, about 10 minutes. Adjust the seasonings to taste and serve with any or all of the accompaniments.

Serves 4

CHAPTER 7

Bountiful
BEAN BAKES,
Comforting
CASSEROLES

Tell me how you like your beans, what you remember about eating them as a child, and I'll tell you where or how you grew up.

Were they pintos, simmered, either to go with, or *in,* chili? You were a Texas child. Were they black beans, and the chile green? You grew up in New Mexico. Were they butter beans or white beans, cooked on top of the stove, with a lump of salt pork, maybe a ham hock, occasionally bacon; did you perhaps crumble cornbread (unsweetened, baked in a skillet) into them? You're a child of the South, or maybe Oklahoma. Were they served with brown rice, after having been cooked with vegetables, a shot of tamari at the end? Oh-ho, I'm guessing you are a child of 1970s-ish alternative parents. Did you grow up eating tofu? Unless you are quite young, there are Asian roots in your family tree, or, again, alternative/hippie parents.

But if those beans were yellow-eyed beans (particularly Maine soldiers, or maybe Jacob's Cattle) or navy beans; if they were baked slowly in a plump bean pot, with a lick of something sweet (molasses, brown sugar, maple syrup) and again, a hunk of salt pork, as well as an onion; if you ate these baked beans once a week, often on a Sunday, usually with sliced sweet, very moist steamed brown bread, you grew into what and who you are in New England.

For most of us, variations on this latter theme are what come to mind when we think "baked beans," for though New England marks their origin, all America, for that matter all the world, is familiar with them (baked beans on toast, though it sounds incomprehensible to many American ears, is a common British comfort food).

But excellent though sweetened baked beans are, the world of slow-baked legumes extends farther. No discussion of beans from the oven could fail to pay homage to the French cassoulet or omit the up-to-the-minute addictive deliciousness of roasted fresh green beans. And though you won't find a recipe for it here, we should at least mention that retro classic: canned green beans, cream of mushroom soup, and canned fried onion rings—the ne plus ultra of the mid-American Hot Dish, a staple in every community cookbook, ubiquitous at certain potlucks to this day. This, too, certainly falls under the rubric of "beans from the oven" (though not, I think, at their finest hour).

And what of bean-rich chilis and stews hiding flavorfully underneath a topping of cornbread; or beans, combined with artful vegetables and seasonings, as savory cobblers or potpies, bursting with self-satisfaction beneath pillowy herbed biscuits? Or of beans as a filling for baked vegetables and leaves as is common throughout the Middle East—picture tomatoes and zucchinis and grape leaves glistening with olive oil, stuffed to plump perfection with a panoply of seasoned legumes, in many recipes mixed with grain. Are you getting hungry yet?

Then there are the basic oven methods of precooking tofu and tempeh. These stalwart soyfoods can be oven-barbecued in sweet-savory sauce, or oven-crisped (nary a bit of deep-frying required). Both create foundational ingredients, good in themselves, but also as beginnings for countless other dishes. The marinated tempeh, for instance, adds toothsome pleasure to comforting vegetable-rich CG's Brunswick New-Stew (page 194), with its jewel-like jalapeño jelly–based glaze. The Oven-Baked Tofu (page 247) shows off in everything from Dragon-style Dan-Dan Noodles (page 147) to the vegan version of

Chicken Salad with Green Beans, Yellow Beans & Creamy Thai Basil Dressing on page 149.

So, having preheated together, let us slide that bean pot or casserole dish or baking sheet into the waiting oven. Let's get golden-brown together. Let's bubble. Let's serve, hot.

"There is much to be said for the succulent little bean—any kind of bean, be it kidney, navy, green, wax, Kentucky, chili, baked, pinto, Mexican, or any other kind. Not only is it high in nourishment, but it is particularly rich in that nutritious value referred to as protein—the stuff that imparts energy and drive to the bean eater and particularly the senators who need this sustaining force when they prepare for a long speech on the Senate floor. . . . I venture the belief that the marathon speakers of the Senate going back as far as the day of the celebrated 'Kingfish,' Senator Huey Pierce Long of Louisiana, and [others who] . . . have spoken well in excess of twenty hours and felt no ill effects, would agree the little bean had much to do with this sustained torrent of oratory."

—Senator Everett Dirksen (R-Illinois), 1933, "An Homage to Beans"

BAKED BEANS

More sweet than savory, smoky, or herbal, each bean clad in a thick sauce rather than a soupy liquid, and finished with a long, slow visit to the oven, these are the iconic beans of New England, now well–known around much of the world.

ɘ ɘ ɘ

Old-Fashioned, Down-Home
ALL-DAY BAKED BEANS

These are "old–fashioned" not just because they're classic baked beans, but because they were included in the original *Bean Book.* They were well loved, so much so that not once, not twice, but three times readers who lost their ancient copies of that book (one to a fire, one to a series of moves, and one in a divorce) wrote me actual pre-e-mail, on-paper letters to beg for a copy of the recipe. "They were the best baked beans I ever had!" one reader wrote, moans and lamentations audible between the sentences.

So, though it's been a mighty long time since pork has touched my lips or even fingertips, here is the recipe again (a vegetarian version, naturally, follows). Among salt-pork users, how much is a matter of huge variation. Some use as little as ¼ pound, the amount I've specified below. But I remember back from researching that first book, that there were some folks who were adamant— adamant!—that anything less than a pound of salt pork was an insult. So, scale up or down as you like. (Of course these objectors are all dead now. *No,* not necessarily from the pork—it was an old-timer thing, and we're talking folks who were old-timers back in the early seventies.)

As I noted back in the first *Bean Book,* homemade baked beans have it all over the canned kind: They're far cheaper and easier on resources, they taste infinitely better, and they fill a home with warmth and gentle fragrance as they bake (especially important in cold-climate winters). All still true. The traditional accompaniment is Steamed Boston Brown Bread (page 219). **Me** **Gf**

3½ cups dried yellow-eye peas (sometimes called soldiers or Maine soldiers) or white beans, picked over, rinsed, and soaked overnight (see page 16)

Mild vegetable oil or bacon fat, for greasing the pot

1 large onion, sliced

1 tablespoon salt (use less if you like, but these beans are happiest when well salted)

½ to 1 teaspoon freshly cracked black pepper, to taste

1½ teaspoons dry mustard

About ⅓ cup packed dark brown sugar, to taste

¼ to ⅓ cup dark molasses, to taste

¼ teaspoon ground ginger

¼ pound salt pork, rinsed very well, drained, patted dry, and diced

❶ Drain the beans and cook them on the stovetop by the method of your choice until almost but not quite tender, 1¼ to 2 hours, depending on the age and variety of the beans. Let cool, then drain through a colander, reserving the cooking liquid.

❷ Preheat the oven to 350°F. Thoroughly grease the inside of a bean pot; you may also use any deep, well-glazed casserole with a tight-fitting lid.

❸ Scatter the sliced onion over the bottom of the pot. Spoon the cooked beans over the onion.

❹ In a large bowl, pour 1 quart (4 cups) of the bean cooking liquid, and whisk in the salt, pepper, dry mustard, brown sugar, molasses, and ginger. Pour this mixture over the beans to just barely cover (add extra bean liquid if needed or hold back some of the mixture if necessary). Scatter the salt pork over the beans, or bury it in the beans if you prefer.

OVEN OR SLOW-COOKER?

Long, slow, at low, steady heat . . . that's how traditional baked beans have always been made, originally in a fire pit or bean hole (see box, page 219) and then in an oven. From Colonial times on, oven-baking made perfect sense in the Northeastern climate where the dish originated: The oven, heated with wood, was burning anyway during the long, cold, gray days of winter. Wisely, baking beans partook of a resource already in play, and added an extra measure of warmth, sustenance, and comfort.

But you don't *have* to make them that way, and especially in warm weather, you won't want to: the 6- to 8-hour baking can be done, instead, in an electric slow-cooker such as a Crock-Pot, set on low. Of course, preparing baked beans this way means you're not baking them in a bean pot, which some would argue lessens baked-bean perfection.

Which method is more environmentally sound? There's no clear answer. If your oven is a newer, more high-end model, it's well insulated and theoretically would use less fuel; otherwise the slow-cooker is the more fuel-conservative choice.

⑤ Lower the oven heat to 250°F. Cover the bean pot, put it in the oven, and let it bake slowly for 7 or 8 hours, adding boiling liquid—water or reserved bean cooking water—as necessary to keep the beans from drying out.

⑥ During the last hour or so, remove the cover so the beans have a chance to develop a nice crust. Serve hot, within a couple of hours of completion. Transfer any cooled leftovers to a covered dish and refrigerate; they'll keep for 3 to 4 days.

Serves 8 to 10

VARIATIONS

Variations on baked beans are numberless; here are a few, growing successively more "out there." Needless to say, it's the more out there ones that greatly appeal to me.

Vegetarian or Vegan Baked Beans: Omit the salt pork from the recipe above or any of those that follow. Vegetarians can use an equivalent amount of butter instead, just as flexible in quantity as the meatist version. Vegans, use veggie margarine or an oil that pleases: olive, peanut, coconut, even toasted sesame if you like. The minimum amount: ½ cup. **Vn Gf**

Vermont-style Baked Beans: No doubt closer to the original Native American baked beans. Substitute ½ to ¾ cup maple syrup for the brown sugar and molasses. **Me** or **Vn**

Baked Beans with Tomatoes or Ketchup: To some, a baked bean without some form of sweetened tomato is just unthinkable. In the last 2 hours of baking, stir in any of the following: 1 cup pureed canned tomatoes (I like the fire-roasted), ½ cup tomato paste (whisked into a little bean cooking liquid), or ¾ cup ketchup (remember, ketchup is quite sweet; you might want to cut back the sweetener if you go this route).

Honeyed Baked Beans: For sweeteners, use just 2 tablespoons each dark brown sugar and dark molasses, and add ½ cup warmed honey. **Me**

Orange Blossom Special Baked Beans: Omit the brown sugar and molasses. Use ¾ cup orange marmalade instead, whisking it into the bean liquid with 1 teaspoon cayenne, 2 tablespoons tomato paste, 1 tablespoon finely chopped chipotle in adobo (optional), the grated zest of 1 orange, and, if available, a few tablespoons orange blossom honey. Save the zested orange and squeeze its juice into the bean pot just before serving. I know this sounds odd, but it's a succulent combo. **Me** or **Vn**

Baked Beans Caribe: I love this one, too. Use 2 onions, and after you add the beans also scatter in about ⅔ cup diced dried pineapple. Here's what you whisk into the bean cooking liquid to pour over the beans: salt, pepper, and dry mustard as above; plus add 1 tablespoon finely chopped or grated fresh ginger, ½ cup dark rum, ⅓ to ½ cup packed dark brown sugar, ½ teaspoon ground cloves, and ½ teaspoon allspice. Substitute ½ cup coconut oil, more if you like, for the salt pork. In the last hour of cooking, stir in ¼ cup frozen pineapple juice concentrate, and when you uncover the beans, sprinkle the top with a little unsweetened coconut. Very fine indeed if you like sweet baked beans with a little kick and pizzazz to them. **Vn**

OLD-TIME YANKEE BAKED BEAN WAYS

Baked beans go back to America's first residents, and those natives taught their ways to the newcomers. Even in 1974, when the students of a folklore class at Bellows Falls Union High School in Bellows Falls, Vermont, undertook an oral history project, there were old-timers whose memories stretched way back (though of course not *all* the way back). The students collected the reminiscences of then-octogenarians (now all deceased, of course) and transcribed them, creating a paperback book called *The Ruddle* (an old New England word for an attic or garage, a place where you store old things you don't use but that just might come in handy some day). From *The Ruddle:*

Mr. Pickard described the way he learned to prepare baked beans: "First, parboil the beans and then put them in a kettle with a smidgin [sic] of ginger and a dollop of mustard (according to taste), then some salt pork and either sugar or molasses. Then bake them but be sure to keep them filled with water while they're baking. [But] the 'loggies' (the loggers who rafted down the Connecticut River at the turn of the last century and well beyond) had a different way of baking beans. They baked them in a bean hole." Judge Bolles described the process which he had seen as a boy: "First, they dug a hole in the ground and lined the hole with rocks, and then they built a fire in the hole and got it real hot. In the meantime, the cook would start cooking the beans in a kettle with the salt pork and get them boiling. After the fire in the hole had gotten real hot, he shoveled the coals out and took his kettle and put it down in the hole and covered it with canvas and dirt. The heat of the rocks would continue to cook the beans, the original fireless cooker."

The process Judge Bolles remembered came straight from the native ways (for more of those, see page 224).

Steamed

BOSTON BROWN BREAD

Steamed Boston brown bread, the traditional boon companion to Yankee-style sweetened baked beans, such as Old-Fashioned, Down-Home, All-Day Baked Beans (page 216).

At first glance (or bite) it's a mystery: What on earth makes this traditional New England bread so moist, tender, and rich? After all, no eggs, oil, or butter are called for, and as for the other ingredients, they're pretty straightforward, too. Well, could it be the dates? Or perhaps it's the dark molasses that holds the secret? Nope. While these and the mix of cornmeal, rye, and wheat flours add to the bread's homespun appeal, the main trick to its density lies in the method by which it is cooked: It's steamed. The steam heat gives the bread its singular texture: intense and solid without being heavy. The batter is ABC simple to put together; the steaming may seem daunting if you haven't done it before, but it, too, is easy.

Traditional Boston brown bread uses a cup each of cornmeal, rye flour, and whole wheat flour, plus ¾ cup dark molasses. If I don't have rye flour on hand, I use a combo of cornmeal and whole wheat flour, and it still comes out very well. I also like mellowing the molasses twang with a little honey or agave. Some people use raisins instead of dates. I don't. Some people do not add nuts. I do.

Before you begin, have ready the cans of your choice (see box, opposite), well washed and dried, the insides sprayed with oil and dusted with cornmeal. Also have ready some aluminum foil, the pot in which you'll be steaming the cans, your trivet or equivalent (again, see box), and one rubber band per can. Check to make sure your pot is large enough so that the lid will still fit tightly once the cans are in place. **Ve** or **Vn**

Vegetable oil cooking spray

1 cup stone-ground cornmeal, plus extra for dusting the coffee cans

2 cups whole wheat flour (or 1 cup whole wheat plus 1 cup rye flour)

1½ teaspoons baking powder

½ teaspoon baking soda

1 teaspoon salt

1 cup pre-diced "cooking" dates (the kind that look, as my long-ago assistant Amber once put it, "extruded")

2 cups buttermilk, yogurt, or soy yogurt (or use soy milk with 2 teaspoons vinegar added)

½ cup warmed blackstrap molasses (see Note)

¼ cup warmed honey or agave syrup (see Note)

Butter, cream cheese, or Neufchâtel cheese, for serving (optional)

1. Put a large tea kettle or pot of water on to boil. Spray your cans or molds with oil and dust them with cornmeal (see headnote).

2. In a large bowl, combine the cornmeal, whole wheat flour, baking powder, baking soda, and salt, and stir well. Add the dates.

3. In a medium-size bowl, whisk the buttermilk together with the molasses and honey.

4. Add the wet mixture to the dry, stirring just enough to moisten well. Scrape the batter into the prepared cans, filling the cans about two thirds of the way full.

5. Place the bread-steaming pot on the stove and set the trivet(s) inside it. Tear the aluminum foil into pieces that are twice as large as the mouth of the cans, fold each in half, and spray one side with oil. Place

the foil oiled-side down on top of the cans, puffing it a bit at the top to give the bread room to rise; secure each piece of foil with a rubber band. Place the cans on the trivet(s).

6 Pour the boiling water into the pot to reach halfway up the sides of the cans. Turn the heat to low (you want to maintain the water at a simmer), and cover the pot. Steam the bread for 2 hours (small molds) to 3 hours (1-pound coffee can–size molds), checking occasionally to add more water as needed. When done, the bread will have risen some, but not enormously, and it will be firm to the touch through its foil cover.

7 Carefully remove the cans from the pot, and let cool on a wire rack for about an hour before reversing out the breads (they will reverse out quite easily). Serve the bread in thick slices, on its own or slathered with the spread of your choice.

Makes 12 to 15 slices

Note: Run the jars of molasses and honey under a hot water tap to warm and loosen their contents before measuring. This will help both to pour more easily.

VARIATION

Untraditional but awfully tasty: Add ½ cup toasted walnuts or black walnuts to the batter. **Ve** or **Vn**

STEAM ON: FINE POINTS

The basic info on how to steam breads is given above, but here's a little further elucidation for those new to the method. Traditional recipes suggest you "place batter into greased pudding molds," but few of us actually *have* a pudding mold, as such. But all of us have cans—and they'll do just fine as pudding molds, thank you very much. The batter for the recipe above will fill one 2-pound coffee can, three 20-ounce cans, four 15-ounce cans, or five 12-ounce cans. Traditional recipes also suggest that you set the batter-filled molds "atop a heat-proof trivet" in a large pot. What, no trivet either? Then how about some old jar-lid rings or some lightly wadded foil?

About the bread-steaming pot: It must be large enough so that even with all the cans/molds in place, the pot's lid will still fit tightly. The trivet or other heat-proof equivalent serves to elevate the molds/cans, preventing direct contact with the bottom of the pot.

The filled molds/cans are half-submerged in simmering water, the pot is covered to trap the steam, and the whole is cooked atop the stove, as directed in the recipe. The great results and characteristic texture of Boston brown bread can *only* be achieved this way.

Old-Fashioned, Down-Home,
BOSTON (MOUNTAIN) BAKED BEANS

Being stubborn and a tinkerer by nature, I didn't give up my beloved childhood Boston baked beans (page 216) just because I had stopped eating meat. By that time I was living in the Ozarks, part of the back-to-the-land movement (which seems to run in cycles; I was in the late 1960s–early 1970s turn of the wheel). I ate many a stovetop-cooked pot of Southern-style beans and cornbread, but still, occasionally, I hankered for the sweeter beans of my youth. I was happy to discover, over time, that salt pork's fatty richness and mouthfeel could be duplicated in a number of ways, peanut butter and tahini being two of the more interesting. One day I amused myself by adding a few dice of tofu to the nearly finished bean pot as a visual joke—to look at it, a dead-ringer, trompe-l'oeil salt pork. I've done this ever since, though the tofu adds nothing to the flavor.

I named this version of the recipe for the Bostons, plural—those mountains, part of the Ozarks, that are among the most dramatic and least developed of that old, old range.

Serve the beans with steamed Boston brown bread (traditional, page 219) or cornbread (pages 166, 167; not traditional, but also wonderful). Some people like to offer ketchup or chili sauce (the sweet, relishy kind, not salsa), too. I also like the molho (page 183) with these. **Gf** **Ve** or **Vn**

1 pound dried white beans (such as navy or Great Northern), picked over, rinsed, and soaked overnight (see page 16)

Vegetable oil cooking spray or oil, for greasing the pot

1 large onion, sliced

1 teaspoon salt

1 heaping tablespoon golden miso (see page 80)

½ to 1 teaspoon freshly ground black pepper

1 tablespoon dry mustard

⅓ cup packed dark brown sugar

¼ cup molasses

¼ cup tomato paste

⅛ teaspoon ground cloves

2 to 4 tablespoons butter, margarine, natural, unhydrogenated peanut butter, or tahini, to taste (optional)

Boiling water or vegetable stock, as needed

2 to 4 ounces firm tofu, cut up into large dice (optional)

Steamed Boston Brown Bread (page 219) or cornbread (see pages 166 and 167), for serving (optional)

Ketchup or chili sauce (the sweet kind), for serving (optional)

1 Drain the beans well, rinse them, and place them in a large, heavy pot. Cover them with water to a depth of 2 inches. Bring to a boil, turn down the heat to a simmer, and let them cook until tender, about 1½ hours. Remove the beans from the heat and carefully drain off the cooking liquid through a colander, reserving it.

2 Preheat the oven to 275°F. Spray a bean pot or other deep, nonreactive casserole with a tight-fitting lid with oil.

3 Scatter the sliced onion in the pot, and add the drained beans.

4 Whisk into the reserved bean-cooking liquid the salt, miso, black pepper, dry mustard, brown sugar, molasses, tomato paste, cloves, and butter, which will partially melt into the still-warm liquid. Pour this mixture over the beans in the pot. The liquid should just barely cover the beans; if it doesn't, add just

---

BOSTON—BUT NOT

Old-Fashioned, Down-Home, Boston (Mountain) Baked Beans

★

Molho à Campanha (page 183)

★

Peter Rabbit's Salad (page 132)

★

Boston Brown Bread (page 219)

★

Maple ice cream and apple sorbet

---

enough boiling water or vegetable stock to achieve this.

5 Cover the pot and bake for 6 hours, checking every once in a while to make sure the liquid level is maintained, and adding more boiling water or vegetable stock as needed.

6 Uncover the beans and stir to distribute the onion at the bottom throughout. Scatter the tofu cubes, if using, over the top of the beans, pressing them in lightly but letting them show, for the visual "salt pork" effect. Let bake for 1 hour more, then serve hot with the bread of your choice. Some people like to offer ketchup or chili sauce with this.

Serves 6 to 8 as a substantial side dish

"The kitchen has two stoves, one gas and one coal, and Esther keeps saying, 'May, don't you think it's time you got rid of that old thing?' Ganny won't listen. She puts her bread to rise on top of the coal stove and bakes her beans in its oven."

—*Mary Cantwell,* American Girl: Scenes from a Small-Town Childhood

THE FIRST BEAN-BAKERS

To most Native Americans, beans were part of a cosmology in which the worldly and spiritual were inseparable. Corn was the primary mythological food/sacrament in this worldview, but beans—protein-rich, such perfect agricultural companions for corn in the garden—played a consistent part; along with squash, these vegetables were called "the three sisters." Many contemporary bean dishes have their origins in the foodways of the Indians of the Southwest. But baked beans, or "bean-hole beans" as they are called to this day throughout Maine, we owe to the native peoples of the Northeast.

Indians throughout what's now New England—the Penobscots, the Abenakis, probably most of the region's First People—went to a lot of trouble to do their beans just right. First, the bean hole was dug: an earthen pit, about three feet deep, three feet wide, and four feet long in the earth. This was lined with flat stones, on top of which a fire was built. After about four hours (and half a cord or so of hardwood), there'd be a bed of coals about a foot deep, resting on the heated stones. Some of the coals were shoveled out and put to one side, and in went the pot of beans—which had been soaked and precooked

in the usual way on an open fire, then doctored with maple syrup and bits of meat, typically venison and/or bear fat. The reserved coals were shoveled around the bean pot, a vessel made of fired clay (earlier still, a thousand-plus years before the Europeans' arrival, the pots were made of carved soapstone). More coals were shoveled over the top, and the whole thing was carefully covered with soil, until not so much as a lick of steam or smoke was visible, completely enclosing the beans in slow, ongoing heat. The soil, if you touched it, was slightly but noticeably warm. Six to eight hours later, the beans were dug out. Feast!

This dish evolved into what we call Boston baked beans. Bear fat became salt pork, molasses replaced maple syrup, and it became a weekly Saturday night tradition in Colonial days. For Puritans kept a Sabbath, not unlike Jews. But while the Jewish Sabbath starts

on Friday night at sundown and ends on Saturday twenty-four hours later, the Puritan Sabbath began at sundown on Saturday and continued until Sunday sunset. For the orthodox in each case, no cooking was allowed on the Sabbath (see Cholent, page 316, for the Jewish bean dish that fulfilled this rule equivalently). Puritan homemakers put their beans on to soak Friday night, gave them a quick precook in boiling water early on Saturday morning to get a further jump on cooking ahead, then transferred them with their seasonings and meat to a bean pot and set them to bake in a brick oven all day Saturday. The beans were ready to be eaten piping hot, with sweet, soft, steamed brown bread that night; no cooking as such involved. Intentional leftovers were returned to the oven. The next day, Sunday, when the family returned from church in the morning, there were the beans,

still warm, ready for breakfast. "Pease porridge hot, pease porridge cold . . .": now you know the ditty's origins.

The faintest remnant of beans-for-breakfast still persists in many New England communities, particularly in Rhode Island and Massachusetts, where they've been hosting hearty May Day breakfast fund-raisers since 1867. But for actual bean-hole cookery, pride of place belongs to Maine, where bean-hole suppers live on in countless community dinners, county fairs, and festivals. Even today, when bean holes are re-created, fairgoers marvel at the aroma of the beans as the pots are lifted out of the ground. The Maine Folklife Center, which does a bean hole for the annual Maine Organic Farmers and Gardeners Common Ground Fair, couldn't resist a little justifiable boasting on their website as they documented their first attempt:

Spectators not only commented on the process and on how good the beans were, but some of them got involved. Especially one photographer who was visiting the fair to get some photos for publication. He stopped at the bean hole and began serving beans to other spectators, giving a running commentary on how delicious they were. Another fairgoer, a restaurant-owner from Massachusetts, was so enthralled he declared the beans "the best food at the fair!" Both pots of beans were finished in an hour as a stream of visitors, drawn by the lovely baked-bean aroma that wafted across the fairgrounds, lined up for a taste.

The Center served samples of bean-hole beans to hundreds of people.

Thank you, Penobscots. Thank you, Abenakis. Thank you, First People, who patiently cultivated beans.

MUSTARD PICKLE BAKED BEANS

These have the traditional sweetness of baked beans, with oomph and texture. The sauce and seasonings of traditional mustard pickles are just made for beans: Once you taste these, you'll wonder why somebody didn't think of this a long time ago. Because so much of the mojo in this particular recipe is in the mustard pickles, the other seasonings are quite simple.

Be sure to choose sweet mustard pickles, the kind that combines cukes, green peppers, baby onions, cauliflower florets, and other vegetables in a sweet-sour golden yellow sauce. Vn

---

3½ cups dried yellow-eyed peas (such as soldiers) or white beans (such as navy beans), picked over, rinsed, and soaked overnight (see page 16)

3 tablespoons olive oil

2 teaspoons salt, plus extra as needed

½ to 1 teaspoon freshly cracked black pepper

4 cloves garlic, coarsely chopped

1 teaspoon to 1 tablespoon chili paste (such as Sriracha or harissa), or use Frank's RedHot Original Cayenne Pepper Sauce or Tabasco sauce

1 pint (2 cups) commercial or homemade mustard pickles

Light or dark brown sugar (optional)

Ketchup (optional)

① Drain the beans and cook them by the method of your choice (see page 217) until almost but not quite tender, 1½ to 2 hours. Let cool, then drain carefully, reserving the hot cooking liquid.

② Preheat the oven to 350°F. Using a little of the oil, thoroughly grease the inside of a bean pot (or any deep well-glazed casserole with a tight-fitting lid).

③ Add the beans to the pot along with the remaining oil, 2 teaspoons salt, pepper, garlic, and 1 teaspoon of the chili paste, and stir together to combine. Add just enough of the hot bean-cooking liquid to barely cover the beans (reserve the extra bean liquid).

④ Lower the oven heat to 250°F. Cover the bean pot, put it in the oven, and let it bake slowly for 5 hours, adding the reserved bean cooking liquid or boiling water as necessary to keep the beans from drying out. Taste the beans: They should be tender, though still pretty bland.

⑤ Open the mustard pickles and put the vegetables in one bowl and the sauce in another (this doesn't have to be a precise division, so don't go crazy over getting every little vegetable out of the sauce). If the vegetable pieces are very large, chop them coarsely into bite-size chunks.

⑥ Stir the sauce from the mustard pickles into the beans, adding a little extra bean liquid if you like. Taste. You may wish to add a little more salt or brown sugar (and one friend who sampled this recipe liked it with a little ketchup on top; she said that when she made it, she thought she'd stir some in, too). This is also your chance to zap things up with the remaining chile paste if you'd like it hotter. Keep baking, covered, for another 2 hours.

7 Remove the lid and stir in the pickles. Continue to bake, uncovered, so the beans have a chance to develop a nice crust, 1 hour more. Serve hot.

Serves 8 to 10 as a substantial side dish

VARIATION

Meatist Mustard Pickle Baked Beans: Scatter ¼ pound diced rinsed salt pork over the beans (or bury it in the beans) when you begin the baking. Or substitute a few slices of chopped raw bacon for the salt pork, and/ or place a few slices of raw bacon over the top of the beans during the last hour of cooking. Or, if you have some leftover ham (somebody or other once described eternity as "two people and a ham"), dice it up and stir it in midway through baking. Me

BAKED LIMAS
with Rosy Sour Cream

I f you are lucky enough to get fresh limas, simply steam them and toss them with a bit of butter and maybe a squidge of lemon juice. But for the frozen kind, you can't do much better than this easy, dairy-rich jazz-up, a simple side dish to make a plainish main dish something special. Even people who swear they hate limas fall for it. Ve

3 boxes (4 ounces each) frozen lima beans, cooked according to package directions until just tender

Vegetable oil cooking spray

1 tablespoon butter

1 onion, chopped

1 cup regular or light sour cream (not fat-free)

3 tablespoons light brown sugar

3 tablespoons ketchup

1 tablespoon sweet pickle relish

Salt and freshly ground black pepper

A few dashes of Tabasco or similar hot pepper sauce

1 Preheat the oven to 325°F. Spray a 3-quart lidded casserole with the oil.

2 Place the cooked limas in a large bowl.

3 In a medium-size skillet over medium heat, melt the butter. Add the onion and sauté until translucent, about 5 minutes. Remove the onion from the heat and add to the limas along with the remaining ingredients, stirring to combine.

4 Transfer the bean mixture to the prepared casserole. Cover and bake for 25 minutes, then uncover and bake for 20 minutes more; the limas will be tender and the dish bubbling hot.

Serves 4 to 6 as a side dish

Simply Terrific

OVEN-ROASTED GREEN BEANS

As you have probably gathered, I love baked beans, don't mind the complications of a cassoulet, and can't resist the occasional slightly frou-froued retro bean-plus-cheese-topped casserole. But all these are primarily winter dishes, for occasional use—just a few times every year. What *will* you find being made in our kitchen all summer long, over and over? When the yellow colander is filled to overflowing with green and yellow beans from the garden, just picked as the setting sun pinked and purpled the sky over the pond, these are my first thought. Simple, delicious, easy, easy, easy, they don't get the kitchen too hot for too long. A huge pile of these and some parsleyed, buttered new potatoes, maybe some sliced garden tomatoes, is a fine summer supper: not for company, just for, as the Rastafarians say, I-and-I.

Use beans that are not too mature for this: They don't have to be the little tiny skinny fillet beans (haricots verts), but neither should they be so large you can see the shape of the actual beans starting to round the pod. Ideally, your beans should all be about the same thickness. This dish is excellent made with Romanos, the flat Italian green beans, too. **Vn** **Gf**

About 1 pound not-too-plump green beans, yellow wax beans, or a combination of the two, tipped and tailed

1 tablespoon extra-virgin olive oil (see Note)

Coarse sea salt

Freshly cracked black pepper

1 Preheat the oven to as high as it will go without defaulting to broil. Place a silicone baking mat in a rimmed baking sheet.

(If you don't have such a mat, use extra oil—3 or 4 tablespoons, and give the baking sheet a good shake halfway through cooking.)

2 In a large bowl, toss the beans with the olive oil, and salt and pepper to taste. Transfer them to the prepared baking sheet, spreading the beans so there's plenty of air space between them and they don't overlap too much.

3 Bake the beans until they are shriveled, browned—sort of unattractive—crispish on the outside, and quite tender within, 18 to 20 minutes (if the hottest you can get your oven before broiling is 450°F, it might be more like 25 to 30 minutes). Serve, hot, right away.

Serves 4 to 6 as a side dish

VARIATIONS

Oven-Roasted Green Beans with Garlic: A few minutes before the beans are all the way done, stir in a clove or two of minced garlic.

Oven-Roasted Green Beans with Tomatoes and Garlic: Toss a handful of halved cherry tomatoes—some yellow, some red—with the green beans in the bowl, adding an extra tablespoon of oil. Add 1 to 2 cloves minced garlic a few minutes before the beans and tomatoes are finished roasting. These are my faves, and I make extra as the beans and tomatoes keep ripening in my garden and freeze the extras in airtight bags for wintertime eating.

The Vernacular Bean

Given how long human beings have depended on beans for sustenance, it's perhaps natural that leguminous phrases abound in our speech. Here's a brief compendium:

★ To be "full of beans" means to be in peak, feisty condition; in good health and/or high-spirits; related to feeling "beany": in a good, energetic mood, on top of one's game.

★ To "bean" is to strike someone in the head with an object, sometimes accidentally. It's usually used playfully and not too seriously: "Hey! You nearly beaned me with that beach ball!"

★ When you give someone "a bean" or "a beaning," you're giving them a piece of your mind; berating, chastising, or criticizing them.

★ Using "the old bean" means using one's head, or brain; thinking perspicaciously.

★ When something "isn't worth a hill of beans" it's useless, worthless.

★ To "know beans" about something, you are knowledgeable about the subject and generally shrewd and smart. If you "don't know beans," you're ill-informed and none too bright.

★ A "bean-counter" is someone so concerned with small details that he or she misses the big picture. Often applied to accountants and middle management bureaucrats.

★ And of course "Spilling the beans" is telling all.

COMFORTING CASSEROLES

The word "casserole" has two meanings. First, a casserole is a vessel (usually lidded, of glazed clay, heat-proof glass or china, or cast iron), in which food is both baked and served. Second, "casserole" is the food itself, cooked in that same baking dish.

Yet colloquially, things expand. A pot roast cooked in a casserole dish is still pot roast, not a casserole, which by common agreement is a dish made up of an artful combination of disparate ingredients, multilayered or mixed together, almost always cloaked with something on top: bread crumbs, grated cheese, a crust, mashed potatoes.

Casseroles are all-embracing. They welcome leftovers and freshly cooked ingredients equally; they look with favor on the contents of bottles you may have squirreled away in the pantry (olives, say). With a little sauce and that appealing topping, suddenly you have the sine qua non of homey comfort food. So easy and utilitarian are casseroles to throw together, the cook may feel she pulled a fast one. But there's no arguing with a contented family, is there?

э   э   э

BAKED BEANS BRAZILIAN
with Olives & Cheese

You want real authentic Brazilian beans? Go to the Fauxjoada on page 196 (well, okay, semi-authentic since my version's meat-free). *This* savory hodgepodge of a casserole has nothing to do with Brazil, but I named it after the country for now-forgotten reasons back in the original *Bean Book* days. It remains an appealing, unsweet baked-bean casserole, studded with green olives and pimentos and topped with cheese. The dish has become spicier over the years, but it still has kind of a retro-hippie feel to it (we did love our cheese-topped casseroles back in the day).

The olives that give the dish its zing are not fancy, expensive French or Greek varieties. Just go to the grocery store and buy a jar of inexpensive "olive mix"— slices and odds and ends of pitted green olives and pimentos.

The main recipe is meatist, the variation vegetarian. Either is nice with brown rice and a salad with a creamy cilantro dressing (see the Thai basil dressing on page 151, and substitute cilantro for the basil) and/or avocado; add some canned hearts of palm to the salad, too, if you have 'em on hand. **Me** **Gf**

3½ cups dried cannellini or navy beans, picked over, rinsed, and soaked overnight (see page 346)

2 to 3 tablespoons olive oil

2 large onions, sliced

4 cloves garlic, chopped

1 tablespoon chile paste such as Harissa (page 266), or Sriracha

1 bay leaf

1 teaspoon salt

½ to 1 teaspoon freshly cracked black pepper

½ pound smoked pork or ham, cubed (optional)

1 cup pimento-stuffed green olive mix, drained well

½ cup finely minced fresh parsley

1 cup (4 ounces) finely grated Monterey Jack cheese

1 Drain the beans and cook them by the method of your choice (see page 217) until barely tender. Let cool slightly, then drain carefully, reserving the cooking liquid.

2 Preheat the oven to 350°F. Using a little of the oil, thoroughly grease the inside of a bean pot (or any well-glazed deep casserole with a tight-fitting lid).

3 In a large bowl, combine the beans, onions, garlic, chile paste, bay leaf, salt, pepper, and the meat, if using. Stir well

and transfer to the bean pot. Pour in just enough reserved bean cooking liquid to not quite cover the beans.

4 Lower the oven heat to 300°F, cover the bean pot, and bake for 2 hours.

5 Uncover the beans and add the olive mix, parsley, and the remaining olive oil, stirring well. Taste for salt and pepper, adding more if needed. Cover again and bake for 1 hour more.

6 Just before serving, remove the bean pot from the oven and sprinkle the cheese over the top. Run the beans under the broiler until the cheese is melty and golden, 1 to 2 minutes, and serve very hot.

Serves 4 to 6 as a main dish

VARIATION

Vegetarian or Vegan Baked Beans Brazilian: Obviously, omit the optional ham or pork. Instead, sauté 8 ounces vegetarian chorizo in a few tablespoons of additional olive oil, over medium heat, turning with a spatula until browned all over, a matter of 5 to 7 minutes. (If the sausage is in links, slice the links after you've sautéed them.) Stir the veggie chorizo into the beans with the olives and parsley. Vegans can omit the cheese over the top and still have a mighty tasty dish. **Ve** or **Vn**

Connecticut

KIDNEY BEAN CASSEROLE

with Mushrooms, Red Wine & Tempeh Bacon

This recipe began life a little blandly: A less spicy, very meatist version appeared in a New England community cookbook I was browsing in my local library. I kept the kidney beans and red wine, nixed the ham and bacon, and amped up the flavor with some of my old faves: garlic, sautéed mushrooms, poblanos, black pepper, tempeh bacon. It would probably be unrecognizable to its original contributor, and it now has less to do with Connecticut than the Baked Beans Brazilian on page 230 have to do with Brazil. But in a global-think world where culinary fusion is lingua franca, there are times when this just doesn't matter.

I suggest you double or triple the garlic–olive oil mix you make in step 1; that way you'll have some left for the garlic bread that is so good with this. (Use a good, crusty, rustic loaf, as grainy as you can get, and almost-but-not-quite cut the slices through in the time-honored garlic bread fashion. Drizzle the garlic oil between the slices, wrap the loaf in foil, and pop it in the oven alongside the beans during their last few minutes of cooking.) If you have any further leftover garlic oil, do be sure to refrigerate it. It keeps, covered, in the fridge for 5 days.

Garlic bread, a salad—with this, such a good dinner. **Vn**

- 3 tablespoons olive oil
- 3 cloves garlic, pressed
- Vegetable oil cooking spray
- ⅓ pound small whole button mushrooms (either ordinary domestic ones or creminis)
- 1½ teaspoons tamari or shoyu soy sauce
- 1 cup hearty red wine, such as a Burgundy
- 2 cans (14.5 ounces each) kidney beans, drained well (save the liquid for soup stock, if you like)

- 1 large onion, finely diced
- 1 poblano pepper, stemmed, finely diced
- Freshly ground black pepper
- 1 tablespoon honey, turbinado or brown sugar, maple syrup, or agave
- ⅓ cup tomato paste
- 1 package (8 ounces) smoked tempeh strips
- Sour cream, light sour cream, or Greek-style yogurt, for garnish (optional)
- Finely minced fresh parsley, for garnish (optional)

1 Preheat the oven to 350°F.

2 In a small bowl, combine 1 tablespoon of the olive oil with the garlic; set aside.

3 Spray a large, heavy skillet with the vegetable oil, and add the remaining 2 tablespoons olive oil. Place it over medium heat, and when the pan is nice and hot, add the mushrooms. Cook, shaking the pan periodically, until the mushrooms are slightly browned, 5 to 6 minutes. Pour the tamari over them and cook, still shaking the pan occasionally, until the mushrooms have browned further and are trying to stick to the pan, about 1 minute more.

4 Spray a nonreactive 2-quart lidded casserole with the vegetable oil. Transfer the mushrooms to the casserole. Deglaze the skillet with 2 or 3 tablespoons of the red wine, stirring to loosen any browned bits from the bottom of the pan. Pour this liquid (the deglaze) into the casserole, too.

5 Add the beans, onion, poblano, lots of black pepper, honey, tomato paste, and remaining red wine and stir very well, making sure there are no little patches of tomato paste. Smooth the top of the beans, and lay the tempeh strips over them.

LONDONDERRY ON THE LAWN

Arugula and romaine tossed with cooked pole beans, red onion slices, and Basic Feisty Vinaigrette (page 132), diced fresh-cooked beets scattered on top

★

Connecticut Kidney Bean Casserole with Mushrooms, Red Wine & Tempeh Bacon

★

Stir-fried Delicata squash

★

Garlic bread

★

Blueberry crisp or Lime Mousse-Custard (page 330)

6 Cover and bake until the beans are good and hot, 30 to 45 minutes.

7 Uncover the beans and brush the tempeh strips with the garlic oil. Bake the beans, uncovered, until the tempeh browns slightly and the garlic is fragrant, another 10 to 15 minutes. Serve hot, garnished if you like with a dollop of sour cream or one of its lighter doppelgängers and a scatter of minced parsley.

Serves 4 as a main dish

> **"A Bean was showing his sore leg to some Eggs and Piefaces in the smoking-room of the Drones Club, when a Crumpet came in."**
>
> *—P. G. Wodehouse describing types of dissipated, monied, but highly amusing generic ne'er-do-wells in Eggs, Beans, and Crumpets, 1940*

VEGETARIAN CASSOULET

No trip to baked-bean land would be complete without a visit to cassoulet, which *may* be the absolute, hands-down best bean dish you have ever eaten. Plump, meltingly soft beans swim in their own rich and delicious sauce of bean liquid, tomato, herbs, aromatics, and olive oil, their texture at play with chunks of hearty sautéed soysage and vegetarian Canadian bacon slices, the whole baked under a crisply crumbed topping. This highly pleasing dish is as noble, delicious, and satisfying as a bean can be. Because traditional cassoulet is both meat-heavy and one of those dishes about which there is passionate opinion, I hesitated to call this garlicky meatless version by that hallowed name. But this cassoulet can, definitively, hold its own against any other.

Now, don't go complaining to me about what a long and complex recipe this is. First, it's worth every minute. Second, long and complicated is simply the nature of cassoulets. Third, comfort yourself by knowing that it's far, far less time-consuming and complex than the with-meat versions. Fourth, there are plenty of good noncomplicated bean recipes here for your pleasure. But cassoulet, deeply pleasurable though it is, is not one of them. **Vn**

---

3 whole sprigs fresh parsley, plus the leaves from 1 bunch of fresh parsley

3 sprigs fresh thyme

2 sprigs fresh oregano

Vegetable oil cooking spray

2½ cups flageolets or dried navy beans, picked over, rinsed, and soaked overnight (see page 348)

About 8 cups vegetable stock or water

3 large onions: 1 left whole, skin on, studded with 3 whole cloves; 2 chopped

2 stalks celery

About 2 heads garlic: 1 head left whole, unpeeled; 5 cloves peeled and minced; 4 cloves peeled and left whole

About 2¼ teaspoons salt

½ cup olive oil

1 package (10 ounces) breakfast-style vegetarian soysage, such as Lightlife Smart Links Breakfast Sausage Style

1 package (10 ounces) Italian-style vegetarian soysage, such as Lightlife Smart Sausages Italian Style

1 package (6 ounces) vegetarian Canadian bacon slices, such as Yves Meatless Canadian Bacon

3 carrots, scrubbed and sliced into ¼-inch rounds

1 can (28 ounces) chopped tomatoes, with their juice

1 teaspoon honey or light brown sugar

1 teaspoon dried red chile flakes

½ teaspoon freshly ground black pepper

1 cup fresh, soft breadcrumbs

1 Bundle the fresh herb sprigs into a bouquet and tie the stems together with a piece of kitchen twine. Spray a large, heavy pot with oil. Drain and rinse the soaked beans and transfer them to the pot, adding the herb bouquet and vegetable stock to cover to a depth of 2 inches. Add the clove-studded onion, celery, and whole head of garlic. Bring to a boil, then lower the heat to a simmer. Cover, and simmer gently for 50 minutes. Add 2 teaspoons of the salt, cover again, and continue simmering until the beans begin softening, 30 to 45 minutes longer.

2 While the beans simmer, spray a large, heavy skillet with oil, add 1 tablespoon of the olive oil, and heat over medium heat. Add the soysages and Canadian bacon and brown, turning until all the sides are nice and golden, about 4 minutes, doing this in batches as needed and setting browned soysage and bacon aside as it's done. When all are cool enough to handle, quarter the Canadian bacon rounds and slice the soysage into ¾-inch pieces.

3 Add another 3 tablespoons of the olive oil to the skillet, and place it over medium heat. Add the chopped onions and sauté until they begin to soften, 3 minutes. Add the carrots and continue cooking, stirring often, for another 4 minutes. Lower the heat slightly, add the minced garlic, and sauté for 1 minute more. Add the tomatoes,

honey, and red chile flakes and cook over low heat for 10 minutes.

4 Meanwhile, back at the beans: Taste them. They should be just barely tender. Once they've reached this point, fish out and discard the clove-studded onion, celery, and herb bouquet. Also fish out the garlic, but don't throw it out; let it cool on the counter.

5 Add the tomato mixture to the beans. When the whole garlic has cooled sufficiently to handle, squeeze out the soft, cooked cloves into the beans (discard the papery skins).

6 Preheat the oven to 300°F. Spray a deep 9½- by 18-inch casserole with oil.

7 In a food processor, combine 1 ladleful of the bean mixture with the whole, peeled garlic cloves, the parsley leaves, and 3 tablespoons of the olive oil. Buzz smooth, and stir into the beans along with the black pepper. Taste the beans for seasoning, adding the remaining ¼ teaspoon salt or more if needed.

8 Spoon half of the beans into the prepared casserole. Scatter the soysage and Canadian bacon over the beans. Top with the remaining beans.

9 Toss the breadcrumbs with the remaining tablespoon of olive oil, and pat them over the top of the beans. Place the casserole in the oven, uncovered, and bake until the beans are bubbling and aromatic, 1½ hours. Remove them from the oven and place under the broiler briefly, until the crumb crust is a deep golden-brown, 1 to 2 minutes at the max. Serve, hot, straight from the casserole.

Serves 8 to 10

SAVORY PIES

"Potpie"—even the word sounds plump, comforting, and homey, doesn't it? Here, this hearty classic home-cooking dish is given new charm, and sometimes spice, while being undergirded with a variety of protein-rich, equally comforting legumes. In all cases you've got two basic components: a savory, moist filling and a crust. I use the word "crust" loosely; a potpie's crust can be biscuits, cornbread, mashed potatoes—and it may top the filling or hide underneath it.

Potpies are potluck perfect. Their unpretentious appeal means you can count on their being crowd pleasers. Plus, they're inexpensive, they travel well, and they can be done mostly in advance. Baking them, of course, in the dish from which you will serve them is what gives them their down-home, peasant-y visual appeal. All versions can be made meatist, vegetarian, or vegan with just a little tinkering. I've offered options for each, as well as make-ahead directions.

ᗧ ᗧ ᗧ

TAMALE PIE DELAHANTY

Tamales: a small bit of spicy filling enrobed in a tube of fluffy corn masa dough (made from masa, the special lime-treated corn flour, used in making tortillas), then individually gift-wrapped in a corn husk or banana leaf and steamed. They're delectable but labor intensive, and they're one of countless remarkable ways poorer people create culinary amazements: resourcefulness in the face of limited resources. The very structure of a tamale means that less of the (more expensive) filling is used in relation to more of the (inexpensive) dough; and yet, who would feel deprived on receiving that steaming hot, neat packet with its charming ribbon of leaf or husk?

Tamale pie, an Americanized first cousin, is a hearty potpie, less time-consuming to make and with a much higher proportion of filling. Its crust is a dough of cooked cornmeal aka polenta. Although you could make it with an anything-goes filling (as in Cornbread Pie à la Hippie, page 239), to me it wouldn't be tamale pie without the distinctively jazzy combination of ground beef or vegetarian equivalent, beans, olives, raisins, green peppers, spices, and a whole bunch of sautéed aromatic vegetables. The way I make the filling has evolved over the years—less fat, without meat, spicier—but the olives, raisins, and peppers remain central, probably because I first heard of the dish in the 1948 novel *Cress Delahanty* by Jessamyn West.

I used to cook the cornmeal mush on the stovetop, a slightly alarming process: big, sudden, spitting, scalding hot bubbles that mess up the stove and usually burn the innocent stirrer a few times. There's a much easier way to make polenta, which you'll find on page 283, and which you can certainly use for the dough (simply use the lesser amount of water called for there). But for this recipe, use precooked polenta, which comes in tubes: Slice it and fit the pieces together to make the crust. **Vn**

2 tablespoons olive oil

1 large onion, chopped

1 carrot, chopped

1 green bell pepper, stemmed, seeded, and chopped

1 poblano pepper, stemmed, seeded, and chopped

1 to 2 jalapeños, stemmed, seeds removed for mildness or left in for heat, chopped

2 cloves garlic, chopped

1½ teaspoons ground cumin

2 tablespoons unbleached all-purpose flour

1 cup vegetable stock, warmed

2 cups commercial salsa, hot or not

8 to 10 ounces precooked spicy-style vegetarian "ground beef," such as Lightlife Mexican Smart Ground

1 to 2 cups cooked or canned pinto or black beans, drained well

½ cup sliced canned black olives (non-fancy)

½ cup sliced green olives with pimentos

½ cup raisins

¼ teaspoon dried oregano

Salt and freshly ground black pepper

Vegetable oil cooking spray

2 tubes (18 ounces each) cooked plain polenta (seasoned only with salt)

❶ Place the olive oil in your largest skillet over medium-high heat. When it's hot, add the onion and sauté until fragrant, about 3 minutes. Add the carrot, green pepper, poblano pepper, and jalapeños and continue sautéing for another 5 minutes. Lower the heat to medium low, add the garlic and ground cumin, and cook, stirring often, until the garlic is very lightly browned, 1 minute more.

❷ Preheat the oven to 350°F.

③ Stir the flour into the sautéed vegetables. Cook, stirring constantly, until the mixture starts to brown, 2 minutes. Whisk in the warm stock and the salsa and bring to a simmer. Let cook, stirring occasionally, for 10 minutes. Add the ground tofu, beans, both kinds of olives, raisins, and oregano. Season to taste with salt (remember the olives are salty) and quite a bit of freshly ground black pepper. Cook, stirring, until the mixture is thick and richly aromatic, about 10 minutes. Remove from the heat. (The filling can be made up to this point, cooled to room temperature, covered, and refrigerated for up to 3 days. Reheat it before you continue.)

④ To assemble the tamale pie, start by spraying a 9½- by 13½-inch (or similar) high-sided baking dish. Unwrap your tubes of polenta and slice them *lengthwise* in long strips about ⅓ inch thick (not in small crosswise rounds, as you'd logically expect). The strips cut from the edge of the tube will be narrow; those from the middle, nice and wide. Line the baking dish with the polenta, fitting the strips onto the bottom and sides, using all the polenta.

⑤ Now spoon the hot filling into the polenta-lined baking dish, cover tightly

---

COOKING CALEXICAN

Mango Margaritas

★

Citrus–Sparkled Bean Salad (page 131)

★

Tamale Pie Delahanty

★

Fresh papaya with lime

---

with aluminum foil, and transfer it to the oven. Bake for 25 minutes, then uncover and bake for 15 minutes more. Remove from the oven, let stand for a few minutes so it can firm up slighty, and serve hot.

Serves 8

VARIATIONS

Meatist Tamale Pie: Substitute a pound or so of well-drained browned ground beef for the tofu. **Me**

Cheese-Topped Tamale Pie: After you uncover the baked tamale pie, top it with 2 cups (8 ounces) grated sharp cheese (a combo of Jack and Cheddar works well) and return it to the oven. **Ve**

"She went into the kitchen which was warm and fragrant with the tamale pie her mother was making. Her mother was at the sink shaking olives from a bottle . . . [she] now began to stir them into her pie. Cress regarded her mother dispassionately. The rain and the steam in the kitchen made her permanent too frizzy. There was a big splash of cornmeal mush across her apron. She was smiling quite happily. Happy, Cress thought, on a spring evening of unutterable beauty, with nothing better to do than make a tamale pie. A pie that will be eaten tonight and forgotten tomorrow . . ."

—*Jessamyn West*, Cress Delahanty

CORNBREAD PIE
À LA HIPPIE

I've made this cornbread-topped deep-dish pie dozens of times, but never the same way twice. It is inherently loosey-goosey. To my taste, the spicier the bean mix, the better.

And speaking of stew, use any juicy, spicy, texture-y bean-vegetable combination you like. I'm a fan of any of the chilis in chapter 5, but you could just as easily (and deliciously) go with any thickish leftover bean soup or stew combined with almost any cooked vegetable, thinned down with stock or diced tomatoes in juice; or undrained canned beans of almost any variety combined with fire-roasted green tomatoes with chiles.

A deeper dish makes for thicker crust, a shallower dish for a thinner, crispier one. Your choice, as is the variety of cheese you feel will work best with your filling (if you use cheese at all). You can also amp the proportion of filling to topping up or down. To me, the best is an ample amount of filling capped by a thin crisp crust of good grainy cornbread, deeply browned. **Ve** **Gf**

Vegetable oil cooking spray

About 2 quarts (8 cups) any juicy bean-vegetable mixture (see headnote)

2 tablespoons melted butter or mild vegetable oil

1¼ cups stone-ground yellow or white cornmeal

½ teaspoon baking powder

¼ teaspoon baking soda

1 cup plus 2 tablespoons buttermilk

A scant ¼ teaspoon salt

1 to 1½ cups (4 to 6 ounces) grated cheese, for melting on top (optional)

1 Preheat the oven to 400°F. Spray a shallow (or deep, but with at least a 3½-quart capacity) baking dish with oil.

2 Heat the bean filling in a medium-size saucepan over medium heat until it's piping hot.

3 In a large bowl, combine the remaining ingredients, whisking swiftly until everything is moistened and well combined, creating a thinnish cornbread batter. Don't smooth it out; don't beat it.

4 Transfer the hot bean filling to the prepared baking dish. Spoon or pour the cornmeal batter over the bean filling, and bake until the top is golden brown, about 25 minutes. If you like, top the baked potpie with the grated cheese and run it under the broiler until nicely, appealingly gratinéed, a matter of minutes.

Serves 6 to 8

SUMMER GARDEN POTPIE
with Cheese-Herb Drop Biscuits

A one-dish meal from the garden: fresh green beans, corn, and other seasonal vegetables in a savory sauce, topped with herbed cheese biscuits. You can vary the sauce easily; slight alterations (which follow the basic recipe) yield different very satisfactory results. Vegans can make the biscuits dairy-free (by using either soy cheese or no cheese); meatists can embellish the sauce with cubes of cooked chicken, beef, or ham. You certainly don't need to cook the vegetables especially for this; part of the beauty of such dishes lies in canny forethought. Deliberately cook more green beans and zucchini (or whatever) a day or two or three before, knowing that they're waiting for you in the fridge (I suggest steaming the green beans and zucchini following the instructions on page 13). Then combining and biscuiting them is quick work—a good cook's sleight of hand.

A prep note: Before you start this, combine the dry ingredients for the biscuits in a large bowl, have the wet ingredients measured but not yet stirred in, and also have the cheese and herbs ready but not yet mixed in. You'll see in the recipe that follows when to combine everything. **Ve** or **Vn**

---

1 quart (4 cups) Velouté Sauce
(recipe follows)

2 cups cooked, very coarsely chopped
green beans

1 to 1½ cups cooked, very coarsely chopped
zucchini (from 1 medium or 2 small
zucchinis)

1½ cups raw fresh corn kernels, cut from
about 3 ears of corn

⅔ cup frozen peas, quick-thawed
in a strainer under hot tap water

Salt and freshly cracked black pepper

Vegetable oil cooking spray

Ingredients (not yet combined) for one recipe
of Cheese-Herb Drop Biscuits (page 242)

---

1 Preheat the oven to 425°F.

2 Combine the sauce and vegetables with salt and pepper to taste in a large saucepan over medium heat. Cook, stirring often, until the whole thing is piping hot. Taste for seasoning and adjust as necessary.

3 Spray an 8- by 12-inch baking dish or casserole with oil. Transfer the filling to the prepared baking dish and put it in the oven so it stays hot while you make the biscuits.

4 Now, prepare the biscuits: Pour the buttermilk into the bowl containing the dry ingredients and quickly combine using as few strokes as possible; you want everything just barely mixed. Sprinkle in the herbs and cheese, and with no more than 2 or 3 stirs, mix them in. The dough will be shaggy and too moist to roll, but it will still hold together nicely.

⑤ Remove the casserole from the oven (use mitts!). Moving quickly, drop the biscuit batter by heaping tablespoonfuls atop the hot filling, leaving some space between the biscuits.

⑥ Return the casserole to the oven and bake until the biscuits are crunchy and golden and the sauce is bubbling, 12 to 16 minutes. Serve ASAP.

Serves 4 to 6

VARIATIONS

Slightly Jazzed-Up Summer Garden Potpie: You can add oomph to any version of this potpie by sautéeing an onion or two with any or all of the following: a chopped carrot, a chopped stalk celery, and 1 to 2 minced cloves garlic (add the garlic at the end of the sauté). Cook these in the same type of fat you used in the sauce, for culinary harmony, and stir them into the sauce in step 2. **Ve**

Summer Garden Potpie with Edamame: Cut back the green beans to a cup, and omit the peas. Add 1⅓ cups cooked, shelled fresh or frozen edamame (see page 26) to the sauce in step 2. **Ve**

Wintertime Potpie, with Mushrooms: Use a dark, rich stock—beef stock if you're so inclined, or mushroom if you're otherwise inclined—to make the velouté. Add a mess of sautéed mushrooms (domestic and/or shiitake) to the filling in step 2, omitting the zucchini and corn. You can also add some diced or shredded leftover beef, or some browned ground hamburger, or some veggie "ground beef" such as Lightlife's Smart Ground, and/or some cooked kidney beans. **Ve** or **Me**

Springtime Potpie, with Mushrooms: Use a light vegetable or chicken stock to make the velouté, and add the juice and finely grated zest of 1 lemon to the completed sauce. Omit the corn and zucchini. Instead, use 2 cups quartered or halved small steamed new potatoes, ½ pound steamed spinach, and the Slightly Jazzed-Up sauté of onion, celery, and carrot, doubling the two latter vegetables. Fresh edible-pod peas (such as sugar snaps or snow peas), barely blanched, replace the frozen peas. Loverly! **Ve** or **Me**

Gardener's Pie: Skip the biscuits and instead top with generous dollops of well-seasoned leftover mashed potatoes dotted with a bit of butter. Bake at 375°F till golden brown, 20 to 25 minutes. **Ve**

Velouté Sauce

4 cups chicken or vegetable stock

Vegetable oil cooking spray (optional)

¼ cup butter

½ cup unbleached all-purpose flour

1½ tablespoons cornstarch

Salt and freshly ground pepper

① Pour all but 2 tablespoons of the stock into a medium saucepan (preferably nonstick), and bring it to a simmer over medium heat.

② Meanwhile, melt the butter over medium-low heat in a medium nonstick skillet or one that has been sprayed with oil. Stir in the flour and cook, uncovered, stirring often, until the flour is slightly golden and aromatic but not darkened, 2 to 3 minutes. This is your roux.

3 Between stirs of the roux, place the reserved 2 tablespoons stock in a small bowl and dissolve the cornstarch in it.

4 Pour the stock into the skillet with the roux, whisking them together so the mixture is lump free. Bring the mixture to a simmer and let it cook, whisking often, until it's the consistency of a very thin sauce or cream soup, about 6 minutes. Raise the heat slightly.

5 Whisk the cornstarch-stock mixture to re-amalgamate the starch and liquid, and whisk this into the hot sauce. It should quickly grow quite a bit thicker. Remove from the heat. Add salt and pepper to taste. Use immediately, or cool to room temperature and refrigerate, covered, for later use. (If the latter, reheat it quickly; extended reheating will cause the cornstarch to lose its thickening power, making your sauce thinner in consistency.)

Makes about 1¼ cups

Cheese-Herb Drop Biscuits

I f you've made conventional rolled-out biscuits, you'll be dubious that this easier, stickier, dropped-from-a-spoon dough can be as good. But it is! A light hand is always important when it comes to biscuit making: Don't overbeat. And yes, you do have to use either butter or a solid vegetable shortening (such as coconut fat or palm oil, the natural alternative to hydrogenated vegetable shortenings such as Crisco) to get a flaky

biscuit. For your herbs, choose a single milder fresh herb (parsley, basil) or better yet, a combo (the two mentioned, plus a few needles of rosemary, a sage leaf, a little fresh oregano and/or thyme and/or marjoram, or some finely chopped scallion). In a pinch, use 3 tablespoons fresh parsley and chopped scallion and a teaspoon of assorted dried herbs. Ve

> 1 cup unbleached white flour
>
> 1 cup whole wheat pastry flour
>
> ⅛ teaspoon cayenne (optional but good)
>
> 2½ teaspoons baking powder
>
> ½ teaspoon baking soda
>
> 1 teaspoon salt
>
> ¼ cup butter, chilled, or vegetable shortening, at room temperature
>
> ¾ cup finely grated very sharp Cheddar cheese (about 3 ounces)
>
> 3 to 4 tablespoons combined minced fresh herbs (see headnote)
>
> 1 cup plus 2 tablespoons buttermilk (2 or 3 extra tablespoons may be needed)

1 Preheat the oven to 425°F. Line a baking sheet with a silicone mat (or use a nonstick baking sheet).

2 Into a medium-size bowl, sift together the flours, cayenne, if using, baking powder, baking soda, and salt. Cut the butter or shortening into pea-size chunks and scatter them over the flour mixture. Quickly cut the fat into the flour with two knives or a pastry cutter. Add the cheese, giving it a couple of cuts to blend it into the flour. Add the herbs and the buttermilk.

3 Stir just until the mixture combines and barely forms a sticky, shaggy ball (this is the point at which you'll be able to tell if you need to add just a bit more buttermilk).

Don't overmix. The secret of a biscuit is to handle it gently, tenderly, lovingly.

4 Drop the dough by heaping tablespoonfuls on the prepared baking sheet. Bake immediately until golden brown and fragrant, 10 to 12 minutes.

Makes about 12 good-size biscuits, or topping for one potpie

VARIATIONS

Vegan Biscuits: Use the vegetable shortening. Omit the buttermilk; instead, place 1 tablespoon vinegar or lemon juice in the bottom of a liquid measuring cup, and add enough plain soy, rice, oat, or almond milk to equal the 1 cup plus 2 tablespoons and possible extra. Omit the cheese. **Vn**

Dill Biscuits: Dill's not exactly a shrinking violet flavorwise, but neither is it overpowering. It does not, however, play well with others. I like to do a chopped fresh dill–only herb biscuit, using Muenster cheese instead of Cheddar. This is particularly pleasing paired with most split-pea soups. **Ve**

SO-GOOD SOYFOODS

S o far all of our bean bakes have completed their journey to becoming dinner in the oven. Here, we take a different approach, using oven baking to *start* the process—at least, for that most exceptional of all beans, the soybean, in two exceptional forms, tofu and tempeh. Soyfoods, as you may know, give us so much; the least we can do is respectfully imbue their culinary properties—neutral flavor, tender texture—with a little pizzazz. When you marinate and pre-bake soyfoods, they come into their own, which is to say, *your* own cooking style and finished dishes, in countless ways. The oven continues to be your friend here.

Basic Oven-Baked
MARINATED TEMPEH

This base preparation assumes you'll use the baked tempeh as part of something else: a stir-fry, a sandwich, part of a filling. For example, in this book you'll find it called for in CD's Brunswick New-Stew, page 194 and Mellow Coconut-Tempeh Curry, page 206. Versatile, endlessly useful, just plain good.

Use any of the optional seasonings singly or in combination up to 3; tweak them depending on how you intend to use the tempeh. **Vn**

MARINADE:

2 tablespoons tamari or shoyu soy sauce

1½ tablespoons vinegar (white, apple cider, balsamic, rice, red or white wine—whatever you have on hand or goes with the flavors of your end-use recipe)

1 teaspoon Pickapeppa or vegetarian Worcestershire sauce (optional, but good)

OPTIONAL SEASONINGS:

1 to 3 cloves garlic, pressed

1 to 2 teaspoons grated fresh ginger

¼ to ½ teaspoon freshly ground black pepper

1 to 2 teaspoons honey or agave syrup

1 to 2 teaspoons toasted sesame oil

½ to 1 teaspoon Tabasco, Sriracha, harissa, or other hot sauce

1 tablespoon ketchup or tomato paste

1 teaspoon ground coriander

TEMPEH:

Vegetable oil cooking spray (optional)

1 cake (8 ounces) tempeh, cut in the size or shape appropriate to your end use

1 Combine all of the marinade ingredients, plus your seasonings of choice, in a nonreactive (glass, ceramic, or enamel-clad) dish or a large zip-top bag. Add the tempeh and let marinate, giving the dish or bag a shake every so often, for 20 minutes to 1 hour at room temp, or up to 2 days if refrigerated. (The longer it marinates, the more flavorful it gets, but this is a matter of convenience more than anything else.)

2 Fifteen minutes before you are ready to cook the tempeh, preheat the oven to 375°F. Spray a rimmed baking sheet generously with oil or line it with a silicone baking mat.

3 Place the marinated tempeh pieces on the prepared baking sheet, allowing plenty of space between them. Bake for 12 to 15 minutes, then flip the pieces over and bake for another 10 minutes. Remove from the oven, and use as desired. The baked tempeh will keep, covered, in the fridge for up to 3 days.

Serves 3 or 4 if used as the main event; possibly many more if used in a stir-fry, spring rolls, pasta dish, or casserole

VARIATIONS

Basic Oven-Baked Breaded Tempeh:
Follow the recipe through step 2. Then, make a breading of ½ cup nutritional yeast and ½ cup flour (wheat, rice, or millet flour all do nicely here, with or without a little cornmeal). Or, you can just use plain nutritional yeast, no flour. Stir 1½ teaspoons sweet Hungarian paprika (or ¼ teaspoon smoked sweet Hungarian paprika), a dash of cayenne, and a little salt and freshly ground black pepper into the breading mixture. Place the breading mixture in a paper bag, add the tempeh a few pieces at a time, and shake-shake-shake (no, not your booty—though, what's the harm?) the tempeh. Place the coated tempeh on the prepared baking sheet and bake as directed. (Leftover breading mix can be refrigerated in a zip-top bag for up to 2 weeks—label it, though!) **Vn**

Basic Oven-Crisped Tempeh: This gives tempeh an exceptionally pleasing crunch. It's messy to make, and you may think *this can't be right* because the egg coating will want to slither off. But you are doing it right, and the resulting crispness—from a no-fry zone!—is worth it for certain dishes. Marinate and bread the tempeh as described. Then, set up two bowls: one containing an egg beaten with 2 teaspoons water and a second with 2 to 3 cups crisp crumbs (bread, cracker, panko, or cornflake crumbs are all terrific). Working with one piece at a time, dip the floured tempeh first in the egg, then in the crumbs, pressing the crumbs in. Place each crumbed piece on the baking sheet, and proceed as directed in step 3, baking an additional 3 to 5 minutes per side. I told you it was messy! But try this over rice with a little Velouté Sauce (page 241) to which you've added 2 to 3 tablespoons nutritional yeast . . . most pleasing. **Vn**

MIDSUMMER LUNCH ON THE LAWN

Basic Oven-Baked Marinated Tempeh on a toasted sesame bun with heirloom tomato slices, fresh avocado, lettuce, and Herbed Tofu Mayo Dip (page 50)

★

Fresh corn, green beans, and sliced cucumber with a drizzle of My Basic Feisty Vinaigrette (page 132)

★

Sea-salted dark chocolate caramels

★

Fresh local strawberries

Three Marinades for Traditional
WATER-PACKED TOFU

Much of the following information I gave in *Passionate Vegetarian.* I repeat it here because it hasn't changed and because I still get asked Tofu 101 questions on a regular basis. So, if you already know all this, skip ahead. If not—welcome.

Marinating tofu, then baking it, takes it from Miss Congeniality to Miss Personality; still congenial, but with a little oomph and ready to go anywhere. It can win the talent contest.

Different varieties of tofu have markedly different characteristics and culinary properties. If you are new to tofu, *read the package!* Any tofu called "silken" or even "soft" should not be used for marinating and baking. (Take advantage of its properties in tofu mayo and in tofu dips, page 49.) Instead, choose traditional, water-packed firm or extra-firm tofu, reduced-fat or not as you prefer. If you want the flavor of the marinade to really infuse the tofu and you like a chewy texture, freeze, then thaw, the tofu before marinating it.

The shape of the tofu slices will be dictated by the dish you intend to use them in, but you definitely want lots of surface exposed so the tofu can soak up the marinade. Usually I do large rectangles about 3 inches long by 2 inches wide, about ¼ to ½ inch thick, but this varies according to the shape of the tofu block and its firmness; sometimes I halve these. This is a good shape when you plan to make an oven-baked tofu, sandwiches, barbecued tofu, or a more elaborately sauced dish. I also use 2-inch triangles and ¾-inch dice not infrequently, usually for stir-fries.

Since most marinades contain vinegar or other acid ingredients, use a nonreactive dish—glass, ceramic, or enamel-clad—or a zip-top bag for marinating.

Traditional Asian-style Marinade for Tofu

This is the mother of all tofu marinades, what almost everyone starts out using. It's certainly not original, but it is good and versatile, leaving you with an already-seasoned product that can be used in all kinds of ways. **Vn**

FOR THE MARINADE:

2 to 4 tablespoons tamari or shoyu soy sauce

2 tablespoons rice wine (mirin) or dry sherry, or, if you prefer a sharper taste, rice vinegar

3 cloves garlic, crushed

1 piece peeled fresh ginger about the size of half your thumb, grated

1 tablespoon honey, agave syrup, or light brown sugar

OPTIONAL SEASONINGS:

Several vigorous grinds of black pepper

Tabasco or Sriracha hot sauce

1 teaspoon toasted sesame oil, or to taste

1 peeled, chopped fresh tomato

12 to 16 ounces traditional water-packed firm or extra-firm tofu

Combine all of the marinade ingredients, including your seasonings of choice, in a nonreactive bowl or large zip-top bag. Place the tofu, sliced according to its intended final use, in the marinade. Let soak for 40 minutes at room temperature, or refrigerate it, turning occasionally, for up to 3 days.

For **Basic Oven-Baked Tofu,** shake the excess marinade off the tofu and bake it as directed in Basic Oven-Baked Marinated Tempeh (or one of its variations) on page 244.

Enough to marinate 12 to 16 ounces of tofu

Smoky Onion-Garlic Marinade for Tofu

This marinade could not be easier or more delicious. It's a great base preparation for any tofu you care to bake in a sweet-spicy-tomato-y or fruity sauce, such as a homemade or purchased barbecue sauce. **Vn**

¼ cup tamari or shoyu soy sauce

1 tablespoon mild vegetable oil, such as corn, canola, or peanut (optional)

1 large onion, peeled and quartered

Cloves from 1 head garlic (if you are in a rush, just use a couple of cloves)

2 tablespoons cider vinegar

2 drops liquid smoke

12 to 16 ounces sliced traditional water-packed firm or extra-firm tofu

Combine all of the ingredients but the tofu in a food processor. Pulse-chop, then buzz, pausing to scrape down the sides of the bowl as needed. The marinade will be thin, with bits of ground onion in it. Place the tofu, sliced according to its intended final use, in a nonreactive dish or large zip-top bag and pour the marinade over it. Let soak for 40 minutes at room temperature, or cover and refrigerate, turning occasionally, for up to 6 days. (Tofu keeps much longer with this marinade than others, because there is a copious amount of it.)

For **Oven-Baked Smoky Onion–Garlic Tofu** shake the excess marinade off the tofu and bake it as directed in Basic Oven-Baked Marinated Tempeh (or one of its variations) on page 244.

Enough to marinate 12 to 16 ounces of tofu

Western, Hippie-style Marinade for Tofu

This tofu marinade was once universal in some circles. It's still a good, useful basic. **Vn**

FOR THE MARINADE:

2 tablespoons tamari or shoyu soy sauce

1 tablespoon cider vinegar

1 tablespoon Pickapeppa sauce

Several vigorous grinds of black pepper

OPTIONAL SEASONINGS:

Tabasco or similar hot sauce

Crushed garlic

1 teaspoon to 1 tablespoon bottled salsa

12 to 16 ounces sliced traditional water-packed firm or extra-firm tofu

Whisk all of the marinade ingredients together in a small bowl, including the seasonings of choice. Place the tofu slices in a nonreactive dish or zip-top bag and pour the marinade over it. Let it soak for 40 minutes at room temperature, or refrigerate it, turning occasionally, for up to 3 days.

For **Basic Oven-Baked Tofu à la Hippie,** shake the excess marinade off the tofu and bake it as directed in Basic Oven-Baked Marinated Tempeh (or one of its variations) on page 244.

Enough to marinate 12 to 16 ounces of tofu

". . . the Food all China abounds in, and which all in that Empire eat, from the Emperor to the meanest Chinese; the Emperor and great Men as Dainty, the common sort as necessary sustenance . . . is called Teu Fu . . . as white as the very Snow . . . Alone, it is insipid, but very good dress'd and excellent fry'd in Butter."

—from the travel journals
of Friar Domingo Navarrete,
a 17th-century Jesuit

New Wave–New Fave
BAKED TOFU OR TEMPEH

I've been doing the previous marinades forever. This new one is first cousin to a good barbecued tofu: piquant, sweet-hot-rich, and scintillatingly tasty. The tofu is baked in the marinade/sauce, which cooks down and coats it, caramelizing them. You'll probably have to soak the baking dish overnight before washing it, but it's worth it. Vary this using fruit juice concentrate instead of honey or sugar, and adding extra ginger, orange zest, or both. For an incendiary smokiness, add chipotle in adobo. **Vn**

⅓ cup natural, unhydrogenated peanut butter (see box, page 323)

⅓ cup tamari or shoyu soy sauce

⅓ cup honey, light brown sugar, maple syrup, or thawed, undiluted frozen apple or pineapple juice concentrate

¼ cup apple cider vinegar

4 to 6 cloves garlic, quartered lengthwise

About 1 tablespoon chopped fresh ginger (optional)

1 to 2 tablespoons tomato paste or ketchup

1 canned chipotle pepper in adobo sauce, ½ teaspoon cayenne, or 1 fresh serrano or jalapeño pepper, de-stemmed

Juice and grated zest of 1 orange (optional, but good)

12 to 14 ounces drained, sliced traditional water-packed firm or extra-firm tofu or tempeh

Vegetable oil cooking spray

❶ Combine the peanut butter, tamari, honey, apple cider vinegar, garlic, ginger, tomato paste, chipotle, and orange juice and zest in a food processor and buzz until the ginger is finely chopped.

❷ To use the marinade, place the tofu in a nonreactive bowl or zip-top bag and pour or spoon this luscious mixture over it. Refrigerate the tofu, covered, overnight.

❸ The next day, preheat the oven to 375°F and generously spray a nonreactive baking dish with oil (I use an 8 or 9 by 12-inch deep glass baking dish).

❹ Place the tofu and its marinade in the baking dish, spreading the marinade as needed so both sides of the tofu slices get a good smear of it. Bake, turning once, until fragrant, firmed up, and golden to deep brown in spots with the marinade considerably thickened, about 30 minutes.

Enough for 12 to 14 ounces of tofu or tempeh

SPRING STIR-FRY AFTER SPIN CLASS

Stir-fry of onions, broccoli, pea pods, baby carrots, and New Wave–New Fave Baked Tofu or Tempeh over quinoa

*

Gingered Asian Green Been Salad (page 132), on a bed of mizuna

*

Coconut sorbet with biscotti

Traditional Asian-style

"CRISPING" MARINADE & METHOD FOR OVEN-BAKED TOFU

This was originally developed for Kung Pao Tofu (page 297), but it's a fine recipe in itself, just asking to be used in any sprightly vegetable stir-fry, as a sandwich filling, or served with brown rice and almost any savory sauce. At first glance you might think this is no different from the Asian-style marinades that appear earlier in this chapter, but the cornstarch makes magic when the tofu is baked at extra-high heat, adding a browned crisp-chewy exterior.

Please note that if making this for the Kung Pao dish, the mirin, cornstarch, and garlic are also needed for the finishing sauce. You may want to measure them out at the same time. **Vn** **Gf**

FOR THE MARINADE:

2 tablespoons mirin (Japanese rice wine) or dry sherry

2 tablespoons cornstarch

3 cloves garlic, crushed

½ teaspoon salt

Several vigorous grinds of black pepper

FOR THE TOFU:

2 packages (8 ounces each) extra-firm or hard-style reduced-fat traditional water-packed tofu, cut into ½ by 1½-inch strips

Vegetable oil cooking spray (optional)

❶ Up to 24 hours but no less than 1 hour before you plan to bake the tofu, combine all of the marinade ingredients in a large bowl, stirring them together well. Add the tofu and toss to coat. Let it stand for at least 40 minutes at room temperature, or cover it and refrigerate it overnight.

❷ Up to 2 hours before serving, line a baking sheet with a silicone baking mat or oil the heck out of it. Lay the marinated tofu strips on the prepared baking sheet, giving them some air space so they're not piled on top of one another.

❸ Preheat the oven to 500°F.

❹ Pop the tofu slices into the hot oven and bake until browned and lightly crisped on the bottom, 10 to 15 minutes, then flip them over and bake for another 5 to 10 minutes. They should be golden brown. Use a spatula to remove the tofu from the baking sheet, and use it however you wish.

Enough for two 8-ounce packages of tofu

CHAPTER 8

Home on the Range

SIMPATICO
SKILLETS
and
STIR-FRIES

Beans are, without a doubt, very much at home on the range.

Stovetop slow-pot beans are cold-weather comfort, simmering in savory liquid, spiced with aromatics, heartened with large chunks of carrot, potato, and, if you're so inclined, meat or chicken. No matter how many feet of snow blanket the ground outside, you know that inside is a safe, warm place where appetites are both whetted and sated.

But besides such slow-food security, stovetop beans are also paradoxically the de-stress, express dinnertime solution to the we're-hungry-now-please-feed-us dilemma. A skillet, a drizzle of oil, a quick sizzling sauté of onions and what-have-you, the sinking-in of the can opener's jaw, that comforting sigh as the seal is broken, the unthinking efficiency of the circular motion you've participated in a million times, then the can's contents—black beans or red, round chickpeas or oval white beans, flattened golden-yellow butter beans—into the skillet. Or perhaps your skillet beans

are in transmogrified form: tofu or tempeh (if you're lucky, previously marinated and baked in any one of the ways described on pages 244–250). In either case, five or ten minutes later, dinner: fast food, slow soul. And again, all is well.

And what about stovetop sides? Most beans that are intended to accompany other dishes begin their transformation from raw to cooked over flame, not in the oven.

Having explored how beautifully beans do in the primal pot of soup and stew, adventure further in the ways of bean over flame, the never-the-same-way-twice panoply of skillet and stovetop. From quick classic Asian stir-fries (pages 294–298) to slow sautés like Greek-style Green Beans (page 284); from old-fashioned sides like Sweet and Sour Wax Beans (page 290) to center-of-the-plate extravagances like a Shiitake, Bean, and Green Ragout (page 282), from down the road and around the world, a wide-ranging universe of leguminous satisfactions awaits us.

SKILLETS

Countless quick skillet zappers and sautés can turn a can of beans, plus whatever vegetables and leftovers are lurking in the fridge (The BEST Vegetable Hash, page 256, being an excellent example) into an almost-instant meal. The trick is an artful hand with the seasonings, and here I'll do my best to guide your hand toward this art. But there are also more intentional sautés, like the garlicky greens-and-beans topping for pasta which, sparked with lemon and heated with dried chile, appears on my table with more regularity than almost any other preparation in this book. And I adore the transformation fresh beans—green beans or yellow, quickly stir-fried in the Asian style or more slowly cooked in the Mediterranean or Indian mode—undergo in a skillet.

But more elaborate skillet–bean transformations await the legume explorer. Chickpea flour makes crepes as tender, pleasing, and versatile as those traditionally made with eggs, becoming an Indian flatbread that will have everyone at the table saying "Are there any more?" Green bean and vegetable fritters, also bound with chickpea flour, start in a skillet and end up, quickly done and savory, as delightful little crispy cakes with elements of Japanese tempura, Indian pakoras, and Chinese eggs-foo-young. These are endlessly versatile and always a crowd-pleaser. Then there are tofu and tempeh, stir-fried with ginger, garlic, sesame, peanut, and chile, in countless pages from the great asparagus-to-zucchini Asian book of kitchen ways.

> "... she spent the better part of her day at work in the kitchen. At home with her mother, meals had been simple—fava beans and olive oil, rghaif and tea, bread and olives, couscous on Fridays, whatever her mother could afford to buy ... "
>
> —*Laila Lalami,* Hope and Other Dangerous Pursuits

But whether cooked in a skillet or wok'd, it comes to the same thing: high heat, the wide-open embrace of a sizzling hot pan, a little oil or other fat, beans plus a pile of good ingredients—and great results, fast. Superb, simpatico, sincerely.

GREEN BEAN & VEGETABLE FRITTERS

I don't use my skillets to fry much these days, but these fritters—another oldie but goodie from the original *Bean Book* (written, after all, when I was a young and calorie-burnin' fool)—are just too tasty to omit. Crispy on the outside, soft and texture-y on the inside, these are irresistible; even people who should know better will go wild eating them, absolutely without self-restraint.

I've updated the recipe a little (I can't even remember the last time I used wheat germ, which was in the original). I've also suggested some dipping sauces, each of which adds its own kind of distinctive, deliciousness to the fritters' allure. Although I've offered the fritters here on the large side, as a main dish, you can also do them petite; miniaturized they are an excellent, and substantial, starter.

Tip, tail, and thinly slice the green beans before measuring them. And feel free to add a little more or less of any of the vegetables, or to mix it up a bit—to use yellow and green beans, for instance, or throw in a little shredded parsnip with the carrot, or use shredded sweet potato instead of carrot, or add some diced red or green bell pepper or fine matchsticks of eggplant, or sliced mushrooms. **Ve**

FOR THE BATTER:

2 eggs

⅔ cup milk

¼ cup chickpea flour (*besan;* see box, page 279)

½ cup whole wheat pastry flour

1 teaspoon salt

A few grinds of black pepper

Dash of Pickapeppa, Worcestershire, or vegetarian Worcestershire sauce

1 tablespoon sugar or maple syrup

FOR THE VEGETABLES:

About ⅓ pound green beans, tipped, tailed, and finely sliced crosswise (1½ cups)

1 carrot, grated

1 onion, very finely chopped, or 3 scallions, derooted, whites and 2 to 3 inches of green finely chopped

½ cup raw fresh corn kernels (cut from 1 ear)

FOR COOKING AND SERVING:

About ½ cup mild vegetable oil, such as corn, canola, or peanut, or more as needed, for frying

Mixed Fruit Salsa (page 181), Thai sweet red chile sauce, and/or plain or flavored Tofu Mayonnaise (page 49), for dipping

1 Set out paper towels or split brown paper bags for draining the finished fritters. Unless you're serving them right out of the skillet, place a baking sheet in the oven set on its lowest setting; you'll stow the completed fritters there to keep them warm until you've finished frying them all.

2 Make the batter: Either buzz all the batter ingredients together in a food processor, pausing to scrape down the sides, until incorporated, or whisk the heck out of them in a large bowl.

3 Stir the vegetables into the batter, making sure everything is well distributed.

4 Place the vegetable oil in a large skillet over medium-high heat and set an instant-read frying thermometer in it. When the oil has reached good frying temperature, 360°F to 365°F, drop in a small spoonful of batter to test it. There should be an immediate sizzling sound and bubbles racing around the fritter, or your oil isn't hot enough. When the fritter sizzles as it should, drop in additional batter by rounded tablespoonfuls, working in batches to avoid crowding the pan. Cook the fritters, turning once with a spatula, until they are golden brown and cooked through, about 3 minutes on each side.

5 Drain the finished fritters on the prepared paper towels and serve immediately, or transfer them, in a single layer, to the baking sheet in the oven to keep them warm. They'll wait, happily, for 15 to 20 minutes. Serve with the dipping sauce of your choice.

Makes 6 to 8 fritters; serves 2 to 3 as an entrée

VARIATION

For extra-light fritters, add 1 teaspoon baking powder to the batter. Or separate the eggs, add the yolks to the other batter ingredients, then stiffly beat the whites and fold them into the vegetable fritter mixture just before frying.

For a vegan version, use 2 eggs' worth of reconstituted Eggscellence Dry Mix (see below) and substitute soy milk or club soda for the milk. **Vn**

. . . .

Eggscellence Dry Mix

1 cup potato starch

¾ cup tapioca flour

¼ cup full-fat soy flour

1 tablespoon baking powder

2 tablespoons xanthan gum

Combine all ingredients thoroughly, sifting together or whisking to combine. Store in a tightly covered jar or double-bagged zip-top in the freezer, where it keeps for up to a year.

To reconstitute: For each egg called for in a recipe, combine the following in a small bowl: 1½ tablespoons Eggscellence Dry Mix, 1½ tablespoons water, and 1 teaspoon liquid lecithin, which is available at natural foods stores. Whisk together very well.

Makes about 2 cups

THE *BEST* VEGETABLE HASH

I'm particular about hashes and have made finding a really good vegetarian one a minor but ongoing culinary mission. I feel I succeeded here, and I hope you'll feel likewise. This, as they say, has got it goin' on: a nice savory sauté of onions, carrots, celery; little cubes of tender and pleasantly starchy potato; good but simple seasonings. The coup de grace? Oddly, it's beans, mashed and used to add heft, flavor, and that perfect hash texture. Top it with a poached egg and, honey, you are going to be thanking me when brunch comes around.

If you want to jazz this up just a little, add half a bunch of fresh parsley and a clove or two of garlic, halved, to the beans when you buzz 'em. **Gf** **Ve** or **Vn**

3 fist-size potatoes, scrubbed well, peeled or not, as you desire, cut into ½-inch (or smaller) dice

2 tablespoons extra-virgin olive oil

1 large onion, diced

2 carrots, diced

½ green bell pepper, stemmed, seeded, and diced

2 stalks celery, with leaves, diced

1 tomato, diced (optional)

1 stalk broccoli, head cut into small florets, stem peeled and diced

1 can (15 ounces) red kidney beans, drained well

Salt and freshly cracked black pepper

Grated extra-sharp Cheddar cheese, for serving (optional)

Poached eggs (1 to 2 per person) or "fillets" of Basic Oven-Baked Tofu or Tempeh (page 244), for serving (optional)

Ketchup, Tabasco or similar hot sauce, and/or salsa, for serving (optional)

BRUNCH ON BEMIS HILL

The Best Vegetable Hash

★

Poached eggs

★

Toasted spelt English muffins

★

Fresh oranges tossed with Grand Marnier

① Fill a medium-size saucepan halfway with water and bring it to a boil. Drop in the potatoes and lower the heat to a brisk simmer, a not-quite-full boil.

② While the potatoes simmer, heat a large skillet over medium-high heat. Add the olive oil and the moment it thins, add the onion. Sauté, stirring often, about 5 minutes. Lower the heat a tad, add the carrots, green pepper, and celery, and sauté until the vegetables are slightly tender, another 5 minutes. Stir in the tomato, if using.

3 Taste a potato; it should be almost or just barely done, not quite 100 percent. Place the broccoli in a colander in the sink (or over a bowl, if you want to catch the potato-cooking liquid for use in a stock—always a good idea) and drain the potatoes over the broccoli (thus precooking the broccoli slightly). Drain the broccoli and potatoes very well, shaking the colander, and add them to the skillet (which you have been continuing to stir at intervals).

4 Continuing to stir the sautéing vegetables regularly, place the kidney beans in a food processor and pulse-chop, pausing to scrape down the sides, until you have a textured puree. Alternatively, you can place the beans in a large bowl and mash them to this same texture with a potato masher.

5 Stir the mashed beans into the sautéing veggies, which will almost immediately thicken up and want to stick. Keep stirring until the mixture is thicker, thick enough so you could shape it into cakes if you were so inclined, 1 to 2 minutes more. Season it with salt and pepper to taste.

6 Serve immediately, hot; if you like, with a sprinkle of grated Cheddar cheese, a poached egg or two, and ketchup, hot sauce, and/or salsa on the table.

Serves 4

ง   ง   ง

Mr. Puppovich's HO-MADE FISHCAKE-STYLE TOFU CAKES

David Levingston and Ellen Greenlaw, two Vermont pan pals, are passionate home cooks who especially enjoy vegetarianizing traditional meat or fish dishes. These cakes—golden and crispy on the outside, tender, chewy, and full of flavory, savory surprises within—can be made large (to serve in a bun) or small (as appetizer-size morsels). If you ever doubted that tofu could be such an obliging chameleon, this recipe will prove it to you; tofu takes on one aspect in the cakes themselves, and another in the creamy tartar sauce that follows. With seasonings full of oomph—minced dill pickle, fresh dill, loads of onion, garlic, and shallot, tamari, mustard, Cajun spices—tofu is anything but bland. Please note that the breadcrumbs in the cakes are soft and serve as a binder, while the panko breadcrumbs in which you dredge the cakes serve to give them their beautiful, crisp golden coating.

It's important to start ahead of time by freezing and then thawing the tofu to render its texture chewy—an essential component of the Ho-Made experience. In fact, everything except the final frying can be done in advance. Leftovers are terrific cold in a sandwich the next day. Ve

1 pound firm or extra-firm water-packed tofu, drained, frozen overnight, then thawed for several hours

2 shallots, very finely minced

¼ red onion, very finely minced

1 teaspoon dehydrated garlic granules (not garlic salt)

1½ sour kosher dill pickles, finely chopped (about ⅓ cup chopped)

1 heaping tablespoon finely minced fresh dill

2 large eggs

1 cup plus 2 tablespoons fine, soft breadcrumbs, preferably wholegrain

1 heaping tablespoon yellow ballpark-style mustard

1½ cloves garlic

About 1 tablespoon tamari soy sauce

½ teaspoon smoked sweet Hungarian paprika, or 2 teaspoons sweet Hungarian paprika

Cajun seasoning to taste (see Note)

Freshly ground black pepper

Salt

Panko breadcrumbs, as needed

Mild vegetable oil, such as corn, canola, or peanut, for frying

Toasted buns (preferably wholegrain with sesame seeds), for serving

Ho-made Tartar Sauce (page 260), for serving

1. Cut each block of tofu in half lengthwise, making 4 rectangles each about the size of a kitchen sponge. With clean hands and applying firm but gentle pressure, squeeze each rectangle over the sink to release as much liquid as possible (it's okay to be dubious if you've never done this before). Crumble the tofu into small pieces into a large bowl.

2. Transfer about one third of the pressed tofu crumbles to a food processor.

3. To the tofu in the bowl, add the shallots, onion, garlic granules, pickles, and dill.

4. To the tofu in the processor, add the eggs, breadcrumbs, mustard, garlic, tamari, paprika, Cajun seasoning, and a generous amount of black pepper. Buzz to form a thick, not quite smooth paste, pausing occasionally to scrape down the sides of the processor bowl. Scrape this paste into the bowl of crumbled tofu.

5. Combine the two tofu mixtures thoroughly. Add salt to taste. At this point you can proceed to the next step (the mixture holds together well even without refrigeration), or cover the bowl and refrigerate the mixture for 1 hour or as long as overnight.

6. When ready to cook, line several plates with paper towels. Let the mixture come

to room temperature, then form it into ten 3-inch cakes, each just shy of an inch thick (make them smaller and thinner if you plan to serve them as a starter; the yield depends on how tiny you go). Spread a layer of panko breadcrumbs on a plate. Press each cake lightly into the panko crumbs to coat it on both sides (you want a moderate, not heavy, coating).

7 Pour the oil into a large skillet to reach a depth of 1½ inches. Place the skillet over medium heat and bring the oil to proper frying temperature (365°F) on an instant-read thermometer. Add the cakes 3 or 4 at a time and fry, turning once, until they are golden brown on both sides, about 3 minutes per side. Adjust the timing downward if you've made your

cakes smaller and thinner. The length of time is best judged by appearance; that nice consistent golden brown is what you're looking for.

8 Place the finished tofu cakes on the paper-towel-lined plates. Serve larger cakes on buns, or put out the smaller cakes as an appetizer (there are mini-buns, too, if you want to go that route). "Enjoy with homemade tartar sauce, and on a bun," David advises. Don't worry, David, we will!

Makes ten 3-inch tofu cakes

Note: I especially like two brands of Cajun spice blend, Tony Chachere's Original Creole Seasoning and River Road Spicy Cajun Seasoning.

WOOF, WOOF!

Therapist David Levingston and his compañera, writer Ellen Greenlaw, have an imagined parallel life in which they feed others. For six months of one year, they lived this life at an area festival or two and at the Saturday Brattleboro (Vermont) Farmer's Market, a much-loved local institution set in a shady grove. Besides produce, plants, and locally made granolas, cheeses, and breads, there are also a dozen or so excellent booths at which to buy something to eat on the spot. The choices vibrate with world flavors: a West African booth vies with Thai, Indian, Middle Eastern, French, and a number of American iterations.

In 2008, one of these booths was David and Ellen's: Mr. Puppovich's Uncommon Delights. One featured item was tilapia-based, pickle-and-anchovy–spiked, panko-crusted "Ho-Made Fish Cakes." But Ellen's a vegetarian, so the two of them set out to make a vegetarian doppelgänger of the popular cakes. "Not to taste *like* fish, exactly," David explains, "but with some of the same basics." Tweak by tweak, they developed snappy tofu cakes (opposite), which debuted at Boston's Bizarre Bazaar festival, selling hundreds and garnering raves in local blogs.

Now, although David and Ellen have backed off from food service, you and I can rave about these irresistible morsels.

Mr. Puppovich? The family dog.

Ho–made Tartar Sauce

This makes enough for one batch of Mr. Puppovich's Ho–Made Fishcake-style Tofu Cakes, but you'll have some left over— ready for the next sandwich that needs perking up. You can simplify the recipe by substituting 1¼ cups conventional prepared mayo for the tofu mayonnaise base, which is what David and Ellen do. But, given that the cakes are fried, to my taste regular mayo feels like overkill in texture as well as calorically: just too much fat. I much prefer this lighter alternative.

This sauce is best made a day or two in advance, to allow the flavors to blend. **Vn**

> 1 recipe Tofu Mayonnaise (page 49)
>
> 2 medium dill pickles, coarsely chopped
>
> 4 sprigs of fresh parsley

> 1 heaping tablespoon chopped fresh dill
>
> 2 tablespoons freshly squeezed lemon juice
>
> 1 thick slice red onion, coarsely chopped
>
> 1 teaspoon vegetarian Worcestershire or Pickapeppa sauce
>
> ½ teaspoon salt
>
> ¼ teaspoon sugar, agave syrup, or honey

Put the tofu mayo in a food processor, add all the remaining ingredients, and pulse-chop 5 to 6 times, pausing to scrape down the sides of the bowl, until the add-ins are finely chopped but not pureed to smoothness. Transfer to a small bowl, cover, and refrigerate until ready to use. It will keep, covered and refrigerated, for 2 to 3 days; just drain off any water that accumulates on the top before using.

Makes about 1¼ cups

ꜩ ꜩ ꜩ

Traditional, Start-Them-the-Day-Before
FALAFELS

At Taiim, the local falafelry in my mother's town of Hastings-on-Hudson, New York, a red poster with a white crown graphic that riffs off of World War II–era British posters advises, "Stay calm—eat falafel." Who wouldn't be calmed by a good falafel? Those crispy-crunchy little balls of well-seasoned fried chickpea are generally served with pita bread, salad, and sauce, generally served as street food, and generally messy. Like the girl with the curl in the middle of her forehead, when falafels are good, they're very, very good, and when they're bad, they're horrid. Why "generally"? Falafel, like any dish people care passionately about, is the source of much debate. It all boils down to this: However they are prepared where you grew up is the only way you believe *real* falafels are done. You may agree that some restaurants or stalls do them better than others, but if you grew up eating them made not with chickpeas but with favas (as in Egypt), or with pickled vegetables (as in Syria and Lebanon), that's the way falafels are supposed to be, period.

But if we are talking "traditional," all Middle Eastern falafels have this in common: they're made with *raw* beans that have been soaked overnight to semi-tenderness, then ground, seasoned, and fried. The frying gives traditional falafels their characteristic exterior crunch; the raw chickpeas gives them their grainy interior texture.

Now, hint #1: Remember the soaking period is *24 hours.* If you want to have falafels for lunch tomorrow, start soaking them at lunchtime today. Hint #2: Unless you are experienced at frying, invest ten bucks and get a thermometer so you can get the oil temp just right. Makes all the difference in the world. And the obvious must be stated: Adjust the seasonings to taste. Your falafel, your call.

This is a large recipe. You could always halve it, but it hardly seems worth the trouble. Besides, no matter how many of these you make, they get gobbled up. **Vn**

FOR THE FALAFEL:

2 cups dried chickpeas

1 small onion, peeled and quartered

4 cloves garlic, crushed with the side of a knife

About 1 cup packed fresh cilantro leaves (from 1 small bunch)

About 1 cup packed fresh parsley leaves (from 1 small bunch)

1 tablespoon ground cumin (preferably freshly ground)

1½ teaspoons ground coriander seed (preferably freshly ground)

¼ to 1 teaspoon cayenne, to taste

¾ teaspoon salt, or to taste

½ teaspoon freshly ground black pepper, or to taste

2 to 4 tablespoons white flour or chickpea flour (optional: only if needed)

½ teaspoon baking soda (optional: only if you use the flour)

FOR FRYING AND SERVING:

Any mild vegetable oil, such as corn, canola, peanut, or grapeseed

Warmed pita breads (preferably wholegrain), for serving

Middle Eastern Chopped Salad (recipe follows), for serving

Tzatziki Yogurt Sauce (recipe follows), for serving

Harissa (page 266), for serving (optional)

Pickled vegetables, such as cucumbers, cauliflower, smoked eggplant, and cabbage (sauerkraut), for serving (optional)

① Place the chickpeas in your largest bowl, add water to cover them to a depth of 3 inches, and soak for 24 hours. The chickpeas will triple in bulk as they absorb the water, so add more water as necessary; you want to make sure they're submerged at all times. They need not be refrigerated, but if the weather is extremely hot, you might want to drain the chickpeas at the 12-hour mark, rinse them well, and cover them with fresh water. (Some soak their chickpeas for only 12 hours, but in my view this makes for heavier, less digestible falafel.)

2 The next day, drain the chickpeas and rinse them thoroughly. Dump them into a food processor with all the other falafel ingredients except the optional flour and baking soda. Alternate between buzzing and pulsing, pausing to scrape down the bowl, until you have a uniformly mixed, but not quite smooth, grainy puree. If the machine seems to be straining, add a tablespoon or so of water, but avoid this if possible.

3 Taste, adjusting seasonings as necessary. Wow, already pretty tasty, right?

4 Texture check! Roll a small amount of the falafel mixture into a slightly-smaller-than-walnut-size ball or flattened patty. The mixture should hold together nicely, making a firm ball, cohering easily, and not falling apart. If it doesn't do this, if it seems too wet, sprinkle the flour, starting with the lesser amount and working up if needed to achieve the exact texture, and then the baking soda over the falafel mixture and quickly knead it in.

5 Proceed with the rest of the batter, making small balls or patties of a consistent size so they'll cook in about the same amount of time. (I prefer the flattened patties, because they seem to me to get done more evenly.) Some do this by hand (like me); some use a small ice cream scoop, and some, a falafel scoop, purchased in Middle Eastern markets. Line up the uncooked falafels on a plate, cutting board, or wax-paper-covered counter.

6 Pour the oil into a wok or a large, high-sided skillet or Dutch oven to a depth of 3 inches and place it over medium-high heat. Place a thermometer in the oil and heat the oil until it registers between 360° to 375°F. (Keep an eye on that thermometer and the flame, and adjust the heat up and down to maintain the proper range; never let the oil get hotter than 375° or cooler than 355°F.)

7 Meanwhile, set up trays lined with paper towels or unfolded brown paper grocery bags. (You'll transfer the cooked falafels to the trays to drain. Keep additional paper towels on hand to blot excess oil from the tops, too.)

8 If it's your first time, fry one falafel experimentally: It should sizzle when you drop it in, the oil around it immediately bubbling. It should also hold together perfectly. Once its underside is browned, 1½ to 2½ minutes, flip it over with a slotted spoon and cook until it's browned all over, 1½ to 2½ minutes more. Fry the remaining falafels in batches, being sure not to crowd them or to cook so many at once that you lower the temp of the oil (the exact number will vary depending on the size and type of pan you are using).

9 Serve hot or at room temperature with the pita, chopped salad, tzatziki, and the harissa and pickled veggies, if using.

Makes 32 to 36 falafels; serves 8

VARIATIONS

Egyptian-style Falafels: Replace the chickpeas with dried fava beans, removing any skins that float to the surface during the soaking; alternatively, use dried split favas (these only need 12 hours soaking, though 24 won't hurt). Or use half dried chickpeas, half dried split favas. **Vn**

Syrian-style Falafels: Add 1 tablespoon powdered sumac, a tangy deep reddish-purple seasoning made from the berries of the sumac plant (available at thespicehouse.com), to the chickpea mixture. [Vn]

West African–style Fritters (Akkra): Substitute dried black-eyed peas for the chickpeas, soaking them for 12 hours. After soaking, swish the black-eyes vigorously and remove any skins that float to the top, then drain them and rinse them well. Omit the garlic, cilantro, parsley, cumin, and coriander; substitute 1 chopped fresh hot red or green chile, for the dried cayenne and add about 1 tablespoon chopped fresh ginger. If you need to add a binder in step 4, use flour or cornmeal. [Vn]

Middle Eastern Chopped Salad

This salad is infinitely variable, but all of the ingredients except the tomatoes should be crispy-crunchy. Yes, there are many variations on the traditional Middle Eastern chopped salad, but this is my version, so don't sass me about it. The quantities are loosey-goosey; how many are you feeding? Just scale up or down. [Ve] or [Vn] [Gf]

- ½ to 1 small onion, peeled, quartered, and finely chopped
- 1 tomato, halved and finely chopped
- 1 cucumber, peeled if skin is at all bitter, quartered lengthwise and coarsely chopped
- ⅛ to ¼ head green cabbage, very thinly sliced (as for slaw), then coarsely chopped
- 1 carrot, coarsely grated
- Sturdy red-leaf or romaine lettuce, thickly sliced
- About ⅓ cup chopped fresh mint, parsley, or cilantro leaves (or a combination)
- ¼ to ½ cup Tzatziki Yogurt Sauce (below), Tahini Sauce (page 265), or Synchronicity Sauce (page 265)

Toss together all of the vegetable ingredients in a large bowl. Add the dressing, beginning with ¼ cup, and toss to combine. Add more dressing if desired.

Makes enough to accompany 4 to 6 servings of falafel

VARIATION

For a more traditional version, omit the carrot and lettuce, and use lemon juice and salt in place of the dressing.

Tzatziki Yogurt Sauce

[Ve]

- 1 cup plain Greek-style yogurt
- Juice of 1 lemon (about 3 tablespoons)
- 1 cucumber, peeled and finely minced
- 1 to 2 cloves garlic, pressed
- Salt, to taste
- 1 to 2 tablespoons finely minced fresh cilantro or mint leaves

Stir together all of the ingredients in a small bowl. Cover and refrigerate for up to 3 days.

Makes about 1½ cups

NEO-TRADITIONAL FALAFELS

I have mixed feelings about the preceding traditional falafel recipe on page 260. They're good—and I eat them a few times a year at Middle Eastern places. But even when made perfectly by traditional methods, they weigh heavily on the digestion, partly because they're fried, partly because the bean is never actually cooked other than the frying. Too, the classic ball shape often means that, unless the cook is experienced with both frying in general and falafel making in particular, the outside is done while the inside is still underdone.

Enter this baked version. You can do it on the spur of the moment, because it relies on canned, not presoaked, chickpeas. It will not weigh on your stomach (and possibly your conscience) like a miniature bowling ball. And the remarkable flavors of the seasonings—both fresh cilantro and ground dried coriander (cilantro) seed, cumin, parsley, a little hot pepper—come through with joyful clarity because they're not obscured by all that grease.

Oh, and did I mention that this is *fast*? Not long ago I made these for a summer supper. Buzz, buzz, shape, shape, and in the oven everything went. Set the timer for twenty minutes and asked David to flip 'em over. Ran down to our pond, swam ten quick laps (twenty lengths). Came back up, took out the falafels, put them in some quickly warmed whole-wheat pitas, quickly chopped the salad and did the dressing. A wonderful warm-weather dinner, forty-five minutes or so start to finish (and very little of that hands-on time), plus a swim . . . You bet I was pleased with myself! **Vn**

FOR THE FALAFEL:

2 cans (15 ounces each) chickpeas, rinsed and thoroughly drained

½ medium-size onion, quartered

3 cloves garlic

1 tablespoon ground cumin

1 teaspoon ground coriander

⅛ to ½ teaspoon ground cayenne or dried red pepper flakes (optional)

½ cup coarsely chopped fresh cilantro

½ cup coarsely chopped fresh parsley

Salt

FOR BAKING AND SERVING:

Vegetable oil cooking spray

Warm pita breads (preferably wholegrain)

Middle Eastern Chopped Salad (page 263), for serving

Tahini Sauce (recipe follows), Tzatziki Yogurt Sauce (page 263), or Synchronicity Sauce (recipe follows), for serving

Harissa (page 266), for serving (optional)

Pickled vegetables, such as cucumbers, cauliflower, smoked eggplant, and cabbage (sauerkraut), for serving (optional)

1 Preheat the oven to 425°F.

2 Combine all of the falafel ingredients in a food processor. Buzz for about 10 seconds, pause to scrape down the sides of the bowl, then continue pulsing until everything has amalgamated into a grainy paste, scraping as needed, maybe 5 to 10 times.

3 Spray a baking sheet with oil (or cover it with a silicone baking mat). Form the falafel mixture into 20 small, flattened patties, each 1½ to 2 inches wide and about ½ inch thick, and place them on the baking sheet as you work.

4 Bake for 20 minutes, flip the falafels over, and continue baking until they are nicely browned on both sides, 10 to 15 minutes more. Remove from the oven and stuff into sliced pitas—allow 2 to 3 falafels per pita half, 4 to 6 total per sandwich—

with the chopped salad and the sauce of your choice spooned into each.

Makes 20 small falafels, serving 4 (with all the fixings)

Tahini Sauce
(TARATOUR)

Vn

1 cup tahini

Juice of 1 lemon (about 3 tablespoons)

1 to 2 cloves garlic, pressed

Salt to taste

Combine all of the ingredients in a small bowl, adding 1 to 2 tablespoons water, as necessary, to achieve the consistency of mayonnaise. Adjust for salt. Cover and store in the fridge for up to 2 days.

Makes about 1 cup

SYNCHRONICITY SAUCE

Here's an idea: Prepare either of the falafel sauces on page 263 and above, but use half yogurt and half tahini. Now stop screaming, traditionalists of one camp or another! I swear this is delicious and in some ways the best of both worlds.

"Your assignment is to knock out the nuclear weapons plant at Falafel Heights. The plant goes on line in twelve hours and is heavily defended. If you have trouble hitting your objective, your secondary targets are an accordian factory and a mime school."

—*From* Hot Shots!, *a 1991 parody of* Top Gun

Harissa

As we all know, some like it hot; others, more so. Some modify their finished falafel sandwiches or platter with a shake of Tabasco, or the equivalent; others prefer a slather of commercial harissa, made of dried, roasted, ground chiles, on the bread. Although I adore the previous, especially the brand made by Les Moulins Mahjoub, there is another school of harissa devotees, which goes for a quickly made, almost salsa-like sauce, as follows. Warning: It is hot enough to take the top of your head off. **Vn** **Gf**

½ pound fresh red chiles, stemmed, seeded (if you wish to reduce heat), and coarsely chopped

6 cloves garlic, crushed

1 teaspoon caraway seeds (optional)

1 teaspoon salt, or to taste

1 to 1½ teaspoons freshly ground black pepper, to taste

1 to 1½ teaspoons ground cumin, to taste

1 teaspoon ground coriander seed

Leaves from 1 small bunch of fresh cilantro (about 1 packed cup)

Juice of 1 lemon (about 3 tablespoons)

1 tablespoon olive oil, plus more as needed

Stir together all of the ingredients in a small bowl. Serve immediately, or transfer to a clean jar, top with a thin layer of olive oil, cover, and keep for up to 2 weeks in the fridge.

Makes ½ to ⅔ cup

"The Latins call a chick-pea Cicer: and the original Cicero, as it appears, had, at the point of the nose, a slight cleft like that of a chick-pea, from which peculiarity he obtained his surname. . . . Cicero . . . when his friends advised him . . . to drop this name and take another, is said to have replied with youthful ardour that he would do his best to prove that Cicero was a more distinguished name than Scaurus or Catulus. During his quaestorship in Sicily he dedicated to the gods a vessel of silver, upon which he had his first two names, Marcus Tullius, engraved. In place of the third he playfully ordered the engraver to carve a chick-pea in relief beside the engraved character."

—*Plutarch,* Lives of the Noble Greeks and Romans

Jamaican Jerk-style
LENTIL-VEGETABLE PATTIES

The Jamaican patty—which is *not* a savory, burger-shaped patty but a dough-wrapped turnover stuffed with a seriously spicy filling—sits at the juncture of Caribbean native foodways and English colonialism. Its ingredients include the islands' fabled incendiary Scotch bonnet chile, local thyme, and allspice, all of which season a filling of beef or goat or vegetable. But wait—what of the curry powder that also rocks and rolls in the patty filling? And what about that flaky dough? Well, the curry got there because the British imported indentured servants from another of their colonies, India, and the servants, in turn, introduced their foodways. As did the English: The turnover concept itself is a version of the ubiquitous but blander British meat pie, such as the Cornish pasty, which uses a similar dough. Jamaicanized, the meat pie as patty is bland no more.

In this recipe, the patty's traditionally high-fat short-crust wrapping is replaced by jazzed-up tortillas. Folded over, tortillas give something of the customary half-round patty shape (though without the fork-crimped edges . . . and indeed, they do not enclose the filling completely), allowing a satisfyingly high proportion of filling to dough. Because traditional patty pastry includes a bit of bright ground annatto, turmeric, curry, and/or paprika, here these spices are added to the merest bit of butter and brushed onto the outside of the tortilla to create a lick of festive color and flavor.

My partner, David, swears these are a dead ringer for the patties he ate regularly when living in the West Indian area of London. Although meat-filled patties are common, so are the vegetable-based fillings favored by both the East Indian and Rastafarian populations of Jamaica. Here, lentils are mixed into a vegetable filling to add protein and heft to the curry savor. An optional but delish yogurt-based sauce in which to dip the patty, bite by bite, stays true to Island spicings while giving a nod to raita, and cools the Scotch-bonnet-curry burn. Ve Vn

FOR THE VEGGIES:

3 medium potatoes, cut into ¼- to ⅓-inch dice (peeled or not as you prefer)

3 carrots, cut into ¼- to ⅓-inch dice

¼ firm, tart apple, such as a Cox's Orange Pippin or a Cortland, cut into ¼- to ⅓-inch dice

FOR THE SEASONING PASTE:

1¾ cups lentils, cooked until tender, then drained well

1 bunch of scallions, derooted, white and about 3 inches of green coarsely chopped

1 cup fresh, soft wholegrain breadcrumbs

1 teaspoon dried thyme

½ Scotch bonnet or habanero chile, stemmed and seeded

3 cloves garlic, peeled

1 teaspoon curry powder (I like extra-hot vindaloo curry powder)

⅛ teaspoon ground allspice

FOR THE SAUTÉ:

1 tablespoon coconut oil, ghee, or any mild vegetable oil

1 large onion, diced

1 tablespoon finely minced or grated fresh ginger

1 teaspoon curry powder (extra-hot vindaloo again)

YAH, MON!

Pumpkin soup with coconut milk

★

*Jamaican Jerk–Style
Lentil–Vegetable Patties*

★

Iced lightly sweetened hibiscus tea

★

Sliced mango with coconut shortbreads

⅛ teaspoon ground allspice

1 to 1½ teaspoons salt, or to taste

FOR THE QUASI-PASTRY:

Vegetable oil cooking spray or ghee, for oiling the baking sheet

1 tablespoon melted butter or ghee (or, for vegans, coconut oil)

1 teaspoon paprika

¼ teaspoon ground turmeric

4 white, whole-wheat, or spelt-flour tortillas (6 inches each), at room temperature

FOR SERVING:

1 recipe Jamaican-Spiced Yogurt Dip (optional, recipe follows)

1 First, prepare the veggies: Bring 3 cups water to a boil in a saucepan over medium-high heat. Drop in the potatoes, and let them cook until almost tender but not quite, 4 to 6 minutes. Add the carrots and cook for 2 minutes more. Lastly, add the apple and cook for another 2 minutes. Remove from the heat, drain well (you can reserve the cooking water for use in a stock, if you like), and set aside to cool.

2 Make the seasoning paste: Place the lentils, scallions, breadcrumbs, thyme, chile, garlic, curry powder, and allspice in a food processor. Pulse-chop several times, pausing occasionally to scrape down the sides of the bowl, then buzz to make a thick, chunky paste. Set this mixture aside, too.

3 Do the sauté: Place the coconut oil in a large skillet over medium heat. Add the onion and sauté until it turns transparent and starts to wilt, about 4 minutes (don't brown it). Add the ginger, lower the heat slightly, and sauté until fragrant, about 1 minute. Add the curry powder and allspice, and sauté for 1 minute more.

④ To the onion mixture add the seasoning paste, the salt, and the veggie mixture. Lower the heat still further and cook for a minute or so to warm and amalgamate everything, turning the mixture over with a spatula. It will be very thick, almost the consistency of unbaked meatloaf. Ta-da! Your patty filling. Taste for salt and adjust seasonings. Set aside. (This part can be done up to 2 days in advance. Store the filling, covered, in the refrigerator. Bring to room temperature before proceeding.)

⑤ About 45 minutes before you plan to serve the patties, begin the quasi-pastry: Preheat the oven to 400° F. Lightly spray a baking sheet with oil or line it with a silicone baking mat.

⑥ Combine the melted butter, paprika, and turmeric in a small bowl. Have a pastry brush handy.

⑦ Now, patty production: Warm a nonstick skillet over low-medium heat. Place a tortilla in the skillet and warm it briefly on one side, just enough to brown it slightly and make it pliable, about 30 seconds. Remove it to the baking sheet, browned side up, while you throw another tortilla in the skillet. As this second tortilla softens, spread one quarter of the patty filling—a very thick layer, ½ inch or so—on *half* of the tortilla on the baking sheet. Fold, pressing the other half of the tortilla over the filling. Voilà: a filled tortilla half-round, something like a turnover, except with the filling showing at the edge. Repeat with the remaining tortillas and filling.

⑧ When all four tortillas have been turned into patties and are resting expectantly on the baking sheet, brush the patties with the spiced butter. Place the baking sheet in the oven and bake until the patties are heated through, 20 to 25 minutes. Serve hot, just out of the oven if possible, with a dab of the yogurt dip on the side, if so inclined.

Makes 4 large turnovers; serves 4

Jamaican-Spiced Yogurt Dip

Use this refreshing, surprising condiment to zap up Jamaican patties or any sandwich. Although the recipe calls for yogurt, you can use mayo or Tofu Mayonnaise (page 49) instead. **Vn**

- 1 lime (preferably organic)
- 1 cup thick, plain Greek-style yogurt
- 2 tablespoons finely chopped fresh parsley
- ¼ cup finely chopped fresh cilantro
- 2 scallions, white and 2 inches of green finely chopped
- 1 clove garlic, pressed

Using a Microplane, if possible, or any fine grater, grate the zest of the lime into a small bowl. Place a strainer over the bowl. Slice the lime in half and squeeze the juice over the zest (using the strainer to catch any seeds). Add all the remaining ingredients, and whisk well. Cover and refrigerate to let the flavors blend, at least 1 hour or up to 3 days.

Makes about 1 cup

Fastest-Gun-in-the-West

HUEVOS RANCHEROS

Look, I know how to make real huevos rancheros from scratch in a number of ways, and you may, too. But there are times in all our lives when we need a few quick down-and-dirty shortcuts. This is one that leaves all comers satisfied—fast. Serve it for brunch or supper; fancy it up with some minced fresh cilantro and a few slices of avocado on top; serve it with warmed corn tortillas or, if you prefer, rice. A plate of sliced melon or fresh pineapple on the side: happy. No one will care that you didn't fire-roast the peppers and tomatoes. **Ve** **Gf**

Vegetable oil cooking spray

3 cups mild to hot commercial salsa
   (be sure it is *not sweetened*)

1 can (15 ounces) black beans, partially
   drained

4 eggs

About 4 ounces (1 cup) grated sharp
   Cheddar or Monterey Jack cheese

Minced fresh cilantro, for garnish (optional)

Avocado slices, for serving (optional)

Warm corn tortillas or cooked rice,
   for serving (optional)

1 Spray a large skillet (one with a tight-fitting lid) with oil, and place it over medium heat. Add the salsa and bring it to a boil.

2 Stir in the beans and their liquid. Let the mixture come back to a boil, then turn down the heat to a high simmer.

3 Use a spoon to make four indentations, to whatever extent possible, in the bean mixture, then break each egg into its own little semi-nest. Lower the heat to a low simmer and cover the skillet tightly.

4 After about 5 minutes, lift the lid. You'll probably need to cover the skillet again and let the eggs cook a little more until they reach the desired stage, which is with the white cooked and the yolk just barely starting to set around the edges and still runny in the center. When the eggs have reached this point, scoop an egg or two and some of the bean mixture onto each serving plate, garnish with the cheese, and use any or all of the go-withs if you like (and you probably will).

Serves 2 to 4

VARIATION

If you have homemade refried beans (see page 271) on hand, heat them (either on the stove or, covered, in the oven) while you simply poach the eggs in the salsa. Serve the refrieds on which the eggs rest magisterially, fixings alongside. Mmmm!

REFRIED BEANS (FRIJOLES REFRITOS) VEGETARIANA

These thick, irresistibly good Mexican-style beans are part of many dishes, many meals, many homes, and many occasions. Usually made from pintos, they can be a side dish (along with rice, they're what make your enchiladas-tamales-chiles-rellenos-or-whatever plate "complete" at a typical Tex-Mex restaurant). But they can also fill those same enchiladas or burritos, or, with rice, cheese, and a salad, be a meal in themselves. "Refried" is a misnomer. They're not "fried" as such at all; not once, and certainly not twice. They're cooked, then cooked a second time in and around a savory sauté, with a sort of semi-mashing taking place (they end up with the texture of mashed potatoes).

Some people like their refrieds very plain, cooking the beans in plain water and using only bacon fat or lard as the medium for both flavoring and frying. My vegetarian approach is less minimalist: Olive oil is the fat, and various spices and aromatics season. As in several other recipes here, I often do the beans for refrieds *borracho,* or drunken; a can or bottle of beer added to the simmering beans does wonderful things for the finished dish.

Completed refrieds freeze beautifully for up to 3 months, tightly covered. If anything, they're even better thawed and reheated. **Vn**

1 pound pinto beans, picked over, soaked overnight (see page 352), drained, and rinsed

3 large onions: 1 coarsely chopped, 2 finely chopped

1 can or bottle (12 ounces) of beer; no need for fancy stuff—whatever you have on hand will do fine

¼ teaspoon chipotle powder

2 tablespoons to ½ cup (see Note) decent olive oil

1 tablespoon cumin seeds

1½ teaspoons salt, or more to taste

1 Place the beans in a large, heavy Dutch oven or soup pot (or in a pressure cooker, if you prefer). Add the coarsely chopped onion, the beer, and enough water to cover the beans to a depth of at least 1¾ inches. Add the chipotle powder (it adds almost no heat, but does contribute a smokiness usually provided by bacon).

2 If using a Dutch oven, bring the beans to a boil, lower the heat to a simmer, and let cook, covered, until the beans are very soft, about 1 hour and 15 minutes. (In a pressure cooker, bring to high pressure, then lower to medium and cook for 15 to 18 minutes, letting the pressure drop naturally.) As always, cooking times vary depending on the age of the beans, but you want them quite tender, with the skin just beginning to peel open. (At this point, if you like, you can cool the cooked beans to room temperature, then refrigerate them overnight for completion the next day.)

3 Drain the beans in a colander, reserving the cooking liquid.

4 Heat the olive oil—start out with 2 to 4 tablespoons and hold the rest back for the moment—in a heavy skillet, preferably cast iron, over medium-high heat. Add the finely chopped onions and the cumin seeds, and sauté until the onions are translucent and the cumin is aromatic, about 5 minutes.

5 Add the strained beans to the skillet, along with about ½ cup of the reserved cooking liquid. With a wooden spoon and a potato masher, begin stirring and mashing the beans in the pan as you continue to cook them, making a rough, thick puree.

Keep adding cooking liquid a little at a time, cooking, stirring and mashing, until the beans rethicken and start to almost stick, then add a little more liquid. This evaporation really adds to the flavor and texture of the refrieds.

6 Add salt to taste—it'll take quite a bit—and the remaining olive oil if you want additional richness. Serve hot.

Serves 4 to 6 as part of a South-of-the-Border dinner

Note: While one *can* make the refried beans with as little as 2 tablespoons of olive oil, they are so much better with more. I'd go for at least ¼ cup, maybe ½ if you're feeling devil-may-care.

VARIATION

Traditional "Meatist" Refried Beans: Substitute lard or bacon fat for the olive oil; you may also cook a small chunk of salt pork with the beans. Omit the beer, chipotle powder, and cumin seeds, using only onion in the sauté.

IT MUST HAVE BEAN A VERY LONG DAY: MY JOURNAL, MARCH 11, 1996

At work on bean section of V cookbook (reader's note: eventually *Passionate Vegetarian*). Deep in bean world, bean research, thought, writing. Day's end. Ned arrived from the inn's front desk.

Me: "Did you know that in ancient Rome all the leading families were named after different types of beans?" Cicero/chick pea, Fabius/ fava, etc.

Ned (deadpan): "Mm," (meditatively). "Were they related to the LL Beans?"

Me (ignorning this): "And lima beans—they're Peruvian. As in Lima, Peru."

Ned: "I always thought those were named after those

British sailors with the vitamin C deficiency." (Note to reader: Meaning limeys, English seafarers rationed a lime a day as a scurvy preventive during extended voyages. Ned knew I'd get the reference.)

Me: "No," (firmly) "You're wrong. You've got the wrong bean. Those, the ones you're thinking of, are navy beans."

CD'S BEANS & GREENS PASTA
with Lemon, Garlic & Chile

Okay, here you are: This is my single favorite go-to, home-cooking, just-us-folks, one-dish meal. I make it all the time—at least once a week, my vast bean (and other) culinary appreciation and repertoire notwithstanding. If, growing tired of coming up with the nightly menu, I say to my companion, "Anything in particular you're in the mood for, David?" I can be pretty sure he'll say, "Well, how about the greens and beans and pasta? We haven't had that in a while." That we actually *have* had it is irrelevant; it's that good.

Why? It's healthy, bold, flavorful, toothsome, easy, and inexpensive. Its main ingredients are just interchangeable enough to ring small variations on, it never ever gets boring. And, oh yes: It is quicker than quick. Put the water on to boil for the pasta, begin the sauté, and everything's done at the same time. Choose a pasta type that's not too delicate. Go with dried, not fresh; eschew angel hair, thin spaghetti, orzo, or tiny stars. Instead, choose any good semolina or whole wheat pasta of medium size: fusilli, ziti, fettuccine, or shells.

Vegans can omit the cheese in this (perhaps substituting nutritional yeast) and still have a fine dish. Ve or Vn

16 ounces dried pasta (see headnote)

2 to 3 whole dried chiles, stemmed and broken in half

3 to 5 tablespoons extra-virgin olive oil

1 large bunch of Swiss chard, rinsed well (but with some moisture still clinging to the leaves), tough ends of stems removed, leaves and tender parts of stems sliced crosswise into ¼-inch ribbons

3 to 5 cloves garlic, chopped

1 lemon, halved

1 can (15 ounces) chickpeas, drained well

Coarse sea salt

Freshly ground black pepper

Finely grated Parmesan cheese, for serving (omit for vegans)

1 Bring a large pot of salted water to a boil and cook the pasta according to the package directions.

2 Meanwhile, set a large, heavy skillet (ideally cast iron) over medium-high heat.

Place the chiles in the skillet and toast, stirring them or giving the pan a shake occasionally, until they darken slightly, 1 to 2 minutes. (You might want to turn on an exhaust vent, if you have one, or throw open the windows; the air gets pretty pungent and cough-producing.)

③ Add 2 tablespoons of the olive oil and then, almost immediately, the still-wet greens. Stir. There will be a big sizzle and the greens will quickly start wilting down, deepening in color. Immediately, just as soon as the greens have been stirred into the chile and olive oil, pop a tight-fitting lid over the skillet. Lower the heat just a bit and let the greens steam in their own liquid for 3 to 4 minutes.

④ Lift the lid and stir in the garlic. Cook for a few minutes more, just to take the edge of rawness off the garlic (don't let it brown), stirring to distribute everything. Then turn off the heat, squeeze half the lemon over the greens (squeeze through a strainer, to trap the seeds), and add the beans. Stir some more to heat the beans through (the pan will still be plenty hot). Add coarse sea salt and pepper to taste.

⑤ When your pasta is done (which might be about now, or midway through lemoning the greens), drain it well. Pile it, steaming hot, onto serving plates and divide the greens and beans over each portion. You can try to pick out the chiles if you like, or warn diners that they are there (if you're using red-stemmed chard, it's quite hard to spot those chiles, so, I repeat, warn those who like their food tamer). Drizzle each portion with a bit of the remaining olive oil. Cut the remaining lemon half into wedges,

and pass them along with the Parmesan at the table.

Serves 4

VARIATIONS

Four major, and many minor, ideas:

Alter the starch: Of course you can use any shape of dried pasta you like (avoiding anything too small), and it can be the usual durum flour pasta, a whole grain, or even a gluten-free pasta (such as those made of corn, rice, or quinoa flour). But here are a couple of other ways to vary the starch component of this dish. You can *add potatoes,* peeled or not as you prefer, diced into ½-inch chunks. Simply drop them into the boiling water along with the pasta and cook until tender; they'll be done when the pasta is. Or, instead of using pasta at all, serve this over Oven-Baked Polenta (page 283), plain or Parmesan'd, or over commercial gnocchi.

Use different greens: Each leafy green has its own flavor, consistency, and cooking time. Each is different, and each is very good. Vary the dish with whichever green looks freshest and best at the market. Ve

* *Collard greens, kale, or Lacinato kale:* Remove tough ribs, stack leaves, roll them up, and slice thin.

* *Turnip or mustard greens:* Remove tough ribs, stack leaves to the extent possible, and slice thin.

* *Broccoli:* Remove the base and rough, tough outer skin of the stems with a knife. Cut the peeled stems into fat matchsticks and the top of the brocc— the head—into medium florets. Cook

as you would the greens, but since broccoli holds less moisture than greens, and takes a bit longer to cook, lift the lid midway through steaming and check; you'll probably need to add 2 or 3 tablespoons water after stirring, so the broccoli can steam to tender-crisp and not burn while doing so. With the last few unlidded minutes of cooking, any remaining water will evaporate.

★ *Broccoli rabe:* Remove the base of the broccoli rabe stems if they are curled back (dried out) or tough. Slice the broccoli rabe—leaves, stems, flowers, and all—crosswise into ¾-inch slices. Some people find broccoli rabe a touch bitter for their taste and choose to blanch it briefly in boiling water; I find the bitterness tonic and delectable.

★ *Escarole:* Pull the escarole leaves off the head and rinse them well. Remove any tough parts at the base of the leaves' center stem. Again, some people blanch escarole because of its bitterness, but I like that quality so I use it raw: your choice. Slice the trimmed escarole crosswise into ½-inch pieces. (If you're unfamiliar with escarole, please see the notes on it in the headnote for Farmer's Market Escarole, page 286.)

Bring on the beans: No particular bean would be disharmonious with any particular green, but here are some of my favorite combos. **Vn**

★ Black-eyed peas with turnip or mustard greens (nice over oven-baked polenta, a sort of New South riff)

CUPBOARD CUNNING

Salad of sliced orange, red onion, and oil-packed olives on a bed of escarole

★

CD's Beans & Greens Pasta

★

Hazelnut gelato with hazelnut biscotti, drizzled with Frangelico

---

★ Cannellini beans with kale, Lacinato kale, or escarole

★ Limas, gigandes, or kidney beans with broccoli or broccoli rabe

★ Navy beans with escarole

Add Italian sausage or soysage: You can add this instead of, or in addition to, the beans. Before you start the sauté in step 3, brown 4 to 6 sweet Italian sausages, either the conventional meat kind or the vegetarian variety (such as those made by Lightlife, Field Roast, or Tofurky) in a little additional olive oil. Remove the browned sausages/soysages from the skillet and slice them crosswise on an angle into ⅓-inch rounds. Wipe out the skillet and proceed as directed (or with any of the variations above). Add the sliced sausage/soysage to the greens and beans at the very end, right before you pile the mixture on the pasta. The sausage/soysage ups the number of servings this dish makes to six. It also makes it a little richer and higher in protein. It's good, and I do make it sometimes, but actually I prefer it without. **Me** or **Vn**

BOK CHOY, BROCCOLI & EDAMAME SKILLET

The greenest skillet you ever saw, this combination—bright in lemon-sparkled flavor as well as verdant color—is perfect when spring-summer cravings hit in midwinter. Very satisfying. Try it with some garlic-buttered (or olive-oiled) whole wheat rotini for a vegetarian main course, or in smaller portions as a side for a grilled chicken breast or lamb chop. **Vn** **Gf**

6 small or 3 medium heads baby bok choy

1 large or 2 or 3 small heads broccoli

Vegetable oil cooking spray

1 to 2 lemons (preferably organic)

1½ cups frozen edamame (do not thaw)

3 tablespoons finely minced fresh parsley

Coarse salt and freshly ground black pepper

1 First, wash the bok choy and trim off and discard the rough base. Chop the white stems crosswise into ½-inch strips and place them in a colander. Slice the leafy greens in strips about the same size and set aside. Next, cut the top of the broccoli into smallish florets and place them in the colander. Peel the broccoli stems and slice the tender inner stems into fat matchsticks. These, too, go in the colander. Rinse everything thoroughly (let a bit of water cling to the vegetables after they drain).

2 Spray your largest lidded skillet with oil and place it over medium-high heat. When the skillet is hot, toss in the contents of the colander. Sauté quickly, about 30 seconds or so, then pop a cover over the vegetables and allow them to steam quickly in their own juices and the clinging water.

3 Meanwhile, finely grate the zest of the lemons into a small bowl. Halve the lemons and juice them over a strainer into the bowl, catching and discarding any seeds. Set aside.

4 Lift the skillet's lid. When the color of the vegetables has deepened slightly and the broccoli is almost but not quite tender-crisp, add the bok choy leaves and the edamame (straight from the freezer). Toss a few times and put the lid back on for 1 to 2 minutes.

5 Lift the lid and toss the vegetables and edamame. By now everything should be done—the broccoli and bok choy stems and edamame tender-crisp, the bok choy leaves wilted—and piping hot. Keeping the heat at medium-high, pour the lemon juice and zest over the vegetables and add the parsley. Stir and toss until the lemon juice is almost evaporated. Season with salt and pepper to taste and serve immediately, very hot.

Serves 4 to 6 as a side dish, 2 to 4 over pasta as a main dish

SOCCA
Chickpea Flatbread

This irresistible Provençal flatbread has a base of chickpea flour and is as simple as it is compellingly good. After you discover how easy it is, and how tasty, I guarantee you will make it over and over again. With edges, bottom, and top crispy-crunchy and golden and a creamy-custardy interior reminiscent of a popover (though it's egg-free), socca is swooningly good as is, straight from the oven. Jazzed up a bit, it makes a pizza that's even better (and easier to prepare) than your classic yeasted wheat dough.

Like my favorite cornbreads, socca begins on the stovetop in a sizzling-hot cast-iron skillet and is then moved to the oven to finish baking. You really taste the olive oil in this bread, so make sure you use a good one that's absolutely fresh. And while we're on the subject, don't resist the temptation to reduce the quantity called for; I tried, and it doesn't work. Though this is definitely not a low-fat recipe, it does work gorgeously for people who are vegan and/or avoiding gluten.

Whether you leave it simple or gild the lily, there'll never be any socca left. Pass it in thin wedges sprinkled with a bit of coarse salt, freshly ground black pepper, and/or a little grated Parmesan, or gussy it up with the toppings on page 278, and you'll be greeted with "Wow!" and "What is this?" and "Can I have the recipe?" and "Where do you buy chickpea flour?" (See the box on page 279 for the answer to this last.) **Vn** **Gf**

1 cup plus 2 tablespoons chickpea flour (*besan*)

½ teaspoon salt

⅓ cup olive oil

Freshly cracked black pepper (optional)

1 Preheat the oven to 450°F. (Make sure you give it time to come up to temperature; the batter comes together almost instantly, and the oven must be really hot before you put in the socca to bake.)

2 In a large bowl, whisk together the chickpea flour, salt, 1⅔ cups water, and 1 tablespoon of the olive oil until smooth. The batter will be quite thin and have a beany aroma.

3 Place your trusty cast-iron skillet over medium heat. When it's good and hot, pour the remaining olive oil into the bottom. If the oil doesn't thin and become a little fragrant almost immediately, let it stay on the stovetop until it does (keep an eye on it—you want it very hot, ripplingly so, but not smoking).

④ Give the batter one last stir, and pour it into the skillet; it should sizzle slightly, and bubble, with rivulets of oil here and there. Grind a little pepper, if using, over the top. Using potholders—remember it's hot!—pop the skillet into the oven.

⑤ Bake the socca until the edge pulls away from the pan and is quite brown and the top is golden and browned in some spots, 25 to 30 minutes. Remove the socca, and run a knife around its edge; it should release from the skillet easily. It will be intoxicatingly tempting.

⑥ Let cool slightly, but not too much. Serve as a snack or starter while it's still quite hot, cutting it into 8 wedges like a pizza. No need to serve it with butter or olive oil.

Serves 4 as a bread, 2 as a pizza

VARIATIONS

Extra-Crisp, Crackerlike Socca: Reverse the finished bread out of the skillet onto a baking sheet and run it under a broiler, watching it closely, until its underside is browned, about 20 seconds. Vn Gf

Rosemary Garlic Socca: Classic flavors, and so good. As the socca bakes, combine 1 to 2 tablespoons olive oil with 3 cloves garlic, crushed, and the needles from one small branch of fresh rosemary. Brush this mixture over the socca as it comes out of the oven. Swoon at the fragrance. Eat, enthusiastically! Vn Gf

Socca Pizza: After the socca has baked for 15 to 20 minutes (its top should be firm), pull it out of the oven and top it with your favorite pizza toppings (see mine below). Slide it back into the oven, or run it under the broiler, until everything is melty and luscious, a minute or two. My two favorite topping combinations:

★ a smear of crushed garlic, caramelized onions, a few chopped fresh or dried figs, and a little crumbled Gorgonzola or other blue-veined cheese, the creamiest you can find. Ve Gf

★ a smear of crushed garlic and caramelized onions to which you've added slivered green pepper and a few bits of chile toward the end. Top with sliced raw plum tomatoes, a scattering of fresh basil, a sprinkle of feta and Parmesan cheeses—and call me for dinner! Ve Gf

---

"It doesn't take much to see that the problems of three little people doesn't add up to a hill of beans in this crazy world. Someday you'll understand that. Now, now . . . Here's looking at you, kid."

—*Humphrey Bogart*, Casablanca

Meet, Greet, and Eat Chickpea Flour

If you aren't acquainted with chickpea flour yet, allow me to introduce you to one of the most pleasure-giving, surprising new ingredients in this book.

It's not really fair to call chickpea flour new, though. While this creamy, pale-yellow flour is still a relative unknown in North America, it's a long-revered part of food cultures in many other parts of the world. In India (where it's called *besan,* pronounced like the English word "basin"—good to know should you need to ask for it at an Indian grocery), it's transformed into snacks (see Bhel of the Ball, page 29), fritter batters (similar to that in the Green Bean & Vegetable Fritters, page 254), and even sweets. But it's no less at home in the Mediterranean, where Socca (see page 277), gigantic chickpea crepes, usually crisp, usually black-peppered, are served finger-burningly hot in southeastern France, especially in Nice. In some versions, too, the chickpea flour is cooked in water to make a polenta-like porridge, which is then set up, sliced, and fried (in which case it's a *panisse,* as in the restaurant) or, less traditionally, baked.

Throughout Italy, a batter almost identical to that used in socca is transformed into *farinata, cecina* (from the *ceci,* Italian for chickpea), or *torta de ceci*—it depends on where you are, how thick or thin the batter is, and how you season it. But a hop, skip, and a jump to Algeria, the batter appears again as *karantita,* with a salutary bit of fiery harissa (page 266) and perhaps a sprinkle of roasted cumin seeds. And it becomes a sweet again in Morocco, Persia (see Sesame-Seeded Chickpea Flour Cookies, or Ghoreyba Soumsoum, page 326, and Rose of Persia Cake, page 334), and other countries throughout North Africa and the Middle East.

American devotees of these cuisines have found their way to chickpea flour, and so have those with dietary restrictions. Avoiding gluten? Chickpea flour is gluten free. A vegan? Chickpea flour can serve as a very handy egg replacer in many recipes (as in the crepes on page 280).

But whether a limited or expanded diet leads you to chickpea flour, you and your body will be happy with it: It's a good source of fiber, magnesium, and copper, and an exceptionally good source of folate and manganese. And it has a whopping 21 grams of protein per cup (white flour, by contrast, has 13).

A few notes on using chickpea flour. As mentioned, it's a very fine, powdery flour, but it lumps easily. Stir any batter made with it very well. You may wish to sift it, too, before adding it. Lastly, it smells decidedly "beany," as in the crepe recipe; it's hard to believe it will cook through properly and not taste of raw beans. But I promise you, it does, beautifully.

Although I'm told one can buy roasted or unroasted chickpea flour, I've only ever run into it unroasted. That's the variety I call for in this book. Find it at any Indian grocery, most large natural foods markets, and sometimes in the gluten-free sections of supermarkets.

NEO-CLASSIC CREPES

Why are these called "neo-classic"? Well, old-o classic crepes are eggy, buttery, delicious, versatile, and high in fat, calories, and cholesterol. These amazing neo's are egg-free and vegan, yet with the delicious, versatile, even buttery qualities that make crepes so well loved.

The secret? High-protein chickpea flour, same as we use in Socca (page 277). It's not as hard to find as you'd think; most natural food markets carry it, as do Indian groceries (there, it's *besan*); and you'll even find it in conventional supermarkets' gluten-free sections. Potato starch is another gluten-free ingredient called for in these crepes; pick it up, too, while you're at it. (Alas, in case you gluten-free folks were getting your hopes up along with the vegans out there, these crepes do contain wheat flour. However, all's not lost: See the glorious gluten-free corn crepes in the variations.)

The batter is buzzed in a food processor; simplicity itself. It'll smell a bit raw-beany, causing you to momentarily lose trust in me: *Can this possibly taste and behave like a traditional crepe?* Well, it can, it does, and your faith will be rewarded.

Crepes are so common they're almost a cliché, yet everything gains instant allure when encased in one: finely diced sautéed onions and mushrooms with thin-sliced cooked green beans, or almost any other vegetable combo you can think of, with or without fine-chopped tofu, tempeh, soysage, or, for you non-v's, chicken, ham, shrimp. Or use some ratatouille, or leftover cooked vegetables bound with a little cheese sauce or tomato sauce or sour cream or white wine sauce or gravy . . . all good. If you like, ladle a little extra sauce atop the finished crepes, top with a bit of cheese and run the whole shebang under the broiler.

That's just the savory route. For the sweet—equally versatile—see the variations. **Vn**

---

2 tablespoons potato starch	**½ cup chickpea flour (*besan*)**
1 teaspoon salt	**2 cups unbleached white flour**
1 tablespoon mild vegetable oil, such as corn, canola, or peanut	**Vegetable oil cooking spray**

❶ Place the potato starch and ½ to ⅔ cup of water in a food processor, along with the salt and vegetable oil. Buzz. Pause, lift the lid, and scrape the sides of the bowl.

❷ Add the chickpea flour and the white flour, and gradually add about 2 cups water, drizzling it in as you start buzzing again and pausing when needed to scrape the sides. When the batter is very smooth, pour it into a bowl, and whisk in as much water as is needed to get it to the consistency of thin cream. Use immediately, or let rest, refrigerated, for up to a week.

❸ Heat a 10-inch skillet or pan (preferably an omelet or crepe pan, with curved sides; use two pans if you have them), regular or nonstick, over medium heat. Spray the pan with oil, or give it a quick swipe with an oil-soaked paper towel. Make sure the pan is really hot—a drop of water sprinkled on the bottom should sizzle and skitter and evaporate in a few seconds. When the pan is hot, pour in 2 to 2½ tablespoons batter, tilting the pan to swirl the batter so it thins out. Let cook until browned on the underneath (the edges will begin to curl up). Allow 1 to 3 minutes for the first side (later crepes will cook a little more quickly). As it cooks, you'll notice the top surface will quickly move, from outer edges to inner, from a pale ivory color and wet appearance to a deeper beige, a little dulled-looking. But even after it's achieved this, it needs to cook slightly longer to get nice and brown underneath; the edges will curl, and if you lift a corner of the crepe with a spatula, you can peek to see that it's nicely browned before you flip it.

❹ Cook for 30 seconds to 1 minute on side two. (The second side never browns quite as attractively as the first; it looks spottier. In most recipes, this second side is used inside, while the prettier side is shown to the public.)

❺ Place the crepes on a cake rack to cool for a minute or two. Once cooled, the finished crepes can be stacked, a piece of waxed paper between them. To freeze the crepes, tightly wrap stacks of ten, label and date, and freeze; use within 2 months.

Makes 26 to 32 six-inch crepes

VARIATIONS

Buckwheat Crepes: Substitute 1½ cups buckwheat flour for 1½ cups of the unbleached flour (so you just use ½ cup unbleached). A soulful, grainy crepe. Vn

Corn Crepes: Substitute 2 cups white or yellow masa harina for the unbleached flour, which (a) gives the crepe a decidedly South-of-the-Border flavor, and (b) makes it gluten-free. This crepe tastes like a cross between a crepe and a corn tortilla, and is just made for a filling of sautéed onion, zucchini dice, chile, fresh corn cut off the cob. Top with a little salsa, grated cheese if you desire, and a garnish of sliced avocado and cilantro. Black beans on the side. Mmmm! Gf Vn

Sweet Crepes: Add a teaspoon or so of vanilla to any crepe batter. Butter, lemon juice, and a dusting of powdered sugar make a quick, fuss-free finish; or get fancy and sauté apples with cinnamon and a little brown sugar, or fresh sliced peaches with a bit of nutmeg and turbinado sugar and a drop of almond extract; or stir sliced fresh strawberries into thick homemade vanilla custard, whipped cream, or soy whipped cream, and fill with that. The more elaborate sweet crepes make a substantial, ooh-ahh finish for a simple soup-and-salad supper.

Ragout of
SHIITAKE MUSHROOMS, BUTTER BEANS & SOUTHERN GREENS

I love, love, *love* this updated combination of some of the best-loved tropes of Southern cooking. It's somehow both old-fashioned and up-to-the-minute, homey and elegant, and it is just perfect over Oven-Baked Polenta with Cheese, page 283 (which, when done by the method I give, could not be simpler). I demo this recipe often in cooking classes.

Sometimes I make this with butter beans, sometimes black-eyes, sometimes Christmas limas or navy beans—it's good with any bean. Why succulent shiitake mushrooms perform such magic with beans when bathed in Italian-style tomato sauce and topped with a tangle of shredded, blanched hearty greens is a mystery—one you will happily ponder bite after bite. An unfussy, colorful, natural, generous-spirited, full-bodied dish. **Gf** **Ve** or **Vn**

Vegetable oil cooking spray (optional)

3 tablespoons olive oil

½ pound shiitake mushrooms, cleaned, tough part of stems removed, coarsely sliced or halved

3 to 4 cloves garlic, pressed

2 cups tender-cooked butter beans (large white lima beans; see page 350)

3½ cups good commercial tomato sauce from a jar (not canned)

Salt and freshly ground black pepper

Honey (optional)

1 bunch of hearty greens such as kale, turnip greens, mustard greens, collard greens, or Swiss chard, washed and sliced crosswise into very slender ribbons

Oven-Baked Polenta with Cheese (page 283), for serving

Freshly shaved Parmesan cheese, for serving

❶ Put a large pot of water, covered, on to boil over high heat.

❷ Spray a large skillet with oil (unless it is nonstick). Place the skillet over medium heat and add the olive oil. When the oil thins slightly, add the shiitakes and sauté until they start to soften, about 3 minutes. Stir in the garlic and cook, stirring, until the mushrooms start to stick to the skillet, a few minutes more.

③ Add the cooked butter beans and the tomato sauce to the skillet, turn the heat to very low, and heat through, stirring occasionally. Taste and correct the seasonings with salt and pepper, maybe a drop of honey. Remove from the heat.

④ When the water is boiling, drop in the sliced greens and blanch them quickly, just until they get limp and their color brightens. (The blanching process is very quick, but timing varies depending on the tenderness of the green and how thin it is sliced. Chard will be done almost instantly; collard greens may take 40 seconds.) Carefully drain the greens in a colander (save the blanching water for stock, if you like) and quickly pour cold water over them to stop the cooking.

⑤ Stir about one quarter of the blanched greens into the hot mushroom ragout, reserving the remainder.

⑥ Serve as follows: A big ladleful of polenta goes in the center of the plate, with the middle slightly hollowed to make a nest for a good-size spoonful of the ragout. Top the ragout with a little tangle of the bright green blanched greens, and lay a few slices of shaved Parmesan along the edges of the plate.

Serves 4 to 6

Oven-Baked Polenta

Polenta lovers will agree with food writer Paula Wolfert, who says this stir-free method of cooking polenta changed her life. Wolfert, in turn, credits the recipe from the back of the package of Golden Pheasant brand polenta. Golden Pheasant's president, Ed Fleming, in turn credits it as "an old

traditional Tuscan peasant recipe." So there you go. Either way, no more pot-sticking, no more big, hot, scary bubbles, no more going stir-crazy. The fancied-up and delectable cheese version follows, as a variation. **Ve** or **Vn** **Gf**

> Vegetable oil cooking spray
>
> 1 cup coarse stone-ground yellow cornmeal
>
> 1½ to 2½ teaspoons salt, to taste

① Heat the oven to 350°F. Spray a baking dish with a capacity of at least 3 quarts with the oil.

② Place the cornmeal and salt in the dish with 4 cups water and stir well. The mixture will separate, the cornmeal sinking to the bottom. Don't worry. Just throw the dish in the oven, uncovered, and forget about it . . . not a second thought until 40 minutes are up. At this point, remove it from the oven, stir the polenta well, and bake for another 10 minutes. Remove the pan from the oven and serve.

Serves 6 to 8

VARIATION

Oven-Baked Polenta with Cheese (or, as we say in the South, Cheese Grits): divine. Add the following to the cooked polenta after it comes out of the oven: 1 tablespoon *each* butter and extra-virgin olive oil, a dash or two of cayenne, ¼ cup heavy cream or plain Greek-style yogurt, and ½ cup *each* freshly grated sharp Cheddar cheese and shredded Parmesan cheese. Grind in a bunch of fresh black pepper, too, if you like it. Serve immediately or keep it warm, covered, back in the oven (turn it down to 200°F). **Ve** **Gf**

Crescent's Superb More-or-Less

GREEK-STYLE GREEN BEANS

I'd tell you to stick a Post-it right here because, once you try these, you'll be making them often—but they're simple enough that after one time through, you'll probably remember how to make them forever. These green beans are cooked to falling-apart-ness in what's essentially a garlic-tomato confit. Every bite is imbued with flavor—garlicky, a little hot, meltingly tender; the kind of good that, with your first bite, you close your eyes and grow silent.

The traditional Greek recipes in which this method is rooted use as much as three quarters of a cup of olive oil—too much for me. The few tablespoons here give flavor and allow the green beans to caramelize. Pretty they are not, but with one bite that is moot. Back in my restaurant days, I once received a proposal of marriage from a guest on the basis of these green beans.

Pay careful attention to the details here. Technique is all. **Vn** **Gf**

1 pound fresh green beans, tipped and tailed

Vegetable oil cooking spray

3 tablespoons olive oil

About 1 tablespoon medium to finely chopped garlic (5 or 6 cloves)

1 large fresh tomato, chopped (I go ahead and leave the skin on and seeds in; if you are fussier than me, remove both and use only the chopped pulp of 2 tomatoes)

Salt and freshly ground black pepper

A few dashes of cayenne

½ to 1 teaspoon dried dill

1. Blanch the green beans: Bring a large pot of water to a boil over high heat. When the water is boiling, add the green beans and cook for 2 minutes. Drain them well, then rinse with cold water, and drain them again.

2. Spray a large, heavy (preferably cast iron) skillet with a tight-fitting cover with oil, and set it over very low heat. Add the olive oil, scatter the garlic over it, and add the blanched green beans (in contrast to most sautés, the green beans are added when neither pan, nor oil, nor garlic, is yet hot). Scatter the tomato over the beans. Don't stir.

3. Still keeping the heat as low as possible, cover the beans and let them just barely cook, without stirring, for about 40 minutes. I know it's hard, but keep on *not* stirring; leave the heat low enough so that nothing burns. If you like, you can push a few beans back to check on the garlic at the bottom of the skillet. It should not be browning, merely cooking very, very slowly. Some of the beans will be browned on one

side, which is good. If this hasn't happened yet, cover again and cook for 10, even 15, minutes more.

④ When the beans are soft, lift the lid and stir gently. It is unlikely, but if there's a noticeable amount of liquid in the skillet, turn the heat up and, stirring gently but constantly, evaporate the liquid off. You want soft, barely-holding-together green beans. They should be slightly shriveled-looking and browned lightly here and there, with a bit of the garlic-tomato jam sticking to them.

⑤ Turn off the heat. Salt and pepper the beans, sprinkle them with the cayenne and dill, stir one more time, and serve. No, no, you don't have to thank me.

Serves 4 to 6 as a side dish

VARIATION

Crescent's More-or-Less Greek-style Green Beans with Gigandes: Gigandes are the truly enormous white lima beans that are typically served at room temperature as an hors d'oeuvre, cooked tender and then braised with a little tomato and a lot of olive oil. But if you soak 2 cups of dried gigandes (see page 348), cook them in a nice savory stock by whatever basic method you like, and then gently stir them into the green beans after they have cooked for about 30 minutes—oh my goodness, what a pleasing vegetarian main dish you have. (If you like, double the olive oil, garlic, and tomato so there will be a bit more with which to coat the gigandes.) This is excellent served with a bulgur or another wholegrain pilaf.

How Done Is Done?

Where vegetable perfection is concerned, I used to be an always-cook-just-to-tender-crisp person. Until, that is, I spent time—thirty-three years, actually—in the South, where meltingly tender, slow-cooked, fresh green beans went a long way toward changing my mind. I was introduced to them in their classic Southern form (slow-cooked, with bacon or salt pork). But when I stopped

eating meat I found an equally delicious flavor-infused softness by cooking them more or less Greek style, with herbs, olive oil, and garlic.

So how done is done? Now I feel that the degree to which a vegetable should be cooked depends on the cook, the vegetable, and the meal. Oh, and the season and course: Skinny little early spring green beans are great when tender-crisp in a salad . . . but let 'em

grow even to adolescence, and slow-cooking is much preferred.

But "shoulds" can be dangerous, in vegetable cooking no less than in anything else. That there can be contrast among different vegetables cooked in different ways is nice, and it's even nicer that one vegetable—the green bean, say—can have so many shades of variation not just in seasoning and cooking method, but in degree of doneness.

FARMER'S MARKET ESCAROLE
with Fresh Yellow & Green Beans

Escarole, a member of the chicory family, counts endive, radicchio, and frisée among its relatives. All share a tonic dose of bitterness, making any one of the clan a nice accent in a salad, but the less-assertive broad-leafed (latifolia) chicory varieties play much more congenially with others. The "others" in this case are fresh green beans, fresh yellow wax beans, a bit of olive oil and/or butter, and a finishing sparkle of mint. With leaves less frilly than those of its cousins, this type of escarole is easy to distinguish. Or, if you're at a farmer's market, talk to the greens farmer, who invariably knows the precise names of the seeds they've planted and tended. Broad-leafed escaroles include Bavarian or Batavian endive, grumolo, scarola, and scarole. (Home gardeners can also grow these as cool-weather crops, at season's start and end, when it's a little chilly; seeds are available from www.seedsofchange.com and www.heirloomseeds.com.)

If you can't find broad-leafed escarole, use broccoli rabe or fresh spinach instead. In either case, you'll have a salutary green side dish, the kind that makes you feel your biceps are rising up into your shirtsleeves. Perfect for spring, with the season's earliest thin beans (not as thin as a pencil lead, nor thick as a pencil—somewhere in between). **Gf** **Ve** or **Vn**

---

2 tablespoons butter, extra-virgin olive oil, or a combination (my preference)

¼ pound thin green beans, tipped and tailed

¼ pound thin yellow wax beans, tipped and tailed

2 large heads escarole, core removed, leaves sliced crosswise into 1-inch pieces, washed very well (or 1 pound broccoli rabe or spinach, tough stems removed, cut into 1-inch pieces)

2 to 3 tablespoons finely minced fresh mint

Salt and freshly ground black pepper

❶ In a large skillet over high heat, melt the butter (with the oil, if using). Add the green and yellow beans, lower the heat slightly, and sauté, stirring often, until the beans are lightly browned, about 3 minutes.

2 Add the escarole. It'll look like there's way too much for the skillet to hold, but pop a lid on the skillet for about a minute (30 to 40 seconds for spinach, 2 minutes for broccoli rabe), and it will quickly wilt down. Remove the lid, raise the heat again, and keep stirring and turning until both the greens and the beans are tender and the liquid has evaporated.

3 Add the mint, salt and pepper to taste, and stir well to distribute the seasonings.

Serves 6 to 8 as a side dish

VARIATION

Sometimes I'll add the grated zest of a lemon plus its juice, stirred in at the end, for a little extra pizzazz. And sometimes I'll add a few cloves of chopped garlic when I stir in the greens. And sometimes I do both. (We love greens and beans around our house. No end to how often we eat them or how we mix 'em up.)

ə   ə   ə

GREEN BEANS T'HORIN

For many years, usually during the inn's off-season, I regularly visited Kerala, the South Indian state whose name means "Land of the Coconut Palms." Almost everything served there contains coconut, and is cooked over a fire started with coconut husks. This Kerala-style dish flavored with coconut and black mustard seeds is sometimes made with very finely chopped cabbage, sometimes with finely chopped green beans; it's home-style cooking, eaten every day or two at the large noon meal. The spice-tempered deliciousness is not at first recognizable as green beans, so transformed is the vegetable by both cut and preparation. It's somewhat dry, unsauced—not at all what most Americans would think of as "Indian food," but deeply good. A single bite takes me back to those formative days in what started out, to me, as very "other": a once-foreign landscape so welcoming and timeless that it is now an intimate part of my heart's geography.

Make sure your knife is sharp and your cutting board is ready. India is a country where labor is cheap; even a lower-middle-class family has a couple of servants—and they do the chopping. The kind of chop needed here is challenging to do right in the food processor, but is essential to the character of the dish;

you'll be doing it by hand. Do it right and the rewards are so satisfying. Serve this with rice and a salad of chopped tomatoes, onions, cucumber, salt, and a squeeze of lime. Or get more elaborate and add Dahl (page 81), Kerala-style Dahl (page 85), or Black-Eyed Peas and Corn in Tomato Masala (page 204). Yogurt and ripe banana with brown sugar for dessert. **Vn** **Gf**

About 1 pound fresh green beans, tipped and tailed

Vegetable oil cooking spray

1 tablespoon coconut oil, or, if unavailable, mild vegetable oil, such as corn, canola, or peanut

1 onion, chopped

1 tablespoon black or brown mustard seeds

2 teaspoons sweet Hungarian paprika

¼ teaspoon salt

⅓ cup dry, unsweetened coconut flakes (see Note)

1 First, prepare the green beans: Stack a handful neatly and slice through it crosswise to make tiny round slices about ⅛ to ¼ inch thick. Don't be tempted to use larger slices; this dish depends on the changed texture and speeded-up cooking time these ultra-thin slices offer. Repeat until all the green beans are sliced. Set aside.

2 Spray a large, heavy skillet (choose one with a tight-fitting lid) with oil, add the coconut oil, and set it over medium heat.

When the pan is hot, add the onion and sauté until softened, about 4 minutes. Add the mustard seeds, raise the heat slightly, and let them cook over medium-high heat, shaking the pan often, until they begin to pop audibly (stand back!), about 3 minutes. Add the paprika and cook, stirring, for 20 seconds. Lower the heat back to medium.

3 Add the sliced green beans and stir well to combine with the onion and seeds, searing the beans slightly. After 20 seconds or so, add the salt and 2 tablespoons water, then pop the lid on the skillet. Lower the heat to medium-low and let cook, stirring now and then and adding extra tablespoons of water if needed, until the beans are tender. (The dish should end up dry, no liquid at all in the pan, though the beans will be moist.)

4 Remove the beans from the heat and stir in the coconut. Serve hot or at room temperature.

Serves 4 to 6 as part of an Indian meal

Note: Dry, unsweetened coconut is available at most natural foods stores.

LEMON-MUSTARD GREEN & YELLOW BEANS

While I adore bean side dishes from the Mediterranean and India, I also relish the many old-fashioned American bean side dishes in my repertoire. I tend to start out with simple cooking methods and treatments, but when my bean harvest starts going completely crazy in midsummer, eventually I rediscover this slightly sweet-tart elaboration that's pure old-time Americana.

If you offer to take a dish to a dinner and are told to provide a side vegetable, you can't go wrong with this or the two recipes that follow. Ve Gf

1 to 1½ pounds mixed green beans and yellow wax beans

1 tablespoon butter, at room temperature

2 tablespoons prepared mustard (I've used both Dijon and good old yellow ballpark-style mustards; the dish came out well with both)

1 tablespoon honey

Juice of ½ lemon

1 tablespoon finely minced fresh parsley

Dash of ground cloves

Salt and freshly ground black pepper

❶ Blanch the beans as follows: Bring a large pot of water to a boil over high heat. When the water is boiling, add the beans and cook them for 2 minutes. Drain them well, saving 1 or 2 tablespoons of the cooking water, then rinse with cold water and drain them again.

❷ While the beans blanch, combine all the remaining ingredients in a small bowl.

❸ Transfer the cooked beans to a serving bowl and toss with the lemon-mustard mixture, adding a tablespoon or two of the bean cooking water to thin the sauce.

Serves 6 to 8 as a side dish

NEW-FASHIONED
DOWN-HOME SUMMERTIME
SUNDAY DINNER

Fried chicken with gravy

★

*Lemon-Mustard Green & Yellow Beans
(or Vegan Sweet & Sour Wax Beans with
Tempeh Bacon & Smoked Salt, page 291)*

★

From-scratch mashed potatoes

★

Platter of sliced garden tomatoes

★

*Blackberry cobbler with vanilla bean
ice cream*

MEATIST SWEET & SOUR WAX BEANS
with Bacon

Y ou can tell how far back in my personal repertoire this one goes: It contains bacon. I include the original here; my current take follows. Although I learned this (after having had it at a now barely remembered Arkansas potluck and tracking down the recipe) with yellow wax beans, there's no reason why it can't be made with green beans, or a combo.

The slightly thickened sauce has a very old-fashioned feeling to it. **Me**

1 to 1½ pounds yellow wax beans, tipped, tailed, and sliced into 1½-inch lengths

2 to 3 slices bacon

1 small onion, chopped

2 tablespoons unbleached white flour

2 tablespoons dark brown sugar (or 1½ tablespoons honey plus ½ tablespoon molasses)

2 tablespoons apple cider vinegar

Salt and freshly ground black pepper

❶ Line a plate with paper towels or a brown paper bag.

❷ Bring a large pot of water to a boil over high heat. When the water is boiling, add the beans and cook them for 2 minutes, or until just tender. Remove from the heat. Drain them well, reserving the blanching water, then rinse with cold water and drain them again. If necessary, add water to the reserved blanching liquid to equal 1 cup.

❸ While the beans cook, place the bacon in a large, heavy skillet over medium heat and fry it, turning occasionally, until crisp, 8 to 10 minutes. Transfer the bacon to the paper-towel-lined plate, and when it's cool to the touch, crumble it and set it aside. Leave the bacon fat in the skillet.

❹ Add the onion to the bacon fat and sauté, still over medium heat, until the onion's slightly browned, about 5 minutes. Sprinkle in the flour and cook the flour in the fat and onion, stirring constantly with a spoon, for 2 to 3 minutes. Gradually pour in the 1 cup bean cooking liquid, stirring, and add the brown sugar and cider vinegar. Cook the sauce, stirring now and again, until thickened, about 3 minutes. Add salt and pepper to taste, going easy on the salt since the salty bacon will be added back in.

❺ Add the wax beans and sprinkle the crumbled bacon over the top. Stir and heat through. Serve, hot or warm.

Serves 6 to 8 as a side dish

VEGAN SWEET & SOUR WAX BEANS

with Tempeh Bacon & Smoked Salt

This nonmeat take on the sweet-and-sour wax beans, opposite, is piquantly delicious in an old-fashioned way. It's similar to the previous recipe, yet it's free of saturated fat as well as being lower in fat, period. The smoked tempeh plus the Bacon Salt, which does not actually contain bacon, really do the trick. Both versions are potluck-appropriate. Vn

1 to 1½ pounds yellow wax beans, tipped, tailed, and sliced in 1½-inch lengths

3 tablespoons mild vegetable oil, such as canola, corn, or peanut

2 to 3 slices tempeh bacon

1 small onion, chopped

2 tablespoons unbleached white flour

2 tablespoons dark brown sugar (or 1 tablespoon plus 2 teaspoons agave syrup plus 1 teaspoon blackstrap molasses)

2 tablespoons apple cider vinegar

Bacon Salt (see box, page 112) or regular salt

Freshly ground black pepper

1 Blanch the wax beans: Bring a large pot of water to a boil over high heat. When the water is boiling, add the wax beans and cook them for 2 minutes, or until just tender. Remove from the heat. Drain them well, reserving the blanching water, then rinse with cold water and drain them again. If necessary, add water to the reserved blanching liquid to equal 1 cup.

2 While the beans cook, heat 1½ tablespoons of the oil in a large, heavy skillet over medium heat. Add the tempeh slices and brown them nicely on both sides, 2 to 3 minutes per side. Remove the tempeh from the skillet and coarsely chop it (it will not be crisp, but tender). Set it aside for later.

3 Add the remaining oil to the hot skillet. In it, sauté the chopped onion until slightly browned, about 5 minutes. Sprinkle in the flour and cook it, stirring constantly with a spoon, for 2 to 3 minutes. Gradually pour in the bean cooking liquid, stirring, and add the brown sugar and cider vinegar. Cook this sauce until thickened, giving a stir now and again, about 3 minutes. Add the Bacon Salt and pepper to taste. (The Bacon Salt is magic here, isn't it?)

4 Add the beans and diced tempeh bacon to the sauce and stir to heat through. Serve, hot or warm.

Serves 6 to 8 as a side dish

DILLED WAX BEANS

nother country-style fresh bean pleasure, from back when I was a young Arkansawyer. This too has sweet-and-sour notes, though less so than either of the sweet-and-sour bean recipes that precede it, as well as piquant fresh dill. Instead of cooking the beans separately and then adding them to the sauce, here the beans cook *in* the sauce. The vegan variation reflects the way I do it now.

With nothing more than a wedge of cornbread, this is a delicious lunch. **Me**

2 slices bacon

1 small onion, very finely chopped

1 to 1½ pounds yellow wax beans, tipped, tailed, and sliced in 1½-inch lengths

About 1½ cups water or chicken stock

1 to 2 teaspoons honey (optional)

1 lemon (preferably organic)

Salt and freshly ground black pepper

2 to 3 tablespoons chopped fresh dill

1 Cook the bacon in a large, heavy skillet (one with a tight-fitting lid) over medium heat just long enough to render the fat and leave the meat a little puckery but still limp—you don't want it crunchy here—about 5 minutes. Remove the bacon from the skillet, coarsely chop it, and set it aside.

2 Add the onion to the bacon fat and sauté it until just slightly translucent, about 1½ minutes. Add the beans and give them a quick stir-fry, too, just enough to coat them with a little of the fat. Add the water and honey, and return the bacon to the pan.

3 Bring to a boil, then turn down to a simmer and cover with the tight-fitting lid.

Lift the lid occasionally to give a stir and check to see if you need to add any liquid. (The beans should be not quite covered with liquid. If you're a devotee of very tender beans, you'll need a long simmer, and more liquid.) Let cook until the beans are tender, about 15 minutes (or as long as an hour for *very* tender beans).

4 While the beans simmer, zest the lemon on a fine grater over a small bowl. Halve the lemon and squeeze half of it through a sieve atop the zest. Set aside.

5 When the beans are done to your taste, lift the lid, and if necessary, raise the heat slightly to boil off any excess liquid (you want no more than ½ inch in the bottom of the skillet). At this point, toss in the lemon zest and juice, and salt and pepper to taste. Lastly, stir in the fresh dill.

Serves 6 to 8 as a side dish

VARIATION

For a vegan take on this, either substitute vegetable oil for the bacon fat, or follow the method given in Vegan Sweet & Sour Wax Beans (page 291). Use agave or maple syrup instead of honey. **Vn**

STIR-FRY WISDOM

L imits. Do they limit us? Or can they, somehow, enlarge who we are, how we live, and what we eat?

The stir-fry is the definitive answer, an answer that's as essential an ingredient as ginger, garlic, or tofu.

In our world, supermarkets sell foods of every season and nationality, both as raw ingredients and as microwaveable finished products. So we tend to forget that traditional recipes always originated *in context,* developing in a particular time and place according to whatever resources and ingredients were or weren't available. And in most times and places in this creaking world's history, that context was limitation.

But, in the face of limitation, human beings often crack the limits, reaching wider-open ways than we would have had everything we "needed" been at our disposal. When you have so little that nothing is really disposable, everything becomes useful.

Enter China.

Throughout most of China's largely rural, hardworking history, and for the vast majority of its people, the greatest limitations were expensive ingredients, cooking fuel, and spare time.

Now, enter the stir-fry.

If you don't have much meat (expensive) but can grow a garden, meals are vegetable-centered. And other than on special occasions when meat is used, it's a seasoning, not a main ingredient. Oil, too, is pricey; you'll use as little as possible, and again, mostly as a seasoning.

If you don't have much fuel, dishes must cook rapidly, at high heat. No big hunks of gravied meat, slow-cooked to tenderness. Instead: ingredients in small, quick-to-cook, bite-size pieces and a small, hot fire, quickly kindled, quickly returning to ash.

Stir-fries developed during the Tang Dynasty (A.D. 618–907) when the typical Chinese oven was a brick box with a chimney and, on top, a single round hole. The wok, round-bottomed and very heavy, fit over and partly into this hole. A single opening, a single pot, meant all those diced ingredients were cooked together over a small, very hot fire, *in* that single pot.

Which brings us to the hot business of the modern-day stir-fry. A little oil in the bottom of the wok, some aromatics, a bit of meat, a lot of chopped vegetables— stir these things together, and don't stop. Otherwise the ingredients will stick to the pan instead of searing deliciously as they make quick contact with the hot metal. In minutes—during some of which you may cover the pan briefly to trap the steam being given off—you've made a dish in which bright natural colors and flavors are retained with fresh vibrancy and textures blend crisp with soft and juicy. All as precious fuel, efficiently used, is conserved.

This combination—bite-size pieces, high heat, quickness—is unique in the cooked dishes of most cuisines (which, of course, developed in their own contexts). It took China's limits, and its people's unlimited creativity, to come up with stir-frying. Its flavors concentrated and harmoniously simpatico, it is unified by the smokiness of the seared bits and best appreciated when eaten the second it's done.

Most of us in America can approximate this only to a point; our burners don't get hot enough and our stoves aren't specifically designed to accommodate woks. Still, we can get satisfyingly close. Here we will, starting with a Basic Asian Tofu Stir-Fry with Bok Choy & Snap Peas (the beans appearing both as tofu and as sugar snaps) below. As the pan sizzles and the kitchen is quickly filled with *wok hei* (Cantonese, loosely, for "breath of the wok"), let's celebrate not only good, fast, healthy dinners in our chronically short-on-time lives, but the wonder of all this. Call it stir-fry wisdom.

Let's start chopping, turn up the heat as high as it'll go, and see how far our limits take us.

ꙮ   ꙮ   ꙮ

BASIC ASIAN TOFU STIR-FRY
with Bok Choy & Snap Peas

Having grown up in the era when being able to make a basic stir-fry and a pot of brown rice was de rigueur, it's hard for me to believe that many don't know how to do it. But just the other day, as I was piling baby bok choy into a bag by the produce counter at the co-op, a young man with a ponytail (probably about the age I was when I learned to make stir-fries) asked me with innocent sincerity, "How do you cook that?" (I must emit some kind of knowledgeable food vibe. I can't tell you how often strangers at the supermarket ask me how to prepare artichokes, or what star fruit tastes like.)

So here goes. Like my beloved Beans & Greens Pasta with Lemon, Garlic & Chile (page 273), you can riff on this to your heart's content.

All Asian stir-fries cook rapidly, at high heat. It is therefore important that all the vegetables be cut up beforehand. In fact, everything should be ready to go before you start cooking: all ingredients prepped, measured, and sitting out on a tray in orderly fashion, with rice (or pasta, or a whole grain) already cooked. Then, the second you finish, it's time to eat, and the kitchen is not in chaos.

One other trick: Don't overload the skillet or wok. You need room and air space for the vegetables to sear properly. Also, don't use too many types of vegetables in any one stir-fry: Three or maybe four, plus the tofu and onion, is plenty. Don't overcomplicate things. In this master recipe, for instance, I've just used carrots, bok choy, and sugar snaps. **Vn**

2 tablespoons peanut oil

2 cloves garlic, minced

About 2 heaping teaspoons finely minced fresh ginger (from a piece a bit smaller than your thumb)

1 onion, sliced vertically into thin crescents

2 carrots, stem end removed, thinly sliced on the diagonal

4 to 6 baby bok choy, tough base removed, white stems cut into 1-inch pieces, green leaves left whole (separate stems and leaves into piles)

¼ pound sugar snap peas, tipped and tailed

8 ounces traditional water-packed firm tofu, drained well and cut into ½-inch cubes

½ cup water, vegetable stock, chicken stock, or beef stock

Your choice of seasoning sauce (see The Nearly Infinite Themes and Variations of a Stir-Fry, page 296)

2 to 3 scallions, derooted, whites and 2 inches of green finely sliced

Cooked rice, for serving

1 Heat 1 tablespoon of the oil in a wok or large skillet with a tight-fitting lid over high heat. Add the garlic and ginger and stand *right over it,* sautéing for about 30 seconds. Scoop out the ginger and garlic with a slotted spoon and set it aside. Add the remaining oil and the onion and cook, stirring constantly, until the onion is slightly browned but still has a bit of shape to it, about 4 minutes. (This is why the technique's called stir-frying, as you may have guessed.)

2 Add the carrots and stir-fry them for 1 minute. Add the bok choy stems and stir-fry with the carrots for another 30 seconds or so.

3 Add the sugar snaps, tofu, and water or stock. Pop on the tight-fitting lid and let the vegetables steam in the liquid until not quite tender, 2 to 3 minutes. Lift the lid, add the bok choy leaves and seasoning sauce, give a good stir, and cover again for about 30 seconds.

4 Add the reserved ginger and garlic and stir-fry madly until everything is steaming, sizzling hot with only minimal liquid (you might need to evaporate some away, or conversely, add a few tablespoons more), about 20 seconds. Taste for seasonings, adjust your sauce ingredients as needed, and serve, sprinkled with the scallions, over or with the rice.

Serves 4

KUNG PAO TOFU
with Honey-Roasted Peanuts & Green Beans

A beyond-basics beautiful dish, this is an updated version of the classic, which, as made in your local Chinese restaurant, is probably scarily high in fat. If you love the flavors but not the calories of King Pao, this far-tastier rendition will please you. It offers the traditional faint heat, sweetness, and ginger freshened up with clean, bright tastes and colors. Tofu, oven-crisped to begin and finished in the skillet, replaces beef or chicken. I use fewer peanuts and I don't fry them. No, honey-roasted peanuts have no honey in them and are not a natural foods item, but somehow they work perfectly here.

Kung Pao Tofu requires a good amount of advance prep; lay out the ingredients on a tray beforehand, following step by step. Your reward: a great dish, quickly put together (the beforehand prep's where the work is). Just know that everything moves really swiftly once the wok is involved, so be prepared to hustle. Warn diners to pick around the chiles; they're for flavor, not for chewing on.

A version of this, with asparagus instead of green beans, appeared in *Passionate Vegetarian.* I almost didn't include it here because it's a bit fussy, but one of the dear, funny things about being a cookbook writer is the way people who know your books and have cooked your dishes react when meeting you. "You're Crescent Dragonwagon? I *love* your . . ." and then they name a dish. I've heard this at least half a dozen times about Kung Pao Tofu—so I'm happily offering it, slightly altered, again.

I also have to repeat one little *Passionate Vegetarian* anecdote: When Ned, my darling and quick-witted late husband, first tasted this, he said, "Wow! This really puts the *pow* in Kung Pao!" **Vn**

1 recipe Traditional Asian-Style "Crisping" Marinade & Method for Oven-Baked Tofu (page 250)

FOR THE TOFU:

2 tablespoons mirin (Japanese rice wine) or dry sherry

1 tablespoon plus 2 teaspoons cornstarch

3 tablespoons tamari or shoyu soy sauce

1 tablespoon plus 1 teaspoon sugar, agave, or honey

⅔ cup vegetable stock

FOR THE FINISH:

Vegetable oil cooking spray

1 tablespoon mild vegetable oil,
  preferably peanut

4 to 6 dried red chiles

2 teaspoons finely minced garlic
  (4 to 6 cloves)

2 tablespoons plus 1 teaspoon peeled,
  finely chopped fresh ginger (from
  a large thumb-size chunk)

½ pound fresh green beans, tipped, tailed,
  and cut diagonally into 1-inch lengths

½ cup water or vegetable stock

1 bunch of scallions, derooted, white and
  2 inches of green, white split lengthwise,
  then all cut into ¾-inch lengths

⅓ cup honey-roasted peanuts

Cooked brown rice, for serving

1 Remember, you start with the tofu already marinated and baked. I'm just saying.

2 Combine all of the sauce ingredients in a large bowl, smushing the cornstarch into the liquid with your fingers to dissolve any lumps. Set aside.

3 Place the sauce, oven-crisped tofu, and all the remaining ingredients except the rice, each in its own little bowl, on a tray or countertop near the stove.

4 Spray a wok or large skillet with a tight-fitting lid with vegetable oil.

5 Heat the oil in the wok over high heat. Let it get very, very hot; it will be fragrant and look sort of thinned out, glazed, and swirly on top. Add the chiles and cook, stirring, until they darken, 1 minute. Working quickly, scoop the darkened chiles out of the pan with a slotted spoon, leaving as much oil as possible in the wok. Reserve the chiles in a bowl.

6 Place the garlic and ginger in the wok and stir-fry until they color slightly; they may try to stick, but ignore that, just keep stirring, 10 to 20 seconds. Add the green beans and stir for 10 seconds. Add the water and immediately pop the lid on the wok. Turn the heat as high as it will go and steam the green beans until they are tender-crisp and the water has almost evaporated. Remove the lid and let any remaining water evaporate.

7 The second the water has evaporated, toss in the scallions. Stir-fry them quickly, about 20 seconds. Give the sauce mixture a vigorous stir to recombine the cornstarch and liquid, and pour it into the hot wok. Cook, stirring constantly, until the sauce becomes a translucent, very thick glaze, about 30 seconds. Add the tofu and peanuts and heat through, stirring, a few seconds more. Serve, hot, ASAP, over the rice.

Serves 4 to 5, with rice

THE NEARLY INFINITE THEMES OF A STIR-FRY

Let's start by just fooling around with seasonings:

★ **BASIC SEASONING SAUCE:** Combine 1 to 2 tablespoons tamari or shoyu soy sauce with 2 to 3 tablespoons mirin (Japanese rice wine) or sweet sherry. A teaspoon of sugar or honey is optional.

★ **BASIC PLUS SESAME:** Cut the oil in the stir-fry back by 1½ teaspoons. Then, make the Basic Seasoning Sauce above, drizzling in 1½ teaspoons toasted sesame seed oil. If you get ambitious, add a tablespoon of toasted sesame seeds.

★ **QUICK SWEET-HOT:** Whisk together 2 tablespoons hoisin sauce and 2 teaspoons Sriracha (hot chile paste). Maybe add a little tamari soy sauce at the end, too.

★ **SWEET-HOT FROM SCRATCH:** Sauté 1 to 3 dried hot Thai red chiles with the garlic and ginger, and remove them at the same time. To the Basic Seasoning Sauce, add 1 to 2 teaspoons sugar or agave syrup. Add the chiles back in for the final stir-fry.

★ **THAI SWEET-HOT HERBAL:** Sauté 1 to 3 dried hot Thai red chiles with the garlic and ginger. Add 2 teaspoons sugar to the Basic Seasoning Sauce. Stir in ¼ cup finely shredded fresh Thai basil and/or cilantro at the last, then garnish with more of the same, plus the scallions and some chopped roasted peanuts.

★ **SWEET-HOT ORANGE:** Combine 2 teaspoons finely grated orange zest, ¼ cup fresh orange juice, 2 tablespoons tamari soy sauce, 1 tablespoon agave syrup or honey, 2 teaspoons Sriracha, and 2 teaspoons cornstarch (smush it in with your fingers).

★ **HOT SWEET-AND-SOUR:** Omit the ginger in step 1 and instead sauté 5 or 6 dried hot Thai red chiles with the garlic, scooping them out when they start to darken in spots. For the sauce, combine 2 to 3 tablespoons white vinegar, 1 to 2 tablespoons sugar, and a grind of coarse salt. Add the chiles back in at the last stir-fry (don't eat 'em).

★ **QUICK SAVORY-SPICY:** Stir together 1 tablespoon black bean garlic sauce, 2 tablespoons chile garlic sauce, 1 tablespoon sugar, and 1 teaspoon tamari soy sauce. Try throwing some minced Thai basil into the stir-fry at the end.

★ **SLIGHTLY THICKENED SAUCE:** Smush 1 teaspoon cornstarch into a tablespoon of water or stock until it's a thin paste. Stir it into any of the above sauces except for Hot Sweet-and-Sour and Quick Savory-Spicy.

Now let's alter the vegetables and tofu:

★ In place of the bok choy stems, add small cauliflower or broccoli florets, green beans cut on an angle into 1-inch pieces, or asparagus tips and tender stems (stems cut on an angle into 1-inch pieces). The bok choy leaves can be replaced by a double handful of spinach, tatsoi, mizuna, or bean sprouts.

★ Instead of carrot, use slivered bell peppers. Replace the bok choy stems with celery, cut into ¾-inch pieces, and replace the bok choy leaves with spinach, bean sprouts, mizuna, or tatsoi. Replace the snap peas with sliced mushrooms.

★ Use marinated baked tofu like the New Wave–New Fave Baked Tofu and the crisp oven-baked tofu on pages 249–250. Or try the Basic Oven-Baked Marinated Tempeh (page 244). Stir these in at the very last.

CHAPTER 9

Beans and Grains

EARTHY
SOUL MATES

"A match made in heaven," we say of a perfect pairing. But heaven's exact nature is a matter of supposition, no? Life in our world is the only thing we know for sure. How much more certain is a match made on earth. In my view, high on a list of such matches are beans (and peas, and other legumes) and grains (most especially rice, corn, and wheat).

These matches are earthy in the sense of being concrete, sensual. They're also deeply rooted in the world's soil and in humanity's long, hungry history. Along the Fertile Crescent, some of our ancient kin ate lentils and barley, while more or less concomitantly our American ancestors were sustained by pintos and corn. Meanwhile, soybeans—often as tofu and tempeh—and rice nourished our Asian roots. No matter which long-ago civilization gave your family its DNA, your early relatives likely thrived on beans and grains.

This was long, long before there was even a name for "protein," let alone for the compounds that make it up, amino acids. Our forebears didn't need to know that nature's jigsaw puzzle put together the legume-grain pieces thus: that the amino acids so abundant in grains are the same as those deficient in legumes, and vice versa; that because of this, their pairing creates high-quality, complete protein— an earthy, earthly match. All our ancestors knew, and all we really need to know now, is how *good* these two foods taste together, how right, and how satisfyingly well this pair feeds us.

Here we'll explore this global coupling (which, besides being culinary perfection when done right, also leaves a smaller environmental footprint than animal-based proteins). Here we're low on the food chain and high on saving money.

These lovable dyads cover beans cooked with grains as well as bean mélanges cooked separately but made to be scooped up and served over grains. Amazing grains, blessed beans. Do I hear an "amen"?

MJEDDRAH

Every time I explore a foodstuff deeply, I discover that dishes become a permanent part of my regular repertoire. This is one of *Bean by Bean*'s top contenders.

While the main ingredients—rice and lentils— are steadfast and stout, be assured that the seasonings make it transcendent. I first came across *mjeddrah* in a novel, Diana Abu-Jaber's *Crescent,* in which the dish and the Iraqi-American protagonist's associations with it are described so rapturously that the culinary Sherlock Holmes game was afoot. Mjeddrah wasn't in any of my Middle Eastern cookbooks, nor in those of the three libraries nearest me. But the good old Internet came through. I found a dozen or so recipes, all similar, all differing slightly, each vague on certain points. This is my worked-out, clarified mjeddrah: definitely fork-food, a moist main-dish pilaf or risotto. The leftovers are even thicker (and, though it seems impossible, even more delicious) the next day. Some people think this is the pot that the biblical Esau sold his birthright for (see box, page 58), and after tasting it, I can understand why.

At Taiim, an Israeli restaurant with a Jordanian chef in Hastings-on-Hudson, New York, mjeddrah is served with a garnish of sliced onions that have been quickly, crisply fried until dark and crunchy (no breading): divine. **Ve** **Gf**

½ cup brown or red lentils, picked over and rinsed

3 tablespoons olive oil

1 large onion, halved vertically and thinly sliced crosswise

2 carrots, chopped

1 stalk celery, with leaves, finely minced

½ cup long-grain brown rice, such as brown Texmati or basmati

½ teaspoon whole or ground cumin

2 cloves garlic, finely chopped

1 small dried red chile, stemmed and broken in half

1½-inch piece of cinnamon stick

Seeds from 2 to 4 whole cardamom pods

Salt and freshly cracked black pepper

1 If you're using brown lentils, bring 2 cups water to a boil in a large pot. Add the lentils, turn off the heat, and let the lentils soak for a few hours. (Skip this if you're using red lentils; they don't need presoaking.)

2 When you get ready to finish the dish—at least an hour before serving, but preferably a day ahead—heat the oil in a large skillet over medium heat. Add the onion and sauté, stirring, for 4 to 5 minutes. Add the carrots and celery and sauté for another 3 minutes. Then scrape the sauté into the pot containing the lentils, along with an additional 3 cups water, the rice, and all the remaining ingredients except the salt and pepper.

3 Bring the mjeddrah to a boil, then lower the heat to a simmer and cook, covered, checking occasionally and adding water as needed, until both lentils and rice are tender, about 1 hour. You're aiming for a thick dish with some liquid (which will be thickened by the rice cooked in it). Try for moist but not at all soupy.

4 When the lentils and rice are tender, add salt and quite a bit of pepper to taste. Remove the chile and discard it, or chop it fine and return it to the mjeddrah. Serve right away or, better yet, refrigerate it, covered, overnight, or set it aside for a few hours at room temperature, and then reheat it. Either pick out the cinnamon stick or warn diners that it's floating around somewhere. (If you were adventurous and made those dark, sweet, crisp onion slices I mentioned earlier, scatter them on now.)

Serves 4 to 6

"Sirine's mother strained the salted yogurt through cheesecloth to make creamy labneh, stirred the onion and lentils together in a heavy iron pan to make mjeddrah, and studded joints of lamb with fat cloves of garlic. . . .

"The smell of food always brought her father into the kitchen. . . . And if it was one of his important favorites—stuffed grape leaves, mjeddrah, or roast leg of lamb—he would appear in the kitchen even before the meal was done cooking. . . . Sirine thought that this was why her mother cooked—to keep her husband close to her, attached to a delicate golden thread of scent."

—*Diana Abu-Jaber*, Crescent

BLACK-EYED PEAS & RICE ONE-POT
with Indian Aromatics

I n India, whether north or south, beans and rice are usually cooked separately. But having fallen in love with Mjeddrah (page 301), it was my pleasure to give the same cooking-together treatment to legumes and grains with several of the vibrant hues from the culinary magic carpet of Indian kitchens. With raita—diced tomato and onion, or cuke and onion, tossed with thick plain yogurt and a little salt—this is a meal. **Gf** **Ve** or **Vn**

½ cup dried black-eyed peas

2 tablespoons ghee or peanut oil

3 onions, thinly sliced

1 carrot, diced

1 green bell pepper, stemmed, seeded, and diced

2 cloves garlic, minced

2 tablespoons minced fresh ginger

½ teaspoon ground turmeric

½ teaspoon cayenne, or 1 to 2 dried hot red chiles, stemmed

2 teaspoons ground cumin

1 teaspoon curry powder

½ cup long-grain brown rice, such as brown Texmati or basmati

1 can (28 ounces) diced tomatoes, preferably fire-roasted, with juices

3 tablespoons raisins

1 tablespoon freshly squeezed lemon juice, or 1 tablespoon tamarind concentrate (see box, page 304) thinned with 2 tablespoons water

Salt and freshly ground black pepper

¼ cup chopped fresh cilantro leaves, for garnish

VARKHALA BY THE SEA

Summer tomatoes tossed with cilantro

★

Cucumber-onion raita

★

Green Beans T'horin (page 287)

★

Grilled pomfret or other mild white fish

★

Black-Eyed Peas & Rice One-Pot with Indian Aromatics

★

Pistachio ice cream with sliced mango

---

❶ Bring 2 cups water to a boil in a large pot. Add the black-eyed peas, turn off the heat, and let them soak for at least an hour, but no more than three. (This amount of time will soften them enough so they cook to tenderness in the same time as the rice.) When you're ready to complete the dish, bring the black-eyes and their soaking water back to a boil, lower to a simmer, and let cook, half-covered, while you continue the recipe.

2 Heat the ghee in a large, heavy skillet over medium heat. Add the onions and sauté, stirring, for 3 to 5 minutes. Add the carrot and bell pepper and sauté for 3 minutes more. Lower the heat, add the garlic, ginger, and spices, and cook, stirring constantly, for 1 minute more. Scrape the sauté into the pot with the black-eyed peas.

3 Add another cup of water to the skillet and bring it to a boil, stirring to loosen any flavor-y remnants from the bottom of the pan. Pour this liquid (the "deglaze") into the pot with the black-eyed peas, along with another cup of water. Add the rice, tomatoes, and raisins.

4 Bring the mixture back to a boil, then lower the heat to a simmer and let cook, covered, over very low heat, for about 1 hour. Uncover and let simmer until the rice and black-eyes are tender, there is very little spare liquid, and your kitchen is steamily aromatic, another 10 to 20 minutes.

5 Remove from the heat and add the lemon juice. Let cool slightly, then add salt and pepper to taste. Serve hot, garnishing each portion with cilantro leaves.

Serves 4 to 6 with raita

TAMARIND: TITILLATINGLY TANGY

Tamarind, related botanically to mesquite and carob, is a large tropical tree that bears copious amounts of plump seedpods, cocoa-brown when ripe. Inside the pod is a seedy, dark brown paste, its texture and color giving rise to one of its common names, "Indian date." But while its appearance and texture are similar, tamarind's flavor is unlike the unadulterated sweetness of dates. It is deliciously tart, with only the merest touch of sweet, with an addictive floral undernote. The paste (or "concentrate") is sold at Indian, African, and Asian markets or online at www.ishopindian.com. It keeps indefinitely. The package or jar may say "seedless," but it's probably not so (though I hear Nirav Tamarind Concentrate is pretty seed-free). No matter; it's still easy to use.

To make *seedless* tamarind paste, pull off a hunk of the sticky paste—2 or 3 tablespoons' worth—and place it in a bowl with an equal amount of warm water. Let stand 5 minutes, then smush it with your fingers a little; it'll mostly melt into a thinnish, soft, dark brown paste. Pour this thinned tamarind paste through a strainer (to catch the seeds) into a second bowl, and there you are.

Even though you'll use tamarind paste only once in a while, it keeps well, so why not keep it on hand?

VERONICA'S JAMAICAN COAT OF ARMS

A version of this recipe appeared in *Passionate Vegetarian,* but it's too good to omit here. I can't give the recipe without mentioning Veronica, the Jamaican housekeeper who kept our family in line for two or three formative years. The Zolotows always remember her fondly. I wrote in *Passionate Vegetarian* about her sashay, Attitude-with-a-capital-A, and highly eloquent lifted eyebrows. I mentioned how Veronica put the dog's dish down, with that eyebrow raise of hers, and called our black standard poodle, Cleo: "Miss Clay-o!" But what I *didn't* say was this: When Cleo would trip eagerly into the kitchen, toenails clicking on the floor, Ver, surveying her, standing hands on hips, never failed to say: "Mon, I have one-t'ird what that dog have, I be one *hoppy* wo-mon."

Veronica returned from her days off laden with foodstuffs. When she fixed rice and peas (Jamaican Coat of Arms), she'd share it with me (though never with my parents). With its faint, haunting coconut-milk flavor and richness and its sui generis spicing, it's equally exotic, pleasing, and soothing. The "peas" are kidney beans, which she stirred every so often as the dish cooked, releasing the starch of both beans and rice, so we ended up with a thick porridge-y mix. This is a fluffy version of that dish (but you can stir it if you want it like Ver's). Ver served rice and peas with long slices of crisp, perfectly fried plantain, another match made on earth. You could fake it, inauthentically, for ease and a nod to tradition, with some unsweetened banana chips. **Gf** **Vn**

1 can (29 ounces) red kidney beans, liquid reserved

1 can (14 ounces) regular or reduced-fat unsweetened coconut milk

1 bunch of scallions, derooted, whites and 1 to 2 inches of green finely chopped

1 to 2 cloves garlic, pressed

3 sprigs fresh thyme or ½ teaspoon dried thyme

Salt and freshly ground black pepper

2 cups converted long-grain rice, such as Uncle Ben's

Boiling water

Fried plantains or unsweetened banana chips, for garnish (optional)

① Open the can of kidney beans, and drain the bean liquid into a 4-cup (or larger) measuring cup. Add the coconut milk and enough water to fill the measuring cup to the 4-cup mark.

② Transfer the liquid to a medium-large saucepan with a tight-fitting lid, and set it over high heat. Bring it to a boil and stir in the beans, scallions, garlic, thyme, salt and pepper to taste, and rice. Check the water level; if need be, add enough boiling water to cover the rice and beans to a depth of 1½ to 2 inches. Bring everything back to a boil, stir once, turn the heat down to a simmer, and let cook, covered, stirring a few times, until the rice is tender, 20 to 25 minutes.

Serve with a side of fried plantains or a sprinkle of banana chips if you like.

Serves 4 to 6

VARIATION

Rasta Rice and Peas: Place one whole Scotch bonnet or habañero pepper, poked a few times with a fork, atop the rice-and-peas mixture before you cover and cook it, so the chile steams with the rice. Do not cut the pepper open; these things are so hot they will take the top of your head off. And be sure to remove the pepper before serving; this way, you get just a little of that good heat and scent and flavor. **Vn** **Gf**

ᕯ   ᕯ   ᕯ

RED BEANS & RICE NOUVEAU CARRÉ

For a long time I made this vegetarian dish using a couple of drops of liquid smoke to give the beans their characteristic smoky taste. That was good—but now there are tastier alternatives. Count 'em; do you see all four ways the requisite smokiness has made its way into this dish? While traditional red-beans-and-rice diehards may scoff at this version, it is really soul-satisfyingly good, and it will also reduce your chances of, to be blunt, dying hard.

I like this a lot. In fact, I wish I had some simmering on the stove at this exact second. Truly. **Vn**

2 cups dried red kidney beans, picked over, rinsed, and soaked overnight (see page 348)

¼ cup olive oil or any mild-flavored vegetable oil, such as corn or canola

2 large onions, chopped

1 large red bell pepper, stemmed, seeded, and chopped

1 large green bell pepper, stemmed, seeded, and chopped

5 stalks celery, chopped

1 carrot, diced

5 to 7 cloves garlic, minced

½ teaspoon dried thyme

1 or 2 bay leaves

1 teaspoon to 1 tablespoon hot sauce such as Frank's RedHot, Crystal, or Tabasco, whichever you're partial to

1½ teaspoons vegetarian Worcestershire sauce

1 teaspoon smoked sweet Hungarian paprika

Cayenne pepper and/or chipotle pepper powder

Freshly ground black pepper

Salt

Bacon Salt (see box, page 112)

½ to 1 pound chorizo-style soysage (I like Lightlife, Tofurky, or Field Roast)

Plenty of hot cooked rice, for serving

4 to 6 breakfast-style soysage links, such as Field Roast Smoked Apple Sage or Lightlife Smart Links (1 per person), browned, for serving (optional)

Chopped scallions, for garnish

① Drain and rinse the beans, place them in a Dutch oven or another large pot, and cover them with water to a depth of about 2 inches. Bring to a rolling boil over high heat, then turn down to a medium simmer and cook, making sure the beans are always adequately covered by water, until they are tender but not falling apart, 45 to 60 minutes. Drain them very well (reserve the cooking water for stock, if you like) and return them to their pot.

② While the beans are cooking, heat the olive oil in a large, heavy skillet over medium-high heat. Add the onions and sauté until they're translucent, about 3 minutes. Add the bell peppers, celery, and carrot and sauté for another 5 minutes. Lower the heat slightly, add the garlic, and sauté, stirring often, for 2 minutes more.

③ Scrape the sauté into the bean pot and add the thyme, bay leaves, hot sauce, Worcestershire, and smoked paprika, as well as the cayenne and/or chipotle and the black pepper (hold back on the salt at this moment). Add enough water to just cover the beans.

④ Bring the beans to a boil, then reduce the heat to a low simmer and cook, half-covered, for 2 hours at least, but preferably for 3 or 4. Give the beans a thorough stir every so often, and when you do, taste and tinker with the seasonings, adding salt and Bacon Salt once the beans are creamy.

⑤ As with so many bean dishes, if you have the time to let the beans cool and then reheat them before serving (adding a little extra water if you refrigerate them overnight), they'll be that much better. But at any rate, about 40 minutes before serving, slice the chorizo soysages on the diagonal, and stir them into the beans.

⑥ When you're ready to plate, remove the bay leaves. Ladle the beans over the steaming hot rice, and if you like, place a freshly browned breakfast-style soysage on the side of each portion. Sprinkle liberally with the chopped scallions and serve. Gooo-ooo-ood! P.S. The smokiness? From the paprika, the Bacon Salt, the veggie chorizo, and the veggie breakfast soysage . . . ta-da!

Serves 4 to 6

RED BEANS & RICE VIEUX CARRÉ

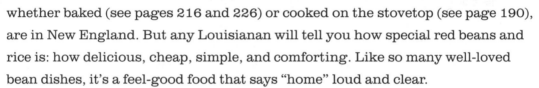

This dish is so quintessentially New Orleans that Louis Armstrong used to sign his correspondence "Red Beans and Ricely Yours." It was traditionally served there on Monday (which was washing day, presumably a busy day, when Mama needed something that could just cook and not need messing with), and it was just as much a part of the culture there as yellow-eye beans, whether baked (see pages 216 and 226) or cooked on the stovetop (see page 190), are in New England. But any Louisianan will tell you how special red beans and rice is: how delicious, cheap, simple, and comforting. Like so many well-loved bean dishes, it's a feel-good food that says "home" loud and clear.

Although the dish is always made with plenty of garlic, and the exact amount is up to you, a New Orleans superstition says that it should always be an odd number of garlic cloves: three, five, seven, eleven, fifteen . . . (I'm for the five-to-seven range, myself.)

My vegetarian version is on the previous page. I learned to make this meat version from a born-and-bred New Orleans waitress who worked in a restaurant where I once cooked. She was small, feisty, and opinionated; a bit cayenne-y herself. Forgive me for not recalling her name—but I do remember her legendary red beans.

Some people cook the beans not in water but in all or part unsalted chicken stock, which does, of course, add another layer of flavor. **Me**

2 cups dried red kidney beans, picked over, rinsed, and soaked overnight (see page 348)

¼ cup bacon fat ("from that morning's bacon," the waitress who remains nameless instructed me)

1 large onion, chopped

5 stalks celery, chopped

1 green bell pepper, stemmed, seeded, and chopped

Minced garlic, to taste (see headnote)

1 large smoked ham hock

½ to 1 pound mild or hot smoked sausage, such as andouille, sliced on the diagonal

½ teaspoon dried thyme

1 or 2 bay leaves

1 teaspoon to 1 tablespoon hot sauce (Frank's RedHot, Crystal, and Tabasco all have their loyal fans)

½ teaspoon Worcestershire sauce

Cayenne pepper

Freshly ground black pepper

Salt

Plenty of hot cooked rice, for serving

6 to 8 grilled links Creole-style hot sausage, chaurice sausage, or chorizo sausage (1 link per person), for serving (optional)

Chopped scallions, for garnish

1 Drain and rinse the beans, place them in a Dutch oven or another large pot, and cover them with water to a depth of about 2 inches. Bring to a rolling boil over high heat, then turn down to a medium simmer and cook, making sure the beans are always adequately covered with water, until they are tender but not falling apart, 45 to 60 minutes. Drain them very well, and return them to their pot.

2 While the beans are cooking, heat the bacon fat in a large, heavy skillet over medium heat. Add the onion and sauté until translucent, about 3 minutes, then add the celery and green pepper and sauté for another 5 minutes. Lower the heat slightly, add the garlic, and sauté, stirring often, for 2 minutes more.

3 Scrape the sauté into the bean pot and add the ham hock, smoked sausage, thyme, bay leaves, hot sauce, and Worcestershire. Add the cayenne and black pepper, but hold off on the salt for now. Add just enough water to cover.

4 Bring the beans to a boil, then reduce the heat to a low simmer. Let the beans cook slowly, half-covered, for at least 2 hours but preferably 3 or 4. Come over and give the beans a thorough stir every so often; when you do, taste for seasonings and adjust (tinkering is part of the New Orleans way of cooking). You want the beans to get creamy and the starch, fat, meat, and seasonings to make their own richly flavored gravy in which the beans swim. When they start getting creamy, taste and start salting.

5 As with so many bean dishes, if you have the time to let the beans cool and then reheat them at serving time, they'll be that much better: Set the pot aside and let the beans cool to room temperature, or cover them and refrigerate them (add a little extra water before reheating them if you refrigerated them overnight). Pick out and discard the bay leaves.

6 When ready to serve, ladle the beans over steaming hot rice, place a grilled fresh Creole-style hot sausage, if using, on the side of each portion, and sprinkle the top liberally with the chopped scallions.

Serves 6 to 8

"In all the ancient homes of New Orleans, and in the colleges and convents, where large numbers of children are sent to be reared to be strong and useful men and women, several times a week there appear on the table either the nicely cooked dish of Red Beans, which are eaten with rice, or the equally wholesome White Beans à la Crème, or Red or White beans boiled with a piece of salt pork or ham."

—The Picayune Creole Cookbook, *1900*

TRADITIONAL HOPPIN' JOHN

Customarily eaten in the South on New Year's Day for good luck, Hoppin' John is an unaffected, inexpensive one-pot: black-eyed peas, rice, sometimes green pepper, salt pork or ham hock or jowls, and onion, stewed together. By most accounts the dish is Afro-Caribbean in origin. Its greatest popularity centers in Lowcountry South Carolina.

In many contemporary African American households, the dish is jazzed up: Spicy sausage may appear instead of or in addition to the ham hock; tomato sauce may be added; the rice and black-eyes may be cooked separately and served with the one over the other. All are iterations of the traditional. Another recurring resonance is its good-luck theme: In some households, a clean, shiny dime is buried in the black-eyed peas before serving. Whoever gets the coin in his or her portion can expect good luck and/or good income in the year to come. (A similar idea plays out in King Cake; see page 336.) Some forego the coin— the spot on each black-eye can represent a coin.

The Brazilian Collard Green Salad (Couve a Mineira) on page 126 is a nice accompaniment and repeats the wish for abundant finances in the New Year: Besides being tasty, the greens represent folded money. And should you have any leftover Hoppin' John, enjoy it the next day, when it's called, by some, "Skinny Jenny" or "Skippin' Jenny." **Me Gf**

2 smoked ham hocks or pork jowls

2½ cups dried black-eyed peas, picked over and rinsed

1 bay leaf

1 onion, chopped

1 to 2 small dried hot red chiles, stemmed and broken in half

2 cups long-grain white rice

Salt and freshly cracked black pepper

1 Place the ham hocks or jowls in a medium-large pot and pour 2 quarts (8 cups) water over them. Bring to a boil and stir in the black-eyed peas, bay leaf, onion, and chiles.

2 Lower the heat to a simmer, half-cover, and cook until the peas are very tender, about 1½ hours. Fish out the ham hocks and set them aside on a cutting board until they're cool to the touch.

③ Add the rice to the peas, stir well once, then cover and cook without stirring until the rice is done, about 20 minutes.

④ While the rice cooks, remove the ham meat from the bones. Discard the bones; chop the meat into bite-size pieces.

⑤ When the rice is tender, turn off the heat and let the pot stand for about 10 minutes. Lift the lid, discard the bay leaf, stir in the meat, and season with salt and pepper to taste. Serve hot.

Serves 6 to 8

VARIATION

Contemporary African American Hoppin' John: Substitute chicken stock for the water, and add 1 cup tomato sauce and a few links of sautéed, sliced spicy sausage (such as andouille, chorizo, or hot Italian) with the rice. Me

ONCE UPON A TIME THERE WAS A DISH WITH AN ODD NAME . . .

Why Hoppin' John? Delightful, if far-fetched, explanations abound:

LEGEND	VERACITY OF SAID LEGEND
In slavery times, part of the good-luck ritual for New Year's Day was to gather the children around and, when the dish was brought out, for them to dance and hop around the table before the family sat down to eat.	It may sound odd, but circular dances and round dishes *are* associated with luck, community, and continuity.
It was named for John, the crippled African American man who hawked a legendary version of the dish on the streets of Charleston, South Carolina, in the decades before the Civil War.	Persistent story, but wholly unverifiable.
Another John had a wife who was a very good cook. When she fixed this dish, he came "a-hoppin."	Yeah, but which John? And how did he and his wife become so well-known?
In old South Carolina you invited guests to come by on New Year's Day for a bite to eat by saying, "Hop in, John."	Also unverifiable.
It's a corruption of the French name for black-eyed peas, *pois pigeons,* which, when pronounced correctly, really *does* sound like hoppin' John.	Possible, but not provable.

Dragon-style

DANCIN' JOHN

I f you grew up with Hoppin' John, you love it; if you met it later in life, you might find it a bit plain. I ate it every New Year's Day from about age sixteen (when I moved to the South) to age twenty-two (when I stopped eating meat). At that point I began reinventing it, for the truth is, it never really did it for me in its original form. This version suits my taste: a happiness-giving dish, full of flavor; chipotles add heat and a touch of characteristic smoke.

Still simple at heart, this is both good and good for you, full of layers of true good flavor. Let the purists squawk; if they taste it, they'll be back for seconds and thirds. (Food writer, fellow vegetarian, and all-around Pan Pal Jill Nussinow calls hers Jumpin' John—love that alliteration!) **Vn**

FOR THE BEANS AND RICE:

2 cups dried black-eyed peas, picked over and rinsed

1 bay leaf

1 dried chipotle pepper, stemmed

½ onion, diced

4 cups (about two 14.5-ounce cans) canned diced tomatoes, preferably fire-roasted, with their juice

Salt and freshly ground black pepper

1½ cups long-grain brown rice

FOR THE SAUTÉ:

3 to 4 tablespoons olive oil

½ large onion, diced

2 carrots, diced

1 green bell pepper, stemmed, seeded, and chopped

1 red bell pepper, stemmed, seeded, and chopped

2 stalks celery, chopped

4 cloves garlic, pressed

FOR THE FINISH AND GARNISH:

3 to 4 links vegetarian chorizo soysage, such as Lightlife or Tofurkey, sautéed and sliced (optional)

Salt and freshly ground black pepper

2 to 3 scallions, derooted, white and 2 to 3 inches of green minced

¼ cup minced fresh parsley

❶ Begin with the beans: Place the black-eyed peas in a Dutch oven with 5 cups water and the bay leaf, chipotle, and the onion. Bring to a boil, turn down to a low simmer, cover, and let cook slowly until the black-eyes are almost tender, anywhere from 50 minutes to an hour and 5 minutes.

❷ When the black-eyes are tender, add the tomatoes, 1 to 2 teaspoons salt, and black pepper to taste. Raise the heat and bring to a boil. Stir in the rice, return to a boil, then lower the heat to a simmer. Cover tightly and let cook for 50 minutes.

❸ Toward the end of the 50 minutes, prepare the sauté: Heat the olive oil in a large skillet over medium heat. Add the onion and sauté until limp and starting to color slightly, 6 to 7 minutes. Add the carrots and cook, stirring, for 3 minutes more, then add the bell peppers, celery, and garlic. Cook, stirring, for 3 minutes more.

④ When the rice and black-eyes have reached their 50-minute-or-tender point, turn off the heat under the pot and let them stand, undisturbed, for 10 minutes. Lift the lid. Scrape the sauté into the rice and black-eyes and stir lightly to incorporate the sautéed vegetables throughout. Add the soysage if you're using it, and stir that in, too. Season again with plenty of salt and black pepper. Serve, hot, sprinkling each portion or the whole serving dish with the scallions and parsley. Have a good year, y'all.

Serves 6 to 8

"IT'S YOUR LUCKY DAY" NEW YEAR'S BRUNCH

Simple Relish Tray:
Carrot and celery sticks, radishes,
deviled eggs, olives

★

Traditional Hoppin' John (page 310)
and/or Dragon-style Dancin' John

★

Brazilian Collard Green Salad (page 126)

★

Black pepper–Cheddar cornbread in a skillet

★

Glazed orange or lemon ring cake,
with compote of sliced oranges,
grapefruits, and pomelos and threads
of candied orange rind

"A pivotal relationship emerged between Jewish and African women. They shared an unlikely alliance as outsiders—Jews because of their religion and blacks because of their race. The kitchen became a 'free zone' where [they] bonded. . . . Within this space, an important blend of southern and Jewish cuisine emerged . . . blended dishes such as lox and grits, sweet potato kugel, collard greens with gribbenes ('cracklins' made from rendered chicken fat), Rosh Hashanah hoppin' john (the black-eyed peas and rice dish traditionally served in January on New Year's day)."

—*Marcie Cohen Ferris,* Matzoh
Ball Gumbo: Culinary Tales
of the Jewish South

MAYA'S MAGIC BLACK BEANS

with Eggplant & Royal Rice

My friend Maya has a way with beans—it's actually *one* way, though she varies it slightly, occasionally substituting other vegetables for the eggplant she usually includes.

But she always starts with two cans of black beans, and they're always Goya black beans. She always uses garlic and her own special combo of seasonings, including ground achiote or annatto seed (see opposite page), ground coriander seed, and cocoa. This (and the eggplant) is no doubt what makes the dish so outstanding and so . . . Maya.

And she always serves it over what, for no particular reason, she calls "Royal Rice"—either a brown rice–wild rice mixture that she buys in bulk at the Lebanon, New Hampshire, co-op, or a Lundberg Jubilee or Country Wild mix. **Vn**

2 cups unseasoned, uncooked brown
rice–wild rice blend

1 teaspoon salt

1 large eggplant

2 tablespoons olive oil or annatto oil
(see box, page 315)

3 cloves garlic, crushed with the side
of a knife and cut into large chunks

2 cans (14.5 ounces each) black beans,
drained of about half their liquid

MAYA'S SEASONINGS:

½ teaspoon ground coriander

¾ teaspoon ground achiote seed
(or achiote paste) if you use olive oil;
omit if you use annatto oil

½ teaspoon unsweetened cocoa powder

¼ to ½ teaspoon garlic powder (see Note)

¼ teaspoon cayenne

A vigorous dash of hot sauce, such
as Tabasco or Frank's RedHot

A MAGICAL MEAL WITH MAYA

*Arugula salad with scallion and avocado,
cilantro-honey dressing*

★

*Maya's Magic Black Beans
with Eggplant & Royal Rice)*

★

Sweet, thick puree of butternut squash

★

Chocolate crème brûlée

1 First, put the rice and salt on to cook according to package directions or your favorite method.

2 While the rice cooks, preheat the oven to 425°F.

❸ Slice the eggplant into ½-inch rounds. Brush the slices lightly on both sides with some of the olive or annato oil, lay them on a baking sheet, and put them in the oven to bake while you continue, about 20 minutes.

❹ Heat the remaining oil in a large skillet over medium heat. Add the garlic, lower the heat, and let cook, stirring often, for about 1 minute. Add the beans, their liquid, and Maya's seasonings, stir well, and raise the heat to medium.

❺ Let the beans simmer, mashing them slightly if you like. (Maya: "It depends if you want your beans thick, goopy, or in between. I like mine in between.")

❻ Check the eggplant. By about 20 minutes of baking, it should be tender. Remove it from the oven, let it cool slightly, and chop it up. Add the eggplant to the simmering black beans. Serve hot, over the hot rice.

Serves 4 to 6

Note: Reader, I balked at the garlic powder. But here's what Maya said: "Yes, yes, I know you disapprove of garlic powder,

"Vegetables in perfection . . . this fruit is called Melanzana and is much esteemed by the Jews in Leghorn (Livorno, Italy). It is much eaten in Spain and the Levant, as well as by the Moors in Barbary. It is about the size and shape of a hen's egg; enclosed in a cup like an acorn; when ripe, of a faint purple color . . . The people here have different ways of slicing and dressing it, by broiling, stewing with other ingredients . . ."

—*Tobias George Smollett,*
Travels Through France
and Italy

CD, but you like my beans and you know I put garlic powder in, on top of the fresh garlic, and if you want to call it my recipe, you *have* to include it. And that's that!"

ANNATTO OIL

Annatto seeds have a lovely, floral-lemon scent, but they are used primarily to add color to dishes. Annatto seeds and oil are available at Latin or natural foods markets, or at Sam's Caribbean, www.sams247.com.

To make your own oil, heat ½ cup peanut or canola oil in a small saucepan over low heat. Add 3 tablespoons annatto seeds and cook, very slowly, for about 5 minutes. (Almost immediately the oil will begin to turn a deep red, the color of cranberries or red wine.) Turn off the heat and let the seeds steep for about 30 minutes. Drain, discarding the seeds, keeping the tinted oil. Store the oil, tightly covered, in the refrigerator, for up to six months.

VEGETARIAN CHOLENT

with Mushrooms, Seitan, Beans & Barley

Cholent was originally cooked overnight on Sabbath eve by religious Jews, for whom it was a clever way of providing a good hot meal while keeping kosher (kosher law forbids cooking on the Sabbath). Those who grew up in families where kosher was kept often say that waking to the warm, savory fragrance of the slowly baking casserole is one of the aromas which most defines and evokes their childhoods.

Since cholent developed over hundreds of years in impoverished Polish and Russian shtetls (small villages to which Eastern European Jews were largely confined), the dish was often vegetarian and was always composed of what was on hand: two or three types of dried beans, a grain (sometimes barley, sometimes buckwheat kasha), potatoes, a few other vegetables. Shtetl life was frequently just a few steps from subsistence, but that doesn't mean it didn't sometimes bring about dishes that were delicious and health-giving. If there was meat, it would likely be a small chunk; all that could be afforded. As Jews emigrated to the U.S. and elsewhere and grew more affluent, the percentage of meat in cholent grew. Today, as we cut back on meat and add more whole grains and beans for health, we are really returning to the traditional, original cholent.

Well, almost. I've jazzed it up a bit. Seitan replaces beef, the seasonings are amped up, and dried mushrooms add their incomparable flavor and texture. Tomaotes—a New World, untraditional ingredient—are also part of my version. Options: You may fix cholent either in the oven or in a large slow-cooker (step 4 of the directions offers full explication).

Both the beans and the mushrooms require presoaking; allow for this in your timing. **Vn**

4 ounces assorted dried mushrooms, preferably a combination of porcini, shiitake, and cèpes (boletes)

About 1½ quarts (6 cups) commercially made mushroom stock

Vegetable oil cooking spray

3 tablespoons olive oil (or, if you prefer, mild vegetable oil)

2 large onions, chopped

2 stalks celery, chopped

2 carrots, chopped

2 parsnips, scrubbed, peeled, and chopped

1½ teaspoons finely grated fresh ginger

½ teaspoon smoked sweet Hungarian paprika

3 cloves garlic, sliced

1 bay leaf

½ cup dried lima beans, picked over, rinsed, and soaked overnight in water to cover (see page 350), well drained

½ cup dried white beans, such as navy beans, picked over, rinsed, and soaked overnight in water to cover (see page 16), well drained

½ cup uncooked pearled barley

1/3 cup lentils

4 small whole new potatoes, scrubbed well and halved

About ½ pound green beans, tipped, tailed, and cut into 1½-inch lengths

1½ cups tomato sauce, homemade, canned, or bottled

1 package (8 ounces) commercially prepared "traditional style" seitan, rinsed well and cut into 1-inch chunks

½ teaspoon freshly ground black pepper, or to taste

1 to 2 teaspoons salt, or to taste

"Then a sentimental passion of a vegetable fashion must excite your languid spleen,
An attachment à la Plato for a bashful young potato, or a not-too-French French bean!"

—*Patience* by Gilbert & Sullivan

1 Begin by placing the dried mushrooms in a small bowl, pouring about 2 cups of the mushroom stock over them, and letting the mushrooms soak until they are tender and the soaking liquid is even darker than it started out, at least 1 hour. If you're planning to bake the cholent (see step 4), preheat the oven to 350°F.

2 Spray a large oven-to-table casscrole or Dutch oven with the oil spray, add the olive oil, and place the pot over medium heat. Add the onions and sauté until they start to soften, 4 to 5 minutes. Add the celery and carrots, and sauté for 2 to 3 minutes more. Add the parsnips and give everything 1 more minute, then add the ginger, paprika, garlic, and bay leaf and sauté for 1 final minute. Pour 4 cups of the mushroom stock over all, and bring to a boil.

3 Add the lima and white beans, plus the uncooked barley, lentils, potatoes, green beans, tomato sauce, seitan, and black pepper. There should be enough liquid to cover the dry ingredients, but you still want 1 to 2 inches of headroom at the top of the pot (remember, the beans and barley will

both swell as they absorb the liquid; add more stock or water if needed). Bring the mixture back to a boil, stir well, and lower the heat to a simmer. Cover the pot tightly.

④ To oven-bake the cholent, turn the preheated oven down to 200°F, transfer the pot from the stovetop to the oven, and let it bake slowly, 7 to 12 hours or overnight (up to 20 hours is traditional). Alternatively, transfer the cholent to the slow-cooker, turn it to high and cook for 1 hour, and then turn it down to low, cover, and let it cook for 7 to 12 hours or overnight. You want tender beans, lentils, and barley, all liquid absorbed, yet not dried out. Once the cholent has reached this point, you can just turn the slow-cooker to "keep warm," and so it will, cozily, for hours.

⑤ When the cholent is done, add the salt (you may need quite a bit), and adjust the other seasonings as necessary. Discard the bay leaf. Serve hot in soup bowls.

Serves 6 to 8

VARIATION

Cholent with a Garnish: Because kosher dietary law forbids the mixing of meat- and milk-based foods, the following variation isn't traditional, and you wouldn't be allowed to do it if you kept kosher and if your cholent contained brisket. It is delicious in the vegetarian version, though! Simply top each bowl of steaming cholent with a generous spoonful of sour cream or thick, unsweetened Greek-style yogurt. Shower this with minced fresh dill. Ve

BEAN FESTIVALS COAST TO COAST

An abridged calendar of the year's leguminous celebrations:

★ Last weekend in June: Emerson, Arkansas, since 1990. **Purplehull Pea Festival.** There's a blessing of this heirloom crop in early June, and the build-up continues, highlighted, some say, by the World Championship Rotary Tiller Race. Plenty of "reci-peas" to sample, too.

★ Second weekend in August: Pullman, Washington, since 1989. **National Lentil Festival.**

A third of all lentils grown in the United States come from the Palouse Region (Eastern Washington and Northern Idaho). That's something to celebrate!

★ Second weekend in September: Portageville, Missouri, since 1948. **Annual National Soybean Festival.** If you're young enough and cute enough, you could be Mr. or Miss Tiny Soybean!

★ Second weekend in October: Rising Sun, Indiana, since 1986. **Rising Sun Navy Bean**

Fall Festival. It's all about the navy bean soup, plus all the rides and goings-on of a classic country fair.

★ Last weekend in October: Mountain View, Arkansas, since 1983. **Annual Arkansas Bean Fest & Arkansas Championship Outhouse Race.** More than 2,000 pounds of Great Value pinto beans cooked over open fires on 30–40 large cast-iron pots on the town square. Live music, contest for Best Beans.

CHAPTER 10

SWEET BEANS

In Which Legumes Dessert You

You say you're surprised that, despite our exploration of the benevolent, bountiful bean, we have come to a chapter on *desserts*? That it didn't occur to you that leguminous generosity could extend from starters, through entrées, all the way to *sweets*?

True, bean-containing desserts do not immediately come to Western minds. But look east: There, sweetened bean pastes (mostly of adzuki) rule. They find their way into pastries, jellies, dessert soups. And ice cream—the Red Bean Ice Cream on page 339 is, in the words of the old Queen song, "guaranteed to blow your mind"—and sweet smoothies, with variations on this theme in Japan, China, Korea, Indonesia, and Thailand. Meanwhile, in India, chickpea flour is a dessert ingredient of choice in a number of buttery confections of fudgelike density and extreme sweetness. Chickpea flour is also key in the lovely, often somewhat shortbread-textured cookies common throughout the Middle East and North Africa, like the Sesame-Seeded Chickpea Flour Cookies (*Ghoreyba Soumsoum*) on page 326.

And now look homeward, angel. Recall, please, that the peanut is a legume. The peanut butter cookie is unequivocally American; if you're lucky, yours have been homemade, embossed with the crisscrossed fork marks that telegraph "I am a peanut butter cookie!" And think about peanut brittle and sweetened popcorn confections (like Cracker Jack) in which peanuts play a part. If you've ever had a slice of peanut butter pie (likely if you live in the peanut-loving South)—well, you've already had beans for dessert. And if you haven't, just wait until you try the White Chocolate and Peanut Butter Banana Cream Pie, page 332.

One more factor made this chapter necessary: The bean-loving, sweet-loving author of this book thinks meals, and cookbooks, are improved by that *un*necessary, so-pleasurable coda known as dessert.

Would you care to join me?

JULIE'S PEANUT BUTTER CUP BROWNIES

These bar cookies of Julie Reimer's are irresistibly chewy, gooey, chocolaty, peanut buttery, impossible to stop eating (as I discovered to my chagrin when she brought them to a potluck). This is her modification, years in the making, of a recipe from *The 55 Best Brownies in the World* by Honey and Larry Zisman (St. Martin's Griffin, 1991). Julie makes it so often that she was able to recite it to me *by memory* at the aforementioned Vermont potluck, though her own kitchen is in Minnesota. There, Julie puts something even more nourishing into young hands: books. She's the kind of librarian you wish you'd had when you were a kid.

No, I don't use peanut butter chips or cook with Reese's peanut butter cups. Yes, they do contain hydrogenated fats (see box, page 323), which I don't eat. Ever. Except here. (Okay, and until recently, in my Thanksgiving pie crusts.)

These brownies freeze well, if you should have leftovers—unlikely. **Ve**

Vegetable oil cooking spray

½ cup (1 stick) butter, at room temperature

¾ cup creamy, natural, unhydrogenated peanut butter (see box, page 323)

2 cups packed dark brown sugar

1 tablespoon pure vanilla extract

4 eggs

4 ounces unsweetened chocolate, melted and cooled to room temperature

1 cup unbleached white flour

1 package (10 ounces) peanut butter chips

24 Reese's peanut butter cup miniatures, unwrapped

① Preheat the oven to 325°F. Spray a 9 by 13-inch pan with oil.

② In a large bowl, using a handheld mixer, cream together the butter, peanut butter, and brown sugar. Beat in the vanilla and eggs. Blend in the melted chocolate, mixing until the batter is uniformly chocolaty. By hand, stir in the flour and peanut butter chips.

③ Spread the batter evenly in the prepared pan. Top with the peanut butter cups in a 4-row-by-6-row pattern.

④ Bake until a toothpick inserted in the center of the brownies comes out more clean than not, 30 to 35 minutes. Don't overbake these; their gooeyness is part of their wonder. Cool completely on a wire rack before cutting. These keep well at room temp, tightly covered (or in a tin), for 5 to 6 days. Which means they're also good for mailing to homesick kids at camp or college.

Makes 12 brownies

JULIE'S PEANUT BUTTER CHOCOLATE CHIP OATMEAL COOKIES

I was so thrilled with the recipe for Julie's Peanut Butter Cup Brownies (page 321) that Julie said, "Well, I'll have to send you the other peanut-butter-chocolate one we love." Less indulgent than the brownies, these are great, homey cookies, perfection when slightly warm and served with cold milk. Any lunch box would be bettered by one or two of these. **Ve**

1 cup (2 sticks) butter, at room temperature

1 cup creamy, natural, unhydrogenated peanut butter (see box, page 323)

1 cup raw (turbinado) sugar

¾ cup packed dark brown sugar

2 eggs

2 teaspoons pure vanilla extract

1½ teaspoons baking soda

2¼ cups unbleached white flour

1½ cups rolled oats (regular oatmeal, not instant)

1 package (12 ounces) semisweet chocolate chips

1 Preheat the oven to 350°F. Line a couple of cookie sheets with parchment paper.

2 In a large bowl, by hand or using a handheld mixer, cream together the butter, peanut butter, and sugars until well combined and a little fluffy. Beat in the eggs and vanilla.

3 Combine the baking soda and flour in a medium-size bowl, and stir it into the butter mixture using a wooden spoon. Then stir in, again by hand (or with your hands—at this point the batter will be pretty stiff), the oats and chocolate chips.

4 Drop the dough by tablespoonfuls (or, if you prefer, shape them by hand into loose balls) onto the prepared cookie sheets, allowing about ¼ inch between cookies (they spread very little).

5 Bake the cookies until they are golden brown, 10 to 13 minutes. Let them cool for 5 minutes on the cookie sheets before transferring them (at least the ones you're not enjoying on the spot) to a rack to finish cooling.

Makes about sixty 2½-inch cookies

SPREAD 'EM! OR DON'T: KNOW YOUR PEANUT BUTTERS

Most major peanut butter brands contain partially hydrogenated oils, or trans fats: oils that have been chemically altered on the molecular level with hydrogen. This changes the oil's consistency from liquid to solid. The resulting substance does not exist in nature and the body really doesn't know how to deal with it: Trans fats raise levels of LDL (bad cholesterol) and lower levels of HDL (good cholesterol). A diet heavy in foods that contain trans fats is clearly, unequivocally linked to increased risk of heart disease. This is more than a question of personal choice; it's a public health issue. Thus, trans fats in foods have been effectively banned in Denmark since 2003, and more recently, in New York City. This is also why one food educator refers to trans fats as "the Darth Vader of processed foods."

Why, then, do peanut butter manufacturers use hydrogenated oils? Solid at room temperature, they keep the oil in PB from separating.

Too, like many "edible foodlike substances" (Michael Pollan's phrase), trans fat–altered peanut butters have a frighteningly long shelf life. So how do you avoid them? Where peanut butter is concerned, it's tricky. It doesn't take much partially hydrogenated oil to serve the manufacturer's ends, so there's a loophole: If the amount of hydrogenated oil is less than 0.5 grams *per serving,* the company can legally say "0 grams of trans fats" or "no trans fats," though of course it's not true. A "serving" of peanut butter is 2 tablespoons; those rascals can get away with putting as much as 8 grams of trans fat in a 16-ounce jar, a jar that comes with a label announcing proudly, "No Trans Fats."

If you want to avoid trans fats, start by reading the list of ingredients on any processed food you buy, nixing all that include "partially hydrogenated" or "hydrogenated." Then go a little further. Choose a natural foods brand that contains just peanuts (preferably organic)

and salt. Such brands usually have about a half-inch of oil at the top. Stir it in when you first open the jar. Once opened and stirred, store the jar in the fridge (which will keep the oil distributed throughout, and will also extend the life of the peanut butter).

Some natural foods brands contain a third ingredient: a little honey, not to sweeten the PB (it's barely detectable as a taste) but to help emulsify the oil, which it does successfully (and without using trans fats). I use and like this type, but vegans will want to avoid it.

What of the freshly ground PB option? You may be surprised to learn I'm not an across-the-board fan of these, because the consumer has no idea how long the peanuts have been sitting out. Though the peanut butter is freshly ground on the spot, the peanuts themselves may not be fresh. One slightly rancid taste of "fresh ground" sent me back to jars. If you do know the peanuts are fresh, or you grind your own in a food processor, great.

Sweet Fava

NUT COOKIES

FAVE DOLCI

S weet favas, or beans of the dead (*fave dei morti*)—we've moved from America to Italy here, with a simple, quietly addictive nut cookie. At first bite you might think,"Good, but doesn't knock my socks off." However, if you are like three certain people (one of whom was me), a batch will be polished off with decaf and good conversation in no time flat. Where *did* those cookies go?

Why "beans of the dead"? Well, fava beans have a history of association with the deceased that goes back to ancient Roman and Greek times, hence these are still made on November first, the traditional Day of the Dead.

Despite the cookie's names, it is beanless. Yet it pays homage to Italy's love of beans: Not much more than ground almonds scented with cinnamon and citrus, these tiny bite-size cookies are deliberately shaped, by hand, into faux favas; rounded, slightly flattened shapes about two-thirds of an inch long, slightly indented at the top. These little pseudo-beans (no one is going to be fooled into thinking they're actual beans, they're too dark and textured) are lovely accompanied by baked apples or pears. Their crunch, simplicity, and not-too-sweet flavor makes them an excellent coffee companion. A labor of love when almonds had to be hand-chopped, with a food processor these are the work of a moment or two. Ve

½ cup minus 1 tablespoon sugar

3½ ounces raw almonds, skin on (about two thirds cup)

½ cup unbleached white flour

¾ teaspoon ground cinnamon (preferably Ceylon or Saigon cinnamon)

1 tablespoon butter, at room temperature

1 egg

Finely grated zest of 1 lemon

1 teaspoon orange flower water (optional; see Note)

❶ Preheat the oven to 350°F. Line a cookie sheet with parchment paper or a silicone baking mat.

❷ Put the sugar and almonds in a food processor. Starting with a pulse-chop (noisy!), then, working up to a steady buzz, grind the nuts and sugar into a coarse, sandy powder. Add the remaining ingredients and pulse a few times more.

❸ Turn out the dough, which will not have come together completely yet, onto a cutting board, and work the ingredients into a stiff, texture-y dough. It will be slightly crumbly but should hold together pretty well.

④ Shape the dough into 6 to 8 small cylinders, each about the length and width of your forefinger. Slice these into little buttons and shape each into a fava bean by indenting one side with your thumb and slightly flattening the other.

⑤ Place the shaped cookies on the prepared cookie sheet. They don't spread, so they can be quite close together.

⑥ Bake until golden brown and quite fragrant, 18 to 20 minutes. Don't overbake them: They burn easily, but even before that they get a little hard and lose their charm. Transfer them to a rack to cool. They'll keep a day or two if put in a tin, but are really best fresh.

Makes 60 small cookies

Note: Orange flower water, sometimes called orange blossom water, is a clear, extraordinarily fragrant distillation of fresh Seville (bitter-orange) blossoms. I use a Lebanese brand, Cortas, which I have found in both conventional and natural foods supermarkets; it's available online, too, at www.Kalustyans.com.

THE LIVELY PYTHAGORAS . . . AND "BEANS OF THE DEAD"

In ancient Rome, so esteemed were legumes that the four leading families took their names from them: Lentullus (lentil), Piso (pea), Cicero (chickpea), and Fabius (fava). Some bean varieties were sacred, offered to the god Apollo. In ancient Greece, besides being eaten, beans were used to cast votes, the white "for," black "against" (you didn't black-ball someone you didn't want in the club; you black-beaned them).

Some cults who believed in reincarnation, most notably the monastic, largely vegetarian followers of Pythagoras, believed human souls traveled to Hades through the stems of bean plants, from there to transmogrify into their next lifetime; it was therefore a sin to eat beans or even walk among the plants. In scholarly circles, the reason for Pythagoras's leguminous prohibition is fiercely debated. It seems unimaginable that the father of mathematics, that most elegant and über-rational discipline, could have believed that you shouldn't walk through a field of favas because your great-grandmother's soul might be on its way to the after-and-before-life. But when Walt Whitman, wrote centuries later, in a wholly other place and time, "I contain multitudes," he clearly spoke for every member of this contradictory human race, including Pythagoras.

SESAME-SEEDED CHICKPEA FLOUR COOKIES
(GHOREYBA SOUMSOUM)

Throughout the Middle East and North Africa you'll find variations of this cookie, which is made from a simple dough combining *toasted* chickpea flour (the toasting is all-important) with wheat flour, fat, and sugar. In this North African version the dough is shaped into fat ropes, rolled firmly in sesame seeds, sliced on the diagonal, and baked to a golden-brown turn. The

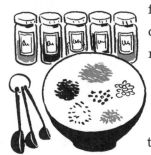

fat is usually a combination of oil and butter, though vegans could replace the butter with Earth Balance or another soy margarine. Western tastes seem to prefer this with a mild oil, but in the region of its origin, olive oil is more often used. I've emphasized the sesame taste by adding a bit of sesame oil, but that's just me; if it isn't you, use an additional tablespoon of oil or butter instead. **Ve** or **Vn**

1½ cups chickpea flour (*besan*; see box, page 279; available at natural foods and Indian foods markets)

½ cup unbleached white flour

¼ teaspoon baking powder

¼ teaspoon salt

½ cup sugar

¼ cup mild vegetable oil, such as canola, corn, peanut, or refined (not toasted) sesame (for a more traditional flavor, use extra-virgin olive oil)

1 tablespoon toasted sesame oil

5 tablespoons unsalted butter or margarine, melted

½ to ⅔ cup hulled sesame seeds

① Preheat the oven to 325°F. Line a cookie sheet with parchment paper or a silicone baking mat.

② Start by toasting the chickpea flour: Place a dry, heavy skillet over medium heat and pour in the chickpea flour. Cook, stirring almost constantly, until the flour darkens and is slightly, toastily, fragrant, 3 to 5 minutes. The second it's done, pour the flour into a food processor (otherwise the residual heat from the pan will continue to cook it, perhaps excessively).

③ Add the white flour, baking powder, salt, and sugar to the food processor. Buzz on and off a few times to blend. Pour in the oils, melted butter, and about 1 tablespoon water and pulse until just combined. You may need to add a bit more water (not much) to make the dough come together into a ball.

④ Turn the dough ball out of the processor and knead it on a lightly floured surface until it is smooth, about 30 seconds. Ready, Freddy.

⑤ Divide the dough ball into six equal parts and roll each into a ball. Roll each ball against the lightly floured surface (the way you made snakes of clay when you were a kid) to make a sausage-shaped log about ¾ inch in diameter and 6 inches long.

⑥ Sprinkle a counter or large cutting board with the sesame seeds and roll each log back and forth in the seeds, turning and pressing lightly to make sure the seeds adhere. Then, with a sharp, thin-bladed knife, slice each roll diagonally into rounds about 1½ inches thick. You'll get about 7 cookies per roll if you press together the little shortened pieces at each end of the rolls to make a single cookie. Transfer the cookies to the prepared cookie sheet.

⑦ Bake the cookies until lightly browned, 12 to 15 minutes, then transfer them to a rack to cool. When cool, they will keep in a tin for up to 3 days. They don't freeze well.

Makes about 40 cookies

ༀ ༀ ༀ

"DON'T HURT YOURSELF" BEAN PIE

Like organized religious movements of every stripe, the American-born Nation of Islam has splintered and fractionated often. During the mid-twentieth century, the period of its greatest growth, it was led by Elijah Muhammad, born Elijah Poole in 1897. One of thirteen children, his parents were emancipated slaves. As Elijah Muhammad, he promoted African American self-reliance, a healthy vegetarian, bean-centric diet, and some fairly out-there beliefs, in my view.

According to Muhammad, not just any bean would do. In his *How to Eat to Live* books (there were two volumes), he spelled it out, "Do not eat field peas, black-eyed peas, speckled peas, red peas or brown peas. Do not eat lima beans, or baby limas. Do not eat any bean but the small navy bean. . . . Simple navy beans [are] one of the best foods that we can eat." His reasoning is not clear; perhaps it is because these other beans were so associated with slavery and poverty?

The bean pie, sometimes called the Muslim bean pie, is a fixture at Black Muslim gatherings, bake sales, and festival food booths and in some neighborhood bakeries. It's made with navy beans and is essentially a rich, sweet, spiced, thickened custard pie, akin to pumpkin pie, but with pureed navy beans instead of pumpkin. Nutmeg and vanilla are always used as flavorings; some cooks occasionally add a bit of cinnamon, ginger, and cloves. It's ridiculously easy to make. Those who've had it remember it fondly and sometimes even pine for it, requesting a periodic fix. Ve

2 cups cooked navy beans (canned are fine), drained well

2 to 3 tablespoons butter, melted (see Notes)

1 tablespoon unbleached white or whole wheat pastry flour

2 eggs

½ teaspoon freshly grated nutmeg

¾ cup sugar

1 cup evaporated milk or half-and-half

2½ teaspoons pure vanilla extract

¼ teaspoon salt

⅛ teaspoon ground cinnamon (optional)

⅛ teaspoon ground ginger (optional)

Tiny smidgen of ground cloves, say ¹⁄₁₆ teaspoon (optional)

1 unbaked 9-inch pie shell, homemade or store-bought (see Notes)

Whipped cream, vanilla ice cream, or vanilla frozen yogurt, for serving (optional)

1 Preheat the oven to 425°F.

2 In a food processor, combine the beans, butter, flour, eggs, nutmeg, sugar, milk, vanilla, and salt. Add the cinnamon, ginger, and/or cloves, if using. Buzz, pausing a couple of times to scrape down the sides of the bowl, to make a smooth puree.

3 When the mixture is uniform, scrape it into the pie shell. Bake for 12 minutes, then lower the heat to 350°F and bake until the crust is golden and the filling is browned and not wobbly in the middle, another 30 minutes or so. Remove the pie from the oven and let it cool on a wire rack.

4 Serve warm or cool, with or without whipped cream. The pie is best eaten the same day, but it will keep, covered with plastic wrap and refrigerated, for up to 2 days. Not that it'll last that long.

Serves 8

Notes: The larger amount of butter adds richness and flavor. Some people go all the way to ⅓ cup melted butter—all-out.

If I'm going with a store-bought crust, I choose a whole wheat, natural, trans fat-free brand from the freezer case.

BEANS THAT AREN'T

Love them we may, call them beans we do, but they are not actual beans. These great pretenders are no kin to Leguminosae family.

★ **CACAO BEANS:** The seeds of *Theobroma cacao,* a tropical evergreen tree 15 to 25 feet tall that originated in the Amazon, and from which we get, of course, chocolate. "Cacao" is how European tongues twisted the native names: the Mayas called it *kawkaw,* the Nahua, *cacahuatl.* Cacao beans resemble large lima beans in shape and come in large poddish seed cases, so it's easy to see how they were misidentified. *Theobroma* means "food of the gods." No surprise there!

★ **COFFEE BEANS:** The seeds of the coffee tree, *Coffea arabica,* also a tropical evergreen tree, which can grow up to 40 feet tall; native to Ethiopia.

★ **VANILLA BEANS:** Fragrant, dried seed pods from the orchid species *Vanilla planifolia* (*Vanilla fragrans*). Its place of origin: the Gulf Coast of Mexico. Vanilla is another lover of the tropics, at home in the humid rain forests of Central and South America, Tahiti, and Madagascar. It grows as a vine, up to 30 feet long. The pods are probably called beans because in shape and size they resemble slightly elongated green beans, though by the time we see 'em, they're dark brown and shriveled.

★ **JELLY BEANS:** A confection consisting of sugar and glucose, starch (usually cornstarch), water, and gelatin. This mixture is mechanically squirted by the hundreds of millions into tiny bean-shaped molds. After being coated with more sugar (to make the firm outer shell of the candy) they're dried. Only then is the color and flavor added.

★ **MR. BEAN:** The clueless title character played by Rowan Atkinson on the eponymous BBC comedy series, which ran for five years. Atkinson has said that various other vegetable-centric names, such as Mr. Cauliflower, were considered before he went leguminous.

★ **L.L.BEAN:** Maine retailer.

★ **THE GREEN BEAN:** My favorite semi-local breakfast-brunch-lunch café, located in Northampton, Massachusetts. Though the bean referred to in the name is the coffee bean (and as we now know, *that's* not really a bean), you'll find plenty of actual beans, in the form of tofu, tempeh, miso, and black beans, all prepared in varied and remarkably appealing big-flavored fashion.

★ **BEANS OF GARLIC:** In some older cookbooks you'll see recipes calling not for a "clove" of garlic but for a "bean." Whatever you call it, it's closer in size to a bean than to a clove, but "clove" won out in the name wars.

★ **BEANBALL:** A baseball colloquialism for a pitch thrown in such a way as to intentionally strike a player on the other team, most often on his or her head (or "bean"). Pitchers who repeatedly throw beanballs are sometimes called headhunters. Beanball is unsporting no matter what you call it, and has nothing to do with beans.

LIME TOFU MOUSSE-CUSTARD

I t's a wonderful thing, isn't it, that a world can contain such heavy caloric pleasures as the White Chocolate & Peanut Butter Banana Cream Pie on page 332 *and* this delectable creamy cloud of delight, piquant with citrus— spoonable, swoonable, but pretty durned healthful? Both are, to my taste, perfect desserts, and either is welcome at my table; but this one appears much more often, since it is healthier. Of all the recipes I've invented over the years, this has to be one of the five or six of which I'm most proud. Why? It's vegan, it's gluten-free, it's free of saturated fat; but more important, it is freely and unadulteratedly delicious, the kind of delicious that brings a whole table of noisy, happy guests to a moment of silent, blissed-out wonder at the first bite. However skeptical you may be of the idea that lime tofu mousse-custard could possibly be this knock-your-socks-off good, well, make it and prepare to be sockless. Don't pass this by.

It's also terrific made with lemon instead of lime. In either case, finely grate the zest of the fruit *before* you juice it. **Vn** **Gf**

¾ cup freshly squeezed lime juice (from 3 to 4 limes)

3 tablespoons cornstarch

2 teaspoons agar-agar (see Notes)

1¾ cups sugar

1 tablespoon plus 2 teaspoons finely grated lime zest (preferably from an organic lime)

1 package (10.5 ounces) silken firm tofu

3 tablespoons raw cashews

2 tablespoons agave syrup

8 paper-thin slices of lime, for garnish

8 fresh raspberries, for garnish (optional)

8 fresh mint leaves, for garnish (optional)

1 Place ½ cup of the lime juice in a small bowl, and whisk into it the cornstarch and agar-agar, making sure it's free of lumps (use your fingers to smush in the cornstarch). Let the mixture sit for 2 minutes.

2 Combine the remaining lime juice with the sugar and 1¾ cups water in a small, nonreactive saucepan, and bring to a boil. Whisk in the cornstarch mixture. The liquid should turn cloudy as you do this, then almost immediately clear up; it will quickly thicken. Turn down the heat to medium-low and let simmer, stirring, for 1 minute. Remove from the heat.

3 Place the lime zest, tofu, cashews, and agave syrup in a food processor and buzz to make a thick, smooth mixture, pausing several times to scrape down the sides of the bowl. You want the cashews really smoothed out. Add the lime juice mixture and buzz again so all is smoothly incorporated.

④ Divide the mousse among small custard cups, ramekins, or sherbet glasses and refrigerate, covered with plastic wrap, until chilled and set up, about 2 hours. Serve with a twist of lime atop each, and, if you like, a raspberry and a mint leaf, too.

Serves 8

Notes: Agar-agar is a vegetarian jelling agent derived from seaweed. It's available at natural foods markets, in different forms: bars, flakes, and powder. I find the latter most satisfactory, and it's what I use here. It serves the function of gelatin, an animal product.

To get the maximum amount of juice, make sure your limes (or lemons) are at room temperature; roll them around on the counter, pressing them lightly against the surface, before you cut them open for squeezing.

ɔ ɔ ɔ

WHITE CHOCOLATE & PEANUT BUTTER BANANA CREAM PIE

In my view, every dessert chapter worthy of the name needs at least one complicated, caloric, but oh-so-worth-it recipe. This is it, and if you are a devotee of old-fashioned cream pies, it's heaven. This began life in a simpler form as a custard pie with peanut butter crumbles—no bananas, no white chocolate—at the Olde Pink House, an antiques-filled restaurant that's an institution in Savannah, Georgia. I've been playing with the recipe since 1984. It's gone from good to out-and-out sublime. It's not a simple quick fix, but it always gets raves, and I have to say, it deserves them.

Make this up to 5 or 6 hours before you intend to serve it, no more, or the bananas will get weepy. But don't do it at the last minute, either; it needs at least 3 hours to cool and set up. I told you it was a bit demanding. Ve

FOR THE PEANUT BUTTER CRUMBLES:

1 cup confectioners' sugar, sifted

¾ cup creamy, natural, unhydrogenated peanut butter (see box, page 323)

1 teaspoon pure vanilla extract

FOR THE CUSTARD:

2½ cups whole milk

4 large egg yolks

¾ cup granulated sugar

¼ cup unbleached white flour

¼ cup cornstarch

6 ounces best-quality white chocolate (see box, page 331), finely chopped

1½ teaspoons pure vanilla extract

FOR THE ASSEMBLY:

1 pie shell (9 inches), baked and cooled

2 ripe bananas, peeled and sliced

1½ cups heavy (whipping) cream, chilled

2 tablespoons Grape-Nuts or Ezekiel 4:9 Whole Grain Flourless cereal; you want small, hard, crunchy nuggets that are unsweetened

① Make the peanut butter crumbles: In a large bowl, using your fingers, mix together the confectioners' sugar, peanut butter, and vanilla to make a crumbly mixture. Divide the mixture in half: one half for the topping, one half to layer with the filling.

② Make the custard: Warm 2¼ cups of the milk in a heavy saucepan over medium heat until it is hot (you want it just under a serious simmer). Meanwhile, in a medium bowl, whisk together the reserved ¼ cup milk, the egg yolks, granulated sugar, flour, and cornstarch until smooth.

③ When the milk is very hot but not boiling, gradually whisk it into the bowl holding the custard mixture until thoroughly combined. Return the whole thing to the saucepan, placing it over medium heat. Whisk and/or stir with a wooden spoon constantly (this allows you to reach the bottom and edges of the pot, where the custard tends to cook first)— really, don't turn your back for a minute. Keep it up until the custard boils and thickens, about 2 minutes.

④ Remove the custard from the heat, transfer it to a clean bowl to stop the cooking, and whisk in the white chocolate and vanilla; whisk until the chocolate is completely melted. Let cool fully.

Cecily: May I offer you some tea, Miss Fairfax?

Gwendolen: [With elaborate politeness.] Thank you. [Aside.] Detestable girl! But I require tea!

Cecily: [Sweetly.] Sugar?

Gwendolen: [Superciliously.] No, thank you. Sugar is not fashionable anymore. [Cecily looks angrily at her, takes up the tongs and puts four lumps of sugar into the cup.]

Cecily: [Severely.] Cake or bread and butter?

Gwendolen: [In a bored manner.] Bread and butter, please. Cake is rarely seen at the best houses nowadays.

Cecily: [Cuts a very large slice of cake, and puts it on the tray.]

—*Oscar Wilde*,
The Importance
of Being Earnest

⑤ Assemble the pie as follows: Sprinkle one quarter of the peanut butter crumbles evenly over the bottom of the baked pie shell. Spoon half the cooled custard over them. Top with the sliced bananas, and then another quarter of the peanut butter crumbles. Spoon the remaining custard over this, mounding it slightly in the center. Cover with plastic wrap and refrigerate for at least 3 hours but no more than 6 hours.

⑥ When ready to serve, uncover the pie. The less delicate among us might well lick the underside of the plastic wrap if no one is watching. Whip the chilled cream in a large, clean bowl until it forms soft, cloudlike peaks; mound it over the pie. Now combine those reserved peanut crumbles with the crunchy cereal in a small bowl. (Just do it. I know it sounds odd. But trust me on this.) Sprinkle these crispy crumbles over the top, and serve with a flourish. This is one pie that is best eaten in one go, the evening of the day it's made. So invite some friends—and make them very, very happy.

Serves 8 extremely lucky people

I'M DREAMING OF A WHITE CHOCOLATE

White chocolate: Some consider it a misnomer, even an abomination. It's true the confection lacks the theobromine-rich cocoa solids that make chocolate brown and bitter, give the cacao plant its botanical name, *Theobroma,* and deliver that slight intoxication chocolate-lovers know and love. But it does have cocoa butter, the cacao bean's fat, another crucial chocolate component, one that contributes richness and meltability and amplifies all the flavors it touches.

I use dark chocolate much more often than white. But white chocolate, much less in-your-face, is also, sometimes, a team player. Its subtleness adds an indefinable, creamy, voluptuous richness. Like all chocolates, it melts when heated and firms when chilled, helping dishes like the White Chocolate & Peanut Butter Banana Cream Pie set up more than they could with thickening alone (white chocolate's setting power, though, is less than that of dark).

"White" is inaccurate; the chocolate is not pure white but a pale, golden off-white, hued by the cocoa butter. Watch out for "white chocolate" that *is* pure white: Its cocoa butter has been replaced with cheaper, inferior fats like hydrogenated oils. These pretenders (sometimes sold as "summer coating") will not have the characteristic white chocolate mouthfeel or flavor. Avoid them. Authentic white chocolate contains cocoa butter, milk solids, sugar, vanilla, and sometimes the soy-based emulsifier lecithin: That's it.

Due to the relatively large percentage of milk solids, white chocolate is persnickety to melt: It's prone to scorching and/or separating, turning lumpy and grainy. This is avoided when, as in this pie, the white chocolate is finely chopped and melted indirectly (by coming into contact with the hot custard mixture).

You can buy white chocolate in pastilles (www.chocolate.com offers them), or ground. (My first choice for the pie is L. A. Burdick's "white hot chocolate"; visit www.burdickchocolate.com.)

ROSE OF PERSIA CAKE

This rich, delectable cake has the texture and grain of pound cake. Moist and tender of crumb, it has the hauntingly floral aroma and flavor only rose water gives. The cake's buttery density is emphasized by the chickpea flour. The recipe combines traditional Iranian ingredients (cherries, pistachios, chickpea flour, that lovely rose water) with a lemon cake recipe that is a family favorite around here. Sift both of the flours before measuring, and then again after. Ve

FOR THE CAKE:

½ cup dried cherries (preferably Bing)

⅓ cup unsweetened sour cherry juice

Vegetable oil cooking spray

1½ cups sifted unbleached white flour, plus 1 tablespoon for the pan

1⅔ cups sugar, plus 1 tablespoon for the pan

1 cup (2 sticks) butter, at room temperature

3 eggs, at room temperature

1½ cups sifted chickpea flour

½ teaspoon baking soda

½ teaspoon salt

¾ cup buttermilk (preferably cultured), or ½ cup plain yogurt whisked with ¼ cup water

2 tablespoons rose water (see Note and box)

2 tablespoons finely grated lemon zest

FOR THE GLAZE:

2 teaspoons rose water

½ cup freshly squeezed lemon juice

1 tablespoon finely grated lemon zest

½ cup sugar

FOR THE GARNISH:

¼ cup shelled pistachios, finely chopped (optional)

1 A few hours before you plan to assemble the cake batter, or even the night before, place the dried cherries in a small bowl, add the cherry juice, and soak to rehydrate the cherries.

2 When you're ready to mix up the cake, preheat the oven to 325°F.

3 Spray a 10-inch tube pan or 12-cup Bundt pan, or even a few small loaf pans, with oil. Combine the 1 tablespoon flour and the 1 tablespoon sugar in a small bowl, and shake this all over the oiled pan to coat. Invert the pan and tap out the excess.

4 In a medium-large bowl, using an electric beater set on high, cream the butter until it's light and fluffy, then gradually add the remaining sugar. Continue beating until the mixture is well combined and even lighter and fluffier. Beat in the eggs, one at a time. Set aside.

5 In a separate large bowl, sift together the remaining white flour with the chickpea flour, baking soda, and salt.

6 Drain the soaked cherries, reserving the cherries and the juice in separate bowls.

7 Combine the buttermilk, rose water, and ¼ cup of the reserved cherry juice (you'll have a small amount of juice left over; reserve it) in a small bowl.

8 Add the flour mixture to the butter mixture, alternating it with the buttermilk mixture, beating together on low speed after each addition just to combine everything; don't overbeat. Stir in the lemon zest and soaked cherries (by hand!) and transfer the batter to the prepared pan.

9 Bake until the top is deeply golden brown, the kitchen is intoxicatingly fragrant, and the cake tests clean, 45 minutes for loaf pans, 1 hour and 10 minutes for a 10-inch tube pan, and somewhere in the middle for a 12-inch Bundt. Let the cake cool in its pan(s) on a rack for 10 minutes while you make the glaze.

10 Combine all of the glaze ingredients plus the reserved cherry soaking liquid in a small saucepan and bring it to a boil, stirring to dissolve the sugar. Turn down the heat and let simmer until slightly thickened, keeping a close eye on it; this should take 4 to 5 minutes. You want the glaze quite liquidy, the better to soak into the cake.

11 Turn the cake out of its pan(s) and onto a serving plate. While it's still warm, slowly pour/spread/spoon about a third of the glaze over the cake, allowing the cake to absorb as much as possible. Poke a few holes in the cake with a toothpick, then pour any remaining glaze over the top. While the cake is still warm and sticky, sprinkle it with the finely chopped pistachios, if using.

Since this cake is so moist, it keeps well, covered, for 3 to 4 days, though the odds are good it'll never last that long. Given its stickiness, a cake dish with its own domed lid is ideal for storing, but plastic wrap will also do.

Serves 12

Note: Rose water can be purchased at www.theindianfoodstore.com.

PERSIAN ROSES

Countless Persian desserts are flavored with rose water, an aromatic liquid whose fragrance wafts throughout the Middle East and India. In Persia—present-day Iran—the nut-filled rose-water pastries enjoyed throughout the region (the one we know best is baklava) are deliberately formed into the shape of a rose, with filo petals and nuts piled in a small central cone to represent stamen and pollen.

Why is the world's best-loved flower so especially revered in Iran? Simple: The rose is a native.

The word "rose" itself is derived from ancient Persian, and the technology by which fresh roses are transformed for use in perfumes, cooking, medicine, and cosmetics was developed there.

The rose fields of Qamsar are legendary: Their flowers are said to have the most exquisite fragrance of all. The rose water created here is considered so superlative throughout the Arab world that it is sent annually to Mecca, where it is used to ritually wash the Kaaba, the cube-shaped central building that devout Muslim pilgrims circle seven times.

KING CAKE
Dragon Style

Here's a cake as round as life itself, traditionally served at the Christian feast day of Epiphany (January 6). It's common in New Orleans, where gateaus range from a fairly plain brioche-type or challah dough twisted into a ring and gaudily decorated with purple, green, and yellow-gold icing or tinted sugar sparkles (traditional Carnival colors) to countless elaborations. Each cake contains a bean—just one, highly purposeful—and the person who gets the piece with the bean becomes "king" or "queen" for the next year (meaning he or she has to provide that year's cake or party).

I take my king cake much farther than slightly dressed-up bread dough, using my recipe for the German *stollen.* Incredibly, devastatingly rich, it's a yeasted, truly kingly pastry—floral with cardamom, wealthy with butter in the dough and glaze. A tiny slice is a dessert fit for royalty, not just a vehicle for the token bean. This cake is what I make when I'm asked to bring a dessert to winter holiday parties. The bean goes in only at Epiphany.

This dough is not as neat and malleable as a simple enriched yeast bread dough would be; you can't braid or twist it, thus it's shaped into loaves. And the browned butter–confectioners' sugar glaze is far more low-key visually than the tricolored icings of New Orleans. It may seem to you fussy to brown the butter, and lord, what a lot of butter it is, after what's already in the cake. But I wouldn't steer you wrong: *Don't skip the browned-butter glaze.*

Start this magical pastry the night before; the dough must be refrigerated overnight. Ve

FOR THE DOUGH:

8 cardamom pods

1 cup milk, scalded

2 scant tablespoons (or two 2¼-ounce packages) active dry yeast

¼ cup warm water

⅓ cup sugar

About 4 cups unbleached white flour

½ cup (1 stick) butter, cold, cut into 8 pieces

½ teaspoon salt

1 tablespoon finely grated lemon zest (preferably from an organic lemon)

1 egg plus 2 egg yolks

½ cup slivered almonds, toasted

FOR THE ASSEMBLY AND FINISH:

10 ounces (1 cup plus 2 slightly scant tablespoons) almond paste

2 large dried beans, either limas or favas

½ cup (1 stick) butter

About 1 cup confectioners' sugar

1 Line two rimmed baking sheets with parchment paper. Set aside. Place the cardamom pods in a small, heat-proof bowl and pour the hot milk over them.

2 While the cardamom infuses the milk, combine the yeast, warm water, and 1 teaspoon of the sugar in a medium bowl. Set aside to let the yeast soften and dissolve, about 10 minutes.

3 Return to the milk, which should still be warm. Squeeze open the now-soft cardamom pods to distribute their small black seeds in the milk. Discard the pods. Stir the warm cardamom milk into the yeast mixture, then beat in 1 cup of the flour until it's incorporated. Cover this mixture, called the "sponge," with plastic wrap and let it rise in a warm place for 30 minutes.

4 While the sponge rises, place 2 cups of the flour and the cold butter, salt, and remaining sugar in a food processor. Pulse 6 to 8 times to combine.

5 When the sponge has had its 30-minute rise, add it to the processor with the lemon zest, egg, and egg yolks. Buzz until the dough is thoroughly mixed, 20 to 30 seconds. Then, with a few quick pulses, add the almonds and another ½ cup of flour. Transfer the dough, which will be quite tender, to a bowl. Refrigerate, covered, overnight.

6 In the morning, punch down the dough and divide it in half. On a flour-sprinkled bread board, gently pull and pat half the dough into a thickish rectangle, about 14 inches long by 10 inches wide.

7 Divide the almond paste in half and set one portion aside for the second cake. Using your hands, scatter an ample line of almond paste bits the length of the dough rectangle, about a third of the way up. Somewhere along the almond paste line, place one of the two beans, pressing it into the dough slightly. Fold the larger portion of the dough over the almond paste, gently enclosing it (and the bean). You now have a narrower, plumpish rectangle. Make it more circular, with your hands. Continuing to round it, carefully transfer the dough to one of the parchment-lined baking sheets.

8 Repeat with the second half of the dough, the remaining almond paste, and bean number 2.

9 Once the rounds of dough are on the baking sheets, let them rise, covered with a clean towel, in a warm place until puffy, though not quite doubled in bulk, another hour or so.

10 In the last 10 minutes of the rise, preheat the oven to 350°F.

11 Bake the cakes until a deep golden brown and beautifully fragrant, 22 to 32 minutes.

12 Toward the end of the baking time, place the ½ cup butter in a small saucepan over medium heat and melt it. Then, lowering the heat slightly and keeping an eye on it, let the butter cook until it's browned and fragrant, about 8 minutes. Don't stir the butter as it browns, but you can shake the pan a little.

13 When the cakes come out of the oven, cool them on racks for about 10 minutes, then spoon the browned butter over the tops. While the surface is still buttery and moist, sift the confectioners' sugar generously over the top. Let cool at least 20 minutes more, by which time the sugar will have set to some degree. Serve, in thin slices, slightly warm or at room temperature. If tightly wrapped and frozen, a king's cake will keep for 2 to 3 months.

Makes 2 cakes, each serving 8 to 10

ᕙ ᕙ ᕙ

GREEN GRAM PAYASAM

There's no American equivalent to *payasam,* a much-loved stovetop Indian pudding, which is semi-liquid, served scaldingly hot, and heavy as all get-out (which is why it may be such an occasional treat). Payasams may be an acquired taste, especially this one, with its base of "green gram," known to us as mung beans. But if you grew up with it, you'll have regular cravings for it. I have to admit that when I lived in India, I did love it once in a while. In the south of India, this is traditionally served on Vishu Day (New Year's Day) and Pongal (harvest festival). **Ve Gf**

1 cup mung beans (labeled "green gram" or "moong" in Indian stores), soaked overnight in 3 cups water, well drained and rinsed

½ cup full-fat coconut milk

½ cup whole milk

½ cup packed dark brown sugar

Seeds scraped from 2 cardamom pods

Dash of salt

¼ cup ghee

❶ Place the soaked, rinsed mung beans in a small, heavy pot and cover with 2 cups cold water. Bring to a hard boil, then lower to a simmer and let cook, uncovered, until the beans are soft, 15 to 20 minutes (they're tiny, so they cook fast).

❷ Add the coconut and dairy milks, brown sugar, cardamom seeds, and salt, and stir well to combine.

❸ Raise the heat slightly. Do not leave the stove! Stand there and stir, constantly, until the sugar has dissolved and the mixture is thick, about 10 minutes.

❹ Stir in the ghee and serve, very hot. You can keep the payasam hot, covered, over very, *very* low heat for up to an hour, but it is not meant to be chilled and reheated, nor, for that matter, eaten cold. Ever.

Makes 6 to 8 small, rich servings

RED BEAN ICE CREAM

A lot of commercial red bean ice creams are just your basic, junky, mass-produced ice creams made with inferior ingredients like gums and thickeners, with a little of the red-bean paste called *anko* stirred in. Not so the following: a custard-based, from-scratch ice cream, enriched with enough anko so that you really get both its flavor and the extra creaminess contributed by its starch. The vanilla is optional; some feel it detracts from the red-beaniness, but I think it enhances it.

If you want to go to town with this one, serve it in scoops sprinkled with a little *matcha* (brightly colored powdered green tea), and offer matcha-flavored meringues (see page 341) alongside; you can make them from the egg whites you'll have left over from the ice cream.

Those who are allergic to dairy products can make this using canned full-fat unsweetened coconut milk: substitute 4 cups for the milk and cream. **Ve** **Gf**

3 cups whole milk

1 cup heavy (whipping) cream

⅔ cup sugar

⅛ teaspoon salt

3 egg yolks

2 tablespoons cornstarch

1¾ cups Anko (red-bean paste; recipe follows)

1 tablespoon pure vanilla extract (optional)

❶ Set aside ¼ cup of the milk in a small bowl. Combine the rest of the milk with the heavy cream and ⅓ cup of the sugar in a heavy, medium-large pot over medium heat. Let the milk mixture get very hot but not quite scalded.

❷ Meanwhile, combine the remaining ⅓ cup sugar, the salt, and the egg yolks in

a heat-proof bowl, and whisk until the yolks thicken slightly and get lighter in color.

❸ Add the cornstarch to the milk you set aside in the small bowl, smushing it in with your fingertips to make an absolutely smooth paste.

❹ When the milk and cream mixture is almost boiling, whisk in the cornstarch slurry, which should thicken the milk almost immediately. Turn the heat down to medium-low.

❺ With a ladle in one hand and a whisk in the other, and a wooden spoon next to the stove, ladle some of the hot milk mixture into the yolk mixture, whisking for all you're worth as you do so. After two ladlefuls have been whisked into the yolk mixture, pour the now-tempered yolk mixture into the pot of hot milk, and whisk the whole thing hard.

6 Now stand there and stir constantly, watching carefully, until the eggs further thicken the milk, though only slightly, 3 to 4 minutes. Because we're doing this over direct heat rather than in a more time-consuming double-boiler, stir mindfully, alternating between the whisk to incorporate everything and the wooden spoon to get into the corners, where the eggs would otherwise tend to cook first.

7 The minute the custard has thickened, transfer it from the pot to a clean heat-proof bowl and whisk in the anko and the vanilla, if using. Let cool to room temperature (if you want to speed this up, set the bowl in a sink partially filled with ice water), then cover it and refrigerate it overnight.

8 The next day, transfer the custard into your ice cream maker and let 'er rip according to the manufacturer's instructions. When the ice cream is done, remove the dasher, fight over who gets to lick it, be nice and share, and transfer the finished ice cream to a storage container. Place the container in the freezer and store until you're just about ready to serve (like all ice creams, this is most full-flavored when softened slightly).

Makes a scant 2 quarts

Asian Desserts Using Anko (Red-Bean Paste)

A thick, sweet bean paste called *anko* or simply *an* is as frequently used in the desserts of Japan, China, Malaysia, and many other Asian countries as, say, chocolate is in the West. If you're trying to wrap your mind around anko, think of it as a slightly starchy jam-like concoction, where beans are sugared and cooked down instead of fruits. Sometimes it's left a little chunky and textured; sometimes it's completely smooth. It's used in *mizu-yokan,* a jellied sweet most often served in summer in Japan, as well as in *manju,* elaborately decorated anko-filled steamed dumplings most often served in fall. And as ice cream has become an all-over-the-world favorite, of course there's red bean ice cream, too—also made with anko.

Anko is most often made with adzuki beans (sometimes spelled minus the z or d), but can also be made with mung or navy beans, resulting, respectively, in a yellowish-brown anko or a gray-beige one. They taste much the same, but I think the dark reddish paste made from adzuki beans is the most appealing.

What do you do with anko? Again, think of it as you would a kind of jam. People who grew up with it even spread it on toast (a fusion snack, in rice-eating cultures). I've used it to fill crepes (a Japanese standard), and instead of jelly in thumbprint cookies (just use your favorite vanilla or almond butter cookie). Here, I've used it in a red bean ice cream that I guarantee will put to shame any commercial ones you may have had.

Anko

Mixing up a batch of anko is simplicity itself. This is slightly less sweet than most Japanese versions. Feel free to add more sugar if you like, though this is plenty for me.

Although most Chinese sweet bean pastes are sieved for extreme smoothness and incorporate oil or lard for a richer mouthfeel, I prefer this method, which is lighter.

> 1 cup dried adzuki beans, picked over, rinsed, soaked overnight in cold water to cover (see page 344), and drained
>
> ½ cup plus 2 tablespoons packed light brown sugar
>
> ½ teaspoon salt

1 Put the soaked beans in a medium-size, heavy pot, cover them with water to a depth of 2 inches, and bring to a boil. Boil the beans for 5 minutes, then drain them through a colander and rinse. Repeat. After the second boil-drain-rinse cycle, cover the beans a third time, this time with 3 cups cold water. Let the beans simmer, uncovered, skimming off any foam that accumulates, until they're tender, 30 minutes to 1 hour.

2 At this point, there should still be plenty of liquid along with the beans in the pot. They need not be covered completely, but they should be, as I say, swimming. If not, add another cup or so of hot water. Stir in the brown sugar and salt and keep simmering the beans gently, stirring them often.

3 Using a potato masher, begin breaking up the cooking beans into a chunky, thick, pastelike mash, stirring more and more

often after this point to prevent sticking. Continue simmering until most, but not all, of the liquid has evaporated; the beans will continue to thicken, absorbing water as they cool. Remove the mashed beans from the heat and set aside. If you want a smooth puree, let the anko cool slightly, then run it through a food processor. Store it, tightly covered, in the fridge for up to a week. **Vn Gf**

Makes about 2½ cups

Matcha Meringues

I've loved meringues since childhood— their crisp outsides, their slightly soft interiors, their sweetness, and the way they just dissolve in your mouth. My mother used to bring home bakery meringues that were studded with walnuts, chocolate chips, and date pieces—my faves.

Meringues are made with just two main ingredients: stiffly beaten egg whites and superfine sugar. Cream of tartar helps maintain the all-important airy structure of the egg whites. The rest: Embellishment.

These pistachio-green *matcha* meringues look like they were colored for St. Patrick's Day, but one taste of that haunting green tea-ness and the French cookie with the Irish looks suddenly transports you to the Far East. This recipe is perfect for using up the three egg whites you'll have left over from the Red Bean Ice Cream on page 339, to which they are a fine accompaniment. **Ve**

> 2 tablespoons matcha green tea powder
>
> ¼ cup confectioners' sugar
>
> 3 egg whites
>
> ¼ teaspoon cream of tartar
>
> ½ cup superfine sugar (see Note)

1 Preheat the oven to 200°F. Place a rack in the center of the oven. Line a cookie sheet with a silicone baking mat or parchment paper.

2 Into a small bowl, sift together the matcha powder and the confectioners' sugar. Set aside.

3 Get out a medium-large bowl and an electric mixer with a whisk attachment (or beaters) and make sure they're scrupulously clean. (Even a trace of fat will mess things up; the egg whites won't reach their desired maximum volume.) Place the egg whites in the bowl and beat them on low-medium speed until foamy. Add the cream of tartar and continue to beat until the whites hold soft peaks. Add the superfine sugar and then the matcha mixture very gradually, a tablespoon at a time. Continue to beat until the meringue holds very stiff peaks. Rub a little between your thumb and forefinger; it should feel smooth, with no discernible grit. If it does feel gritty, the sugar isn't fully dissolved, so keep beating until it feels smooth between your fingers.

4 If you're using parchment paper (and not a silicone baking mat), here's a neat trick: Put a teeny dab of meringue on the underside of each corner of the paper. This will keep it from curling or sliding off the sheet.

5 Though you can pipe the meringue through a pastry bag fitted with a ½-inch tip and create nice neat rows of meringues that are each about 1 to 1½ inches in diameter, I usually use two spoons to place mounds of the meringue mixture onto the prepared cookie sheet.

6 Bake the meringues until they are a slightly deeper pale green than when you put them in, and are crisp and firm on the outside, 1½ to 1¾ hours. To ensure even baking, rotate the baking sheet from front to back about halfway through the baking time.

7 Turn off the oven and open its door a crack. Leave the meringues in the oven to finish drying overnight. In dry weather, the meringues will keep in a tin for up to a week.

Note: If you just have regular granulated white sugar, dump it in a food processor and buzz it to superfineness, about 30 seconds.

Makes about 2 dozen 1- to 1½-inch meringues

A Few Last Words from the Author

The bean itself is a wheel of life everlasting, as we said in the very beginning of this book, and back to which we loop as we close.

Wherever you are in your life's cycle—sprouting or green, cooked or raw, waiting out some personal or actual winter or celebrating spring or midsummer—I wish you the faith, through famine and feast, that you too, and our bean-eating, bean-loving race, will not just survive but thrive. That you will grow again, to nourish and be nourished, feed and be fed, love and be loved, as the wheel spins us through our brief sojourn here and we take our places at the vast, ever-changing table.

—Crescent Dragonwagon,
Westminster West, Vermont

Basic Beanery

NAME(S)	ORIGIN & CHARACTERISTICS	SOAKING & COOKING
Adzuki (AKA ADUKI, AZUKI, RED COWPEA, RED ORIENTAL)	Himalayan native, now grown throughout Asia. Especially loved in Japan. Small, nearly round red bean with a thread of white along part of the seam. Slightly sweet, starchy. Lower in oligosaccharides.	**SOAKED, CONVENTIONAL STOVETOP:** 40 minutes. **UNSOAKED, CONVENTIONAL STOVETOP:** 1¼ hours. **SOAKED, PRESSURE COOKER:** 5–7 minutes. **UNSOAKED, PRESSURE COOKER:** 15–20 minutes.
Anasazi (AKA CAVE BEAN AND NEW MEXICO APPALOOSA—THOUGH IT ISN'T ONE)	New World native (present-day junction of Arizona, New Mexico, Colorado, Utah). White speckled with burgundy to rust-brown. Slightly sweet, a little mealy. Lower in oligosaccharides.	**SOAK?** Yes. **CONVENTIONAL STOVETOP:** 2–2½ hours. **PRESSURE COOKER:** 15–18 minutes at full pressure; let pressure release gradually. **SLOW-COOKER:** 1½ hours on high, then 6 hours on low.
Appaloosa	New World native. Slightly elongated, curved, one end white, the other end mottled with black and brown. Holds its shape well; slightly herbaceous-piney in flavor, a little mealy. Lower in oligosaccharides.	**SOAK?** Yes. **CONVENTIONAL STOVETOP:** 2–2½ hours. **PRESSURE COOKER:** 15–18 minutes; let pressure release gradually. **SLOW-COOKER:** 1½ hours on high, then 6–7 hours on low.
Black-eyed pea (AKA BLACK-EYES, LOBIA, CHAWALI)	West African native, now grown and loved worldwide. An ivory-white cowpea with a black "eye" across the indentation. Distinctive ashy, mineral-y taste, starchy texture.	**SOAK?** Optional. **SOAKED, CONVENTIONAL STOVETOP:** 20–30 minutes. **UNSOAKED, CONVENTIONAL STOVETOP:** 45–55 minutes. **SOAKED, PRESSURE COOKER:** 5–7 minutes. **UNSOAKED, PRESSURE COOKER:** 9–11 minutes.

★ *All cooking times are approximate. The older the bean is, the longer it will take to cook. Always taste for tenderness about three-quarters of the way through the shorter suggested time when using a conventional pot or slow-cooker. When using a pressure cooker, stop the cooking at the earlier end of the cooking range, let pressure release gradually, open, and taste. If not tender, reseal the lid and bring it back up to high pressure for the remaining time.*

AVAILABILITY	SUBSTITUTES	USAGE
Widely available in natural foods markets and Asian groceries.	Mung beans can and often do serve as a substitute—similar taste and cooking time—but visually quite different.	Sweetened and made into a paste, used in many Asian desserts, including moon cakes and ice cream. Cooked with sticky rice (Japan). Cooked with butter and sugar as a pudding (Somalia). Bean of choice for dahls in North India.
Occasionally available in natural foods markets, specialty foods stores. Online: Purcell's Mountain Farm; Rancho Gordo; Bob's Red Mill; Adobe Milling of Dove Creek.	Pinto, pink, tepary, "real" appaloosa. Though different visually and tastewise, navy and black beans work functionally.	Usually in stews with Southwestern seasonings (chile, cumin, garlic, onion, peppers). Sometimes used in baked beans in the Southwest (often added: ham, bacon, or salt pork). In Southwest, often served at festivals honoring Native Americans.
Not in most supermarkets. Online: Rancho Gordo; Bob's Red Mill; Purcell's Mountain Farm.	Pinto, pinquito, anasazi, tepary. Though different visually and tastewise, navy and black beans work functionally.	Usually cooked as a stew, with Southwestern seasonings (see above). Often ham, bacon, or salt pork is added. Also sometimes used in baked beans in the Southwest.
Widely available in supermarkets.	All cowpeas share about the same cooking time, though each differs slightly in flavor. Lady, crowder, cream, clay, and pigeon peas, or goat's eye or asparagus beans work in black-eyed pea recipes.	*Akkra,* a deep-fried fritter (Africa). *Buñelo,* a similar fritter (Colombia). *Chèotâutráng,* a sweet pudding (Thailand). Tossed with olive oil, vegetables, and lemon (Greece). As Hoppin' John and Texas Caviar (U.S.). In many regional curries (India). Also a traditional side dish for a meal of cod and potatoes (Portugal).

Yields for virtually all dried beans: 1 cup dried beans, peas, or lentils equals 2¼ to 2½ cups cooked.

NAME(S)	ORIGIN & CHARACTERISTICS	SOAKING & COOKING
Black bean (AKA TURTLE BEAN, BLACK VALENTINE, *FRIJOL NEGRO, FEIJÃO PRETO*)	New World native. Shiny, true black uncooked; cooking liquid turns smoky-purplish. Creamy texture when cooked. Flavor has an unusual, faintly sweet note, reminiscent of some chocolate.	**SOAK?** Yes. **CONVENTIONAL STOVETOP:** 1½–2 hours. **PRESSURE COOKER:** 15–18 minutes at full pressure; let pressure release gradually. **SLOW-COOKER:** 1½ hours on high, then 6–7 hours on low.
Cannellini (WHITE KIDNEY BEAN; ALSO AVAILABLE AS FLOUR, OR *BESAN*)	New World (Argentina) native, now much loved and used in Italy. White, slightly elongated. Creamy texture, pleasingly bland, slightly nutty.	**SOAK?** Yes. **CONVENTIONAL STOVETOP:** Cook at a full, hard boil for 10 minutes, then cook slowly 1½–2 hours. **PRESSURE COOKER:** 11–13 minutes; let pressure release gradually. **SLOW-COOKER:** Boil on stovetop for 10 minutes, then transfer to cooker for 1 hour on high, then 6–7 hours on low.
Chickpea (GARBANZO, CECE, CECI, CHANNA)	Middle East (probably Turkey) native. Round, pale yellow to light brown, with a ridge on one side. Slow to cook, holds its shape well, has a pleasant, nutty flavor and slightly mealy texture.	**SOAK?** Yes. **CONVENTIONAL STOVETOP:** 2–3 hours. **PRESSURE COOKER:** 12–15 minutes; let pressure release gradually. **SLOW-COOKER:** 2 hours on high, then 6½–7½ hours on low.
Desi dahl ALSO AVAILABLE AS FLOUR, OR *BESAN*.	*Desi dahl* is a second variety of chickpea—smaller, firmer, darker, more wrinkled, a staple of Indian home cooking; used in channa dahl.	

AVAILABILITY	SUBSTITUTES	USAGE
Widely available in supermarkets.	For cooking properties, interchangeable with most New World beans, including cranberry, pinto, navy, and many more. But for flavor and color, nothing else looks or tastes like black beans.	*Feijoada* (Brazil). *Moors y Christianos* soup (Cuba). In New Mexico, served with every Southwestern plate by default. Common in chili, especially chili mole; and in soup, often with sherry (U.S.). Excellent in bean-burgers; flavor compatible with mushrooms.
In some supermarkets. Online: Purcell's Mountain Farm; Rancho Gordo.	Interchangeable with most New World beans, but navy and Great Northern are closest visually.	Often used in minestrone, *pasta e fagioli*, and other Tuscan bean soups. Also marinated and used as an appetizer or addition to salad (Italy).
The European/Middle Eastern variety is widely available.	The chickpea is sui generis. It's one of the slowest-cooking beans (second only to the soybean) and is shaped like no other bean, with a flavor and texture like no other bean. If you fall in love with a chickpea recipe but want to make it with some other bean, fine; just adjust cooking time according to the bean cooked. You'll have a good result, it just won't be chickpea-ish.	Base for hummus and falafel, and used in many soups (Middle East). Used in countless curries, especially with potato and cauliflower, as well as a plain dahl (India). The whole cooked beans, in sugar syrup, are also eaten as a sweet and used in a variety of desserts (Philippines). Part of most three-bean salads, and often a component of bean-burgers (U.S.).
Desi dahl is available at any Indian market. *Besan* is available at many natural foods markets, Indian groceries, and through Bob's Red Mill.	See comments above.	*Desi dahl*, curried, is classic Indian home cooking. Flour is an ingredient in batter for deep-fried vegetables (India). Used in shortbreadlike cookies (Persia/Iran), and in flatbreads (*panelle*, Sicily; socca, France).

NAME(S)	ORIGIN & CHARACTERISTICS	SOAKING & COOKING
Cranberry (AKA BORLOTTI, TONGUES OF FIRE, DRAGON'S TONGUE)	New World (Colombia) native. Ivory or tan, beautifully mottled with striations of red, burgundy, even bright pink. A melting, creamy texture; a little nutlike; very pleasing.	**SOAK?** Yes. **CONVENTIONAL STOVETOP:** 1½–2 hours. **PRESSURE COOKER:** 11–13 minutes. **SLOW-COOKER:** 1½ hours on high, then 6 hours on low.
Fava (AKA BROAD BEAN, HORSE BEAN, BELL BEAN, WINDSOR BEAN) SOLD WHOLE WITH SKIN ON, OR SPLIT, SKIN REMOVED. FOR FRESH FAVAS, SEE PAGE 44.	North Africa native. Shaped like fat, bumpy lima beans, dried favas are usually golden brown, with the occasional ivory bean. Tough-skinned, they must be peeled after soaking. Smooth, creamy, a little buttery, with a trace of bitterness.	**SOAK?** Yes, for whole favas. No, for split, peeled favas. **EXTRA STEP FOR WHOLE BEANS:** After soaking, pop each fava out of its skin, discarding the skins. **CONVENTIONAL STOVETOP:** whole peeled favas, 1–1¾ hours; peeled and split, 40 minutes. In either case, cook until disintegrated and creamy. **CANNOT BE PRESSURE-COOKED.** **SLOW-COOKER:** whole peeled favas, 1 hour on high, then 3–4 hours on low. Peeled and split favas, 40 minutes on high, then 2–3 hours on low. In either case, cook until disintegrated and creamy.
Flageolet	New World native, an immature kidney bean, grown, developed, and adored in France. Smallish beans are pale green, with an occasional ivory one sneaking in; turn ivory-golden when cooked. Creamy, agreeable.	**SOAK?** Yes. **CONVENTIONAL STOVETOP:** 1¾–2¼ hours. **PRESSURE COOKER:** 15–20 minutes. **SLOW-COOKER:** 1¾ hours on high, then 6–7 hours on low.
Gigande (GIANT LIMA, GIANT BUTTER BEAN, *ELEPHANTE*, ELEPHANT BEAN)	New World origin, but bred and now primarily grown and eaten in Greece. Shaped like a giant lima, this is a huge, sweet-starchy white bean.	**SOAK?** Yes. **CONVENTIONAL STOVETOP:** 1¼–1½ hours. **PRESSURE COOKER:** 11–13 minutes. **SLOW-COOKER:** 1½ hours on high, then 6–7 hours on low.
Great Northern	New World native. A white bean, slightly larger than the navy bean, bland, meltingly textured, starchy.	**SOAK?** Yes. **CONVENTIONAL STOVETOP:** 1½–2 hours. **PRESSURE COOKER:** 11–13 minutes. **SLOW-COOKER:** 1½ hours on high, then 6–7 hours on low.

AVAILABILITY	SUBSTITUTES	USAGE
Not in most supermarkets. Online: Purcell's Mountain Farm; Rancho Gordo; Bob's Red Mill.	If you're substituting visually, pinto beans look very similar to cranberry, but are quite different in taste. Cannellini or red kidney beans are closer taste-alikes, but don't look like cranberry beans.	*Barbunya,* with slow-cooked tomatoes, vegetables, lots of olives (Turkey). Used in soups and stews, often with spicy sausage (Portugal). Sometimes in *fagioli* and in a hearty Piedmontese risotto with sausage (Italy).
At Middle Eastern and specialty foods stores; at some natural foods markets. Online: Shamra sells two varieties of whole dried favas and one split. Whole dried favas also available through Purcell's Mountain Farm and La Tienda. Peeled, split fava available through Kalamala, where they are called "yellow favas" (Golchin).	The closest approximation for the flavor and texture of dried split favas is cooked yellow split peas. But to true fava lovers, there is no substitute.	*Ful Medames,* favas cooked with oil, cumin, lemon, and onions, often for breakfast (Egypt). *Baghalee polo,* rice cooked with favas (Persia/Iran). *Skordalia,* garlicky fava bean dip (Greece). In stews, and made into flour (Ethiopia). *Bagiana,* a fava soup with onions, garlic, beet greens, olive oil, and lard (Italy). A single fava bean baked in a cake for luck (many countries).
Hard to find; available at some specialty foods stores. Online: Rancho Gordo and Purcell's Mountain Farms.	Cannellini beans are a good substitute, and navy beans are fine in a pinch.	Traditional in cassoulet, as well as cooked and mashed and served like mashed potatoes with lamb (France). Good in soups, and also cooked, marinated, and served as a salad or starter.
Available in Mediterranean specialty foods stores. Online: Purcell Mountain Farms.	While baby or Fordhook limas would work as a miniature substitute visually; the whole point of this bean is its unique size, shape, and texture.	With garlic, olive oil, tomatoes, and fresh dill as a side dish or starter (Greece). Also excellent in soups.
Readily available.	Navy beans or cannellini.	Often used instead of navy beans in baked beans, soups, or pies. Since it holds its shape well and is a bit larger than navies, it's sometimes cooked and used marinated in salads.

NAME(S)	ORIGIN & CHARACTERISTICS	SOAKING & COOKING
Kidney bean (RED BEAN, CHILI BEAN, *RAJMA*)	New World native. Kidney shaped, shiny dark-red seed coat. Cooks up creamy, with a little sweetness. Mild in flavor.	**SOAK?** Yes. **CONVENTIONAL STOVETOP:** Cook at a full, hard boil for 10 minutes, then cook slowly 1½–2 hours. **PRESSURE COOKER:** 11–13 minutes; let pressure release gradually. **SLOW-COOKER:** Boil on stovetop for 10 minutes, then transfer to cooker, 1 hour on high, then 6–7 hours on low.
Lentil SEE "LUSCIOUS LENTILS & OTHER LOVABLE LITTLE LEGUMES," PAGE 354.		
Lima, baby (BUTTER BEAN, *HABA*)	New World (Peru) native. Flattened, parchment-white, smaller bean. Smooth, creamy, a little sweet. Cooked, they're quite soft and don't hold their shape well.	**SOAK?** Yes. **CONVENTIONAL STOVETOP:** 1¼–1¾ hours. **PRESSURE COOKER:** 10–12 minutes. **SLOW-COOKER:** 1 hour on high, then 6 hours on low.
Lima, large (Fordhook)	Larger version of the above. Cooking times, et al, apply, but the larges hold their shape better than the babies when cooked.	
Lima, Christmas (AKA POPE'S BEAN, CHESTNUT LIMA)	New World (Peru) native. Large, flattened, parchment-white, mottled with a deep burgundy. A little sweet, slightly mealy, with a distinct chestnut-like flavor. Hold their shape better than other limas.	**SOAK?** Yes. **CONVENTIONAL STOVETOP:** 1¼–1¾ hours. **PRESSURE COOKER:** 10–12 minutes. **SLOW-COOKER:** 1 hour on high, then 6 hours on low.
Mung (MOONG, GREEN GRAM, MOOG) SPLIT MUNG BEANS, THEIR SEED COATS REMOVED, ARE CALLED *MOONG DAHL*, AND ARE YELLOW.	India/Pakistan native. Small, almost round, green with a small white stripe along part of its seam. Mild and starchy, a tiny bit mealy.	**SOAK?** Optional. **SOAKED, CONVENTIONAL STOVETOP:** 40 minutes. **UNSOAKED, CONVENTIONAL STOVETOP:** 1¼ hours. **SOAKED, PRESSURE COOKER:** 5–7 minutes. **UNSOAKED, PRESSURE COOKER:** 15–20 minutes.

AVAILABILITY	SUBSTITUTES	USAGE
Readily available.	Cannellini (for flavor and texture), pintos for looks.	Used in many curries (India). Used in New Orleans's famed red beans and rice, and always present in three-bean salads (U.S.).
Readily available.	Navy beans.	In stews, with chicken, lamb, or beef. In rice dishes made with fresh limas in season and dried the rest of the time, including *Dami-e Baghala,* with turmeric, and *Shevid Baghali,* with fresh dill (Persia/Iran). As a "soup bean" with ham, served with cornbread, and in Brunswick Stew (U.S., South).
Readily available.	Navy beans, though they're smaller	As above. And fresh Fordhook are divine—chestnutty and sweet.
Available in some specialty foods stores and natural foods markets. Online: Rancho Gordo or Purcell Mountain Farms.	No other beans have the distinctive look, size, and chestnut flavor of Christmas Limas.	Marvelous in any bean soup, also excellent creamed. Cooked, mashed, sweetened, and covered with whipped cream, they're a dead ringer for the chestnut puree that is key to the French dessert Mont Blanc.
Available at any natural foods store or market.	Adzuki beans—very similar in cooking properties, texture, and taste, but visually different.	Often used for sprouting. Green gram, a mild curry served with whole wheat dosa (South India). *Ginisang mongg,* mung bean soup with shrimp (Philippines). Sweetened, mixed with coconut milk, as dessert (Vietnam, Thailand, Philippines, Indonesia). Mung bean starch is used to make transparent or cellophane noodles, popular throughout Asia.

NAME(S)	ORIGIN & CHARACTERISTICS	SOAKING & COOKING
Navy (PEA BEAN, HARICOT)	New World native. Smaller white bean. Soft but not creamily so. A pleasant neutral flavor, bland, a little starchy.	**SOAK?** Yes. **CONVENTIONAL STOVETOP:** 1½–2 hours. **PRESSURE COOKER:** 12–14 minutes. **SLOW-COOKER:** 1 hour on high, then 6–7 hours on low.
Pigeon pea (CONGO PEA, GANDULE). WHEN SPLIT, *TOOR DAHL.*	An African native and a Caribbean fave. A small rounded bean, beige or golden, speckled with brown. Slightly sweet, a little mealy.	**SOAK?** Optional. **UNSOAKED, CONVENTIONAL STOVETOP:** 45–60 minutes. **SOAKED, CONVENTIONAL STOVETOP:** 25–35 minutes. **UNSOAKED, PRESSURE COOKER:** 9–11 minutes. **SOAKED, PRESSURE COOKER:** 7–9 minutes. **UNSOAKED, SLOW-COOKER:** 1 hour on high, then 6–7 hours on low. **SOAKED, SLOW-COOKER:** 1 hour on high, then 2–3 hours on low.
Pinto	New World native. Pink-buff bean mottled with a deeper brown-burgundy. It cooks up plump, creamy, a little sweet, mild.	**SOAK?** Yes. **CONVENTIONAL STOVETOP:** 1½–2¼ hours. **PRESSURE COOKER:** 11–13 minutes; then let pressure release gradually. **SLOW-COOKER:** 1 hour on high, then 6–7 hours on low.
Rattlesnake	New World native, a pinto relative, variegated in much the same way, except the pink/burgundy tones are more purely brown/dark brown. Plump, creamy, a little sweet. Slightly intensified pinto bean flavor.	**SOAK?** Yes. **CONVENTIONAL STOVETOP:** 1½–2¼ hours. **PRESSURE COOKER:** 11–13 minutes; then let pressure release gradually. **SLOW-COOKER:** 1 hour on high, then 6–7 hours on low.
Soybean: FOR NOTES ON EDAMAME, SEE PAGE 25; SOY SAUCE AND MISO, SEE PAGE 80; AND AS MEAT ANALOGS, SEE PAGE 243.		
Tepary	A New World native, the tepary grows successfully in drought conditions; small, flattish bean with a dense texture. Available in both brown and white varieties, the latter slightly sweeter.	**SOAK?** Yes. **CONVENTIONAL STOVETOP:** 1¾–2½ hours. **PRESSURE COOKER:** 18 minutes; then let pressure release gradually. **SLOW-COOKER:** 1½ hours on high, then 6–7 hours on low.

AVAILABILITY	SUBSTITUTES	USAGE
Readily available.	Great Northern, cannellini, baby lima.	The bean traditionally used in U.S. Senate Bean Soup and in baked beans. Much loved in Great Britain, it's also favored in the U.S. Black Muslim communities use it in a sweet bean pie.
At most markets where there is a Latino, African, or Caribbean population (also canned, from Goya). Online: Purcell Mountain Farms.	Any cowpea (medium-size hot-climate bean): Black-eyed, crowder pea, goat's eye bean, asparagus bean, lady pea, cream pea, clay pea. Though they differ some in flavor, cooking times are about the same.	*Toor dahl* is the bean of choice in many dahls, de rigueur in the thin hot soup/sauce called *sambhar* (India). *Moro de Guandules,* rice and pigeon peas; in stew, with plantain (Dominican Republic). Bean, as well as its leaves, is used in many spicy stews known as *w'aats* (Ethiopia).
Widely available.	Pinto's flavor is unique, but red kidney, appaloosa, rattlesnake, cranberry, and anasazi beans all work well.	The default bean used for refrieds in Tex-Mex restaurants. Excellent in chilis of any type, soups, and any Southwestern-seasoned casserole.
Hard to find, though some specialty foods stores have them. Online: Purcell Mountain Farms.	Pinto.	See above.
Not widely available, though some specialty stores carry it. Online: Rancho Gordo; Purcell Mountain Farms.	Its flavor and looks are unique, but pinto, kidney, black, and navy beans would all work well in recipes calling for it.	An excellent soup bean, it pairs nicely with Southwestern flavors and vegetables. Often cooked with a ham bone or chunk of salt pork.

Luscious Lentils & Other Lovable Little Legumes

All lentils are descendants of the natives of the Middle East. But as they traveled, they adapted to the particular soils and climates of their adopted homes, with varieties becoming quite distinctive. Of course lentils are renowned in soups and stews, but they're also good cold in salads, cooked in a stew or sauce to be served over grains, pureed to be part of dips, or mashed to add textural heft, flavor, and protein to various veggie burgers and loaves. As you'd expect from such travelers, lentils work well with a range of flavorings: Mediterranean, North African, Indian. Though they can be used interchangeably, here are a few notes on the varieties.

I've also included several quick-cooking legumes that are technically peas, not lentils.

NAME	COOKING NOTES	LOCALE
Brown lentil BROWNISH GREEN, TINY DISC	Used in classic American lentil soups; will work well in any lentil recipe. Hold their own with strong, wintery flavors: wild rice, full-flavored mushrooms. Good in croquettes and burgers because they easily cook to mushiness. Cook tender in 30 to 45 minutes.	Raised in American Northwest; found in typical supermarkets.
Black or Beluga lentil NAMED FOR ITS PASSING RESEMBLANCE TO CAVIAR, ABOUT THE SIZE AND SHAPE OF BLACK PEPPERCORNS	Small and round, these cook in 20 to 30 minutes and have a nice nutty flavor. They hold their shape well and become shiny black when cooked. Visually striking in salads or with pale grains. Cooked separately and stirred in at the last, they are an excellent addition to risottos, both tasty and attractive.	Raised in Idaho; available at specialty foods markets and online through Purcell Mountain Farms and Indian Harvest.
Spanish or Pardina lentil ABOUT A THIRD THE SIZE OF A CONVENTIONAL BROWN LENTIL	These tiny discs hold their shape nicely when cooked. Their flavor is slightly richer than that of brown lentils, and they hold up nicely with tomato sauces and curry spices, but also work well anywhere you'd use brown lentils. They cook in 25 to 35 minutes.	They used to be imported from Spain but are now grown in Idaho and the American Northwest, too. Available at specialty foods markets and online through Purcell Mountain Farms and Indian Harvest.

★ *All cooking times are approximate. The older the bean is, the longer it will take to cook. Always taste for tenderness about three-quarters of the way through the shorter suggested time when using a conventional pot or slow-cooker. When using a pressure cooker, stop the cooking at the earlier end of the cooking range, let pressure release gradually, open, and taste. If not tender, reseal the lid and bring it back up to high pressure for the remaining time.*

NAME	COOKING NOTES	LOCALE
Green lentil (LENTILES DU PUY)	Slightly smaller than brown lentils, and even more flavorful than the domestics. They also cook tender in 30 to 45 minutes.	Until recently they were imported from France, where they are grown in volcanic soil, but they're now grown in Idaho, too. Available at specialty foods markets and online through Purcell Mountain Farms and Indian Harvest.
Red lentil A STUNNING, VIBRANT CORAL ORANGE WHICH MUTES TO A STILL-PRETTY GOLDEN YELLOW WITH COOKING	These are actually split, skinned brown lentils. They cook up quickly into a tender and indistinct mass. Try them anywhere you'd use split peas, or in any dahl, or in veggie burgers. Their texture rules them out for salads. They'll cook in 20 to 25 minutes, and are relatively low in gas-forming compounds.	A native of the Middle East and widely grown in India as well as the American Northwest. Available at Indian, Middle Eastern, and specialty foods markets; online through Purcell Mountain Farms.
Split pea PALE GREEN DISC, SKINLESS AND THIN (BECAUSE IT IS SPLIT)	A variety of yellow or green peas, grown for drying (distinct from garden peas, which are intended to be eaten fresh). Halved down the natural split in the center. Split peas cook in a quick 30 to 40 minutes, and are relatively low in gas-forming compounds. Of course they're a classic and so-good legume for soup. Because they, too, cook to mushiness, their texture rules them out for salads.	A native of the Middle East and widely grown in India as well as the American Northwest. Available at many supermarkets, as well as at Indian, Middle Eastern, and specialty foods markets; online through Purcell Mountain Farms.
Yellow split pea SLIM YELLOW DISC	Used much more often in India than in America as the basis for soupy, spicy, pleasing dahl, an all-purpose Indian dish of a thousand regional variations. Bright in color, they seem to suggest bright, spicy flavorings—they're also often part of Moroccan and Tunisian tagines to accompany couscous, but you can swap green for yellow or yellow for green in any recipe, Eastern or Western. Cooking time's 30 to 40 minutes. Because they, too, cook to mushiness, their texture rules them out for salads.	A native of the Middle East and widely grown in India as well as the American Northwest. Available at many supermarkets, as well as at Indian, Middle Eastern, and specialty foods markets; online through Purcell Mountain Farms.

Yields for virtually all dried beans: 1 cup dried beans, peas, or lentils equals 2¼ to 2½ cups cooked.

Index

Conversion Tables

APPROXIMATE EQUIVALENTS

1 stick butter	8 tbs / 4 oz / ½ cup
1 cup all-purpose presifted flour or dried bread crumbs	5 oz
1 cup granulated sugar	8 oz
1 cup (packed) brown sugar	6 oz
1 cup confectioners' sugar	4½ oz
1 cup honey or syrup	12 oz
1 cup grated cheese	4 oz
1 cup dried beans	6 oz
1 large egg	about 2 oz or about 3 tbs
1 egg yolk	about 1 tbs
1 egg white	about 2 tbs

Please note that all conversions are approximate but close enough to be useful when converting from one system to another.

WEIGHT CONVERSION

U.S./U.K.	METRIC	U.S./U.K.	METRIC
½ oz	15 g	7 oz	200 g
1 oz	30 g	8 oz	250 g
1 ½ oz	45 g	9 oz	275 g
2 oz	60 g	10 oz	300 g
2 ½ oz	75 g	11 oz	325 g
3 oz	90 g	12 oz	350 g
3 ½ oz	100 g	13 oz	375 g
4 oz	125 g	14 oz	400 g
5 oz	150 g	15 oz	450 g
6 oz	175 g	1 lb	500 g

LIQUID CONVERSION

U.S.	IMPERIAL	METRIC
2 tbs	1 fl oz	30 ml
3 tbs	1½ fl oz	45 ml
¼ cup	2 fl oz	60 ml
⅓ cup	2½ fl oz	75 ml
⅓ cup + 1 tbs	3 fl oz	90 ml
⅓ cup + 2 tbs	3½ fl oz	100 ml
½ cup	4 fl oz	125 ml
⅔ cup	5 fl oz	150 ml
¾ cup	6 fl oz	175 ml
¾ cup + 2 tbs	7 fl oz	200 ml
1 cup	8 fl oz	250 ml
1 cup + 2 tbs	9 fl oz	275 ml
1¼ cups	10 fl oz	300 ml
1⅓ cups	11 fl oz	325 ml
1½ cups	12 fl oz	350 ml
1⅔ cups	13 fl oz	375 ml
1¾ cups	14 fl oz	400 ml
1¾ cups + 2 tbs	15 fl oz	450 ml
2 cups (1 pint)	16 fl oz	500 ml
2½ cups	20 fl oz (1 pint)	600 ml
3¾ cups	1½ pints	900 ml
4 cups	1¾ pints	1 liter

OVEN TEMPERATURES

°F	GAS MARK	°C	°F	GAS MARK	°C
250	½	120	400	6	200
275	1	140	425	7	220
300	2	150	450	8	230
325	3	160	475	9	240
350	4	180	500	10	260
375	5	190			

Note: Reduce the temperature by 20°C (68°F) for fan-assisted ovens.